HASHTAG ACTIVISM AND WOMEN'S RIGHTS

Are Social Media Campaigns Really Making Laws Better for Women and Girls?

Reilly Anne Dempsey Willis

First published in Great Britain in 2025 by

Bristol University Press
University of Bristol
1–9 Old Park Hill
Bristol
BS2 8BB
UK
t: +44 (0)117 374 6645
e: bup-info@bristol.ac.uk

Details of international sales and distribution partners are available at bristoluniversitypress.co.uk

© Bristol University Press 2025

British Library Cataloguing in Publication Data
A catalogue record for this book is available from the British Library

ISBN 978-1-5292-4128-0 hardcover
ISBN 978-1-5292-4130-3 ePub
ISBN 978-1-5292-4131-0 ePdf

The right of Reilly Anne Dempsey Willis to be identified as author of this work has been asserted by her in accordance with the Copyright, Designs and Patents Act 1988.

All rights reserved: no part of this publication may be reproduced, stored in a retrieval system, or transmitted in any form or by any means, electronic, mechanical, photocopying, recording, or otherwise without the prior permission of Bristol University Press.

Every reasonable effort has been made to obtain permission to reproduce copyrighted material. If, however, anyone knows of an oversight, please contact the publisher.

The statements and opinions contained within this publication are solely those of the author and not of the University of Bristol or Bristol University Press. The University of Bristol and Bristol University Press disclaim responsibility for any injury to persons or property resulting from any material published in this publication.

Bristol University Press works to counter discrimination on grounds of gender, race, disability, age and sexuality.

Cover design: Liam Roberts Design
Front cover image: Liam Roberts Design

For Dave.

For John.

For Henry.

For Jim.

And for Roger. But just a little bit.
Like a page or two.

Contents

List of Figures and Tables		vii
Preface and Content Warning		ix

1	**Introduction**	**1**
	#Introduction	1

2	**Research Framework**	**6**
	Fourth wave feminism and digital feminist activism	6
	The spiral model of human rights change theory	8
	Criticisms of the spiral model	9
	The role of social media	16
	Research design	24
	Conclusion	28

3	**Negative Outcomes: #stopstoning, #letwomengotostadium**	**34**
	#stopstoning campaign overview	35
	#letwomengotostadium campaign overview	37
	Context	39
	Legal outcomes	40
	Twitter characteristics	53
	Conclusion	59

4	**Status Quo: #farkhunda, #sendeanlat, #mydressmychoice**	**61**
	#farkhunda campaign overview	61
	#sendeanlat campaign overview	63
	#mydressmychoice campaign overview	64
	Context	66
	Legal outcomes	67
	Twitter characteristics	91
	Conclusion	99

5	**Tactical Concessions: #delhigangrape and #niunamenos**	**100**
	#delhigangrape campaign overview	100

	#niunamenos campaign overview	101
	Context	103
	Legal outcomes	104
	Twitter characteristics	126
	Conclusion	133
6	**Possible Success: #women2drive**	**134**
	#women2drive campaign overview	134
	Context	137
	Legal outcomes	138
	Twitter characteristics	149
	Conclusion	156
7	**Aggregate Analysis and Conclusions**	**157**
	Campaign 'groupings' based on outcomes	157
	Statistical analysis	161
	Overall models	181
	Ideal Twitter campaign behaviours	185
	The future of the hashtag	185
	Final thoughts: are social media campaigns really making laws better for women and girls?	188
	Appendix: Design Challenges and Technological Solutions	190
	References	200
	Index	244

List of Figures and Tables

Figures

3.1	Timeline of Tweets in #stopstoning and #letwomengotostadium	55
3.2	Consistently used words, #stopstoning	58
3.3	Consistently used words, #letwomengotostadium	58
4.1	Number of Tweets per day, status quo campaigns	93
4.2	Sentiment over time, #sendeanlat	97
4.3	Consistently used words, #farkhunda	98
4.4	Consistently used words, #sendeanlat	98
4.5	Consistently used words, #mydressmychoice	98
5.1	Number of Tweets per day, #delhigangrape and #niunamenos	127
5.2	Positivity and peaks, #niunamenos	130
5.3	Positivity and peaks, #delhigangrape	131
5.4	Consistently used words, #delhigangrape	132
5.5	Consistently used words, #niunamenos	132
6.1	Number of Tweets per day up to 1,000, #women2drive	150
6.2	Number of Tweets per day up to 200, #women2drive	151
6.3	Profiles of the 100 most active users, #women2drive	153
6.4	Positivity over time, #women2drive	154
6.5	Consistently used words, #women2drive	155
7.1	Relationship between changing messaging and UN dialogue	171
7.2	Relationship between total number of days of campaign and overall legal outcomes (log scale)	173
7.3	Relationship between number of active days and overall legal change	176
7.4	Relationship between World Justice Project rankings and overall legal change, excluding Saudi Arabia	178
7.5	Relationship between replies and legal outcomes	182
7.6	Relationship between likes and institutionalization	183
7.7	Relationship between overall campaign score and overall legal change	184

Tables

2.1	Overview of initial study campaigns	26
2.2	Definitions of variables	29
2.3	Research map	32
3.1	Reliable reports of stoning in Iran, 2001–2017	47
4.1	Number of active days, status quo campaigns	93
5.1	Conviction rates of femicides, Argentina, 2014–2016	119
7.1	Overview of statistical tests	163
7.2	Summary of significant relationships, user profiles	166
7.3	Summary of significant relationships, messaging content	170
7.4	Summary of significant relationships, Tweets per day	174
7.5	Partial correlations, Tweets per day	174
7.6	Summary of significant relationships, Tweets per day, after partial correlations	175
7.7	Summary of significant relationships, engagement metrics	180
7.8	Correlation between overall campaign score and legal change	184
7.9	Ideal campaign behaviours	186

Preface and Content Warning

TW: sexual violence, rape, femicide (gender-based murder).

The book you are about to read explores some truly harrowing examples of violence against women and girls, including sexual violence, rape and femicide (gender-based murder). The campaigns studied all began after a 'spark' incident, an incident that was so horrific people couldn't stand by any longer. I present enough detail of the spark incident to understand the campaign, but I try not to spend more time than necessary on the incidents themselves so as not to perpetuate the spectator approach which can continue the cycle of violence for the victim. However, parts of this book may still be difficult to read.

It is also important to recognize that these are some of the worst examples of individual violence against women. This book explores the extremes of violence and power carried out by a very small fraction of the world's population. I ask you therefore not to perpetuate *any* harmful gendered stereotypes against men *or* women stemming from the contents of this book.

I would finally like to acknowledge Michael, Andri, and Adriana for their incredible part in this beast.

1

Introduction

#Introduction

Hashtag campaigns have become part of everyday life, with people even using the word 'hashtag' in general conversations (as in 'How are you today?' 'Hashtag feeling tired'[1]). News outlets use social media posts from both the general public and from well-known figures to report on top stories. That which trends becomes a headline.[2] Official political announcements which used to be exclusive to broadsheets are made on social media first.[3] When working as a human rights advocate, campaigning for policy changes to improve the lives of women and girls, I noted a distinct and extremely rapid transition in the world of non-governmental organizations to social media. Every campaign suddenly 'had' to have a social media drive. Rather than asking our organization's members to go out and volunteer locally (as we had done in the past) we were now asking them to send a Tweet, like a Facebook post, or sign a change.org petition, and for most members this meant targeting a foreign country. Participation may have increased, but our understanding of the potential outcomes had not. Monitoring and evaluation rigour was nigh on impossible with social media. As a practitioner, without assessments or even a general idea of the actual outcomes of these campaigns, I felt as though our responsibility as advocates for women and girls was at risk. Thus, the idea for this research was born – to find out what these social media campaigns were *really* doing to improve laws for women and girls in the long term.

---

[1] At the time of writing, the author can confirm that this is a true statement.

[2] Joan Donovan and danah boyd, 'Stop the Presses? Moving From Strategic Silence to Strategic Amplification in a Networked Media Ecosystem' (2019) American Behavioral Scientist 000276421987822.

[3] Bart Cammaerts, 'Protest Logics and the Mediation Opportunity Structure' (2012) 27 European Journal of Communication 117.

At the time of writing this book, there were over five billion individuals using the internet, representing a 64.4 per cent global penetration rate, with over four and a half billion of these users active on social media.[4] This is a 3 per cent increase in just one year with numbers more than doubling in ten years.[5] These numbers, however, mask significant inequalities.[6] While 74 per cent of North Americans, 84 per cent of Northern Europeans, and 84 per cent of Western Europeans actively use social media, only 27 per cent of Central Asians, 7 per cent of Middle Africans, 8 per cent of East Africans, 13 per cent of West Africans, and 33 per cent of Southern Asians are social media active.[7] Are we starting to see the possible problems? The majority of social media users are, statistically, in the Global North, but social media advocacy campaigns tend to target the Global South. Concerns are imminent about the ability of the domestic voice – those most affected by the campaigns – to play a significant role in the campaign, compounded by social media functionalities and platform designs which may favour the elite.[8] Whose voices are we really hearing?

Equally, statistics show that in every region in the world, men are using the internet more than women. The gender gap is even more pronounced in the Global South.[9] This added layer of inequality creates another complex concern when using social media for women's rights campaigns, where platforms themselves are often built on inequalities which most adversely affect what tend to be already silenced voices. Social media platforms themselves are criticized for embedding heteronormative patriarchy or preferences for mainstream feminisms into the very fabric of their functionalities.[10] (These concepts are explored more fully in Chapter 2.)

---

[4] We Are Social, 'Digital 2023' (We Are Social UK, 26 January 2023) https://wearesocial. com/uk/blog/2023/01/digital-2023/, accessed 9 November 2023.

[5] Ibid.

[6] International Telecommunication Union, 'Measuring Digital Development: Facts and Figures 2022' (2022) https://www.itu.int/hub/publication/d-ind-ict_mdd-2022/, accessed 9 November 2023.

[7] 'Digital in 2018: World's Internet Users Pass the 4 Billion Mark' (We Are Social UK, 30 January 2018) https://wearesocial.com/uk/blog/2018/01/global-digital-report-2018, accessed 4 October 2018.

[8] Kate Ott, 'Social Media and Feminist Values: Aligned or Maligned?' (2018) 39 Frontiers: A Journal of Women Studies 93.

[9] International Telecommunication Union (n 6).

[10] Tegan Zimmerman, '#Intersectionality: The Fourth Wave Feminist Twitter Community' (2017) 38 Atlantis: Critical Studies in Gender, Culture & Social Justice 54; Reilly Anne Dempsey Willis, 'Habermasian Utopia or Sunstein's Echo Chamber? The "Dark Side" of Hashtag Hijacking and Feminist Activism' (2020) 40 Legal Studies 507; Reilly Anne Dempsey Willis, 'Whose Story Is It Anyway? Hashtag Campaigns and Digital Abortion Storytelling' in Tom Vine and Sarah Richards (eds), *Stories, Storytellers, and Storytelling* (Springer International Publishing, 2022) https://doi.org/10.1007/978-3-031-07234-5_7, accessed 14 November 2023; Abigail Locke, Rebecca Lawthom and Antonia Lyons,

INTRODUCTION

To understand the relationship between hashtag campaigns and legal change for women and girls, this study looks at one million Tweets across eight campaigns targeting domestic legal change in seven countries. The campaigns included in this study are:

1. #stopstoning – calling for changes to the law in Iran which sets stoning as a form of the death penalty for women accused (often falsely) of adultery.
2. #letwomengotostadium – advocating for the lifting of a ban on women attending men's volleyball matches in Iran, seen as an affront to women's autonomy and equality.
3. #farkhunda – the brutal mob murder of a young woman in Afghanistan, in the presence of police, was caught on film and went viral on social media. The resulting hashtag campaign in her name called upon the government to strengthen law enforcement to protect women from violence, particularly in the public sphere.
4. #sendeanlat – rates of femicide in Turkey have been steadily rising for many years. When a young woman was raped and murdered on a bus, her story led to the campaign #sendeanlat, which roughly translates into 'share your story'. The campaign specifically called upon the government to repeal a law which allowed mitigation in many femicide cases based on 'provocation'.
5. #mydressmychoice – a woman in Nairobi was publicly and violently stripped naked because she was wearing a mini-skirt. This incident was also videoed and went viral on social media. The ensuing hashtag campaign advocated for stronger laws to protect women from violence and more action from frontline law enforcement.
6. #delhigangrape – when a young woman was brutally gang raped and murdered on a bus in India, her story ignited outcry via social media. The campaign demanded that the government strengthen laws and law enforcement, particularly in the courts, to protect women and girls.
7. #niunamenos – machismo culture in Argentina is often blamed for the high rates of femicide. After a report of a young woman murdered because of her gender, activists turned to social media to catalyse the country. The campaign had very clear demands for changes and improvements to the laws around femicide, including the establishment of a national registry of femicide.
8. #women2drive – for decades, a religious decree banned women from driving in Saudi Arabia. Activists decided to use social media to

---

'Social Media Platforms as Complex and Contradictory Spaces for Feminisms: Visibility, Opportunity, Power, Resistance and Activism' (2018) 28 Feminism & Psychology 3.

reinvigorate their campaign, filming themselves driving and posting the videos online. The campaign took off, demanding that the ban be lifted.

It is important to recognize that the attention drawn to issues highlighted in social media campaigns will be necessarily different than the potential effects from traditional media. Social media, organic in nature, allows the framing and attention on an issue to reflect, at least to some extent, society's views more so than traditional (edited and curated) media or organizationally hierarchical campaigns. The visibility of hashtag campaigns and the relationship between social media and news outlets opens all sorts of awareness-raising doors that are harder to open with offline campaigns. These are, of course, not without drawbacks, which are explored in detail in Chapter 2. All of the campaigns in this study either started with or became popularized via a hashtag in a Tweet and continued to be driven by the use of Twitter (now X) in particular. The campaigns were known more by the hashtag than any other descriptor. The campaigns sought to use mass public support and pressure, both domestic and transnational, to force governments to act. They all set out to improve the lives of women and girls through domestic legal change. Yet very little is known about the long-term influence on or relationship with law – positive, negative, or neither. This research seeks to understand the full range of potential outcomes through a large-scale, comparative study to determine whether campaigns originating in and driven by hashtags on Twitter are associated with legal change. This research therefore takes a unique and innovative approach to measuring and modelling the relationships between hashtag campaigns and domestic legal change.

The study is designed to test the three theories: the theory of legal change embedded in the spiral model of human rights change and theories of media effects and social media campaigns, using an analytical lens drawn from fourth wave feminism and digital feminist activism theory. This study builds upon the body of scholarship critiquing the spiral model for its underrepresentation of domestic voice and overly simplistic view of long-term, meaningful legal change, coupled with literature which critiques the use of social media for feminist activism and traditional media effects theories.[11] Ultimately, the study seeks to identify a 'package' of campaign characteristics that are most closely

---

[11] Malcolm Gladwell, 'Small Change' (*The New Yorker*, 10 April 2010) http://www.newyorker.com/magazine/2010/10/04/small-change-malcolm-gladwell, accessed 14 March 2016; Malcolm Gladwell and Clay Shirky, 'From Innovation to Revolution: Do Social Media Make Protests Possible?' (2011) 90 Foreign Affairs 153; Clay Shirky, *Here Comes Everybody: How Change Happens When People Come Together* (updated with a new chapter, Penguin Books, 2009); Clay Shirky, 'The Political Power of Social Media: Technology, the Public Sphere, and Political Change' (2011) 90 Foreign Affairs 28.

aligned with positive legal change to create an 'ideal' hashtag campaign. Equally important, the study will identify risky campaign behaviours which are correlated to negative outcomes. Although this study uses Tweets to analyse the campaigns, the results can be extrapolated across many social media platforms.

The main study, in all, took place from 2015 to 2020. Tweets from the campaign start dates (which varied) up until November 2016 were retrospectively collected in 2017 and 2018, with a brief update to outcomes in 2023. A total of 1,051,525 unique Tweets were collected, with 743,671 Tweets in the final analysis (the exclusions are discussed in Chapter 2 and in the technical appendix) alongside over 1,500 pieces of legal evidence. This study has drawn together a substantial body of evidence to analyse the relationship between hashtag campaigns and legal change for women and girls.

The book proceeds as follows. Chapter 2 provides the scholarly foundation for the research design and analysis, using theories of legal change, critiques of social media activism and media effects theories, all through the lens of fourth wave feminism and digital feminist activism. Chapters 3, 4, 5, and 6 explore each campaign in detail, analysing long-term legal change and hashtag campaign behaviours using vast bodies of evidence. Chapter 7 pulls all the campaign analyses together to draw some tentative conclusions about the relationship between hashtag campaigns and long-term legal change for women and girls, thus attempting to answer the question: are social media campaigns really making laws better for women and girls?

2

Research Framework

This chapter sets out the framework and design of the study, first exploring the theories structuring the work and then moving into the specifics of how data were collected and analysed.

This work is underpinned by three main theoretical frames: theories of legal change and media effects/social media theory, viewed through a fourth wave feminism and digital feminist activism lens. These three theories, woven together, provide the understanding for research design, structuring the study, and guiding the analysis and conclusions.

Fourth wave feminism and digital feminist activism

Although the research design in this study is primarily built on theories of legal change and social media theory, it is also analysed through an overarching feminist lens. Digital feminist activism is torn between celebrating (if cautiously) the emergence of new spaces for collective action and hearing the voices of the subaltern,[1] and decrying the replication of patriarchal structures and hierarchies which continue to silence true feminist perspectives.[2] Through a mosaic lens of the work of Nancy Fraser, Sara

---

[1]   Kate Ott, 'Social Media and Feminist Values: Aligned or Maligned?' (2018) 39 Frontiers: A Journal of Women Studies 93; Ann Travers, 'Parallel Subaltern Feminist Counterpublics in Cyberspace' (2003) 46 Sociological Perspectives 223; Nancy Fraser, 'Rethinking the Public Sphere: A Contribution to the Critique of Actually Existing Democracy' (1990) Social Text 56; Carrie A Rentschler, '#MeToo and Student Activism against Sexual Violence' (2018) 11 Communication Culture & Critique 503; Carrie A Rentschler, 'Bystander Intervention, Feminist Hashtag Activism, and the Anti-Carceral Politics of Care' (2017) 17 Feminist Media Studies 565; Carrie Rentschler, '#Safetytipsforladies: Feminist Twitter Takedowns of Victim Blaming' (2015) 15 Feminist Media Studies 353.

[2]   danah boyd, 'Can Social Network Sites Enable Political Action?' (2008) International Journal of Media and Cultural Politics 241; danah boyd, *It's Complicated: The Social Lives of Networked Teens* (Yale University Press, 2014); Heather Lang, '#MeToo: A Case Study in Re-Embodying Information' (2019) Computers and Composition,

Ahmed, and, to some extent, Clare Hemmings, it is possible to conceptualize social media spaces as catalysts for feminist activism, providing the ingredients for subaltern counter-public formation, the visibility of harms, and an anti-feminist backlash which often strengthens movements.[3] In this light, campaigns could potentially be associated with positive change.

Yet the elite, patriarchal heteronormativity of social media is inescapable. Platforms are far from neutral. As profit-making entities, they are designed to 'push' more than 'pull', creating echo chambers which replicate destructive social structures and power dynamics, silencing non-dominant voices and amplifying that which makes money, not that which drives change.[4] There are heightened concerns about non-cis, non-white, non-Western representation in digital spaces. This debate is clearly manifested in this research – are these campaigns truly representing women's voices? How can they possibly overcome the structural and economic inequalities built into the very platforms that they use? Can we even truly *be* digital feminist activists? Kaba et al pose an equally challenging question: 'How can social media exist independently of the dynamics and forces of oppression that structure

---

https://linkinghub.elsevier.com/retrieve/pii/S8755461519300222, accessed 23 August 2019; Kaitlynn Mendes, Jessalynn Keller, and Jessica Ringrose, 'Digitized Narratives of Sexual Violence: Making Sexual Violence Felt and Known through Digital Disclosures' (2019) 21 New Media & Society 1290.

[3] Fraser (n 1); Cinzia Arruzza, Tithi Bhattacharya, and Nancy Fraser, *Feminism for the 99 Percent: A Manifesto* (Verso, 2019); Sara Ahmed, 'Beyond Humanism and Postmodernism: Theorizing a Feminist Practice' (1996) 11 Hypatia 71; Sara Ahmed, 'Deconstruction and Law's Other: Towards a Feminist Theory of Embodied Legal Rights' (1995) 4 Social & Legal Studies 55; Sara Ahmed, *Living a Feminist Life* (Duke University Press, 2017); Clare Hemmings, 'Affective Solidarity: Feminist Reflexivity and Political Transformation' (2012) 13 Feminist Theory 147; Clare Hemmings, ' "But I Thought We'd Already Won That Argument!": "Anti-Gender" Mobilizations, Affect, and Temporality' (2022) 48 Feminist Studies 594; Reilly Anne Dempsey Willis, 'Habermasian Utopia or Sunstein's Echo Chamber? The "Dark Side" of Hashtag Hijacking and Feminist Activism' (2020) 40 Legal Studies 507; Reilly Willis, 'Whose Story Is It Anyway? Hashtag Campaigns and Digital Abortion Storytelling' in Tom Vine and Sarah Richards (eds), *Stories, Storytellers, and Storytelling* (Springer International Publishing, 2022) https://doi.org/10.1007/978-3-031-07234-5_7, accessed 14 November 2023.

[4] Ott (n 1); boyd, *It's Complicated* (n 2); boyd, 'Can Social Network Sites Enable Political Action?' (n 2); Joan Donovan and danah boyd, 'Stop the Presses? Moving From Strategic Silence to Strategic Amplification in a Networked Media Ecosystem' (2019) American Behavioral Scientist 000276421987822; Gail Lewis and Clare Hemmings, ' "Where Might We Go If We Dare": Moving beyond the "Thick, Suffocating Fog of Whiteness" in Feminism' (2019) 20 Feminist Theory 405; Lang (n 2); Cass R Sunstein, *#Republic: Divided Democracy in the Age of Social Media* (Princeton University Press, 2017); Tarleton Gillespie, 'The Politics of "Platforms"' (2010) 12 New Media & Society 347.

the world at large? The answer is simple: it does not and cannot.'[5] Here we also must raise concerns about the rejected victim–saviour dichotomy and ask: are these campaigns colonialism in disguise, pushing a 'gender equality' agenda which is defined and driven by white Western women?[6] Hemmings presents an uncomfortable truth: 'the fantasy of white, Western rescue of passive brown female victims of unconscionable brown patriarchs is a key mode through which colonial violence is displaced and refashioned as ethical'.[7] With these perspectives, the outlook for these campaigns could equally be bleak.

The spiral model of human rights change theory

The primary theoretical frame for this work is the spiral model of human rights change theory and critiques thereof. In 1998, Margaret Keck and Kathryn Sikkink published a ground-breaking book in transnational advocacy, where they outlined their 'boomerang model'.[8] The model used a visual metaphor of a boomerang to describe the relationship between domestic civil society and transnational advocacy networks (TANs) in advocating for domestic change. The metaphor envisions domestic groups 'boomeranging' out to transnational networks to exert foreign pressure on domestic governments. This theory opened significant doors to the work of TANs and marked a watershed moment in activism research.

Shortly thereafter, the boomerang model formed the baseline for the development of a more detailed, predictive model. Risse et al pulled together

---

[5] Mariame Kaba, Andrea Smith, Lori Adelman, and Roxane Gay, 'Where Twitter and Feminism Meet' (*The Nation*, 17 April 2014) https://www.thenation.com/article/arch ive/where-twitter-and-feminism-meet/, accessed 13 November 2023.

[6] Julian Go, 'Thinking against Empire: Anticolonial Thought as Social Theory' (2023) 74 The British Journal of Sociology 279; Walter D Mignolo, 'Prophets Facing Sidewise: The Geopolitics of Knowledge and the Colonial Difference' (2005) 19 Social Epistemology 111; Walter D Mignolo, 'Coloniality and Globalization: A Decolonial Take' (2021) 18 Globalizations 720; Walter D Mignolo and Fábio Santino Bussmann, 'Coloniality and the State: Race, Nation and Dependency' (2023) 40 Theory, Culture & Society 3; Veeran Naicker, 'The Problem of Epistemological Critique in Contemporary Decolonial Theory' (2023) 49 Social Dynamics 220; Sujata Patel, 'Anti-Colonial Thought and Global Social Theory' (2023) 8 Frontiers in Sociology, https://www.frontiersin.org/articles/10.3389/ fsoc.2023.1143776, accessed 13 November 2023; Christian Borch, 'Crowds, Race, Colonialism: On Resuscitating Classical Crowd Theory' (2023) 90 Social Research: An International Quarterly 245; Yunana Ahmed, 'Political Discourse Analysis: A Decolonial Approach' (2021) 18 Critical Discourse Studies 139.

[7] Clare Hemmings, 'Resisting Popular Feminisms: Gender, Sexuality and the Lure of the Modern' (2018) 25 Gender, Place & Culture 963.

[8] Margaret E Keck and Kathryn Sikkink, *Activists beyond Borders: Advocacy Networks in International Politics* (Cornell University Press, 1998).

a series of case studies on human rights change to identify consistent patterns, trends, and outcomes. The result was the spiral model of human rights change.[9] The model, again using a visualization, resembles a spiral moving across three groups of horizontally aligned actors (domestic state, domestic civil society, and international actors) and through five vertically aligned phases of change. Again, the pivotal element of the model, *necessary* for change, was (and still is) the influence of the international actors. The model was revisited in 2013, and, although some clarifications were suggested, the basic tenets of the model were upheld through additional case studies and scope condition identification.[10] Since its first publication, the spiral model has been tested, interrogated, and both critiqued and lauded as a revolutionary approach to activism.

Broadly, the theoretical model tracks how states move from human rights repression to denial, to tactical concessions, to prescriptive status, and finally to rule-consistent behaviour. Transnational actors and foreign pressure are essential to the model when moving from repression to denial, and again from denial to tactical concessions. Since the development of this model, some scholars have also found that the continued presence of transnational advocacy is critical to move from tactical concessions through to norm institutionalization.[11]

The glue holding the model together is the networking between international groups and domestic groups. The international groups are responsible for exerting the pressure necessary to move the domestic regime through a process of legal change; some pressure from the 'bottom up' is needed from domestic groups, but the lynchpin of the model is the leverage provided by the international network. The theory seeks, 'ultimately, to specify the causal mechanisms by which international norms affect domestic structural change'.[12]

Criticisms of the spiral model

Evan Shor provides a blunt but accurate overview of the critiques of the spiral model: it is 'too crude, deterministic, and holds a somewhat naively

---

[9] Thomas Risse, Stephen C Ropp, and Kathryn Sikkink (eds), *The Power of Human Rights: International Norms and Domestic Change* (Cambridge University Press, 1999).

[10] Thomas Risse-Kappen, Stephen C Ropp, and Kathryn Sikkink (eds), *The Persistent Power of Human Rights: From Commitment to Compliance* (Cambridge University Press, 2013).

[11] E Neumayer, 'Do International Human Rights Treaties Improve Respect for Human Rights?' (2005) 49 Journal of Conflict Resolution 925; Kathryn Sikkink, *A Typology of Relations Between Social Movements and International Institutions* (The American Society of International Law, 2003).

[12] Risse, Ropp, and Sikkink (n 9) 19.

optimistic view'.[13] An in-depth survey of scholarship testing and critiquing the spiral model resulted in the identification of five primary categories of broadly agreed upon weaknesses, some of which reflect tenets within the digital feminist activist literature:

1. an overemphasis of international (Western) actors coupled with a lack of recognition of the power of domestic actors;
2. ignoring the risk of government backlash against foreign involvement, particularly of a Western nature;
3. a general problem of progression, where many states do not move through to the final phases of the model (without recognition in the model of this problem);
4. although there are some scope conditions present in the model's description, these conditions do not give adequate treatment to domestic capacity;
5. the model's reliance on naming and shaming without seriously taking into account the role of other incentives (that is, material).

These critiques, coupled with the critiques of social media, are the cornerstones of this book, informing the choice of variables used to test the utility of international, Twitter-driven hashtag campaigns for domestic human rights change. This chapter therefore culminates in the production of a 'research map' which matches the theoretical spiral model critiques to the identified risks of campaigning via social media. This research map is revisited throughout the book to frame, understand, and interpret results in light of this theoretical framework.

Domestic actors

Many scholars and studies focus on the spiral model's lack of prioritization of domestic factors, echoing concerns about non-majority women's voices being silenced in elite social media spaces. It is the voices of those most affected by changes that need to feature front and centre for a campaign to be successful, and the feminist literature discussed earlier finds that does not always happen on social media.

Muñoz's work in Mexico found that the work of transnational groups was equalled by the work of domestic groups, and it was this combination that led to positive change, more so than had the TANs dominated change as specified by the spiral model.[14] Encarnación applied the spiral model to

---

[13] Eran Shor, 'Conflict, Terrorism, and the Socialization of Human Rights Norms: The Spiral Model Revisited' (2008) 55 Social Problems 117, 122.

[14] Alejandro Anaya Muñoz, 'Transnational and Domestic Processes in the Definition of Human Rights Policies in Mexico' (2009) 31 Human Rights Quarterly 35.

the gay rights movement in Argentina, and came to the conclusion that it was the work of the domestic movement that was critical to change.[15] Another interesting perspective was presented in Cheng's work, where she found that human rights change was achieved in Taiwan, but this meant that the Taiwanese people had to adopt Western norms and approaches which were not conducive or reflective of domestic culture or desires.[16] In the Israeli context, despite the theoretical applicability of the model, long-term change was not achieved in part because the work was supported by domestic activists, but not by the broader domestic citizenry.[17] Cizre identified similar problems in the Turkish context whereby the intervention of TANs resulted in domestic non-governmental organization dependency on foreign funding, which alienated them from the wider society.[18] In her work examining the model in Colombia, Brysk finds that the nature of the violations meant that the government was able to effectively silence the voice of international actors, that the presence of TANs may have increased the violence, and indeed that the human rights norms in question needed to be broadly accepted by domestic society on the whole, not just activist groups.[19] The combination of these elements in the Colombian context meant that human rights change was not possible.

Domestic regime is also potentially underspecified in the spiral model's theories. Both Schwarz and Heo find that domestic regime change was the most critical component in achieving change, not the role of TANs.[20] This will later be shown to be a critical variable in this study as well. Schwarz, in particular, criticizes the model for having, essentially, just one independent variable – the involvement of TANs. He finds that, in reality, the process is much more dynamic and domestically driven. Similarly, Chase tested the model's applicability in Yemen, and found that the lack of recognition of

---

[15]   Omar G Encarnación, 'International Influence, Domestic Activism, and Gay Rights in Argentina' (2013) 128 Political Science Quarterly 687.

[16]   Isabelle Cheng and Lara Momesso, 'Look, the World Is Watching How We Treat Migrants! The Making of the Anti-Trafficking Legislation during the Ma Administration' (2017) 46 Journal of Current Chinese Affairs 61.

[17]   Andreas Laursen, 'Israel's Supreme Court and International Human Rights Law: The Judgement on "Moderate Physical Pressure"' (2000) 69 Nordic Journal of International Law 413.

[18]   Umit Cizre, 'The Truth and Fiction About (Turkey's) Human Rights Politics' (2001) 3 Human Rights Review 55.

[19]   Alison Brysk, 'Communicative Action and Human Rights in Colombia: When Words Fail' (2009) Colombia Internacional 36.

[20]   Rolf Schwarz, 'The Paradox of Sovereignty, Regime Type and Human Rights Compliance' (2004) 8 The International Journal of Human Rights 199; Man-ho Heo, 'Mongolia's Political Change and Human Rights in Five-Phase Spiral Model: Implications for North Korea: Mongolia's Political Change and HR' (2014) 29 Pacific Focus 413.

the importance and influence of domestic actors, both government, activist, and non-activist, may explain the lack of human rights change.[21]

Although the spiral model carves important space for domestic civil society, the crux of the model is the strong-arm intervention from international actors. This runs the risk of returning to the now-rejected 'victim–saviour' dichotomy with postcolonial overtones, where TANs and other international actors must come 'to the rescue' and use their power and clout to pressure domestic governments to change.[22] Hints of colonialism again dance at the margins.[23]

While this pressure is necessary, it is *not* both sufficient *and* necessary. Rather, these critiques find that it is the domestic drive and voice which are the cornerstones of change. Although there may be a place for TANs to exert pressure, this pressure must stem from domestic roots and must reflect the voice of the people who will be most affected by any change, or lack thereof.

Target government backlash

Stemming from the potential underspecification of the role of domestic actors, a similar critique finds that the over-reliance on foreign actors runs the very real risk of domestic government backlash, aligning with digital feminist literature discussed earlier which finds that opening social media spaces opens doors more to harassment, abuse, and backlash than meaningful dialogue and change. Goodman and Jinks generally find that the model is part of a dynamic process and does indeed lead to predictions about the nature of human rights change, however they also discuss the model's lack of attention to potential backlash.[24] Similarly, Jetschke also broadly upholds the model, but raises concerns over the model's ability to open the door to government counter-framing of issues.[25] Sikkink applies the spiral model in the US setting in the 2013 revisit, and again although her research applies to

---

[21] Anthony Tirado Chase, 'The State and Human Rights: Governance and Sustainable Human Development in Yemen' (2003) International Journal of Politics, Culture, and Society 213.

[22] Makau W Mutua, 'Savages, Victims, and Saviors: The Metaphor of Human Rights' (2001) 42 Harvard International Law Journal 201.

[23] Lewis and Hemmings (n 4); Hemmings (n 7); Go (n 6); Mignolo, 'Prophets Facing Sidewise' (n 6); Mignolo, 'Coloniality and Globalization' (n 6); Mignolo and Bussmann (n 6); Naicker (n 6); Patel (n 6).

[24] Ryan Goodman and Derek Jinks, 'How to Influence States: Socialization and International Human Rights Law' (2004) 54 Duke Law Journal 621.

[25] Anja Jetschke, 'The Power of Human Rights a Decade after: From Euphoria to Contestation?' in Thomas Risse-Kappen and Stephen C Ropp (eds), *The Persistent Power of Human Rights: From Commitment to Compliance* (Cambridge University Press, 2013).

more authoritarian governments, she finds that backlash in the US context was damaging to the process.[26] Returning to her study in Colombia, Brysk notes that the involvement of international actors may have fuelled some of the human rights violations carried out by the state, particularly in the government's use of violence against both domestic and foreign actors.[27] Though not directly seen in his work in Argentina, Encarnación highlighted how many other Latin American countries purposefully rejected gay rights as a Western, American ideal which derailed any domestic movement.[28] Again, we see similarities with digital feminist activist thought.

Particularly as Western bias and influence appears to become less and less palatable to non-Western countries, the sustained international involvement specified by the model runs the risk of sparking domestic regressive backlash. Governments have been seen to purposefully and intentionally act out in response to the 'foreign meddling' in domestic affairs. Without due accord to the position and voice of domestic actors, the spiral model not only overlooks but indeed paves the way for this kind of backlash, which can have devastating long-term effects. Particularly in social media, which tends to be seen as a Western tool (and statistically remains so[29]), the possibility of government backlash is exacerbated. Once again, the echoes of colonialism are hard not to hear.[30]

Lack of progression

In his study in Saudi Arabia, Alhargan found that the model was an excellent representation of the first three phases, but that it deviated when progressing beyond tactical concessions.[31] Jetschke and Liese in their work also find issues with progression.[32] Again, they find that the first three phases hold true, but phases four and five can be problematic. Brysk in another study on sexual politics found that there was a stalling effect between commitment

---

[26] Kathryn Sikkink, 'The United States and Torture: Does the Spiral Model Work?' in Thomas Risse-Kappen and Stephen C Ropp (eds), *The Persistent Power of Human Rights: From Commitment to Compliance* (Cambridge University Press, 2013).

[27] Brysk (n 19).

[28] Encarnación (n 15).

[29] 'Digital in 2018: World's Internet Users Pass the 4 Billion Mark' (We Are Social UK, 30 January 2018) https://wearesocial.com/uk/blog/2018/01/global-digital-report-2018, accessed 4 October 2018.

[30] Hemmings (n 7).

[31] Raed A Alhargan, 'The Impact of the UN Human Rights System and Human Rights INGOs on the Saudi Government with Special Reference to the Spiral Model' (2012) 16 The International Journal of Human Rights 598.

[32] Anja Jetschke and Andrea Liese, 'The Spiral Model: How Does It Score After Ten Years?', *Workshop: The Power of Human Rights – Ten Years After* (2009).

and compliance.[33] Shor not only found a lack of progression as problematic, but indeed identified countries which in fact *regressed*. He therefore takes issue with the unidirectionality of the model introduced earlier in addition to the potential for lack of progression.[34]

At many points in the development of the spiral model, the researchers tracked a government through to phase 4 (prescriptive status) and concluded that, with time, the government would indeed move into phase 5 (rule-consistent behaviour).[35] Additionally, in some cases the establishment of phase 5 has been less than thorough. Governments are considered to have institutionalized said norms if they 'talk the talk' but we do not truly know if they 'walk the walk'.[36] In other words, true institutionalization needs to be measured and examined much more specifically. Too many times, governments have dipped their toes in the metaphorical water of human rights norms but then failed to fully institutionalize the normative change which would positively affect domestic civil society.

If campaigns at times struggle to move governments from prescriptive status through to rule-consistent behaviour, the fickle and capricious nature of social media then becomes an area of significant concern. In the simplest of terms, if a campaign that is strategically and hierarchically managed and operated fails to institutionalize human rights norms, how could a social media campaign, moving quickly and passing in and out of public attention, possibly be successful in instituting long-term meaningful change?

Domestic capacity

Domestic capacity has also been examined as a potential weakness in the spiral model. Borzel and Risse explore the applicability and utility of the model in limited statehood contexts. They find that the model is still relevant, but with less impact on a government with limited capacity.[37]

---

[33] Alison Brysk, 'Changing Hearts and Minds' in Thomas Risse, Stephen C Ropp, and Kathryn Sikkink (eds), *The Persistent Power of Human Rights* (Cambridge University Press, 2013).

[34] Shor (n 13).

[35] Risse et al (n 9).

[36] Beth A Simmons, 'From Ratification to Compliance: Quantitative Evidence on the Spiral Model' in Thomas Risse-Kappen and Stephen C Ropp (eds), *The Persistent Power of Human Rights: From Commitment to Compliance* (Cambridge University Press, 2013).

[37] Tanja Borzel and Thomas Risse, 'Human Rights in Areas of Limited Statehood: The New Agenda' in Thomas Risse-Kappen and Stephen C Ropp (eds), *The Persistent Power of Human Rights: From Commitment to Compliance* (Cambridge University Press, 2013).

Of note, their work points out that the model only really has two options for governments: deliberate non-compliance or compliance. There is no scope in the model for non-compliance *not* due to deliberate state decisions. Goldsmith and Krasner come to a similar conclusion about the model ignoring national capabilities.[38] Shor's exploration is equally fascinating, where he finds that the model does not leave any room for security threats or differentiation of domestic practices. This lack of accommodation for domestic capacity issues, either due to potential conflict or differing practices, renders the model problematic in his view.[39]

Although the second incarnation of the model attempted to address some of the capacity criticisms, it remains a weak point.[40] The model does not appropriately accommodate the practicalities of domestic government capacities. In other words, there are cases where the government, for lack of a better word, *wants* to change but lacks the capacity to do so. Capacity may be infrastructure related or power related, but either way the government is in a position where it cannot progress through the model. The model does not allow for this kind of 'deviation' where domestic capacity becomes a significant variable which impacts on final outcomes.

International Twitter-driven hashtag campaigns are even less likely to be able to accommodate for domestic capacity. Governments are targeted by social media users with little to no knowledge of the ability to implement change. The pseudo-mob mentality on social media does not stop to think about whether change is even possible before demanding domestic change. Again, this risk is potentially exacerbated if the campaign is foreign-driven. If domestic capacity does indeed dictate whether a campaign will be successful or not, a Twitter-driven hashtag campaign could face even greater challenges.

Incentives

Krebs and Jackson present a strong argument that, when it comes to governments instituting change, persuasion alone usually is not enough.[41] This could be even more exacerbated when looking at unpalatable women's rights campaigns. Linde's work applying the model to the Czech Republic found that, while reputational damage did play a critical role given the political environment and timing, in reality economics played more

---

[38] Jack Goldsmith and Stephen D Krasner, 'The Limits of Idealism' (2003) 132 Daedalus 47.
[39] Shor (n 13).
[40] Risse-Kappen et al (n 10).
[41] Ronald R Krebs and Patrick Thaddeus Jackson, 'Twisting Tongues and Twisting Arms: The Power of Political Rhetoric' (2007) 13 European Journal of International Relations 35.

important part than persuasion alone.[42] When looking at corruption in Kenya, Bachelard found that not only did the spiral model not take account of material incentives for *positive* change, but in fact did not take account of the possible role of material incentives for *not changing*, particularly in a context dealing with corruption.[43] Similarly, Goldsmith and Krasner also highlight the potential role of material interests which are not accounted for in the model.[44] Snyder and Vinjamuri also discuss the need for both carrot and stick in the institutionalization of change, something which the model does not fully address.[45]

The current model discounts and ignores the very real importance of incentives other than reputational damage. Rather than building the role of incentives into the model, the model chooses to ignore this aspect. For example, some of the case studies did indeed show that incentives, in the end, were part of the movement towards rule-consistent behaviour, but the model instead seems to place causality on the sustained pressure from international actors and TANs.[46]

International Twitter-driven hashtag campaigns will rely almost exclusively on reputational harm and naming and shaming as incentives for change. This kind of pressure, while certainly useful, may not rise to the level necessary to institute long-term, meaningful domestic change.

The role of social media

A media effects framework helps to conceptualize some of the macro-level questions this book seeks to address: what effect does social media have on individuals? Does it influence their decision to participate in the campaign at a population level (in terms of the population of the campaign)? How does the media affect the manner in which they participate (that is, do they reply, do they retweet, do they write their own original Tweet?) Is there an impact on how often they engage with the campaign? The answers to these questions then have an additional cyclical effect by feeding into the social media campaign and altering the influence at individual level. As social

---

[42] Robyn Linde, 'Statelessness and Roma Communities in the Czech Republic: Competing Theories of State Compliance' (2006) 13 International Journal on Minority & Group Rights 341.

[43] Jérôme Y Bachelard, 'The Anglo-Leasing Corruption Scandal in Kenya: The Politics of International and Domestic Pressures and Counter-Pressures' (2010) 37 Review of African Political Economy 187.

[44] Goldsmith and Krasner (n 38).

[45] Jack Snyder and Leslie Vinjamuri, 'Trials and Errors: Principle and Pragmatism in Strategies of International Justice' (2003) 28 International Security 5.

[46] Risse et al (n 9).

media is user-driven, there is a bi-directionality of influence that continues, changes, and flows over time. This research certainly does not purport to answer all of these questions, but it is firmly situated in the knowledge that the relationships of influence and effect are a complex, interwoven web. Castells explains this as a 'multimodal' system, both 'synchronous and asynchronous'.[47] Perloff presents a thoroughly visceral picture of the interactions: 'a complex, labyrinth-like area in which perceptions become reality, reality is enshrouded by perceptions, and perceptions hinge on the very important factor of whether you are considering the media's impact on other people or yourself'.[48]

Similar to the critiques of the spiral model, this chapter now turns to a critical approach to understanding the role of social media in activism and campaigning for women's rights. This research explores five specific risk areas identified in social media campaigning: the elite-driven, heteronormative patriarchal nature of social media (in particular in digital feminist activism), the organic, and potentially chaotic, approach to framing, the proven 'fickleness' of trends and campaigns on social media, the potential for a damaging lack of knowledge and understanding of the domestic situation from foreign online campaigners, and the perception of domestic governments of the lack of risk and investment from (foreign) online campaign participants.[49]

Elite-driven, heteronormative, patriarchal structures specified in digital feminist literature

It is well established that communication has a 'fundamental' relationship with power structures.[50] Social media is driven, shaped, and built by a global elite which tend not to reflect non-Western or non-majority values.[51]

---

[47] Manuel Castells, 'Communication, Power and Counter-Power in the Network Society' (2007) 1 International Journal of Communication (19328036) 238, 246.

[48] Richard M Perloff, 'Mass Media, Social Perception, and the Third-Person Effect' in Jennings Bryant and Mary Beth Oliver (eds), *Media Effects: Advances in Theory and Research* (Routledge, 2008) 252.

[49] Reilly Dempsey Willis and Benjamin Mason Meier, 'Framing the Position of Social Media in the Local Institutionalization of International Human Rights Norms' in Thorsten Bonacker, Judith von Heusinger, and Kerstin Zimmer (eds), *Localization in Development Aid: How Global Institutions Enter Local Lifeworlds* (Routledge, 2017).

[50] Castells (n 47) 238; see also Manuel Castells, *Networks of Outrage and Hope: Social Movements in the Internet Age* (second edition, Polity Press, 2015).

[51] Chrysi Dagoula, 'Mapping Political Discussions on Twitter: Where the Elites Remain Elites' (2019) 7 Media and Communication 225; Sebastian Stier, Wolf J Schünemann, and Stefan Steiger, 'Of Activists and Gatekeepers: Temporal and Structural Properties of Policy Networks on Twitter' (2018) 20 New Media & Society 1910; Ott (n 1); Grant Blank, 'The Digital Divide Among Twitter Users and Its Implications for Social Research' (2017) 35 Social Science Computer Review 679.

Although there is (and definitely was) some argument that social media is potentially *less* elite-driven than traditional media,[52] current approaches recognize the continued power imbalances even in new digital media. The very code which operationalizes the platforms comes from a Western, capitalist, predominantly white male world, laden with unconscious (and perhaps conscious) bias.[53] Using these platforms to address issues affecting non-white women in non-Western countries seems a paradox which is hard to accept. This is compounded by the algorithms and filter bubbles which are meant to personalize or even monetize the user experience, leading to 'echo chambers' which may be closed to non-dominant discourse.[54]

Here I reiterate the digital feminist activism debate – are social media platforms potential spaces for new collective actions, cultivated and curated by subaltern counter-publics challenging visible anti-feminist dominant discourse? Or are these platforms so entrenched in capitalist profit-making that all we see are the amplifications of the elite white Western voice (with the fantasy of feminist 'unity'[55]) through echo chambers, filter bubbles, and anti-feminist algorithms?[56]

Additionally, as evidenced by the statistics presented in Chapter 1 of this book, social media still tends to be dominated by users from the Global North.[57] In this study, despite efforts to identify and analyse a campaign targeting a domestic law in the Global North, the vast majority of hashtag campaigns target countries in the Global South. Ireland (#repealthe8th) is in the Global North but was excluded from the final study as it was not as driven by Twitter as the other campaigns were. Argentina is arguably a 'Global North'/Western/developed country and is the only campaign in this study where the target government is not in the Global South. Therefore, there is indirect evidence suggesting that many international Twitter-driven campaigns continue to target countries in the Global South. Viewed in light of the critique of the spiral model that it underemphasizes the role of domestic

---

[52] For a discussion on the elite-driven nature of traditional media, see, for example, Piers Robinson, 'The CNN Effect: Can the News Media Drive Foreign Policy?' (1999) 25 Review of International Studies 301, 303–4. For a discussion on the potential of social media for non-dominant discourse, see, for example, Castells (n 47).

[53] Ott (n 1); Gillespie (n 4); Mendes et al (n 2).

[54] Willis, 'Habermasian Utopia or Sunstein's Echo Chamber?' (n 3).

[55] Lewis and Hemmings (n 4); Mignolo, 'Prophets Facing Sidewise' (n 6).

[56] Ott (n 1); Gillespie (n 4); boyd, *It's Complicated* (n 2); boyd, 'Can Social Network Sites Enable Political Action?' (n 2); Donovan and boyd (n 4); Mendes et al (n 2); Hemmings (n 7); Lewis and Hemmings (n 4).

[57] 'Digital in 2018: World's Internet Users Pass the 4 Billion Mark' (n 29).

actors and domestic voices and anticolonial schools of thought, looking at social media campaigns this is likely to be of even more concern.[58] With social media dominated by users from the Global North, and campaigns targeting countries in the Global South, the likelihood of domestic users and voices being 'drowned out' by foreign influence is high. Equally, the platforms are designed in an elite-driven way which reduces the likelihood of non-Western, non-elite voices gaining visibility.

Social media is organic and chaotic

By definition, social media is 'social' because content is user-driven (though see discussion on the underlying algorithms and filter bubble which act as gatekeepers for some messages to emerge and others to die off – not all users have equal access).[59] 'Messaging is organic, created and promulgated by users', and likely to be a subsection of elite users at that.[60] According to Castells, 'it is self-generated in content, self-directed in emission, and self-selected in reception by many that communicate with many'.[61] No longer do the knowledge-based hierarchies of advocacy networks or the expertise levels of epistemic communities apply; rather an elite hierarchy which is unmanaged dictates the rules.[62] This does not mean that there is no scope for organizationally driven framing, but there are no guarantees that users will carry the messaging as set out by formal advocacy networks.[63] Therefore there is little control over the messaging which will dominate the campaigns or 'earn' visibility through the platforms themselves.

---

[58] Go (n 6); Mignolo, 'Prophets Facing Sidewise' (n 6); Mignolo and Bussmann (n 6); Mignolo, 'Coloniality and Globalization' (n 6); Naicker (n 6); Patel (n 6).

[59] Sarah Joseph, 'Social Media, Political Change, and Human Rights' (2012) 35 Boston College International and Comparative Law Review 145; Bart Cammaerts, 'Protest Logics and the Mediation Opportunity Structure' (2012) 27 European Journal of Communication 117.

[60] Anjali S Bal, Chris Archer-Brown, Karen Robson, and Daniel E Hall, 'Do Good, Goes Bad, Gets Ugly: Kony 2012' (2013) 13 Journal of Public Affairs 202.

[61] Castells (n 47) 248.

[62] Steven Livingston, 'The CNN Effect Reconsidered (Again): Problematizing ICT and Global Governance in the CNN Effect Research Agenda' (2011) 4 Media, War & Conflict 20; Castells (n 47) 248; Malcolm Gladwell, 'Small Change' (*The New Yorker*, 10 April 2010) http://www.newyorker.com/magazine/2010/10/04/small-change-malcolm-gladw ell, accessed 14 March 2016; E Schwarz, '@hannah_arendt: An Arendtian Critique of Online Social Networks' (2014) 43 Millennium – Journal of International Studies 165.

[63] Giselle A Auger, 'Fostering Democracy through Social Media: Evaluating Diametrically Opposed Nonprofit Advocacy Organizations' Use of Facebook, Twitter, and YouTube' (2013) 39 Public Relations Review 369.

The 'noisiness' of a multitude of competing frames is also identified as problematic in the media effects literature.[64] There is little control over how messaging evolves, changes, or fluctuates over time. As stated by a feminist writing about the #delhigangrape campaign: '[f]eminist voices have been a part of these projects, but the chorus of slogans made it difficult to decipher who was saying what'.[65] This differs significantly from the more traditional work of TANs where framing and messaging are carefully and strategically constructed and crafted to suit particular purposes. Constructed messaging is, ideally, sensitive to domestic context and reflective of domestic society. Organic and potentially elite-driven social media messaging, which can be retweeted thousands of times, is user-generated and may not reflect those strategic choices or sensitivities.[66] As Joseph writes, 'social media can also spread bad ideas and content just as it can spread good ideas and content'.[67] Another area of concern is the ability of counter-narratives or repressive regimes to co-opt or thwart an advocacy campaign.[68]

'Fickleness' of social media

Social media campaigns could potentially lack persistence, coming and going faster than meaningful change demands. This risk draws down from the 'CNN effect', a theory which holds that the speed of the spread of news with modern technology has a potential 'policy forcing' effect on decision makers.[69] According to Gilboa, this effect can mean that 'media pressure on reluctant governments are most likely to result in minimalist policies aimed at defusing pressure for interventions on the ground'.[70] Governments can no longer make carefully considered decisions, but rather are forced to respond with almost immediate effect, sometimes to reports that are ill-founded or lacking in evidence.[71] The media effects literature identified this

---

[64] Maxwell E McCombs, Donald L Shaw, and David H Weaver, 'New Directions in Agenda-Setting Theory and Research' (2014) 17 Mass Communication and Society 781; Robinson (n 52).

[65] Debolina Dutta and Oishik Sircar, 'India's Winter of Discontent: Some Feminist Dilemmas in the Wake of a Rape' (2013) 39 Feminist Studies 293, 295.

[66] Donovan and boyd (n 4).

[67] Joseph (n 59) 173.

[68] Beth A Simmons, 'Preface: International Relationships in the Information Age' (2013) 15 International Studies Review 1; Willis, 'Habermasian Utopia or Sunstein's Echo Chamber?' (n 3); Willis, 'To Tweet or Not to Tweet: How Hashtag Campaigns Open Spaces for Counter-Narratives' (2018) The Society of Legal Scholars Annual Conference at Queen Mary, University of London.

[69] Eytan Gilboa, 'The CNN Effect: The Search for a Communication Theory of International Relations' (2005) 22 Political Communication 27.

[70] Ibid, 334.

[71] Gilboa (n 69); Livingston (n 62); Robinson (n 52).

as problematic simply when television became more connected via satellite feeds; this effect when mapped onto social media is likely to increase.

Media effects studies also highlight the so-called 'sleeper effect', whereby the influence of the media on individuals may not manifest for quite some time.[72] With the speed at which social media moves, this sleeper effect could problematize the long-term potential of the influence. Hashtags which are trending today may not trend next week or may not even be around next month. Research has shown that the average lifespan of a Tweet, including retweets, is just 18 minutes.[73] Social media experts recommend that campaigns for business or marketing last between 45 days and nine months.[74] Using these metrics as indicators of users' general social media attention span, this indicates that hashtag campaigns are at risk of being relatively short-lived. If longevity is a concern of advocacy campaigns under the spiral model, then campaigns on social media are even more uncertain to progress through to rule-consistent behaviour. Information spreads quickly, including erroneous or false Tweets.[75] In fact, the pace of social media has even been characterized as 'dangerous' to international law, in direct conflict with the slow and methodical pace of international justice.[76] In her work on exploring the use of social media in Iran after the 2009 elections, Naghibi found that the Iranian protests dominated North American media – until the death of Michael Jackson.[77] Western attention cared about the Iranian protests, but only until the King of Pop overdosed.

---

[72] Elizabeth M Perse and Jennifer L Lambe (eds), *Media Effects and Society* (second edition, Routledge, 2017).

[73] 'When Is My Tweet's Prime of Life? (A Brief Statistical Interlude)' (*Moz*, 12 November 2012) https://moz.com/blog/when-is-my-tweets-prime-of-life, accessed 10 December 2018; 'The Life Span of a Tweet: Why Fast Isn't Fast Enough in a Crisis' (*Stanton Communication*, 16 March 2017) https://stantoncomm.com/life-span-tweet, accessed 10 December 2018.

[74] 'Multi-Channel Marketing: How Long Should Campaigns Last?' (Technology Therapy™ Group, 12 January 2015) https://technologytherapy.com/long-multi-channel-advertis ing-campaigns-last/, accessed 10 December 2018; 'How Long Does a Typical Social Media Campaign Last?' (Ignite Social Media – The Original Social Media Agency, 7 February 2008) https://www.ignitesocialmedia.com/lifestyle/how-long-does-a-typical-social-media-campaign-last/, accessed 10 December 2018.

[75] Joseph (n 59); Felicity Morse, 'Bring Back Our Girls: Boko Haram Should Be Scared of a Hashtag' (*The Independent*, 13 May 2014) http://www.independent.co.uk/voices/comment/the-bring-back-our-girls-campaign-is-working-boko-haram-should-be-sca red-of-a-hashtag-9360830.html, accessed 11 December 2018.

[76] Marta Poblet and Jonathan Kolieb, 'Responding to Human Rights Abuses in the Digital Era: New Tools, Old Challenges' (2018) 54 Stanford Journal of International Law 259; boyd, 'Can Social Network Sites Enable Political Action?' (n 2).

[77] Nima Naghibi, 'Diasporic Disclosures: Social Networking, NEDA, and the 2009 Iranian Presidential Elections' (2011) 34 Biography 56.

Lack of knowledge of the domestic context or voice

Somewhat derivative of the first social media risk outlined in this section, with many hashtag users likely being foreign there is a major concern that individuals are campaigning blindly, without any knowledge of the domestic context, voice, or desires. This is a particular concern when we already know how difficult it is to hear some women's voices. Research has shown that the vast majority of social media activity is in 'entertainment'; this could blur the lines between serious advocacy campaigns and personal desires for online identity creation.[78] One researcher has even gone so far as to refer to social media activism as a 'narcissistic compulsion to self-disclose'.[79] A powerful quote on this topic comes from a commentary on the #bringbackourgirls campaign:

> The dualistic construction of women as worthy of political recognition due to their relationship to a more privileged agent [comparing the girls to Obama's daughters] works powerfully in the age of hashtag activism through its ability to draw emotional response and impassioned reaction from a non-contiguous and apathetic populous. ... The enthusiastic Western adoption of #BringBackOurGirls must also be treated skeptically for its failure to consider its own imperial dynamics.[80]

Perhaps it is worth reiterating Hemmings' insight here: 'the fantasy of white, Western rescue of passive brown female victims of unconscionable brown patriarchs is a key mode through which colonial violence is displaced and refashioned as ethical'.[81] Not only would this render these campaigns ineffective, this perspective goes so far as to label them as 'colonial violence'. In other words, rich, elite Western countries exerting a new form of power over non-white or non-Western countries which may have been exploited through colonial rule or the slave trade.

No 'risk' to campaign participants

One of the main tenets of the slactivist literature (that which critiques using social media as 'slacker activism') is that true activism is rooted in the personal risk that activists take when participating in a campaign – arrest, losing a job, marking their identity, even potential physical harm.[82] Gladwell

---

[78] Schwarz (n 62).

[79] Naghibi (n 77) 59.

[80] Meredith Loken, '#BringBackOurGirls and the Invisibility of Imperialism' (2014) 14 Feminist Media Studies 1100.

[81] Hemmings (n 7) 966.

[82] Gladwell (n 62); Donatella Della Porta and Mario Diani, *Social Movements: An Introduction* (second edition, Blackwell Publishing, 2006).

makes this eminently clear when he writes: 'Facebook activism succeeds not by motivating people to make a real sacrifice but by motivating them to do the things people do when they're not motivated enough to make a real sacrifice.'[83] This personal risk or sacrifice, in traditional campaigning, underscores to the governments how important the issue is to voting citizens.[84] From a feminist perspective, there is also something particularly important about using the physical female body in acts of protest.[85] Although there is extensive research exploring how 'collective identity' and community building can be achieved in protest movements on social media and how this may translate into some offline political activity,[86] the efficacy of this new kind of protest is contested.[87] The disruption caused by social media protests is, arguably, less damaging to domestic governments.[88]

Although for some there is risk even in participating in online campaigning (see particularly Chapter 6), for many there is no real risk.[89] This lack of risk translates into a lack of incentive for the domestic government to change. The only incentive for governments to change is the naming and shaming pressure, which may extend from social media into traditional media. However, as critics of the spiral model point out, other incentives may be necessary to truly push a domestic government to change. The lack of risk and associated incentives in social media campaigns may simply not rise to the level necessary to see long-term, meaningful, institutionalized change. When researching the impact of social media on an early campaign, Save Darfur, the researchers found that:

---

[83] Gladwell (n 62).

[84] Sidney Tarrow, *Power in Movement: Social Movements, Collective Action, and Politics* (Cambridge University Press, 1994); Joel Penney, 'Social Media and Symbolic Action: Exploring Participation in the Facebook Red Equal Sign Profile Picture Campaign' (2015) 20 Journal of Computer-Mediated Communication 52.

[85] Karina Eileraas, 'Sex(t)Ing Revolution, Femen-Izing the Public Square: Aliaa Magda Elmahdy, Nude Protest, and Transnational Feminist Body Politics' (2014) 40 Signs 40.

[86] Manuel Castells, *Networks of Outrage and Hope: Social Movements in the Internet Age* (second edition, Polity Press, 2015); Paolo Gerbaudo, *Tweets and the Streets: Social Media and Contemporary Activism* (Pluto Press, 2012); Paolo Gerbaudo and Emiliano Treré, 'In Search of the "We" of Social Media Activism: Introduction to the Special Issue on Social Media and Protest Identities' (2015) 18 Information, Communication & Society 865; Stefania Milan, 'From Social Movements to Cloud Protesting: The Evolution of Collective Identity' (2015) 18 Information, Communication & Society 887.

[87] Schwarz (n 62); Maria Bakardjieva, 'Do Clouds Have Politics? Collective Actors in Social Media Land' (2015) 18 Information, Communication & Society 983.

[88] Della Porta and Diani (n 82); Cammaerts (n 59).

[89] Malcolm Gladwell and Clay Shirky, 'From Innovation to Revolution: Do Social Media Make Protests Possible?' (2011) 90 *Foreign Affairs* 153; Gladwell (n 62); Della Porta and Diani (n 82).

Considering the extraordinary size of this movement (1.2 million members), the influence and accessibility of the world's largest social medium (Facebook), and the moral urgency of the social issue at stake (genocide), the amount and quality of activism that resulted from the myriad online interactions among Cause members were extraordinarily modest.[90]

Research design

Research questions

With this three-part theoretical grounding, this research therefore sets out to answer the following questions:

1. Can international campaigns originating in and driven by hashtags on Twitter contribute to domestic legal change in women's rights?
2. If so, which campaign behaviours are associated with change?

At the time the study was designed, Twitter was generally perceived by academics as an accessible, reliable, and valuable site for data mining and analysis.[91] While these campaigns were present on other platforms, Tweets were used as indicators of the campaigns as a whole and provided a researchable window via a vast and accessible data set. The Appendix in this book goes into detail around data collection and analysis, demonstrating the design tools used to attempt to overcome some of the critiques of the algorithms used in Twitter. The future of the hashtag given the 2023 changes to the platform are discussed in Chapter 7.

Campaign selection

With the overarching framework and architecture built, the next and perhaps most crucial step in the research was the selection of hashtag campaigns.

---

[90] Kevin Lewis, Kurt Gray, and Jens Meierhenrich, 'The Structure of Online Activism' (2014) Sociological Science 1, 4.

[91] Steven Ovadia, 'Exploring the Potential of Twitter as a Research Tool' (2009) 28 Behavioral & Social Sciences Librarian 202; Luke Sloan and Anabel Quan-Haase, *The SAGE Handbook of Social Media Research Methods* (SAGE, 2017); Tyler McCormick, Hedwig Lee, and Emma Spiro, 'Using Twitter for Demographic and Social Science Research: Tools for Data Collection and Processing' (2017) 46 Sociological Methods & Research, https://journals-sagepub-com.uos.idm.oclc.org/doi/full/10.1177/004912411 5605339?casa_token=K4lvY7ipluQAAAAA%3AwF-Z75tcF63ueaY5HCM1SiXzOg97G fSHs_59ItqA5FTt3Lzi-TQfPwa6xjXd-qA1_QO_QZ_upls5, accessed 26 April 2024; Reilly Dempsey Willis, 'Exploring the Relationship between Global Twitter Campaigns and Domestic Law: Methodological Challenges and Solutions' (2021) 30 Information & Communications Technology Law 3.

A large-scale mapping exercise was undertaken to identify possible hashtag campaigns for women's rights across the given time period (from when hashtags began to be widely used in 2009 until 2016). Fifty-one campaigns were initially identified. Through an iterative process, a set of distinct selection criteria was then developed:

1. international attention;
2. more than 1,000 Tweets;
3. seeking specific domestic legal change (either repealing an existing law, passing a new law, or implementing an existing law) in the area of women's rights;
4. originating in, and continuing to be driven by, Twitter and the hashtag.

Selection criteria four was pivotal to the study. These are all campaigns which 'took off' with a Tweet sometime before 2016. Some campaigning may have been ongoing before the original Tweet, but the campaigns did not garner significant attention until the hashtag campaign emerged on Twitter. Therefore, these campaigns all *originated in* and are *rooted in* Twitter via a hashtag. The campaigns then all had to continue to be *driven* by Twitter and the hashtag. This means that the campaigns centred on social media – they were referred to by the hashtag (that is, it was not generally known as, say, Ni Una Menos, it was referred to as #niunamenos, similar to the #MeToo movement, though that campaign does not seek specific legal change in a single target country and thus was not selected), activities were organized on social media, activists shared information and knowledge on Twitter using the hashtag, key messages were developed and spread via Twitter and the hashtag (though see discussion on the non-neutrality of Twitter later in this chapter), and this continued drive and focus on social media was clear throughout the entire lifespan of the campaign. This, by no means, is to claim that there were no other campaign activities taking place, but rather that there is something inherently different about campaigns which originate in and continue to be driven by Twitter. They are Twitter-*based* and Twitter-*driven* hashtag campaigns, not Twitter-*only* campaigns. The role of social media in mobilizing, messaging, and framing is different from campaigns which are not driven by Twitter and the use of the hashtag. It is this difference which necessitates study to help understand the role of social media driven campaigns in legal change.

Of the initially identified 51 campaigns, all fit criteria one. Nineteen campaigns were excluded on criteria three, as they sought to raise awareness and dialogue, but not to change specific domestic law. Eight campaigns were excluded for targeting legal change, but not in one specific domestic location (one of which also failed on criteria two). Five were excluded for campaigning for general domestic legal change, not specific. Four were

Table 2.1: Overview of initial study campaigns

Campaign	Target location	Legal change sought
#delhigangrape	India	Strengthening laws protecting women from sexual violence, including prosecutions
#farkhunda	Afghanistan	Strengthening laws prosecuting perpetrators of violence against women and improving frontline policing to protect women and girls in public spaces
#letwomengotostadium	Iran	Call for a change to law which bans women from entering sporting stadiums to watch men's volleyball
#mydressmychoice	Kenya	Properly implementing existing laws protecting women from violence, particularly in the public sphere
#niunamenos	Argentina	Strengthening laws protecting women from femicide, including prosecutions
#sendeanlat	Turkey	Strengthening laws protecting women from femicide, including prosecutions
#stopstoning	Iran	Repealing a law which calls for stoning as a form of capital punishment
#women2drive	Saudi Arabia	Lifting a ban on women driving
#malala	*Pakistan*	*Strengthening laws around girls' access to education*
#notacriminal	*Ireland*	*Decriminalization of abortion*

Note: Factual details of the spark incidents of each campaign are presented in the relevant campaign chapters.

excluded for focusing on individual cases and not changes in the law as a whole. Two were excluded for having multiple hashtags. This left a possible list of 13. The target number of campaigns was ten, given data collection and time constraints. Three more were excluded from the final list to ensure a range of geographic targets and issues in focus. The final list of ten is presented in Table 2.1.

During the process of data collection and initial analysis, two further campaigns were excluded, #malala and #notacriminal. #malala, although the largest and arguably most 'famous' campaign in the study, was excluded as the content of the Tweets significantly lost focus on girls' right to education in Pakistan. The hashtag quickly changed and became focused on Malala herself as a spokesperson, activist, and role model for girls' rights in general. This therefore meant the campaign failed to meet the original selection criteria. Initial analysis of #notacriminal Tweets showed that this hashtag was subsidiary to another hashtag, #repealthe8th. Tweets for #repealthe8th were then collected. Legal data was collected for this campaign and it became very clear that this campaign was not driven by Twitter, but rather was a 'traditional' advocacy campaign using a multitude of tools and strategies. Twitter was just one. The campaign was therefore, in the late stages of the study, excluded. This left eight campaigns for the final analysis.

The exclusion of #notacriminal is particularly important, as it underscores the careful consideration and attention paid to ensuring that the campaigns in the study were rooted in *and driven by* Twitter and the hashtag. By excluding this campaign well into the study, this shows how the selection criteria were rigorously, consistently, and objectively applied throughout. This also shows that it is possible to clarify the differences between a campaign that is driven by Twitter and a campaign which merely uses Twitter.

Including the two excluded campaigns, 1,051,525 unique Tweets were collected. After #malala and #notacriminal were excluded, a total of 743,671 Tweets were analysed.

Variable selection

Variables were selected from a dual process of identifying metrics to measure the desired characteristics from the research map and assessing available data. An initial list of 25 potential variables were identified based on the theoretical framework only. These were then compared to the data available through a matching process, resulting in a variable map containing 22 variables, five to measure context, 12 independent variables from Twitter data, and five dependent variables to measure legal change. All variables used in this study are therefore derived from and analysed through the three-part theoretical framework of legal change, social media, and feminism.

Context variables were identified to ensure that country characteristics could be examined. Independent variable/Twitter data included the following information: date of the Tweet, content of the Tweet, author of the Tweet, and the number of times it was liked, retweeted, or replied to. From the most 100 prolific users in each campaign, additional information was collected on location, profile, number of campaign Tweets, number of Tweets ever sent, and number of followers. This data generated a total of 513 parameters for study.

Finally, an initial list of five legal categories was set to measure the dependent variable of legal change and outcomes. This list included hard law, soft law, budget allocation, judicial involvement, and UN reporting. As the data was collected and analysed, the list was reduced down to four and amended: legislative change, institutionalization (including government discourse, soft law, and budgets), law enforcement (to cover both police involvement and the courts), and UN dialogue. These categories adequately covered the data which was available while providing ample evidence for quantifying legal change. Throughout the process of data collection, cleaning, and analysis, some adjustments and modifications were necessary. The final variable map, as shown in Table 2.2, included eight context variables measured across 14 parameters, seven Twitter variables measured across ~500 parameters, and four legal variables measured across 150–200 pieces of evidence per campaign.

Data collection and took place across 2017 and 2018, with Tweets from up until November 2016 collected and analysed. The main study, in all, took place from 2015 to 2020, with a brief update in 2023.

Using composite scores

For each variable, a process was also undertaken to distil the rather large number of parameter components down to one composite score. For the independent variables, parameters which were ordinal, scaled, and most reflected the research questions were identified. The numerical data was then divided into quintiles for each parameter, and each campaign given a score of 1–5 based on the quintiles. These were reversed for negative parameters. The average of these scaled scores provided the composite score in each independent variable for each campaign. In other words, those measures that could be represented numerically were 'sliced' into five equal sections to give a ranking of one to five.

Creating composite scores can be useful but brings the risk that nuanced information will be lost. For this reason, while the composite scores were analysed in detail, this was not at the expense of the individual parameters. The overall composite score comprised of persistence, engagement, users, and messaging/norms (context and sentiment are not 'scaled' and therefore cannot be used in a regression analysis).

Readers interested in the specifics of these methods are encouraged to visit the Appendix for more information on the data collection and analysis, and an important discussion about correlation versus causation.[92]

Conclusion

In sum, the selected variables and null hypotheses can be mapped together (see Table 2.3).

This chapter has served to provide a full account of the development of the research framework (though again for more technical details please see the Appendix), starting from theory and moving into methodology and execution.

---

[92] Willis (n 91).

RESEARCH FRAMEWORK

Table 2.2: Definitions of variables

Variable	Description
Context	
Months to regime change	The number of months between the start of the campaign and the next election, collected from publicly available information.
Gender Development Index	Gender Development Index, as developed from the United Nations Development Programme (UNDP).[a] This score looks at health, knowledge, and living standards. Index is from the year the campaign started.
Gender Inequality Index	The Gender Inequality Index is also UNDP and measures differences between men and women in reproductive health, empowerment, and economic status.[b] Index is from the year the campaign started.
Gender Gap Index	The Gender Gap Index is produced by the World Economic Forum and uses parameters in Economic Participation and Opportunity, Educational Attainment, Health and Survival, and Political Empowerment.[c] Index is from the year the campaign started.
Political Terror Scale Amnesty International (AI)	The Political Terror Scale measures political terror as violations of basic human rights to the physical integrity of the person by agents of the state within the territorial boundaries of the state in question. The AI indicator uses information taken from Amnesty International's State of the World's Human Rights Report.[d] The score is taken from the year the campaign started.
Political Terror Scale US State	The Political Terror Scale measures political terror as violations of basic human rights to the physical integrity of the person by agents of the state within the territorial boundaries of the state in question. The US State indicator uses the information published by the United States Department of State in the Country Reports on Human Rights Practices.[e] The score is taken from the year the campaign started.
Gender equality civil society organizations	The number of national 'civil society organizations' registered with the United Nations Economic and Social Council that specify work on Millennium Development Goal 3 (gender equality). Due to availability of data, this variable is from 2017.
Treaty status	The number of International Human Rights Treaties, including Optional Protocols, that have been signed and ratified by the country before 2017. The score is out of 13.
CEDAW status	Specifically measures engagement with the Convention on the Elimination of All Forms of Discrimination Against Women (CEDAW) and its two Optional Protocols. Score is from 2017 and is out of a possible 3.
CEDAW Decl/ Reserv	The total number of declarations and reservations to CEDAW as of 2017. The higher the number the less engaged the country is with CEDAW.

(continued)

Table 2.2: Definitions of variables (continued)

Variable	Description
Relative capacity score, agri	The relative capacity score is somewhat experimental and aims to measure government performance from a social science perspective. The relative capacity score 'agri' approximates the ability of governments to appropriate portions of the national output to advance public goals, using mining and agriculture. The score for all countries is from 2013 due to the availability of data.[f]
Relative capacity score, work	The relative capacity score is somewhat experimental and aims to measure government performance from a social science perspective. The relative capacity score 'work' gauges the capacity of governments to mobilize populations under their control using activity rate of population. The score for all countries is from 2013 due to the availability of data.[g]
World justice project Open Government Index	The Open Government Index aims to measure how 'open' a government is based on the perspective of the people. It measures across publicized laws and government data, the right to information, civic participation, and complaint mechanisms. The data available is from 2015.[h]
Internet access	Captured by the World Bank, this measures the number of individuals using the internet as a percentage of the total population. This measure is from the year the campaign started.[i]
Legal	
Legislation	As a key outcome variable from the spiral model is legislative change, it is crucial to look at this variable as an indicator of 'success' of the campaigns.[j] To this end, relevant laws and legislation were identified and collected from before the campaign and after the campaign started. Change was measured against the stated goals of the campaigns. As a criterion for inclusion in the study was a clear legal goal, each campaign therefore had a stated desired change in some form of legislation. This aspect of the legal analysis was, therefore, fairly straightforward.
Institutionalization	Beyond simply hard law legal change, advocates are well aware that soft law is needed to move from rhetoric to implementation on the ground. This measure indicates the regime's willingness to institutionalize the norm. To gauge how the domestic government *really* addressed the issues in the question, a wide range of documentation and reporting was collected and analysed from before and after the campaign. This ranged from policies and regulations intended to implement the law (for example, a national strategy on violence against women), budgetary information (for example, how much money does the government spend on programmes to reduce violence against women?), evidence of government discourse relating to the campaign and the issue (press releases, interviews, media reports), non-governmental organization documentation providing domestic insight into the 'on the ground' situation for women and girls, and any other relevant and reliable

RESEARCH FRAMEWORK

Table 2.2: Definitions of variables (continued)

Variable	Description
	information discovered through a snowballing technique. When read together, these various pieces created a mosaic picture of how far changes had been institutionalized to benefit women and girls domestically. Change was measured by how much the picture 'aligned' with the goals of the campaign.
Law enforcement	The involvement of courts has been cited as an important aspect of institutionalizing norms and moving from phase 3 to phases 4 and 5 of the spiral model.[k] Proper use of law enforcement and litigation can 'make or break' how the norm is activated on the ground. When this research first began, the intention was to focus purely on case law relevant to each campaign. However, when in-depth research on the legal change began in earnest, it became very clear that frontline policing was equally important to measuring legal change. To that end, and as much as feasible, information was collected on the actions of police and rates of prosecutions, as well as case law and judicial decisions.
UN dialogue	The final area of law used to measure legal change was the state dialogue with relevant UN treaty bodies. This stemmed from the innovative methodology developed by Meier and Kim in their work on water and sanitation.[l] This process of coding and using state reports to explore the role of international human rights norms in domestic governance provided another important dimension to the measurement of legal change. Analysing what is and is not reported by the state opens a fascinating window on how the government approaches the issue in question, particularly in an international context. Reviewing the language used in UN reporting from the government also gave exceptional insight into the institutionalization of norms, both positive and negative.
Campaign behaviours	
Number of Tweets	Number of Tweets in each campaign (duplicates removed)
Number non-English	The number of Tweets which are not in English.
% non-English	The percentage of Tweets which are not in English.
Persistence	28 different measurements of activity throughout the campaign
Engagement	39 measurements of likes, replies, and retweets
Users	357 different measurements of users and the campaign drivers
Content	71 measurements of the content of the Tweets

Notes: [a] United Nations, 'Gender Development Index', https://hdr.undp.org/gender-development-index, accessed 29 November 2023.

[b] United Nations, 'Gender Inequality Index', https://hdr.undp.org/data-center/thematic-composite-indices/gender-inequality-index, accessed 29 November 2023.

(continued)

Table 2.2: Definitions of variables (continued)

[c] 'Global Gender Gap Report 2023' (World Economic Forum) https://www.weforum.org/publications/global-gender-gap-report-2023/, accessed 29 November 2023.

[d] 'The Political Terror Scale' (The Political Terror Scale) https://www.politicalterrorscale.org/, accessed 29 November 2023.

[e] Ibid.

[f] 'TransResearch Consortium' (TransResearch Consortium, 15 September 2022) https://transresearchconsortium.com, accessed 30 November 2023.

[g] Ibid.

[h] 'Open Government Around the World' (World Justice Project) https://worldjusticeproject.org/open-government-around-world, accessed 30 November 2023.

[i] 'World Bank Open Data' (World Bank Open Data) https://data.worldbank.org, accessed 30 November 2023.

[j] Mark Goodale and Sally Engle-Merry (eds), *The Practice of Human Rights* (Cambridge University Press, 2007).

[k] Thomas Risse, Stephen C Ropp, and Kathryn Sikkink (eds), *The Power of Human Rights: International Norms and Domestic Change* (Cambridge University Press, 1999).

[l] Benjamin Mason Meier and Yuna Kim, 'Human Rights Accountability Through Treaty Bodies: Examining Human Rights Treaty Monitoring for Water and Sanitation' (2015) 26 Duke Journal of Comparative and International Law 139.

Table 2.3: Research map

Theoretical grounding	Independent variable(s)	Null hypothesis (that which this research sets out disprove)
Spiral model lack of focus on domestic actors/overemphasis on Western approaches; social media is elite-driven and non-neutral; campaigns may be dominated and/or driven by elite international actors, drawing from digital feminist activism critiques	Twitter profiles of 100 most prolific users in each campaign	Campaigns dominated by foreign actors will be more successful
Potential government backlash; lack of message tempering due to organic nature of medium; Hemmings' 'colonial violence' approach to feminist activism	Content analysis	Consistency of messaging in Tweets will not affect campaign outcomes
Lack of long-term progression; 'fickleness' and speed of social media	Persistence (Tweets per day)	Persistence of Tweets in Twitter-driven campaigns do not affect campaign outcomes

Table 2.3: Research map (continued)

Theoretical grounding	Independent variable(s)	Null hypothesis (that which this research sets out disprove)
Ignores domestic capacity issues; lack of knowledge of domestic context; colonial concerns from feminist literature	Context (various indicators of domestic political context and situation for women)	Domestic context has no impact on campaign success
Ignores material or nuanced incentives; does not present enough incentive for change to domestic government	Engagement (reply, retweet, and like data)	Campaigns driven by 'likes' will have the same impact as campaigns driven by replies (replies used as a proxy for engagement/investment/risk in campaign, as opposed to a simple click to like)
Theoretical weaknesses in spiral model and feminist scholarly concerns are amplified in social media driven campaigns	Combined quantified variables	Twitter variables have no relationship to campaign outcomes

This chapter has shown the theoretical grounding of the research design, building upon fourth wave feminist work and the literature on digital feminist activism read in conjunction with the body of literature which critiques the spiral model of human rights change theory. These critiques, alongside the academic concerns with social media campaigning and media effects literature, provide the theoretical lynchpin of this research, informing methodological choices, variable selection, and analysis throughout the entire process. At every stage, the research is tied back to these theoretical critiques to frame the understanding of whether and how international Twitter-driven hashtag campaigns affect domestic legal change for women's rights within these lenses of digital feminism, legal change, and media effects. The chapters which follow present each campaign in detail, exploring the context, legal outcomes, and Twitter characteristics.

3

Negative Outcomes: #stopstoning, #letwomengotostadium

In the chapters which follow each of the campaigns are explored in detail, grouped together by outcomes.

Two of the eight campaigns in this research showed negative outcomes after the social media activity – #stopstoning and #letwomengotostadium. Both targeted legal change in Iran. After the #stopstoning campaign there was a change in the law which allowed judges to hand down a sentence of stoning more easily than before the campaign started. Analysis of government statements and legislative reports (discussed in detail later) uncovered indications that the changes to the law were made, at least in part, as backlash against the Western media attention. Reliable reports from Amnesty International, Iran Human Rights, and National Council of Resistance of Iran (NCRI) show that more women have been stoned to death since the campaign started than before. #letwomengotostadium saw no changes to the law while activists appear to be more rigorously targeted for arbitrary arrests and unnecessarily lengthy detentions, again more so after the campaign started than before. Women's rights in Iran came to the forefront with the 2022 protests, with hundreds of arrested, killed, or sentenced to death.[1] The situation for women's rights in this country is dire.

---

[1]   Philip Loft, 'One-Year Anniversary of the Mahsa Amini Protests in Iran' (14 September 2023) https://commonslibrary.parliament.uk/one-year-anniversary-of-the-mahsa-amini-protests-in-iran/, accessed 8 November 2023; Nazanin Boniadi, 'One Year On, Iranian Women Are Still Fighting' (*TIME*, 14 September 2023) https://time.com/6313431/iran-women-defiant-amini-anniversary/, accessed 17 November 2023; Human Rights Watch, 'Iran: Mass Arrests of Women's Rights Defenders' (Human Rights Watch, 19 August 2023) https://www.hrw.org/news/2023/08/19/iran-mass-arrests-womens-rig hts-defenders, accessed 8 November 2023; Philip Loft, '2022 Iran Protests: Human Rights and International Response' (26 May 2023) https://commonslibrary.parliament.uk/resea rch-briefings/cbp-9679/, accessed 8 November 2023; Philip Loft, 'Mahsa Amini Protests

It is of the utmost importance to lay out, at the outset, the *differences* in outcomes. At first blush, it could very easily have been concluded that the regressive results were not related to the characteristics of the Twitter campaigns but were simply down to the closed and authoritative nature of the target domestic government – Iran. However, two findings disprove this theory and allow for the continued examination of the Twitter campaigns. First, there were differences in degrees of regression *between* the two Iranian campaigns. If the only influencing variable were the target country itself, then the outcomes of the two campaigns would have been much more similar. Although both campaigns showed regressive outcomes, there were very important differences in the degree and range of regressive outcomes that indicates that something *else* is at play other than just the closed nature of the target Iranian government. Second, Iran shows domestic context which is similar, and in some instances even better, than other countries in the study. This again underscores that, while of course the nature of the target government is an important variable, other variables are needed to explain the full breadth of differences.

It is also important to note that while Twitter was technically banned in Iran, it was still used as a key advocacy tool for *transnational* campaigns, aiming to connect domestic voices to international pressure. The number of domestic voices present in the campaigns (again explored in more detail later in this chapter) demonstrates that, although banned, Twitter was commonly used via simple workarounds by advocates in Iran, underscoring the spiral model of human rights change.[2]

#stopstoning campaign overview

Stoning is a type of judicial execution condoned by the majority of states and non-governmental organizations.[3] A small number of countries continue to use this practice, primarily through religious doctrine justifications. As these executions are considered unlawful internationally, reports and statistics are difficult, though not impossible, to obtain.[4] These cases also bring up

---

in Iran 2022' (7 October 2022) https://commonslibrary.parliament.uk/mahsa-amini-prote sts-in-iran-2022/, accessed 8 November 2023.

[2] Sheera Frenkel, 'Iranian Authorities Block Access to Social Media Tools' (*The New York Times*, 3 January 2018) https://www.nytimes.com/2018/01/02/technology/iran-prote sts-social-media.html, accessed 28 December 2018.

[3] Amnesty International, 'Iran End Executions by Stoning' (2008) MDE 13/001/2008; Amnesty International, 'Iran Executions by Stoning' (2010) MDE 13/095/2010.

[4] Amnesty International, 'Stoning: Global Summary' (2010).

issues around access to justice and judicial reform.[5] The law in Iran allows for death by stoning for a handful of crimes, mostly involving adultery. The story that sparked the international hashtag campaign was that of Sakineh Mohammadi Ashtiani. Sakineh was found guilty of adultery in 2006 and sentenced to death. While she confessed on television to adultery and involvement in her husband's murder, the confession is highly contested. It is argued that Sakineh was under duress at the time.[6] Sakineh's case, like many others, was compounded when her defence attorneys were also arrested and held in detention.[7] According to Amnesty International, which was active in Sakineh's case, Iranian officials have a 'track record' of bringing criminal charges against anyone attempting to defend individuals such as Sakineh.[8] Although Amnesty regularly releases reports and calls to action for women at risk of stoning, this particular case sparked international outrage and the hashtag campaign emerged. Domestic activists, repressed on the ground domestically, turned to social media and social networks to organize and progress the cause internationally.[9]

While Sakineh herself was eventually released and then acquitted, other women were not. Many Iranian women are sentenced under false accusations and more women are sentenced to stoning than men.[10] The majority of stonings are for women, who are generally more vulnerable due to systemic discrimination, illiteracy, economic injustices, and social injustices.[11] Differences in stoning sentences based on gender is listed as one

---

[5] Amnesty International, 'Iran End Executions by Stoning' (n 3); National Council of Resistance of Iran, 'Women in Pursuit of Justice: Arbitrary Trends and Illegal Proceedings Victimizing Female Political Prisoners in Iran' (2017).

[6] Amnesty International, 'Iran Stoning Sentence Suspension Not Enough' (8 September 2010).

[7] Amnesty International, 'Fears Grow for Iran Stoning Case Lawyer and Son' (3 November 2010); Amnesty International, 'Iran Must End Harassment of Stoning Case Lawyer' (28 July 2010).

[8] Amnesty International, 'Fears Grow for Iran Stoning Case Lawyer and Son' (n 7).

[9] Mahboubeh Abbasgholizadeh, ' "To Do Something We Are Unable to Do in Iran": Cyberspace, the Public Sphere, and the Iranian Women's Movement' (2014) 39 Signs 831.

[10] For a dramatic interpretation of a harrowing true story, the documentary film *The Stoning of Soraya M.*

[11] See, for example, Amnesty International, 'Iran End Executions by Stoning' (n 3) 6–7; Amnesty International, 'Iran Executions by Stoning' (n 3) 3; Mohammad Nayyeri, 'Gender Inequality and Discrimination: The Case of Iranian Women' (Iranian Human Rights Documentation Center, 2013) 11; Maryam Hosseinkhah, 'The Execution of Women in Iranian Criminal Law: An Examination of the Impact of Gender on Laws Concerning Capital Punishment in the New Islamic Penal Code' (IHR, 2012); Rochelle Terman and Mufuliat Fijabi, 'Stoning Is Not Our Culture: A Comparative Analysis of Human Rights and Religious Discourses in Iran and Nigeria' (The Global Campaign to Stop Killing and Stoning Women, 2010) 8; International Federation for Human Rights (FIDH), 'Iran/

of the laws which contradicts the Convention on the Elimination of all forms of Discrimination Against Women (CEDAW) as per Iranian authorities.[12] Because men are legally and religiously allowed to engage in polygamy and temporary marriage, they have mitigating factors to excuse what otherwise would be charged as adultery. Women are not afforded these allowances.[13]

The impression left is that Sakineh was spared specifically because of the international attention, but that this left the hard-line conservatives and religious clerics angry at the foreign interference. Reports of clandestine local stonings carried out under provincial judges' sentences have increased since the campaign, seemingly in response. Mahmood Amiry-Moghaddam, the spokesperson of Iran Human Rights, said: '[W]e hope that the international attention that Mrs. Ashtiani's case has received, will also be directed towards all the others sentenced to death by stoning and will continue until this barbaric punishment is removed from the penal law.'[14] This quote summarizes very well the overall campaign and the effect that was had on the law in Iran. The law remains part of the penal code in 2023.[15]

#letwomengotostadium campaign overview

Women in Iran have not been allowed to attend certain male sporting events since the revolution. A particular ban on attending men's football matches was put in place in 1979. That ban was then extended in 2012 to men's volleyball matches. The ban is intended to protect women from foul language and the potentially uncouth environment in sporting events. However, volleyball had always been seen as quite a family friendly sport and the ban sparked outrage among women.

The #letwomengotostadium campaign began in 2014, just before a large international volleyball tournament was to be held in Tehran. No women were allowed in the stadium in 2014; amidst several arrests of

---

Death Penality: A State Terror Policy' (2009); Justice for Iran, 'Gender Discrimination at Its Worst: An Overview of the Discriminatory Laws of the Islamic Republic of Iran in Family Life: Submission to the United Nations Working Group on Discrimination against Women in Law and in Practice' (2014).

[12] National Council of Resistance of Iran, 'CEDAW: Why the Iranian Regime Does Not Join CEDAW? A Study by the Women's Committee of the National Council of Resistance of Iran' (2016) 3.

[13] Ibid, 4.

[14] Iran Human Rights Documentation Center, 'At Least 7 Stonings Implemented by the Iranian Authorities in the Past 4 Years. 14 More Sentenced to Stoning' (21 August 2010) https://iranhr.net/en/articles/603/, accessed 17 November 2023.

[15] Iran Human Rights Documentation Center, 'Death Penalty Annual Report 2022' (2022) https://iranhr.net/media/files/Rapport_iran_2022_PirQr2V.pdf, accessed 6 November 2023.

women attempting to enter was one British Iranian woman who was later imprisoned. Her case garnered much international attention. Although the President and the Vice President for Women's Affairs announced in early 2015 that the ban would be lifted for the summer tournament, just days before the event the sporting authorities reneged and said that women would not be allowed in. Some foreign women were allowed in the stadium, but no Iranian women. The ban was again tested in February 2016 when another international tournament was held in Kush. The international volleyball association (The Fédération Internationale de Volleyball [FIVB]) stated that it would cease awarding tournaments to Iran if women were not allowed in, but again in the eleventh hour the Iranian authorities announced that women would continue to be banned and the FIVB backed off, claiming that cultural issues were outside its remit. Women were allowed to watch from a rooftop café for a time, but even that was closed off by the end of the tournament. The FIVB came under pressure again in 2017 before the February tournament; this time it took a hard line and said that it would cancel all international tournaments in Iran if women were not allowed. Women were thus allowed into the stadium for the February tournament on Kush Island in 2017. However, since that time only very limited numbers of women have been allowed to attend any tournaments, including the major summer tournament in Tehran.[16] Although related more to football than volleyball, in 2019 Sahar Khodayari self-immolated on the steps of the courthouse and tragically died from her injuries one week later. She had been arrested after wearing a wig to disguise herself as a man to enter the Azadi Stadium to watch her favourite football team. She was imprisoned for three days and, after her release but before her trial, she took her own life when she learned that she could face prison time for her actions.[17] This

---

[16] 'Iran: Progress on Ban for Women at Stadiums' (Human Rights Watch, 28 June 2018) https://www.hrw.org/news/2018/06/28/iran-progress-ban-women-stadi ums, accessed 16 November 2023; Nancy Gillen, 'Iran Continues to Get Away with Discriminatory Policy towards Female Spectators' (*Inside the Games*, 17 October 2020) https://www.insidethegames.biz/articles/1099687/iran-get-away-with-gender-dis crimination, accessed 6 November 2023.

[17] Nada Altaher, 'Iranian Woman Denied Soccer Stadium Access Dies after Setting Herself on Fire' (*CNN*, 10 September 2019) https://edition.cnn.com/2019/09/ 10/football/iran-football-women-sahar-khodayari-spt-intl/index.html, accessed 12 December 2019; 'Iranian Woman Facing Prison for Sneaking into Soccer Match Burns Herself to Death' (*CBS*, 10 September 2019) https://www.cbsnews.com/news/ the-blue-girl-iran-woman-caught-sneaking-soccer-stadium-dies-setting-herself-fire- rather-than-prison/, accessed 12 December 2019; 'Iranian Female Soccer Fan Dies after Setting Herself on Fire' (*NBC News*, 10 September 2019) https://www.nbcn ews.com/news/world/iranian-female-soccer-fan-dies-after-setting-herself-fire-n1051 896, accessed 6 November 2023; James Dorsey, '#Bluegirl: Iranian Football Fan Who Set Herself on Fire Indicted FIFA & Iran' (*Global Village Space*, 13 September 2019)

tragedy underscores how women are treated in Iran and how deep the discrimination and its effects run.

Context

As introduced earlier, it must be first explored whether the negative outcome of these campaigns was based on context of the target domestic country, both being Iran. The initial thought would be that as the two campaigns with negative outcomes were targeting the same domestic government, it would be the domestic context that explained the negative outcomes. However, an in-depth exploration of the context variables indicates the Iran is not significantly different from other countries in the study which showed more positive change. Although the context for Iran is not particularly good, the important aspect for this study is that the context is not significantly *different* from more successful countries. This does not indicate that the poor outcomes were based on the target government or domestic political situation alone.

The World Justice Project index of openness does have a statistically significant relationship to outcomes (explored in more detail in Chapter 7). Here, Iran showed the lowest scores. This indicates that governments which are more 'open' and transparent in general are more likely to respond positively to social media campaigns. However, as will be seen throughout this volume, the campaigns themselves do matter *in addition* to the openness of the government. It is possible that had the Twitter campaign behaved differently, more positively, or at least less negatively, changes could have been seen.

Iran is also the only country in the study that has not signed or ratified CEDAW and has only ratified six international human rights treaties. This was less than other countries in the study. As seen in the exploration of the dialogue with United Nations (UN) treaty bodies later in this chapter, Iran exhibits scepticism of the (perceived) Western-driven nature of the international human rights regime. The anti-Western rhetoric and discourse seen in reaction to the social media campaigns was certainly echoed in the dialogue with treaty bodies.

Therefore, the contextual picture does not significantly set Iran apart from other countries in the study. We can see that the lack of openness of the government most likely played a part, but again it is not likely that this was the sole reason for the negative legal outcomes, nor the degree of regression. Although Iran does stand out for its lack of engagement with the UN human

---

https://www.globalvillagespace.com/bluegirl-iranian-football-fan-who-set-herself-on-fire-indicted-fifa-iran/, accessed 6 November 2023.

rights mechanisms, this alone does not explain why the campaigns in this country were less successful than the others. Rather, it is more an indication of Iran's reticence towards what are perceived as Western-driven norms and foreign intervention, a finding that is in line with the critique of the spiral model and the overall impressions of the campaigns – a possible patriarchal response in line with Hemmings' points about colonial violence.[18]

Legal outcomes

These two campaigns showed the poorest legal outcomes. #stopstoning showed substantial regression in legislation, law enforcement, and the representation of women's rights norms in UN dialogue. #letwomengotostadium led to no changes in the law coupled with evidence of regression in institutionalization and law enforcement. Both campaigns brought out conservative hard-liners and exposed government discourse which is hostile to 'Western' influences, the perceived goals of the Twitter-driven campaigns. Law enforcement was, and remains, likely used as a tool to reassert domestic patriarchal power as a tool of resistance against perceived colonial violence.[19]

Legislation

Although neither campaign showed positive change in legislation, #stopstoning showed more distinct regression. Before the #stopstoning campaign, stoning to death was a penalty prescribed for adultery while married.[20] Under *Shari'a* law, which came into force after the 1979 Islamic Revolution,[21] sexual activity outside of marriage is considered to be *hadd* crime; sexual intercourse between a man and a woman who are not married is *zina*. *Zina* is punished as a *hadd* crime, which is 100 lashes or death by stoning.[22] The Islamic Penal Code was officially adopted in 1991, and explicitly allowed for death by stoning.[23] Guilt must be proved by confession

---

[18] Clare Hemmings, 'Resisting Popular Feminisms: Gender, Sexuality and the Lure of the Modern' (2018) 25 Gender, Place & Culture 963.

[19] Ibid.

[20] See, for example, Amnesty International, 'Iran End Executions by Stoning' (n 3); Amnesty International, 'Iran Executions by Stoning' (n 3); Extra-Legal Executions in Iran, 'Capital Offenses in the Islamic Republic of Iran: Submission to the UPR' (2009); Hosseinkhah (n 11); Mohammad Nayyeri, 'The Question of "Stoning to Death" in the New Penal Code of the IRI' (IHR, 2012).

[21] Hosseinkhah (n 11).

[22] Nayyeri (n 11) 10.

[23] Islamic Penal Code 1991 Articles 83 – prescription of punishment, 63 – crimes, 102/ 104 – methods, 68/71/74/81/105 – burden of proof. See, for example, Hosseinkhah (n 11); Terman and Fijabi (n 11) 18–19; Justice for Iran, 'Mapping Stoning in Muslim

four times in front of a judge, or testimony by four male eyewitnesses or three men and two women, or the 'knowledge' of the judge.[24] A moratorium on stoning was passed in 2002, but it was ignored by many judges, and the moratorium did not affect the written law.[25] In September 2003, a law was passed which appeared to undermine the moratorium.[26] The practice came back into being more acutely after the defeat of the reformist party and the election of President Ahmadinejad.[27] Amnesty reports that the Deputy Head of the Judiciary has made highly anti-Western remarks in defence of stoning as an appropriate punishment based on religious law and beliefs.[28]

Although the penal code has been reformed since the start of the campaign, it still allows for execution by stoning. The drafting of the New Islamic Penal Code began in 2007, in anticipation of the 2012 expiry date for the 1991 code. It was approved in 2011. While stoning has been explicitly removed from the new penal code, this does not mean that stoning is outlawed. Rather, the code is silent on the matter, which therefore allows judges to interpret *Shari'a* law as they choose. Article 167 of Iran's Constitution gives this power: 'In case of the absence of any such law, [the judge] has to deliver his judgment on the basis of authoritative Islamic sources and authentic fatwa.' Therefore, the silence in the constitution means that execution by stoning is still legal in Iran. The crime of adultery is still considered *hadd* within the penal code, although the crime of *zina* is no longer specifically mentioned.[29] Stoning is also referenced in other Articles (172 and 198) of the new code which again adds to the clarity that it is indeed allowable under the new code.[30]

Context' (The Global Campaign to Stop Violence against Women in the Name of Culture, 2012).

[24] Amnesty International, 'Iran: New Executions Demonstrate Need for Unequivocal Legal Ban of Stoning' (2009); Amnesty International, 'Iran End Executions by Stoning' (n 3) 3; Nayyeri (n 20); Hosseinkhah (n 11); Terman and Fijabi (n 11).

[25] See, for example, Amnesty International, 'Iran: New Executions Demonstrate Need for Unequivocal Legal Ban of Stoning' (n 24); International Federation for Human Rights (n 11); Justice for Iran (n 23).

[26] Amnesty International, 'Death Penalty/Stoning: Mokarrameh Ebrahimi' (9 July 2007).

[27] Terman and Fijabi (n 11) 20.

[28] Amnesty International, 'Iran End Executions by Stoning' (n 3) 4.

[29] Hosseinkhah (n 11); Nayyeri (n 20); Human Rights Watch, 'Iran: UPR Submission' (2014); Justice for Iran (n 11); 'Iran's New Penal Code Retains the Punishment of Stoning' (18 May 2013) http://justice4iran.org/publication/call-for-action/iran-new-penal-code-stoning/, accessed 17 November 2023; National Council of Resistance of Iran, 'Iranian Regime's 20-Year Conduct since Beijing Platform for Action and Accountability to International Community' (2015) 30.

[30] Hosseinkhah (n 11); Justice for Iran (n 11); Human Rights Watch, 'Iran: Proposed Penal Code Retains Stoning' (3 June 2013).

Note 4 of Article 221.5 of the 2007 draft stated: '[if] the enforcement of stoning should create disturbance and prove damaging to the regime, the verdict of stoning ... could be changed to execution'. This was completely removed from later drafts, notably after the campaign began.[31] Ali Shahrokhi, Head of the Judicial and Legal Commission of the Islamic Consultative Council, has stated: 'it is in the best interest of the regime if certain [penalties] under the law of Hudud, namely stoning, are not *referenced* in the Code' (emphasis added).[32] Officials have since stated that the reference to stoning was removed specifically in response to the negative international attention: 'Some people in the international arena have a very biased view of stoning and used it against Iran. They meant that stoning is a violation of human rights. Stoning is only removed from the law but it still exists in Sharia and cannot be removed from the Sharia.'[33]

#letwomengotostadium campaigned for a different kind of legal change – lifting a ban which technically is not legally binding. However, there are some policing regulations which are in place which treat the ban as law and therefore, in practice, it takes on a legally binding nature. The ban is still very much in effect for the majority of Iranian women and it seems that neither the domestic nor the international pressure was enough to push the government to legislative change.

Institutionalization

Neither campaign showed positive change in the evaluation of institutionalization. In both campaigns, there is ample evidence of the government rejecting the perceived Western ideals. Though this represented no change from before the campaign in #stopstoning, in #letwomengotostadium it was the campaign itself which brought out the reactions from hard-line religious conservatives, at times in opposition to the ruling government. Again, this seems to be a reaction to 'foreign' social media activism seen as being driven by Western, white, elite women, highlighting and even aggravating the fissure between elected government and powerful religious leaders.

Prior to the #stopstoning campaign, officials were already vocally disparaging of the 'Western' perspective on stoning: 'The real and fabricated images of stoning in the foreign media and their destructive impact on

---

[31] Hosseinkhah (n 11).

[32] Ibid.

[33] Iran Human Rights Documentation Center, 'Annual Death Penalty Report 2012' (2012) 17.

Islam and Iran are well-known.'[34] It was also reported that just after the UN General Assembly passed a moratorium on the death penalty, Iranian officials said it was 'part of the West's wanton attempts to export to other countries ideological issues of their own particular interest'.[35] It has been suggested that central Iranian government had instructed provincial courts to remain silent on the use of stoning since 2001.[36] Many feminist scholars warn of these 'blinders' in social media campaigning, potentially doing more harm than good.[37]

Government discourse was similar once the campaign began, exposing the tensions between foreign relations and provincial authorities. As one example, the Iranian Embassy in London issued a statement specifically aimed at the international community stating that Sakineh would not be stoned; just a few days later the head of the provincial judiciary said that the sentence of stoning was still in place.[38] Quotes from religious leaders continued to show this rejection of so-called 'Western' influence. For example, the head of Iran's Human Rights Committee dismissed the focus on the stoning sentence as Western 'propaganda'.[39]

The lack of institutionalization of international women's rights norms was quite evident in the government's report on the 20-year review of the implementation of the Beijing Platform for Women. In listing identified obstacles to eliminating violence against women, the state proffered reasons such as victim reluctance to report incidence to the police, lack of women's awareness, women's avoidance of pursuing cases due to 'personal views and family culture', and the 'promotion of violence and using "women" as a "means" through foreign media'.[40] This kind of rhetoric places the blame on women victim/survivors and completely avoids any suggestion of underlying root causes, discrimination, or inequalities. Similarly, in relation to the refusal

---

[34] 'Emad Baghi's "The Bloodied Stone"' (Center for Human Rights in Iran, 2 August 2008) https://www.iranhumanrights.org/2008/08/baghibloodiedstone/, accessed 17 November 2023.

[35] Extra-Legal Executions in Iran (n 20).

[36] US State Department, 'Country Reports on Human Rights Practices for 2016' (2016) https://www.state.gov/j/drl/rls/hrrpt/humanrightsreport/index.htm#wrapper, accessed 13 April 2017.

[37] Hemmings (n 18); Gail Lewis and Clare Hemmings, '"Where Might We Go If We Dare": Moving beyond the "Thick, Suffocating Fog of Whiteness" in Feminism' (2019) 20 Feminist Theory 405.

[38] Amnesty International, 'Action Appeal' (2010).

[39] Hugh Tomlinson, 'Ashtiani Freed after 9 Years on Death Row' (*The Times*, 19 March 2014) https://www.thetimes.co.uk/article/ashtiani-freed-after-9-years-on-death-row-5gk8c3nnds7, accessed 17 November 2023.

[40] The Vice Presidency for Women & Family Affairs, 'National Review on Women's Status in the Islamic Republic of Iran (Beijing+20)' (2015) 29.

to sign and ratify CEDAW, the state holds that too many rights contained within the treaty are in contradiction to Islam.[41] This kind of discourse and approach shows a complete rejection of international women's rights norms, even when those norms seem to be accepted and desired by domestic women.[42] This rejection appears to be similarly exhibited both before and after the campaign, showing no change in the long term.

#letwomengotostadium appears to show a negative change in government discourse and institutionalization in response to the campaign itself. There is very little evidence of the government's approach to women attending men's volleyball matches before the ban came into effect, although it can be speculated that it was not seen as problematic given that football matches had been banned since 1979, but volleyball was not banned until 2012. What is known is that the ban was 'designed to shield women from men's rowdiness in sport stadia and to pre-empt the temptation of genders mixing'.[43] This kind of statement shows a highly paternalistic and stereotyped approach to women. Just before the campaign began, Ayatollah Khamenei stated that: '[T]he westerners have, for a variety of reasons, misunderstood the issues of women, but have succeeded through their propaganda machine to promote their incorrect and destructive understanding of women throughout the world while suppressing any opposite voice.'[44]

The campaign itself seemed to open the door for exposing the tensions between elected government officials, particularly those in charge of foreign relations, and domestically focused male religious leaders. In June 2014, the (then) Minister for Women's Affairs Molaverdi announced in an interview that the ban was *not* actually socially accepted and that the government would review its legality.[45] In April 2015, government official Abdolhamid

---

[41] One non-governmental organization goes so far as to hold that the regime 'say CEDAW is an attempt by the West to globalize its culture and that western standards of human rights and women's rights could not be accepted and implemented by the World of Islam. Denying universality of human rights, Ali Khamenei, the mullahs' supreme leader, believes that acceptance of such western prescriptions are against Islamic dignity and are counter-productive, because the regime would have to surrender to the instructions of "Arrogant Powers" and endorse them' (National Council of Resistance of Iran (n 12)).

[42] National Council of Resistance of Iran (n 12).

[43] James M Dorsey, 'Bowing To Pressure: Iran Grants Women Spectators Access To Sporting Event' (*Huffington Post*, 19 February 2017) http://www.huffingtonpost.com/entry/bowing-to-pressure-iran-grants-women-spectators-access_us_58a92da2e4b0fa149f9ac73d, accessed 16 November 2023.

[44] 'West's Approach to Women Issues "Profoundly Deviant": Leader' (The Iran Project, 20 April 2014) http://theiranproject.com/blog/2014/04/20/wests-approach-to-women-issues-profoundly-deviant-leader/, accessed 16 November 2023.

[45] Leila Mouri, 'My Share, Half of Azadi: Let Iranian Women Go to Stadium' (*Huffington Post*, 19 June 2014) http://www.huffingtonpost.com/leila-mouri/my-share-half-of-azadi-le_b_5508962.html, accessed 16 November 2023; دستور حسن روحانی برای بررسی حضور بانوان،

Ahmadi, Iran's Deputy Minister of Sports and Youth Ministry, told the Islamic Republic News Agency that plans were in place to lift the ban. This was seemingly confirmed by Molaverdi. Opposition in government, Babak Dinparast, then immediately stated that there were no plans in place to lift or change the ban. This back and forth continued throughout 2015.[46] In June of that year, a law enforcement spokesperson confirmed the ban was still in place and had legal status.[47] The chairman of Tehran Islamic seminaries council, Ayatollah Rashad, said that 'given the improper physical and moral conditions of stadiums for women, their presence is not in the interest of society'.[48] In the week leading up to the June 2015 tournament, religious groups produced flyers which called women attempting to attend the event 'sluts' and 'prostitutes' and claimed that 'on Friday there will be blood'. Similar sentiments were posted on social media sites as well.[49] The fissure between the elected government officials and the male religious leaders was excruciatingly clear, with the religious power seeming to dominate.

Molaverdi was very public with her reaction to this particular incident, notably taking to Facebook to state that the government had been pressured by the religious leaders, claiming that the hard-line conservative pressure came 'from those who were denounced two years ago by voters, and who had crawled into their cave of oblivion for eight years'.[50] The post was confirmed as her own. Molaverdi said (also on Facebook) that the publication of the flyers was by: '[T]hose who call themselves followers of God ... and which used words that one loathes to repeat, clearly constitute several offences under the law. ... Even if one day our beloved girls and women forgive this crowd, they will never forget them and keep these days in their historical memory.'[51]

'در سالن مسابقات والیبال' (*Mehr News Agency*, 17 June 2014) http://www.mehrnews.com/news/2313394/دستور-حسن-روحانی-برای-بررسی-حضور-بانوان-در-سالن-مسابقات-والیبال, accessed 29 November 2023.

[46] 'Rouhani Minister Expresses Outrage That Women Were Banned from Attending Iran-US Volleyball Match' (Center for Human Rights in Iran, 23 June 2015) http://www.iranhumanrights.org/2015/06/rouhani-minister-women-volleyball/, accessed 16 November 2023.

[47] Ibid.

[48] 'Senior Cleric Opposes Women's Presence in Sports Stadiums' (The Iran Project, 13 June 2015) http://theiranproject.com/blog/2015/06/13/senior-cleric-opposes-womens-presence-in-sports-stadiums/, accessed 16 November 2023.

[49] 'Female Iran VP Scolds Hardliners over Volleyball Ban' (*Middle East Eye*, 20 June 2015) http://www.middleeasteye.net/news/female-iran-vp-scolds-hardliners-over-volleyball-ban-411944926, accessed 16 November 2023.

[50] Ibid. See also Human Rights Watch, 'Iran: Volleyball Federation Should Penalize Ban on Women' (Human Rights Watch, 2 July 2015) https://www.hrw.org/news/2015/07/02/iran-volleyball-federation-should-penalize-ban-women, accessed 16 November 2023.

[51] 'Female Iran VP Scolds Hardliners over Volleyball Ban' (n 49).

An interview with the FIVB in November 2015 seemed to indicate the support from central government to lift the ban was strong and noted that resistance was instead from the religious hard-liners.[52] A women's rights activist summed up the situation and the lack of institutionalization in September 2016:

> So the ban exists for one reason only and that reason is neither cultural nor historical, but political. Ali Khamenei and his regime want to curtail women's rights further and further, in accordance with their religious convictions. ... With regards to women's rights, Rouhani's term has indeed been a huge disappointment, especially because he made many promises in 2013, which included the potential easing of the stadium ban. ... In July, the regime promised that women could purchase tickets and attend the international volleyball matches again, but when the online sale began, a 'sold out' alert appeared. So the problems have not changed.[53]

Law enforcement

These campaigns both led to highly regressive tactics used by law enforcement officials, both frontline and in the judiciary. In #stopstoning, there were reported increases in the number of stoning sentences handed down after the campaign, while in #letwomengotostadium there were ample reports, some quite egregious, of increases in arbitrary arrests and detentions.

Collecting information about stoning sentences is difficult given the clandestine nature of how they are carried out, particularly in rural settings. However, three organizations are considered reliable for reporting on stonings: Amnesty International, Iran Human Rights, and NCRI (based on their methods and recognition as valid organizations). Their findings for the years surrounding the campaign are summarized in Table 3.1.

---

[52] 'Convincing Iranian President Hassan Rouhani, a relative moderate who has notably improved Iran's relations with the Western world and has also enhanced women's rights by appointing female Foreign Ministry spokespersons since he assumed office in 2013, is unlikely to prove too difficult. The situation is complicated by the power still held by conservative religious figures, including the Supreme Leader Ali Khamenei.' Nick Butler, 'Exclusive: FIVB "Hopeful" Ban on Women Attending Volleyball Matches in Iran Will Be Lifted by February' (*Inside the Games*, 27 November 2015) http://www.insidethega mes.biz/articles/1032038/exclusive-fivb-hopeful-ban-on-women-attending-volleyball-matches-in-iran-will-be-lifted-by-february, accessed 16 November 2023.

[53] Quantara, 'Iran's Stadium Ban on Women: Excluding the People' (9 September 2016) https://en.qantara.de/content/irans-stadium-ban-on-women-excluding-the-peo ple, accessed 16 November 2023.

NEGATIVE OUTCOMES

Table 3.1: Reliable reports of stoning in Iran, 2001–2017

Year	Amnesty International reports: stonings	Iran Human Rights annual reports: stonings	NCRI reports
2001	2 or 3 women stoned		
2006	1 woman and 1 man stoned		
2008			
2009			
2010			
Total	*4 women stoned over a 10-year period*		
Campaign starts			
2011			
2012		4 women stoned	
2013			2 women stoned
2014			
2015			
2016			
2017			
Total	*6 women stoned over a 7-year period*		

Although the numbers shown in Table 3.1 are relatively small, they do indicate a 115 per cent increase from before to after the campaign, notably in the years closer to the peak of the campaign. While it cannot be said with any certainty that the increases were a reaction against the social media campaign, what is clear is that the campaign did not achieve its goal of ceasing the use of stoning as a punishment.

Iran Human Rights recounts that a 2019 directive issued by the Head of the Judiciary provided a detailed description of how stonings should be carried out.[54] Reliable reports continue to demonstrate the use of stoning, as a Tehran court reportedly sentenced a woman to stoning as recently as 2021.[55] Executions on the whole continue to increase in

---

[54] Iran Human Rights (n 15).

[55] 'A Tehran Court Sentences a Young Mother to Stoning, Execution' (NCRI Women Committee, 8 November 2021) https://women.ncr-iran.org/2021/11/08/a-tehran-court-sentences-a-young-mother-to-stoning-execution/, https://women.ncr-iran.org/2021/11/08/a-tehran-court-sentences-a-young-mother-to-stoning-execution/, accessed 16 November 2023.

Iran.[56] The stoning sentence for Sakineh herself was eventually lifted, however activists were sceptical, concerned that her case would be treated differently than others.[57]

The most regressive outcome of the #letwomengotostadium campaign specifically focusing on volleyball was the arrest of British Iranian Ghoncheh Ghavami. She attempted to enter the June 2014 tournament and was temporarily detained but released. She was then called back to the police station, purportedly to collect her phone, and was rearrested. She was kept in solitary confinement for over a month where she was allegedly interrogated and mistreated with significant failings in due process.[58] She was eventually released in November 2014, after six months of detainment without charge. It has not gone unnoticed that the woman targeted for arrest and detention relating to the activism was a *British* Iranian national, perhaps sending a message about foreign involvement in issues deemed to be solely of domestic concern.[59] The lengthy detainment showed a marked change in law enforcement, which can be correlated in time to the climax of the campaign. Since then, at most major volleyball tournaments (and other sports for that matter), there are usually a small number of women arrested for attempting to enter the stadium, however they are generally detained for a short amount of time and are released.

We also must recount again Sahar Khodayari's self-immolation after her arrest and detainment in 2019.[60] Although not directly tied to this campaign (as she was attending a football match), this underscores the very real impact these bans have on women in Iran.

UN dialogue

Both campaigns revealed a negative relationship between the state and the UN human rights mechanisms. There seemed to be some movement from the Iranian government towards international women's rights norms in the early 2000s, however this changed dramatically after the stoning issue

---

[56] Hedia Zaalouni, 'Annual Report on the Death Penalty in Iran: Alarming Increase in Executions' (WCADP, 18 September 2023) https://worldcoalition.org/2023/09/18/ann ual-report-iran-2022/, accessed 6 November 2023.

[57] Amnesty International (n 6).

[58] Human Rights Watch, 'Ghoncheh Ghavami: The Shifting Goal Posts of Iran's Hardliners' (Human Rights Watch, 21 October 2014) https://www.hrw.org/news/2014/10/21/ ghoncheh-ghavami-shifting-goal-posts-irans-hardliners, accessed 16 November 2023.

[59] Although space does not allow for a full discussion, it is important to note the complex political history of the British-Iranian relationship. See, for example, Īraj Pizishkzād and Dick Davis, *My Uncle Napoleon: A Novel* (first edition, Mage Publishers, 1996).

[60] Dorsey (n 17).

garnered international attention. The government's response was highly defensive and anti-Western. As relating to equality principles and the #letwomengotostadium campaign, little to no change was detected. It is also important to keep in mind that Iran has not signed or ratified CEDAW, is only party to six human rights treaties, does not allow for any individual complaints, and has several reservations lodged around the supremacy of Islam.

Of particular note is the 2005 Mission to Iran by the Special Rapporteur on Violence Against Women.[61] She confirmed what discourse tended to indicate in other reports – that women do have access to education, employment, and health, but that it is very much under 'strict surveillance and within well-defined boundaries'.[62] She specifically addressed the issue of stoning:

> The death penalty, particularly by stoning, has been a major area of concern. The Special Rapporteur received numerous reports of women on the death row, sentenced mainly for sexually or morally oriented offences such as adultery. … Their stories reflect gender biases in the attitudinal and institutional structure of the country within which they, some still children, have become labelled criminals.[63]

She went on to raise concerns that despite the moratorium, stoning remained legal and was still handed down as a sentence.[64]

By 2008, the Special Rapporteur began issuing urgent appeals for women sentenced to death by stoning.[65] The Iranian government replied that stoning was an important deterrent which was fundamental to Islam. Stoning is seen as different from execution, serving a more specific religious purpose, and therefore sufficiently justified to maintain the sanctity of the family.[66] The government also stated that three stoning sentences had been overturned but did not address the other four cases in the Special Rapporteur's appeal.

---

[61] Human Rights Council, 'Report of the Special Rapporteur on Violence against Women, Its Causes and Consequences: Mission to the Islamic Republic of Iran' (2006) UN Doc E/CN.4/2006/61/Add.3.

[62] Ibid, 25.

[63] Ibid, 41.

[64] Ibid, 43.

[65] Human Rights Council, 'Report of the Special Rapporteur on Violence against Women, Its Causes and Consequences, Yakin Ertürk Addendum Communications to and from Governments' (2008) UN Doc A/HRC/7/6/Add.1.

[66] Human Rights Council, 'Report of the Special Rapporteur on Violence against Women, Its Causes and Consequences, Yakin Ertürk Addendum Communications to and from Governments' (2009) UN Doc A/HRC/11/6/Add.1 para 302.

Generally, after the campaign started, the reports show a regression in dialogue, with more open defensiveness and antagonism towards the West. The first reporting cycle after Sakineh's case rose to international prominence was with the Committee on the Elimination of Racial Discrimination in 2010. The Committee specifically asked Iran to address the issue of Sakineh's case.[67] After the state outlined the myriad ways in which her case was legitimate, the Iranian representative went on to say 'that the case did not fall within the scope of the Committee's mandate. The media had politicized the case and used it as an opportunity to disseminate negative propaganda about his country'.[68]

The most egregious evidence of the state's hostility towards the UN human rights mechanisms was in the 2013 state reply to the Committee on Economic, Social and Cultural Rights' list of issues. The state wrote that one of the Committee's questions was 'a fictitious and irrelevant claim'[69] and went on to say: 'We believe question 4 goes beyond the content of the Covenant, and are amazed to see this question.'[70] Later, in relation to marital rape, the state reports that ' "[m]arital rape" is a concept that goes beyond commitments of the State party to the Covenant. Moreover, there is no international agreement or consensus on the wording of this concept and the "marital rape" is beyond the scope of the Covenant'.[71] Further on, when discussing divorce, one of the acceptable grounds used as an example by the government was 'beating or other forms of continuous abuse by the husband that is not normally tolerable by the wife are examples of undesirable conditions'.[72] These public, recorded statements taken together do not reflect discourse from a state which is institutionalizing international norms on women's rights and eliminating all forms of violence against women. If this is the kind of dialogue that the state uses to defend its human rights record, one can imagine what the situation is like on the ground. The open and blatant antagonism towards the UN system and its 'Western' values was made very clear in these examples.

The Special Rapporteur on the Situation in Iran[73] in March 2014 writes that, in an interview with an Iranian lawyer:

---

[67] Committee on the Elimination of Racial Discrimination, 'Summary Record of the 2016th Meeting' (2011) UN Doc CERD/C/SR.2016 paras 38, 47, 50.

[68] Committee on the Elimination of Racial Discrimination, 'Summary Record of the 2017th Meeting' (2010) UN Doc CERD/C/SR/2017 para 25.

[69] Committee on Economic, Social and Cultural Rights, 'Replies of the Islamic Republic of Iran to the List of Issues' (2013) UN Doc E/C.12/IRN/Q/2/Add.1 para 5.

[70] Ibid, 7 referring to issues around sexual orientation and gender identity.

[71] Ibid, 39.

[72] Ibid.

[73] In 2011, the UN approved and appointed a Special Rapporteur in the situation of human rights in the Islamic republic of Iran. Human Rights Council, 'Resolution Adopted by

The lawyer recalled that Iranian law allows for women who report rape to be prosecuted of adultery [and a possible sentence of stoning] in cases where they are unable to convince a judge of their charges, given that the allegations imply that the women had engaged in extra-marital relations. The lawyer also pointed out that rape cases were very difficult to prove and put women wishing to report the crime at risk of being prosecuted for a capital offence, which likely deterred women victims from coming forward.[74]

The report then brings to light the increases in executions more generally, and specifically notes that in 2013 at least 28 women were publicly hanged. The report also corroborates that the new penal code still allows for the death penalty, specifically stoning, in crimes of adultery.[75] The 2015 report raised similar concerns.[76] The 2016 report specifically mentions that the new penal code still allows for stoning, and that there was a stoning sentence for adultery handed down in 2015. The government claimed that the sentence had been commuted, while continuing to argue that stoning is perfectly legitimate to uphold the tenets and values of Islam.[77]

The 2015 Universal Periodic Review state report attempts to paint women's rights in a very positive light,[78] yet the antagonism between the state and the international community was again rife:

Iran views the 'Resolution on the Situation of Human Rights in Iran' and the appointment of the Special Rapporteur, as a political,

---

the Human Rights Council' (2011) UN Doc A/HRC/RES/16/9. The first report was published in September of that year. The Special Rapporteur drew specific attention to the rights of women, citing issues around the worth of women, family, and marriage laws, targeting of women's rights activists, and notably referring to government statements which seemed to blame women's dress for incidents of violence against women. Human Rights Council, 'Report of the Special Rapporteur on the Situation of Human Rights in the Islamic Republic of Iran' (2011) UN Doc A/66/374 para 56. The Special Rapporteur also drew attention to the widespread use and increase in executions, many done in secret or without due process. Notably, however, no mention is made of stoning or the death penalty as applied to women in particular.

[74] Human Rights Council, 'Report of the Special Rapporteur on the Situation of Human Rights in the Islamic Republic of Iran' (2014) UN Doc A/HRC/25/61 para 79.

[75] Ibid, 16.

[76] Human Rights Council, 'Report of the Special Rapporteur on the Situation of Human Rights in the Islamic Republic of Iran' (2015) UN Doc A/HRC/28/70.

[77] Human Rights Council, 'Report of the Special Rapporteur on the Situation of Human Rights in the Islamic Republic of Iran' (2016) UN Doc A/HRC/31/69 para 15.

[78] Human Rights Council, 'Universal Periodic Review National Report Iran' (2014) UN Doc HRC/WG.6/20/IRN/1 para 77.

discriminatory, and unfair process that is based on double standards. Unfortunately, this process is being pursued by certain Western countries as a means to achieve their political wills. Such a biased approach, visibly contradicts human rights principles and norms that were drafted to promote and protect these ideals.[79]

While the state report is silent on the matter of the death penalty, both the compilation report and the stakeholder report reiterated previous concerns. Iran rejected recommendations calling for in-country visits, and rejected all 38 recommendations to repeal or change the death penalty.

#letwomengotostadium draws from many of the same reports, albeit with a different issue focus. The same overarching findings apply, whereby Iran does not exhibit full engagement with the international human rights mechanisms or norms, though some promising progress was seen in the early to mid-2000s. More recent reports show a regression in engagement and a re-emergence of nationalistic, religious norms.

Issues relating to women's rights to enter stadiums and participate in sporting events as supporters were raised as far back as 1993, when the Human Rights Committee raised concerns about a prohibition on women practising sport in public.[80] Nearly a decade later, in 2010, the state report to the Human Rights Committee was still using language which reinforced traditional gender stereotypes and the primacy of women's roles in the family.[81]

Once the campaign began, the dialogue changed. The 2015 Human Rights Committee summary report specifically addresses the issue of Ghavami's arrest and detention.[82] Again in 2016 the Committee on the Rights of

---

[79] Ibid, 118.
[80] Comments of the Human Rights Committee 1993 (CCPR/C/79/Add25) para 13.
[81] Human Rights Committee, 'Third Periodic Reports of States Parties: Iran' (2010) UN Doc CCPR/C/IRRN/3 paras 217, 219, 225. Another good example (though just one of many) of Iran's approach to placing women within the context of the family comes in the 2011 CESCR state report: 'Based on the provisions of paragraph 3 of its terms of reference stressing the importance of "policy making and planning for the consolidation of sacred family unit through facilitating the formation of family, protecting its sanctity and basing family relations on the Islamic law and ethics" and also benefiting from the teachings of the Holy Quran and the traditions of the Holy Prophet Mohammad (peace be upon him), the provisions of the Constitution of the State and other laws and regulations in force in the Islamic Republic of Iran, the women's social and cultural council has formulated policies on the formation, consolidation and elevation of family.' Committee on Economic, Social and Cultural Rights, 'Second Periodic Report Submitted by States Parties Islamic Republic of Iran' (2011) UN Doc E/C.12/IRN/2 para 148.
[82] Human Rights Council (n 76) para 150.

the Child raises the issue of women's access to sports.[83] Notably, the 2015 Universal Periodic Review reports do not give the issue much attention.[84] Although access to sport for women was raised as a concern, it was about women's *participation*, not equality in access as a fan.

Across all four legal variables, the situation is the same or worse after the social media attention. The disparaging remarks about the West and foreign media seem to indicate a strong backlash against these campaigns in line with feminist literature and the risks of colonial violence.[85] In particular, removing stoning from the penal code and making it more subjective, with direct reference to Western media attention as the driving force behind this decision, goes some way to showing a correlation between social media activity and regression for women's rights. For #letwomengotostadium, the arrest and detention of Ghavami, a British Iranian, at the climax of the campaign again sends a message about the Iranian government's reaction to Western interference. At the very least, it is clear that neither campaign made a positive difference as, in 2023, stoning sentences continue and the majority of women are still not allowed to enter stadiums.

Twitter characteristics

These were the two smallest campaigns in the study, with 1,093 (#stopstoning) and 7,173 (#letwomengotostadium) Tweets analysed. Analysis indicates that the campaigns were just big enough to garner a baseline level of international attention which appeared to lead to backlash against foreign interference, but not big enough to rise to the level of combined foreign and domestic pressure needed to push for positive change. These campaigns showed high proportions of non-domestic users and, given that these are not English-speaking countries, a relatively high proportion of Tweets in English. Across all of the Twitter variables, these two campaigns showed a marked lack of persistence, low levels of engagement, and high proportions of non-domestic users. These characteristics opened the door to backlash (against the foreign intervention) without repercussions, with the lack of domestic drive providing no incentives or pressure.

It is therefore possible that the negative foreign attention combined with the lack of domestic pressure created an environment conducive to government backlash, contributing to the regressive outcomes explored in

---

[83] Committee on the Rights of the Child, 'Concluding Observations on the Combined Third and Fourth Periodic Reports of the Islamic Republic of Iran' (2016) UN Doc CRC/C/IRN/CO/3-4 para 79.

[84] Human Rights Council, 'Report of the Working Group on the Universal Periodic Review: Islamic Republic of Iran' (2014) UN Doc A/HRC/28/12.

[85] Lewis and Hemmings (n 37); Hemmings (n 18).

this chapter. This is one of the key critiques of the spiral model and echoes some of the more sceptical digital feminist activism literature. The model does not allow any room for the very real risk that governments may exhibit a negative backlash against the transnational pressure, leading to outcomes which can be more negative than positive. These campaigns seem to provide empirical evidence of this risk. This is also one of the major risks inherent in social media campaigns. There is no control over who will and who will not participate in a campaign. It is impossible when a campaign starts in earnest to predict whether there will be enough domestic pressure alongside a balanced amount of transnational pressure. These campaigns very much illustrate these risks.

Persistence (Tweets per day)

#stopstoning and #letwomengotostadium showed poor indicators of persistence. These campaigns did not have the long-term investment that the other campaigns had, despite the fact that #stopstoning was the longest running campaign in the study.

#stopstoning showed a very low variation in the number of Tweets per day, with an average of 0.46 (indicating the high number of days with 0 Tweets) and a standard deviation of 5.09 – meaning that across the campaign the majority of days had somewhere between zero and five Tweets per day. This, compared to other campaigns, is very low. Of note, the only two #stopstoning peaks were organizationally driven by Women Living Under Muslim Law (WLUML). The first occurred when WLUML started a change. org petition for Sakineh and again when WLUML organized a 'Thunderclap' social media event to gather support and attention. Other days with small peaks revolved around landmarks in Sakineh's case. Interestingly, there was only Tweet when she was released and pardoned for good behaviour. #stopstoning simply did not attract the same levels of sustained attention as the other campaigns. It may be because it started fairly early, in 2010. This was only four years after Twitter began. Other campaigns which started after Twitter had become more popular may have seen better success in gathering supporters.

#letwomengotostadium had higher peaks and more fluctuation in both domestic and international attention, indicating interest and involvement, but overall the campaign did not sustain the peak levels. There were only two peak days and one peak period, centred around the annual tournament in Tehran. The rest of the campaign was relatively quiet, with just a handful of Tweets keeping the momentum, exhibiting similar characteristics to #stopstoning. Also of note, there was very little social media attention when the British Iranian woman was released, although some international media

Figure 3.1: Timeline of Tweets in #stopstoning and #letwomengotostadium

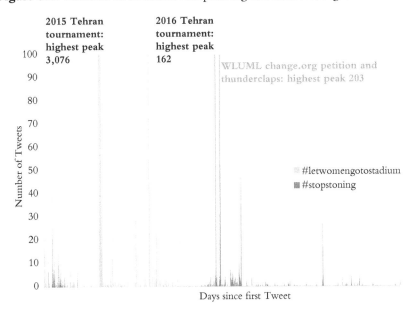

outlets did pick up the story. Both campaigns showed very long periods of complete inactivity as shown in Figure 3.1.

Two of the most prominent variables in this study are the number of days in the campaign with more than zero Tweets and the number with more than five Tweets. Campaigns with more 'active' days throughout showed much more positive legal change. Overall, this tells us that while peaks may matter in gathering attention, continued and sustained activity matters too. The Iranian campaigns showed the greatest numbers and proportions of inactive days, thus not showing the kind of pressure needed for the government to institute change.

Engagement (retweets, likes, and replies)

The #stopstoning campaign had an exceptionally low reply to Tweet ratio; it did not therefore spark much dialogue or inter-user engagement. Very few users replied to Tweets in the campaign. There was a higher ratio of retweets to Tweets, at 1.55. This means that for every Tweet there were between one and two retweets. These ratios show a general lack of engagement with the campaign. #letwomengotostadium produced a different but equally important engagement metric in the extraordinarily high ratio of likes to Tweets at 6.78. This was consistently high during both peak and non-peak periods. For comparison, other campaigns ranged from 0.2 to 2.7, thus underscoring the exceptional nature of this campaign's level of like activity.

The striking level of likes in #letwomengotostadium errs towards Gladwell or Morozov's theories on slactivism.[86] Similarly, #stopstoning showed very low levels of replies. Neither campaign produced dialogue or debate, indicative of the lack of sustained attention and engagement. Again, these factors all remove any pressure or incentive on governments to institute change. If the campaign does not spark attention or engagement with followers, then the drivers of change are not likely strong enough to pressurize the government.

Users (profiles of 100 most active users)

These campaigns showed the lowest percentages of domestic users, one of the central critiques to the spiral model. Here, the lack of domestic drive (alongside the lack of persistence and engagement) likely allowed the government backlash without repercussion. Having such low percentages of domestic users in the top 100 (1 per cent and 32 per cent, respectively) rendered these campaigns particularly foreign. These campaigns were not driven or 'owned' by Iranian women. This lack of domestic voice is likely associated with a negative impact on the end result. These campaigns are striking examples of the harm that can result from a campaign which is perceived as 'Western' pushing for change in a non-Western setting, coupled with an absence of domestic voices. Quotes and actions from the Iranian governments, both in relation to these campaigns and on women's rights in general, showed a very clear backlash against foreign interventions. Had these campaigns been more domestically driven, *and* had they garnered inescapable international attention which rose to the level of incentivizing change, then perhaps the legal outcomes would have been different. However, they ended up sitting in a void of sorts, with just enough foreign voices to spark backlash from the Iranian government, but not enough domestic and international attention to necessitate change.

Digging deeper into the profiles of the 100 most active users, there is another interesting, and perhaps damaging, aspect. In both campaigns, Tweets from the 100 most active users made up a larger proportion of the total campaign than seen in other, more successful, campaigns. Although this is partially due to the smaller number of Tweets and users overall, it

---

[86] Malcolm Gladwell, 'Small Change' (*The New Yorker*, 10 April 2010) http://www.newyorker.com/magazine/2010/10/04/small-change-malcolm-gladwell, accessed 14 March 2016; Malcolm Gladwell and Clay Shirky, 'From Innovation to Revolution: Do Social Media Make Protests Possible?' (2011) 90 Foreign Affairs 153; Evgeny Morozov, 'The Internet' (2010) 179 Foreign Policy 40; Evgeny Morozov, *The Net Delusion: How Not to Liberate the World* (Allen Lane, 2011).

still indicates that the campaign was driven by a relatively small user group, which we now know was also foreign.

Coding the profiles into broad categories showed some interesting results in both campaigns, though particularly in #stopstoning. This campaign was overwhelmingly foreign-driven; most of the foreign users were individuals or organizations (such as WLUML). Non-domestic individuals accounted for 51 per cent of the Tweets sent from the 100 most active users and 24 per cent of the reach. Non-domestic organizations came in at 28 per cent and 36 per cent. Notably, there was a group of European Union politicians who became very active in the campaign. However, as we have seen in reactions from the Iranian government, this Western involvement was not particularly well received. It can be speculated, given the Iranian government's discourse and rhetoric, that social media from Members of the European Parliament would not be the kind of pressure that would lead to positive legal change.

#letwomengotostadium was also heavily non-domestic, though not as striking as #stopstoning. The largest category of users in the top 100 were non-domestic individuals. Although there were numerically fewer domestic individuals (16 compared to 28), they were far more prolific in their campaign activity, accounting for 34 per cent of the Tweets from the 100 most active users. #letwomengotostadium did show less regressive results than #stopstoning, perhaps because of the stronger representation of domestic individuals in the campaign. It is possible that this drive from individuals prevented #letwomengotostadium from the level of regression seen with #stopstoning. In other words, this level of individual activity perhaps did succeed in putting some pressure on the government – not enough to warrant change, but enough to curb some of the potential backlash seen in #stopstoning.

The active organizations in the #stopstoning campaign notably had further reach (that is, more followers) than active organizations in any other campaign – 380,814 compared to the other campaigns which ranged from 3,681 (#women2drive) on the lowest end to the high end at 132,943 from #niunamenos. This indicates that high levels of activity from organizations with far reach does not equate to higher levels of positive change. These organizations were also more active, proportionally, in #stopstoning than in other campaigns (responsible for 28 per cent of the most active users' Tweets as compared to 1–19 per cent in other campaigns). Perhaps as the active organizations in #stopstoning were overwhelmingly foreign, this reach and activity level actually worked against the campaign, promulgating the saviour–savage dichotomy which sparked regressive backlash from the Iranian government.[87]

---

[87] Makau W Mutua, 'Savages, Victims, and Saviors: The Metaphor of Human Rights' (2001) 42 Harvard International Law Journal 201.

Content analysis

The analysis of content paints a varied but interesting picture. Both campaigns showed a fairly high presence of organically emerging but consistent framing and messaging. Figures 3.2 and 3.3 are visual representations of the words most oft-used across the whole of the campaign; the larger the font the more the word appeared in Tweets.

As seen earlier in this chapter, many of the peaks in #stopstoning are related to organizationally driven activities, such as Thunderclaps. It is interesting to see that so many of the Tweets in this campaign contained words such as please, sign, today, and petition. It is also notable that the hashtags #VAW and #humanrights and the word countries were consistent in the campaign, showing perhaps the high level of non-domestic users (these are very 'global' terms). #letwomengotostadium showed very subject specific words, such as stadiums, volleyball, enter, gym, game, and ban or banned. The consistent messages in these two campaigns were very different from each other. #stopstoning overall showed a more global campaign focus, while #letwomengotostadium was very focused on the domestic issue.

Figure 3.2: Consistently used words, #stopstoning

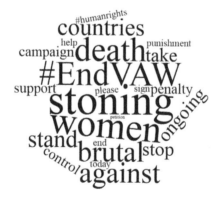

Figure 3.3: Consistently used words, #letwomengotostadium

Organic framing and messaging, as defined in this study, are those words which emerge from the campaign but come and go based on time periods. In other words, they are the topics which everyone 'talks about' for a few days, then they wither away. The high presence of these organic messages is negatively associated with government backlash, specifically in dialogue with UN treaty bodies. #stopstoning showed the highest presence of organic framing and the most government backlash of any campaign. It is likely that this relationship emerges from the lack of controlled messaging on social media.

Interestingly, #stopstoning began domestically focused, with many specific cases and women referenced. Over time, it appears that the campaign took on a more 'global' tone, which may relate to the findings earlier in this chapter regarding the lack of domestic focus and the lack of domestic drive in this campaign. It appears that the Tweet contents reflect this characteristic of this campaign, which is likely to have contributed to the backsliding effect.

#letwomengotostadium told a more domestic story, at times with reference to the religious fundamentalism against which the campaigners were fighting and specific domestic politics (that is, 'Rouhani'). This may be why there were some positive outcomes in the campaign. However, the overall messaging seems very 'factual' relating to sporting events themselves. Perhaps the lack of strong framing and messaging in this campaign contributed to the overall lack of change.

Across all the campaigns, the per cent of international norms which are present to any extent is statistically significant. These campaigns, unsurprisingly, showed very little representation of international women's rights norms. #stopstoning in fact showed the least number of international norms at just 23 per cent. By way of comparison, #women2drive showed 86 per cent. This lack of invoking international norms seems to relate to a lack of success.

Conclusion

In short, these two campaigns illustrate the theoretical critique of the spiral model on the risk of government backlash coupled with Hemmings' work on elite white feminism and colonial violence.[88] The characteristics of the Twitter campaigns opened the door to this risk which was manifested in the regressive outcomes, albeit to different degrees. Both campaigns lacked in persistence and engagement, and the low levels of activity that did occur were non-domestically driven, the crux of feminist critique. Although consistent messaging was exhibited, without persistence, engagement, or domestic pressure, in essence, it did not matter. The #stopstoning campaign is associated with a change in the penal code which now allows for stoning

---

[88] Lewis and Hemmings (n 37); Hemmings (n 18).

to be used at the discretion of local judges, and evidence indicates that more women have been stoned since the campaign began than before, particularly in the years immediately after the campaign peak. The dialogue with UN treaty bodies manifested hostility towards Westernism, thus unsurprising that a campaign which is perceived as Western-driven would not be associated with positive outcomes. Similarly, #letwomengotostadium has not led to changes in the ban bar one isolated incident, yet more egregious examples of arbitrary arrest and detention have been seen in reaction to the campaign.

4

Status Quo: #farkhunda, #sendeanlat, #mydressmychoice

The next group of campaigns showed, on balance, little to no change. There were gains in some areas and losses in others, rendering the situation for women and girls on the ground no different than before the campaigns. While the gains and losses differed in each campaign, these campaigns showed striking similarities in Twitter behaviours. They all gained significant attention in the timeframe immediately after the spark incidents, but very quickly faded from public consciousness. It appears as though this initial mass interest led to some small changes but without continued public pressure or interest the governments were free to ignore the long-term goals of the campaigns, once again manifesting both critiques of the spiral model of human rights change theory and, to some extent, media effects theory. Feminist critiques were perhaps less evident in these campaigns.

#farkhunda campaign overview

On 19 March 2015, an Afghan mob attacked and killed Farkhunda Malikzada in the streets of Kabul. She had been in an altercation with a caretaker at a shrine, and he loudly accused her of burning the Koran. He was illiterate and it later emerged was selling illegal items from the shrine. She was, in fact, a religious scholar. A mob of men formed and beat her, stoned her, threw her off a building, drove over her body, burned her, and left her in the dry riverbed. Police were present but were unable to stop the mob. The incident was caught on video and shared online. Some officials, believing her guilt, endorsed the incident in the aftermath. It quickly became clear that she was innocent, and the resulting outrage led to one of the largest protests ever in Afghanistan. It did not go unnoticed that the attack was not carried out by Taliban, but rather by 'normal' Afghan men, wearing jeans and T-shirts.[1] One news commentator shared this insightful perspective on the protests and their portrayal on social media: '[A]n extremely disturbing selfie mania, the narcissistic tradition of our generation, found its way among the crowd. Pictures with the signs. Pictures with the crowd. Tweet. Tweet. Tweet. It all became about "me, myself, and I".'[2]

The focus of the campaign was on the lack of law enforcement, including police and their perceived impunity, as well as a call for proper and transparent trials of those involved.[3] Unfortunately, the international public pressure led to hasty trials, the verdicts of which were then overturned on procedural matters. In other words, in response to the public attention, the trials were rushed, botched, and overturned, leading to perceptions of impunity for men. Criticism of the government's approach was clear.[4] Afghani advocate Noorjahan Akbar stated:

> When we began speaking out along with thousands of Afghans around the world, we hoped that Farkhunda's murderers would be brought to justice and that her case would set a precedent for the legal system to protect the safety and rights of Afghan women. But a year later, the lack of justice has had significant implications for women's rights in Afghanistan, where the majority of perpetrators of violence against women never face legal repercussions. The government's failure to maintain justice has emboldened criminals and left Afghan women more vulnerable to violence.[5]

---

[1]   Special Inspector General for Afghanistan Reconstruction, 'Report to the United States Congress' (2016) 10; Zarghuna Kargar, 'Farkhunda: The Making of a Martyr' (*BBC News*, 11 August 2015) http://www.bbc.co.uk/news/magazine-33810338, accessed 29 November 2023.

[2]   'Farkhunda's Murder: A National Tragedy' (*TOLOnews*, 28 March 2015) https://www.tolonews.com/opinion/farkhundas-murder-national-tragedy, accessed 16 November 2023.

[3]   'Thousands March in Kabul Demanding Justice for Woman Killed by Mob' (*The Guardian*, 24 March 2015) https://www.theguardian.com/world/2015/mar/24/farkhu nda-thousands-march-in-kabul-demanding-justice-for-woman-killed-by-mob, accessed 29 November 2023; 'Afghan Woman Lynched by Mob Becomes Rights Symbol' (*CBS News*, 5 April 2015) https://www.cbsnews.com/news/afghan-woman-farkhunda-lync hed-mob-rights-symbol/, accessed 29 November 2023.

[4]   Human Rights Watch expressed concern over the quick trial: 'This trial leaves the impression that the Afghan government wants a quick and dirty process to get this case out of the headlines and move on – rather than real justice and a real examination of how such a terrible attack could have happened'. 'Farkhunda Murder: 4 Sentenced to Death' (*TOLOnews*, 6 May 2015) https://www.tolonews.com/afghanistan/farkhunda-murder-4-sentenced-death, accessed 16 November 2023.

[5]   Noorjahan Akbar, 'A Year Later, Still No Justice for Farkhunda' (*Foreign Policy*, 1 April 2016) https://foreignpolicy.com/2016/04/01/a-year-later-still-no-justice-for-farkhunda/, accessed 16 November 2023.

#sendeanlat campaign overview

On 11 February 2015, Turkish student Özgecan Aslan was murdered. A bus driver attempted to rape her, and when she fought back, he killed her. He called his father and a friend who both then attempted to assist the driver in covering up the murder and disposing of the body. Her body was not found until 13 February. No lawyer would agree to defend the perpetrators, and all three were convicted and given aggravated life sentences without the possibility of parole. The driver was given additional time but was subsequently murdered in prison.

The hashtag #sendeanlat emerged, which means 'share your story', as a way for women to show how many have been affected by violence or femicide in Turkey.[6] The hashtag led to several protests and rallies in Turkey and around the world to raise awareness of the high rates of violence against women in Turkey.[7] Özgecan's murder and resulting hashtag campaign

---

[6] Helen Davidson, 'Rape and Murder of Young Woman Sparks Mass Twitter Protest in Turkey' (*The Guardian*, 17 February 2015) http://www.theguardian.com/world/2015/feb/17/turkish-woman-ozgecan-aslans-sparks-anti-violence-campaign-sendeanlat, accessed 29 November 2023; Mustafa Akyol, 'The Monsters among Us' (*Hürriyet Daily News*, 18 February 2015) http://www.hurriyetdailynews.com/the-monsters-among-us.aspx?pageID=449&nID=78486&NewsCatID=411, accessed 17 November 2023; Umut Uras, 'Turkey Women Share Harassment Stories after Grim Murder' (*Al Jazeera*, 16 February 2015) http://www.aljazeera.com/news/2015/02/150216101649506.html, accessed 29 November 2023; Jim Roberts, 'Turkish Women Launch Twitter Campaign against Sexual Violence' (*Mashable*, 16 February 2015) http://mashable.com/2015/02/16/ozgecan-aslan-sparks-sexual-violence-hashtag/, accessed 17 November 2023; 'Turkish Women Relate Sexual Harassment Stories via Social Media' (*Hürriyet Daily News*, 16 February 2015) http://www.hurriyetdailynews.com/turkish-women-relate-sexual-harassment-stories-via-social-media-.aspx?pageID=238&nID=78413&NewsCatID=341, accessed 17 November 2023; 'Turkish Women Share Stories of Abuse' (*BBC News*, 17 February 2015) http://www.bbc.co.uk/news/blogs-trending-31504416, accessed 29 November 2023; Charlotte Alfred, 'Women in Turkey Share Devastating Stories of Sexual Harassment in #Sendeanlat Twitter Campaign' (*Huffington Post*, 17 February 2015) http://www.huffingtonpost.com/2015/02/17/turkey-sendeanlat-twitter-campaign_n_6699702.html, accessed 29 November 2023.

[7] Davidson (n 6); Miriam Wells, 'Attacks on Women Continue In Turkey Despite Protests Over Student's Brutal Murder' (*VICE News*, 21 February 2015) https://news.vice.com/article/attacks-on-women-continue-in-turkey-despite-protests-over-students-brutal-murder, accessed 17 November 2023; Meredith Hoffman, 'Protests Across Turkey Denounce Violence Against Women After Student's Brutal Murder' (*VICE News*, 15 February 2015) https://news.vice.com/article/protests-across-turkey-denounce-violence-against-women-after-students-brutal-murder, accessed 17 November 2023; 'Thousands Protest Murder of Özgecan Aslan' (*Hürriyet Daily News*, 18 February 2015) http://www.hurriyetdailynews.com/thousands-protest-murder-of-ozgecan-aslan-.aspx?pageID=238&nID=78520&NewsCatID=341, accessed 17 November 2023.

became flashpoints of anger about the rising levels of femicide, the lack of prosecutions, and, in particular, loopholes in the Turkish laws that allowed many perpetrators to secure reduced sentences or easy appeals. Laws were in place to address the issue of femicide, but they were not being implemented or making a difference on the ground. Stemming from the hashtag campaign, 'Özgecan's Law' was proposed, which was intended to prevent the reduction of sentences of perpetrators but was never passed into law. The campaign seems to have led to prosecution in this particular case, but no reduction in the numbers of femicide victims nor a meaningful change in the law.[8] Deeply rooted patriarchy and pushback against the West were also exposed in the government's discourse around women and equality.[9]

#mydressmychoice campaign overview

On 7 November 2014, a woman was publicly stripped and beaten at a bus stop in Nairobi, Kenya. She was called 'Jezebel' and was accused of 'tempting' men in the area, based on a perception of the clothing she was wearing. The attack was videotaped, and the video quickly went viral online. In the aftermath, more public strippings took place.[10] It became clear that this type of incident was not new in Kenya, but in this case posting the video on social media pushed activists to take action.[11] The hashtag resulted in a large-scale public protest in Nairobi, with both women and men turning out to say no

---

[8] Caitlinrose Fisher, 'Legislation Is Not Enough: Turkey Fails to Enforce Its Violence Against Women Laws' (*Global Rights for Women*, 10 April 2015) https://web.archive. org/web/20170329062905/http://globalrightsforwomen.org/2015/04/10/legislation-is-not-enough-turkey-fails-to-enforce-its-violence-against-women-laws/, accessed 17 November 2023.

[9] Mehmet Yilmaz, 'Why the Insistence on "Turkish-Style" Rules?' (*Hürriyet Daily News*, 9 March 2016) https://www.hurriyetdailynews.com/opinion/mehmet-y-yil maz/why-the-insistence-on-turkish-style-rules-96240, accessed 17 November 2023; 'Explained: How Özgecan's Murder United, Divided Turkey' (*Hürriyet Daily News*, 17 February 2015) http://www.hurriyetdailynews.com/explained-how-ozgecans-murder-united-divided-turkey.aspx?pageID=238&nID=78414&NewsCatID=509, accessed 17 November 2023.

[10] Pamilerin Beckley, '#Mydressmychoice v #Nudityisnotmychoice' (*Go Woman Africa*, 18 November 2014) https://web.archive.org/web/20190219025838/http://gowomanafrica. com/mydressmychoice-vs-nudityisnotmychoice/, accessed 16 November 2023.

[11] Indhira Santos, '#MyDressMyChoice: Tackling Gender Discrimination and Violence in Kenya One Tweet at a Time' (World Bank Blogs, 16 March 2015) http://blogs.worldb ank.org/developmenttalk/mydressmychoice-tackling-gender-discrimination-and-viole nce-kenya-one-tweet-time, accessed 16 November 2023.

to this kind of violence against women.[12] On the one side, activists saw the public stripping as an act of violence against women, calling for stronger enforcement of existing laws. On the other side, conservatives used the incident of public stripping to call for new 'decency' laws to be passed, to control what women can and cannot wear in public.[13] The counter-narrative in this campaign was very strong, and though male-dominated it was not solely men who were advocating for decency laws.[14] This counter-narrative aligned with much of the feminist digital activism literature, demonstrating the pushback and violence activists experience online. A similar issue was then deliberated in neighbouring countries Uganda and Namibia.[15] Although extensive debate in the government ensued, it seems that none of the campaign goals were fully realized.

---

[12] Dana Regevil, 'Kenya's #MyDressMyChoice rally' (*dw.com*, 17 November 2014) http://www.dw.com/en/mydressmychoice-kenyans-hold-rally-to-support-woman-beaten-for-wearing-miniskirt/a-18069645, accessed 11 October 2017.
The campaign officially called for the following:
- Immediately investigating and arresting all perpetrators of the attacks; urgently deploying police squads to public bus stations to prevent gender violence, including harassment.
- More aggressively cracking down on those inciting violence and similar attacks on women, whether in public or on social media, pursuant to Section 96 of the Penal Code.
- Comprehensively and urgently addressing the Kenyan Government's obligation to combat violence against women, including: community sensitization and awareness campaigns, regulatory action to ensure accountability of bus operators, and necessary legal reforms to strengthen the 2006 Sexual Offenses Act in light of these offenses.
- Urging the media to exercise caution in sharing the graphic videos of the women being attacked and stripped, as the videos re-victimize and stigmatize the survivors and are emboldening copycat criminals. Ultimately, these videos should be treated as evidence of criminal activity. ('Stop the Violent Attacks on Women: #MyDressMyChoice' (*Equality Now*) https://web.archive.org/web/20181018124310/https://www.equalitynow.org/stop_the_violent_attacks_on_women_mydressmychoice, accessed 16 November 2023)

[13] Zoe Kelland, '#MyDressMyChoice – Protests in Kenya after a Woman Is Publicly Stripped' (*Global Citizen*, 20 November 2014) https://www.globalcitizen.org/es/content/mydressmychoice-protests-in-kenya-after-a-woman-is/, accessed 16 November 2023; Dan Moshenberg, '#MyDressMyChoice' (*Africa Is a Country*, 14 November 2014) http://africasacountry.com/2014/11/mydressmychoice/, accessed 16 November 2023; Catherine Wambua-Soi, 'My Dress, Whose Choice?' (*Al Jazeera*, 31 December 2014) http://www.aljazeera.com/blogs/africa/2014/11/99751.html, accessed 16 November 2023.

[14] Basia Cummings, 'Kenyans Protest after Woman Is Beaten and Stripped in Public' (*The Guardian*, 17 November 2014) http://www.theguardian.com/world/2014/nov/17/kenya-mydressmychoice-protest-woman-stripped, accessed 29 November 2023; 'Stop the Violent Attacks on Women: #MyDressMyChoice' (n 12); Reilly Anne Dempsey Willis, 'Habermasian Utopia or Sunstein's Echo Chamber? The "Dark Side" of Hashtag Hijacking and Feminist Activism' (2020) 40 Legal Studies 507.

[15] Cummings (n 14); Moshenberg (n 13).

Context

This group covers a very wide range of geopolitical, socioeconomic, and demographic environments. It is also important to note the delicate political situations in Afghanistan and Turkey in particular – Afghanistan's post-Taliban relationship with the United States is complex and intricate, and Turkey's ongoing relationship with the European Union is equally fragile. Generally, there are no discernible patterns in looking at the basic context variables for these three countries. Turkey and Kenya showed some of the highest gender equality indices of all eight campaigns, outranked only by Argentina. This indicates that simply having a more equal society does not necessarily indicate that an online women's rights campaign will be successful. Afghanistan reported worse indicators of baseline gender equality than Iran yet showed more positive outcomes.[16] This is an interesting finding, as it could have been hypothesized that countries with a better starting point for women would be more inclined to move towards more positive change. However, this group of countries disproves that hypothesis on both ends – the countries with better indicators of gender equality did not show positive change, and the country with indicators showing the highest level of gender inequality did not show the most negative legal outcomes. Another finding of note is the presence of women's rights civil society organizations in these countries. These countries all have a strong domestic movement with a healthy level of civil society activity. Perhaps this prevented the countries from more negative legal outcomes.

---

[16] One day before her murder, Amnesty International issued a statement concerning the risks of violence against women in public in Afghanistan and the lack of law enforcement available to protect them. Amnesty International, 'UNAMA Mandate Extension a Clear Reminder to Prioritise Human Rights in Afghanistan' (2015) 3. The roots of violence against women in Afghanistan are deep and troubling. See, for example, Asad Kosha, 'Farkhunda, Victim of a Society of Oppressors and the Oppressed' (*Radio Salam Watandar*, 17 March 2016) https://web.archive.org/web/20170218014 541/http://salamwatandar.com/english/Article.aspx?a=19458, accessed 16 November 2023. Women were often targeted during the civil wars in the 1980s and 1990s, and when the Taliban took control the plight of women was even worse. After the fall of the Taliban in late 2001, violence against women was widely practiced and tolerated. Amnesty International, 'Afghanistan Women Still under Attack – a Systematic Failure to Protect' (2005); Human Rights Watch, 'The "Ten-Dollar Talib" and Women's Rights Afghan Women and the Risks of Reintegration and Reconciliation' (2010). The attack on Farkhunda was 14 years into the new regime, less time than the entirety of the Taliban rule.

Legal outcomes

These campaigns showed, on average, little to no legal change. Gains made in some areas were counter-balanced by negative outcomes in other areas. #farkhunda showed particularly poor judicial outcomes but with somewhat positive legislative changes, #sendeanlat showed almost no change with the law proposed by the campaign never even voted on by the government, and #mydressmychoice showed slightly poor outcomes in the courts with slightly positive indications in the institutionalization of ending violence against women. On the whole, very little changed for women and girls living in Afghanistan, Turkey, or Kenya.

Legislative change

Current legislative frameworks in Afghanistan are generally quite new, many passed since the fall of the Taliban in 2001. While the Constitution continues to prioritize Islam, it also has several articles protecting women's equality and bodily integrity.[17] Afghanistan passed a progressive law to end violence against women in 2009 (EVAW),[18] however there is a large divide between legislating and implementation on the ground.[19] Amnesty International found that the government was under international pressure to legislatively address violence against women, but that simply passing the law did not translate into changes on the ground.[20] The United Nations Assistance Mission in Afghanistan (UNAMA) reports also cite many weaknesses of the law.[21] Major problems exist with the categorization of cases and the

---

[17] Islamic Republic of Afghanistan The Constitution of Afghanistan 2004 ss 22, 24, 44.

[18] Law on Elimination of Violence against Women (EVAW) 2009.

[19] Human Rights Watch, '"I Had to Run Away" The Imprisonment of Women and Girls for "Moral Crimes" in Afghanistan' (2012) 104.

[20] Amnesty International (n 16) 4; Amnesty International, 'Too Many Missed Opportunities: Human Rights in Afghanistan under the Karzai Administration' (2014) 2; Amnesty International, 'Back-Tracking, Compromises, and Failed Pledges – Human Rights Sidelined in Afghanistan. Amnesty International Submission to the UN Universal Periodic Review' (2014) 7.

[21] United Nations Assistance Mission in Afghanistan, 'Still a Long Way to Go: Implementation of the Law on Elimination of Violence against Women in Afghanistan' (2012) 11–12. As also reported by SIGAR, 'Many elements of the 2009 law seek to terminate the customs, traditions, and practices that allow or encourage violence against women. However, UNAMA found that many law enforcement authorities were either unaware of the law or were unwilling to enforce it, resulting in the persistence of acute gender inequity'. Special Inspector General for Afghanistan Reconstruction, 'Report to the United States Congress' (2011) 84.

continued use of traditional dispute resolution mechanisms.[22] Using EVAW as a basis for judgement in court happened in just 4 per cent of relevant total reported cases.[23]

The law is legally binding as it was passed by the president, but it never went before parliament. Efforts to later strengthen the law then put it to parliament where it was met with heated conservative backlash.[24] One MP stated that he was 'surprised that the president had issued the decree in the first place and hinted that the law was an attempt by foreigners to impose western values on Afghan society'.[25] Before the law could be overturned or overruled, it was sent back to Commissions for redrafting and clarifying. This is a good indication of the tensions in the Afghan government, with one side driven by international pressures and incentives and the other supported by domestic religious conservatives. This makes progress in the area of women's rights and violence against women particularly difficult, not entirely dissimilar from Iran (though with a more complex relationship to the West), where tensions between central government and hard-line conservatives are palpable.

After the attention the campaign brought to the issue, efforts to implement a new draft law on harassment of women intensified, intended to clarify some of the identified ambiguities in the EVAW law.[26] Activists at the time felt that the new law, rather than clarifying the EVAW, was actually duplicative and perhaps contradictory, covering some of the same crimes but in two different pieces of legislation.[27] The laws were for a time in flux, with strong groups lobbying for progressive and supportive laws and conservative groups lobbying for more traditional laws which are, arguably, less favourable for

---

[22] United Nations Assistance Mission in Afghanistan, 'A Long Way to Go: Implementation of the Elimination of Violence against Women Law in Afghanistan' (2011) 21–26; United Nations Assistance Mission in Afghanistan (n 21) 48; United Nations Assistance Mission in Afghanistan, 'A Way to Go: An Update on Implementation of the Law on Elimination of Violence against Women in Afghanistan' (2013) 21–22.

[23] United Nations Assistance Mission in Afghanistan, 'A Long Way to Go: Implementation of the Elimination of Violence against Women Law in Afghanistan' (n 22) 10.

[24] Special Inspector General for Afghanistan Reconstruction, 'Report to the United States Congress' (2013) 139; Amnesty International, 'Too Many Missed Opportunities: Human Rights in Afghanistan under the Karzai Administration' (n 20) 3; Afghan Women's Network, 'Beijing+20 Afghanistan Civil Society Progress Report' (2015) 21.

[25] Special Inspector General for Afghanistan Reconstruction (n 24) 139.

[26] Ehsan Qaane, 'Harassment of Women in Afghanistan: A Hidden Phenomenon Addressed in Too Many Laws' (Afghanistan Analysts Network, 2 April 2017) https://www.afghanistan-analysts.org/harassment-of-women-in-afghanistan-a-hidden-phenomenon-addressed-in-too-many-laws/, accessed 16 November 2023.

[27] Ibid.

women.[28] A report from UNAMA in 2020 confirmed this continued tension, with some evidence of slow improvements from 2018 to 2020 but with many failures of the justice system to fully address violence against women.[29]

There was, in the aftermath of the campaign, therefore a potentially positive change in the efforts of the government, at least to some extent, to improve the existing law and to implement those changes in the judicial system. However, the improvements were not always in agreement with the recommendations of women's rights groups, nor were they implemented properly by the authorities or the courts.[30] Since this study was conducted, the political situation in Afghanistan has changed dramatically, with significant ongoing concerns about the treatment of women under the Taliban rule.[31]

Moving to Turkey and the issues in the #sendeanlat campaign, there is a similar situation with legislative outcomes. Turkey had previously been praised for progressively legislating on violence against women.[32] However, in

---

[28] AWN Shadow report in 2016 stated: 'The implementation of gender sensitive laws and policies remains limited, hindered by conservative forces, which consider women's empowerment against the traditional values of Afghanistan as a country. There is a growing fear among women's rights activists for the roll back of women's rights that have been gained in the 15 years, as commitments made by the government continues to remain on paper alone' (Afghan Women's Network Annual 2nd report on Convention of the Elimination of All Forms of Discrimination Against Women (CEDAW) In Afghanistan, 2016, para 23, available at: https://awn-af.org/wp-content/uploads/2022/09/AWN-Annual-2nd-report-on-CEDAW-In-Afghanistan.pdf).

[29] UNAMA, 'In Search of Justice for Crimes of Violence against Women and Girls' (2020) https://unama.unmissions.org/sites/default/files/in_search_of_justice_for_crimes_of_violence_against_women_and_girls.pdf, accessed 7 November 2023.

[30] United Nations Assistance Mission in Afghanistan, 'Justice through the Eyes of Afghan Women: Cases of Violence against Women Addressed through Mediation and Court Adjudication' (2015).

[31] Patricia Gossman, 'I Thought Our Life Might Get Better' (Human Rights Watch, 2021) https://www.hrw.org/report/2021/08/05/i-thought-our-life-might-get-bet ter/implementing-afghanistans-elimination, accessed 7 November 2023; Fahima Sirat, 'Violence Against Women: Before and After the Taliban' (OHRH, 15 March 2022) https://ohrh.law.ox.ac.uk/violence-against-women-before-and-after-the-tali ban/, accessed 16 November 2023; 'Afghanistan: UN Experts Say 20 Years of Progress for Women and Girls' Rights Erased since Taliban Takeover' (OHCHR, 8 March 2023) https://www.ohchr.org/en/press-releases/2023/03/afghanistan-un-experts-say-20-years-progress-women-and-girls-rights-erased, accessed 16 November 2023.

[32] 'The last decade has witnessed a ground-breaking shift in the legal approach to violence against women in Turkey, as almost all the inadequate or discriminatory provisions mentioned above have been changed. The primary driving force for these reforms has been the advocacy and lobbying efforts of a strong women's movement in Turkey. These reforms have not only brought forth significant legislative advances, but also have led to a visible shift in terms of public discussion and attention to violence against women and challenging prevalent attitudes and constructs.' Good Practices in Legislation on Violence against Women in Turkey and Problems of Implementation 2008 (EGM/GPLVAW/2008/EP13) 2.

a 2011 Human Rights Watch report, the government's response to domestic violence was uncovered as contradictory and full of gaps.[33] This included a penal code provision which allowed for sentence mitigation based on 'provocation' or 'incitement'.[34] The report goes on to highlight the mistrust most women felt towards the police and the relevant authorities.[35]

This is echoed in a quote from a woman in Afghanistan when told about the new harassment law and the ability to lodge complaints: 'That would make me happy. But what would really be a big help is if the policemen themselves didn't harass me.'[36] The problem therefore, similar to Afghanistan, is in implementation, particularly by authorities and the courts.[37] For example, the Turkish law (Law No. 6284) provides for restraining orders and temporary protective measures, but the statistics show that many of the femicides occurred despite these mechanisms being in place. In 2016, 6 per cent of femicides were of women with existing protection orders, and 9 per cent were killed despite asking for protection orders or when the orders expired – 15 per cent in total.[38] The same was true in the past with 10 per cent in 2015,[39] 8.9 per cent in 2014,[40] and 13.5 per cent in 2013.[41]

---

[33] Human Rights Watch, ' "He Loves You, He Beats You": Family Violence in Turkey and Access to Protection' (2011).

[34] Ibid.

[35] 'Law enforcement officers often prioritize preserving family unity, and push battered women to reconcile with abusers rather than pursuing criminal investigations or assisting women in getting protection orders.' Ibid, 31.

[36] Mina Habib, 'New Afghan Law Targets Sexual Harassment' (Institute for War and Peace Reporting, 8 March 2017) https://web.archive.org/web/20170823165516/https://iwpr.net/global-voices/new-afghan-law-targets-sexual-harassment, accessed 16 November 2023.

[37] Republic of Turkey, 'Report Submitted by Turkey Pursuant to Article 68, Paragraph 1 of the Council of Europe Convention on Preventing and Combating Violence against Women and Domestic Violence (Baseline Report)' (2017); Mattia Gallo and Selin Cagatay, 'Fighting for Women's Rights in Turkey' (*International Viewpoint*, 21 February 2015) http://www.internationalviewpoint.org/spip.php?article3891, accessed 17 November 2023.

[38] Çiçek Tahaoğlu and Begüm Baki, 'Men Kill At Least 261 Women, Girls in 2016' (*Bianet – Bagimsiz Iletisim Agi*, 3 February 2017) http://www.bianet.org/english/women/183255-men-kill-at-least-261-women-girls-in-2016, accessed 17 November 2023.

[39] Çiçek Tahaoğlu, 'Men Kill over 284 Women in 2015' (*Bianet – Bagimsiz Iletisim Agi*, 16 February 2016) http://www.bianet.org/english/women/172165-men-kill-over-284-women-in-2015, accessed 17 November 2023.

[40] Çiçek Tahaoğlu, 'Men Kill 281 Women in 2014' (*Bianet – Bagimsiz Iletisim Agi*, 20 January 2015) http://www.bianet.org/english/women/161678-men-kill-281-women-in-2014, accessed 17 November 2023.

[41] Çiçek Tahaoğlu, 'Men Kill 214 Women in 2013' (*Bianet – Bagimsiz Iletisim Agi*, 9 January 2014) http://www.bianet.org/english/women/152706-men-kill-214-women-in-2013, accessed 17 November 2023.

Again, very similar to the situation in Afghanistan, a new law was proposed in the aftermath of the #sendeanlat campaign which was never passed. It was known as 'Özgecan's Law' and would have amended the Turkish Criminal Law Article 82 to specify gender-based killing, as well as amending Articles 85–86 and 106 to reflect gender-based killing.[42] The proposed law changed the permissibility of postponing punishment in the Execution Act, particularly on the grounds of mental illness as statistics show this is abused as a justification in femicides.[43] Finally, the law called for changes to sentencing to ensure that perpetrators are not released early.[44] The government promised to pass the law in 2015 but it was delayed on more than one occasion, and in fact has never been passed.[45]

In the years since the study was conducted, the situation for women and girls in Turkey has declined. Rates of femicide continue to rise, and in 2021 President Erdoğan withdrew from the Istanbul Convention (a Council of Europe convention on eliminating violence against women).[46] In a horribly familiar case, university student Pinar Gultekan was murdered by her ex-boyfriend in 2020 – and, once again, activists protested.[47] Once again, the 'unjust provocation' mitigating factor was applied in the courts. There are

---

[42] 'Platform Law Proposal Full Text to Stop the Murder of Women' (We Will Stop Femicide, 27 June 2015) https://kadincinayetlerinidurduracagiz.net/haklarimiz/2251/kadin-cinaye tlerini-durduracagiz-platformu-yasa-teklifi-tam-metni, accessed 17 November 2023.

[43] Ibid.

[44] Ibid; Agence France-Presse, 'Three Men Get Life Sentence for Murder and Attempted Rape of Student in Turkey' (*The Guardian*, 4 December 2015) https://www.theguard ian.com/world/2015/dec/04/three-men-life-sentence-murder-student-turkey-ozge can-aslan, accessed 29 November 2023; 'Femicides on the Rise as Watchdog Releases First Quarter Figures' (*Hürriyet Daily News*, 7 April 2016) http://www.hurriyetdailyn ews.com/femicides-on-the-rise-as-watchdog-releases-first-quarter-figures.aspx?pageID= 238&nID=97398&NewsCatID=339, accessed 17 November 2023; Christina Asquith, 'Ozgecan Aslan and Violence Against Women in Turkey' (*The New York Times*, 23 February 2015) https://www.nytimes.com/2015/02/24/opinion/ozgecan-aslan-and-violence-agai nst-women-in-turkey.html accessed 29 November 2023.

[45] 'Sign the Petition' (Change.org) https://www.change.org/p/özgecanyasası-çıksın-yasalar-kadınları-korusun-ba-yildirim, accessed 17 November 2023; 'Sadece 2016'da 236 Kadın #25Kasım' (Change.org) https://www.change.org/p/%C3%B6zgecanyasas%C4%B1-%C3%A7%C4%B1ks%C4%B1n-yasalar-kad%C4%B1nlar%C4%B1-korusun-ba-yildi rim/u/18584990, accessed 17 November 2023.

[46] The Advocates for Human Rights, 'Turkey CEDAW Alternative Report DV Femicide' (2022) https://www.theadvocatesforhumanrights.org/Res/FINAL%20Turkey%20CE DAW%20Alternative%20Report%20DV%20Femicide.pdf, accessed 7 November 2023.

[47] Burcu Karakas, 'Turkey Faces up to Femicide' (*dw.com*, 19 June 2022) https://www. dw.com/en/turkeys-femicide-problem-all-eyes-on-court-verdicts/a-62165754, accessed 17 November 2023.

ample stories which continue echo the same failings.[48] The government went so far as to try to shut down the non-governmental organization pushing for legal change (We Will Stop Femicide) but the effort failed in court.[49] The issue is as much in focus now as it was in 2015, with no meaningful change.

Finally, turning to Kenya, once again a very similar legislative picture exists. Fairly robust laws were in place to protect women from violence, yet violence continued. After the campaign, a new law was proposed to bolster existing legislation, but it was rejected by parliament. Prior to the campaign, in 2006, Kenya had enacted the Sexual Offences Act, the first legislation in Kenya to recognize sexual harassment as a crime. It covers a wide range of sexual offences, importantly with commensurate minimum sentences, an improvement over the discretion previously allowed under the penal code.[50] The Sexual Offense Act of 2006 was intended to be a major improvement over previous laws. It took many iterations and debates to reach a point of majority support.[51] Yet, once again, problems in implementation by authorities and judges allowed violence against women to continue.[52]

After the campaign, some progress was initially made with a handful of legislative updates to protect women passed by parliament.[53] But a new

---

[48] AI Monitor, 'Fury in Turkey as Convicted Wife Killer Murders Third Victim' (6 January 2023) https://www.al-monitor.com/originals/2023/01/fury-turkey-convicted-wife-killer-murders-third-victim, accessed 17 November 2023; Human Rights Watch, 'Interview: How Turkey's Failure to Protect Women Can Cost Them Their Lives' (Human Rights Watch, 2022) https://www.hrw.org/news/2022/05/26/interview-how-turkeys-failure-protect-women-can-cost-them-their-lives, accessed 7 November 2023.

[49] France24, 'Turkey Drops Bid to Close Leading Women's Rights Group' (*France 24*, 13 September 2023) https://www.france24.com/en/live-news/20230913-turkey-drops-bid-to-close-leading-anti-femicide-group, accessed 17 November 2023.

[50] Ruth Aura, 'Kenya Law: Situational Analysis and the Legal Framework on Sexual and Gender-Based Violence in Kenya: Challenges and Opportunities' (Kenya Law) http://kenyalaw.org/kl/index.php?id=4512, accessed 6 November 2017.

[51] 'Legislating against Sexual Violence: The Kenyan Experience' (Choike.org) https://web.archive.org/web/20101207010147/http://www.choike.org/nuevo_eng/infor mes/4717.html, accessed 16 November 2023; Agency for Cooperation and Research in Development, 'Making the Law Count: Kenya: An Audit of Legal Practice on Sexual Violence' (2009) 17.

[52] 'The novel provisions within the SOA may lead one to conclude that all loopholes in the law have been sealed, that SGBV cases are now easily prosecuted in the Kenyan legal system and that survivors are now benefitting from a gender and survivor friendly judicial process in Kenya. However, the law still has some challenges in applicability.' Agency for Cooperation and Research in Development (n 51) 17.

[53] 'There has been some progress to get justice for women being publicly assaulted in Kenya. In late December 2014, the Security Laws (Amendment) Act of 2014 became law. While there are serious issues surrounding provisions in the law that run counter to protecting human rights, Article 17 criminalizes these strippings.' 'Stop the Violent Attacks on Women: #MyDressMyChoice' (n 12).

proposed law, the Sexual Offences (Amendment) Bill 2016, was rejected by MPs in February 2017.[54] The amendments were intended to criminalize unwanted contact and bargaining around sexual attacks.[55] The bill was supported by women's rights groups. It was reported that mostly male ministers rejected the amendments, claiming that the amendments could be easily misinterpreted. Although there were parts that had support, such as establishing specialized units in police stations, the bill was thrown out in its entirety.[56]

The issue of decency laws is still ripe. Of note, before #mydressmychoice, there was a proposed bill in a Kenyan county to 'ban the miniskirt'.[57] Then in 2015, not long after the campaign, some universities in Kenya began to pass and enforce dress codes on campus which called for 'decent' dressing.[58] One commentator posited that '[p]erhaps these schools are "protecting" their students from self-styled "fashion police" who have attacked and stripped women on the streets of Nairobi and other major towns in Kenya … in the-not-so-distant past over what they consider "inappropriate dressing"'.[59] In September 2017, county employees in two counties in Kenya were ordered to 'dress decently'.[60] Similar tactics were used in neighbouring Uganda,

---

[54] Daniel Psirmoi, 'MPs Reject Changes to Sex Offences Law' (*The Standard*) https://www.standardmedia.co.ke/article/2001229527/mps-reject-changes-to-sex-offences-law, accessed 16 November 2023.

[55] The Sexual Offences (Amendment) Act 2016 included the following amendments:
   • Defining 'indecent act' more broadly, including unwanted touching or exposure.
   • Increasing fines.
   • A provision whereby perpetrators are excluded from care work.
   • Tightens provisions for plea bargaining, so that individuals who sought to cover up their crime have a minimum sentence.
   • More special units and training for law enforcement.
   • Sex education in schools.

[56] Psirmoi (n 54).

[57] Duke Mangera, 'Kenyan Politician Wants to Ban Miniskirts and Tight Trousers' (Index on Censorship, 12 March 2014) https://www.indexoncensorship.org/2014/03/kenya-county-wants-ban-miniskirts-tight-trousers/, accessed 16 November 2023.

[58] ArtMattersInfo, 'Kenyan Universities Call for "Decent" Dressing and Grooming' (ArtMatters.Info, 18 November 2015) http://artmatters.info/2015/11/kenyan-universities-call-for-decent-dressing-and-grooming/, accessed 16 November 2023.

[59] Ibid.

[60] Steve Njuguna, 'County Staff Asked to Dress Decently' (*Daily Nation*, 3 September 2017) http://www.nation.co.ke/news/Nakuru--Nyandarua-counties-ask-staff-to-dress-decently/1056-4081652-11cjwvdz/index.html, accessed 16 November 2023; Morris Kiruga, 'Understanding Africa's "Fashion Gestapo": Miniskirts, Maxi Skirts Make-up, and Long Beards' (*MG Africa*, 5 December 2014) https://web.archive.org/web/20180401162426/http://mgafrica.com/article/2014-12-04-understanding-africas-fashion-police/, accessed 16 November 2023.

where a dress code was passed in 2017 for civil servants.[61] Also in Uganda, an anti-pornography bill (which is also known to be used as a decency law to regulate women's attire) was also then reviewed but passed muster and is still in force.[62]

Since this study was conducted, the situation in Kenya is much the same. Reports of intimate partner violence were particularly harrowing during the COVID-19 pandemic, exacerbated by the economic instability of many women who became wholly financially dependent during lockdown.[63] Once again, the government is responding by introducing new policies and to fully implement existing legislation, however most groups and advocates are sceptical as the country has a long history of having positive legislation and policies on the books, but with a lack of implementation on the ground.[64]

There were very similar legislative outcomes across all three of these campaigns. Fairly robust and modern laws on violence against women existed prior to the incidents which sparked the campaigns. However, significant problems in implementation of these laws were identified in all three countries which allowed for the spark incidents of violence against women to occur. This continues to be the case in 2023. The attention these campaigns brought to the issues seemed to result in proposed changes

---

[61] Patience Atuhaire, 'Mini-Skirts and Morals in Uganda' (*BBC News*, 9 July 2017) http://www.bbc.co.uk/news/world-africa-40507843, accessed 29 November 2023; Anneeth Kaur Hundle, 'Uganda's Colonial-Style Dress Code' (*Al Jazeera*, 14 August 2017) http://www.aljazeera.com/indepth/opinion/2017/08/uganda-colonial-style-dress-code-17080 8072148083.html, accessed 16 November 2023.

[62] Thair Shaikh, 'Uganda Bans Miniskirts as MPs Pass Anti-Pornography Bill' (*The Independent*, 19 December 2013) http://www.independent.co.uk/news/world/africa/no-thighs-please-uganda-bans-miniskirts-as-mps-pass-anti-pornography-bill-9016686.html, accessed 29 November 2023; but see 'Women Free to Wear Miniskirts – Lokodo' (*Daily Monitor*, 16 January 2014) http://www.monitor.co.ug/News/National/Women-free-to-wear-miniskirts---Lokodo/688334-2148738-v2a1ai/index.html, accessed 16 November 2023.

[63] Juliana Nnoko-Mewanu, 'I Had Nowhere to Go' (Human Rights Watch, 2021), https://www.hrw.org/report/2021/09/21/i-had-nowhere-go/violence-against-women-and-girls-during-covid-19-pandemic-kenya, accessed 7 November 2023; Human Rights Watch, 'Kenya: Survivors of Gender-Based Violence Lack Help' (21 September 2021) https://www.hrw.org/news/2021/09/21/kenya-survivors-gender-based-viole nce-lack-help, accessed 7 November 2023; Yohannes Dibaba Wado, 'Violence against Women in Kenya: Data Provides a Glimpse into a Grim Situation' (*The Conversation*, 19 October 2021) http://theconversation.com/violence-against-women-in-kenya-data-provi des-a-glimpse-into-a-grim-situation-170109, accessed 16 November 2023.

[64] Equality Now, 'Kenya Just Committed to Ending Gender Based Violence in Five Years. Here's How They Plan to Do It' (*Equality Now*, 10 August 2021) https://www.equality now.org/news_and_insights/kenya_just_committed_to_ending_gbv_in_5_years_here_s _how_they_plan_to_do_it/, accessed 16 November 2023.

to the existing laws, intended to fill gaps and improve implementation. In Afghanistan, the new law is in effect but has been met with criticism from advocates and thus far has not made much difference on the ground; with the political changes in the country the situation is now bleak. In both Turkey and Kenya, the proposed new laws failed in parliament. While in Turkey the government seems to be less committed to reducing femicide and gender-based violence, in Kenya major issues remain in the gap between legislation and implementation, particularly evidenced during COVID-19 lockdowns. These campaigns did not achieve the desired legislative changes.

Institutionalization

Starting again with Afghanistan and #farkhunda, some positive changes were seen in the institutionalization of women's rights norms after the attention drawn to the issue by social media. In the years leading up to her murder, the Afghan government was continually criticized for not doing enough to protect women. In 2011, Trust found that Afghanistan was the world's most dangerous place for women.[65] In 2012, the Afghan Women's Network stated that it was 'concerned that there is a lack of genuine commitment by the government to protect women's rights'.[66] According to Special Inspector General for Afghanistan Reconstruction (SIGAR), there were warnings that women's rights could face serious challenges and backsliding with the withdrawal of US troops in 2014.[67] Then, just four days before Farkhunda's murder, President Ghani was in Washington, DC giving a speech to the US Congress in which he spent significant time emphasizing the importance of equality for women.[68] Given the complex history and delicate relations with

---

[65] 'The World's Most Dangerous Countries for Women 2011' (Trustlaw, 15 June 2011) https://web.archive.org/web/20180711002531/http://news.trust.org/spotlight/the-worlds-most-dangerous-countries-for-women-2011, accessed 16 November 2023.

[66] Afghan Women's Network, 'Afghanistan CEDAW Shadow (NGO) Report' (2012) 27–28.

[67] Special Inspector General for Afghanistan Reconstruction (n 24) 140; Amnesty International, 'Strengthening the Rule of Law and Protection of Human Rights, Including Women's Rights, Is Key to Any Development Plan for Afghanistan: Open Letter to Participants in the International Donors Conference on Afghanistan in Tokyo' (2012).

[68] 'A mental and cultural revolution must take place over the treatment of women in and by our society. There is no point talking about how much we respect women's honour, if we let it go unpunished or allow harassment in our streets. We've signed the global conventions to end discrimination again women and we will implement them vigorously but work is still need to convince our [people?] that protection of women's rights is part and parcel of their own quest for social justice. I as the leader of Afghanistan am personally committed to work with the mullah, activists, and top leaders of our country to bring about this mental change.' John Boehner, *President Ashraf Ghani of Afghanistan's Address to a Joint Meeting of Congress*, https://www.youtube.com/watch?v=cgqc7MO9zl0, accessed 22 July 2024.

the West, and the United States in particular, Ghani's speech may very well have been an act of lip service rather than an actual indication of domestic political will to change. It could also be indicative of the domestic tensions in Afghanistan, between elected government officials determining foreign policies and religious leaders focused domestically, similar to Iran, and reflecting the theoretical critiques of the spiral model identified by Borzel and Risse regarding lack of domestic capacity.[69] Either way, the government had not made efforts to improve women's rights in the years leading up to Farkhunda's death.

The #farkhunda incident therefore was, sadly, not surprising. The government did make some attempts after the campaign to make progress in the institutionalization of the elimination of violence against women. For example, the High Commission and Commissions for the Elimination of Violence Against Women 'increased' from 2014 to 2016, a 'trust fund' was established to deal with cases of violence against women, a department in the Attorney General Office was created to combat violence against women, and there was the adoption of a regulation for the prevention of sexual harassment.[70] The government spoke about the importance of awareness-raising, stating they were using schools and media outlets to reach the general population.[71]

However, once again, frontline change did not seem to follow. SIGAR undertook interviews with Afghan women in 2016 to learn more about progress and challenges. Security was the main challenge that women reported. Interviewees reported that there was a 'backlash' and that violence was on the rise.[72] 'Several women recalled the murder of Farkhunda Malikzada, pointing out that the men who beat Farkhunda to death were not Taliban. These were young guys in jeans with iPhones. The hatred and the grudge they had against women is very powerful.'[73] After the campaign, women recounted feeling less secure, with the knowledge of what Afghan men are capable of.[74] On one positive note, interviewees also felt that violence against women was, in the years following the campaign, being reported more because of the media attention.[75]

---

[69] Tanja Borzel and Thomas Risse, 'Human Rights in Areas of Limited Statehood: The New Agenda' in Thomas Risse-Kappen and Stephen C Ropp (eds), *The Persistent Power of Human Rights: From Commitment to Compliance* (Cambridge University Press, 2013).

[70] Islamic Republic of Afghanistan, 'Progress Report on Women's Status and Empowerment and National Action Plan (NAP 1325)' (2016) 7.

[71] Ibid, 27.

[72] Special Inspector General for Afghanistan Reconstruction (n 1) 9.

[73] Ibid.

[74] Ibid, 10.

[75] Ibid, 16.

Turkey showed a similar pattern. While Afghanistan was balancing a delicate relationship with the United States, Turkey was balancing a delicate relationship with Western Europe based on its desire to integrate with the European Union. Therefore we see government lip service to 'Western' issues such as women's rights and eliminating gender equality, however little to no effort to institutionalize norms.[76] Feminist discourse analysis can uncover the 'true' approach of those in power, with the prime minister himself having been quoted as saying that men and women cannot be in equal positions.[77] He also made comments about women's duty as mothers, disparaging feminists.[78] These underlying and harmful stereotypes of women used by the government have been labelled as 'anti-female' by women's groups and were in fact blamed for the rising incidents of femicide.[79] In recent years, the government has been much more outspoken about rejecting some of these ideals, culminating in the decision to withdraw from the Istanbul Convention.

Officially, there were two national action plans to combat violence against women in Turkey.[80] Although these action plans called for the establishment of many support services and shelters, civil society criticized the continued

---

[76] Jonny Hogg, 'Fight against Domestic Violence Stalls in "Patriarchal" Turkey' (*Hürriyet Daily News*, 23 July 2014) http://www.hurriyetdailynews.com/fight-against-domestic-violence-stalls-in-patriarchal-turkey.aspx?pageID=238&nID=69455&NewsCatID=339, accessed 17 November 2023.

[77] Selin Girit, 'Özgecan'ın Ölümü Kadına Yönelik Şiddette Milat Olur Mu?' (*BBC Türkçe*, 20 February 2015) http://www.bbc.com/turkce/haberler/2015/02/150220_ozgecan_aslan, accessed 29 November 2023; Nuray Babacan, 'Erdoğan's Remarks on Gender Equality Stir Fury' (*Hürriyet Daily News*, 26 November 2014) http://www.hurriyetda ilynews.com/erdogans-remarks-on-gender-equality-stir-fury-.aspx?pageID=238&nID=74820&NewsCatID=338, accessed 17 November 2023; Davidson (n 6); 'Turkey President Erdogan: Women Are Not Equal to Men' (*BBC News*, 24 November 2014) http://www.bbc.co.uk/news/world-europe-30183711, accessed 29 November 2023; 'Turkish President Erdoğan Says Gender Equality "against Nature"' (*Hürriyet Daily News*, 25 November 2014) http://www.hurriyetdailynews.com/turkish-president-erdogan-says-gender-equality-against-nature.aspx?pageID=238&nID=74726&NewsCatID=338, accessed 17 November 2023; Yunana Ahmed, 'Political Discourse Analysis: A Decolonial Approach' (2021) 18 Critical Discourse Studies 139.

[78] 'Our religion regards motherhood very highly. Feminists don't understand that, they reject motherhood.' 'Turkey President Erdogan: Women Are Not Equal to Men' (n 77); 'Turkish President Erdoğan Says Gender Equality "against Nature"' (n 77).

[79] 'Turkey's Femicide Problem' (17 May 2015) https://web.archive.org/web/20230120024848/https://harvardpolitics.com/turkeys-femicide-problem/, accessed 17 November 2023; Bianet, 'BİANET (Independent Communication Network) Shadow Report to GREVIO' (2017).

[80] Çiğdem Tozlu and Asuman Göksel, 'WAVE Violence against Women Country Report Turkey' (2016) https://notus-asr.org/wp-content/uploads/2016/05/WAVE_Report_Turkey_FINAL_EN_6March2016-3-3.pdf.

lack of implementation and institutionalization.[81] Some went so far as to find that the policies created overly bureaucratic systems which made more problems than were solved.[82] The government also replaced the Ministry for Women and Family with the Ministry of Family and Social Policies in 2011, removing women's issues from the ministry.[83] Again, this shows the underlying lack of political will to engage with women's rights issues, which has become more and more prominent with time.

Just days after Özgecan's murder, the Ministry of Family and Social Policies announced a series of actions to renew and implement the national action plan on the fight against violence against women, including the establishment of more women's shelters and an impact analysis of the focus of the campaign, Law No. 6284.[84] However, a report found that the national action plan had not, in fact, been renewed.[85] There appeared to be significant lip service from both ruling party and opposition parties on eliminating violence against women, verbally addressing both prevention and prosecutions in the months and years following the campaign.[86] Time has shown that these discussions were and continue to be short-lived and lacking in teeth.[87] There is also some

---

[81] Ibid, 39.

[82] Ibid.

[83] Christina Asquith and Sophia Jones, 'Turkish Women Rising' (*Ms. Magazine Blog*, 23 March 2017) http://msmagazine.com/blog/2017/03/23/turkish-women-rising/, accessed 17 November 2023; Human Rights Watch, 'Turkey: Backward Step for Women's Rights' (Human Rights Watch, 2011) https://www.hrw.org/news/2011/06/09/turkey-backw ard-step-womens-rights, accessed 17 November 2023.

[84] Law to Protect Family and Prevent Violence Against Women 2012 (6284); 'Turkish Family Ministry Plans Stronger Action Plan to Combat Violence against Women' (*Hürriyet Daily News*, 18 February 2015) http://www.hurriyetdailynews.com/turkish-family-minis try-plans-stronger-action-plan-to-combat-violence-against-women-.aspx?pageID= 238&nID=78548&NewsCatID=341, accessed 17 November 2023.

[85] Bianet (n 79) 9.

[86] 'Turkish PM Pledges to Act on Women Killings' (*Hürriyet Daily News*, 16 February 2015) http://www.hurriyetdailynews.com/turkish-pm-pledges-to-act-on-women-killi ngs.aspx?pageID=238&nID=78388&NewsCatID=338, accessed 17 November 2023; Emily Feldman, 'Violence against Women in Turkey: Erdogan Takes a Surprising Stand' (*Mashable*, 19 February 2015) http://mashable.com/2015/02/19/erdogan-violence-agai nst-women/, accessed 17 November 2023.

[87] 'Turkey's Femicide Problem' (n 79); US State Department, 'Country Reports on Human Rights Practices for 2016' (2016) https://www.state.gov/j/drl/rls/hrrpt/humanright sreport/index.htm#wrapper, accessed 13 April 2017; Bianet (n 79) 8; 'Turkish Leaders Celebrate International Women's Day' (*Hürriyet Daily News*, 9 March 2015) http:// www.hurriyetdailynews.com/turkish-leaders-celebrate-international-womens-day--- ---.aspx?pageID=238&nID=79370&NewsCatID=338, accessed 17 November 2023; 'Erdoğan Says Turkey's Main Opposition Leader "Politicizes" Murder of Özgecan' (*Hürriyet Daily News*, 18 February 2015) http://www.hurriyetdailynews.com/erdogan-says-turk eys-main-opposition-leader-politicizes-murder-of-ozgecan.aspx?pageID=238&nID= 78483&NewsCatID=338, accessed 17 November 2023; 'Erdoğan Urges Muhtars to

indication that the government may have taken action against the media in the aftermath of the incident, attempting to quell the negative attention.[88] This is compounded by the more recent action of the government to attempt to shut down We Will Stop Femicide and other activist organizations.[89]

Finally, moving to Kenya and #mydressmychoice, the commonalities in legal outcomes for this group of campaigns continue. Yet again, there were policies and programmes in place intended to address the issue of violence against women but implementation and governmental institutionalization were lacking. A poll from 2010 underscored how little these laws and policies were changing experiences for women and girls, with 48.2 per cent of women fearing sexual harassment from a household member.[90]

National guidelines on the management of sexual violence were intended to ensure a rights-based, multiagency holistic approach to supporting victims of sexual violence, in particular addressing a dignified procedure for the collection of evidence.[91] But again, gaps between policy and implementation were significant. One non-governmental organization attempted to identify why this gap is so problematic in Kenya, and found a range of challenges and barriers, including many issues around inadequate resourcing, limited capacity, and sociocultural issues.[92] This was echoed in the work produced by a Task Force set up to oversee the implementation of the Sexual Offences Act.[93]

The president did take some action in the immediate aftermath of the spark public stripping incident, launching a new national framework towards response and prevention of gender-based violence, which was intended to coordinate efforts across sectors towards a more effective and efficient approach.[94] Of note, the framework specifically draws down from

---

Protect Women from Violence' (*Hürriyet Daily News*, 11 March 2015) http://www.hurriy etdailynews.com/erdogan-urges-muhtars-to-protect-women-from-violence-.aspx?pag eID=238&nID=79480&NewsCatID=338, accessed 17 November 2023; 'Is Life Getting Worse for Women in Erdogan's Turkey?' (*BBC News*, 4 March 2015) http://www.bbc. co.uk/news/world-europe-31709887, accessed 29 November 2023.

[88] There were 50 per cent fewer reports on violence against in the first 100 days of 2017 than there had been in 2016. 'This fall in press reports, even as violence against women was increasing, is another sign of violence against women. The closure of a number of media outlets and restrictions in press freedom in Turkey likely played a role in this situation', stated the report. '173 Women Killed in Turkey in First Five Months of 2017: Report' (*Hürriyet Daily News*, 5 June 2017) http://www.hurriyetdailynews.com/173-women-killed-in-turkey-in-first-five-months-of-2017-report.aspx?pageID=238&nID=113 936&NewsCatID=509, accessed 17 November 2023.

[89] Karakas (n 47); France24 (n 49).

[90] Santos (n 11).

[91] Aura (n 50).

[92] Agency for Cooperation and Research in Development (n 51); Aura (n 50).

[93] Human Rights Center, 'Sexual Offences Act: Implementation Workshop' (2012) 13.

[94] Aura (n 50).

international norms found in the Convention on the Elimination of all Forms of Discrimination Against Women, the Beijing Platform for Action, and the Nairobi Forward-Looking Strategy.[95] This coincided with the country's first 16 days against violence against women national campaign. This pattern repeated after COVID-19 – reports of domestic violence exploded, so the government announced a new commitment to ending gender-based violence, with little expectation of change on the ground.[96]

The #mydressmychoice campaign, similar to the other status quo campaigns, clearly pushed government officials to address the issue and denounce the public stripping[97] including, notably, a Tweet from the president.[98] However, in this particular campaign, the attention also prompted the counter-narrative to address the issue, where 'local news reported various interviews with local men who think that the mobs did the right thing', arguing that there is 'moral decay in society' and that the victim learned a lesson.[99] Others were critical of the movement out of a belief that a woman wearing a miniskirt lacks 'decency'.[100]

Despite all the attention to both sides of the decency debate, it seems little has changed.[101] In 2017 a commentator reported that, upon interviewing women, seven out of ten were still worried about what they wore based on where they were going.[102] In other words, women still feel as though they need to dress more conservatively in the cities where the perceived risk of harassment is higher.

---

[95] Ibid.

[96] Equality Now (n 64).

[97] Santos (n 11).

[98] Emmanuel Igunza, 'Stripping Videos Outrage Kenyans' (*BBC News*, 26 November 2014) http://www.bbc.co.uk/news/world-africa-30217462, accessed 29 November 2023.

[99] Willis (n 14).

[100] Santos (n 11).

[101] On 16 November 2016, two Nairobi gubernatorial candidates appeared on television for a live debate. The male candidate not only called the female candidate a 'socialite bimbo' but also stated 'You are so beautiful, everybody wants to rape you.' A few days later, the same female candidate attended an event wearing a black dress which showed her thighs, sparking debate on social media: 'One Twitter commentator posted: "Her mode of dressing is alarming. Why behave like a teenage girl?" The candidate replied "My great grandmother walked with less than I do. So did Eve. No apologies to make." Twitter reactions from the counter-narrative included the words "Bimbo," "spreading your womanhood," "dresses like she's in a brothel", "My dress my choice makes some people walk half naked", "As much as we condemn Miguna (male candidate), let our women carry themselves in an unquestionable manner".' Rachel Wambui, 'Is your dress really your choice' (*Daily Nation*, 3 March 2017) https://nation.africa/lifestyle/satur day/Is-your-dress-really-your-choice/1216-3835390-c1h5aj/index.html, accessed 16 November 2023.

[102] Ibid.

Across all three countries, again, we see a very similar picture in the institutionalization of women's rights before and after the hashtag campaigns. Policies and programmes were in place, but with the government lacking either the will or the capacity to prioritize meaningful change. Violence against women was rampant in these countries despite the various action plans, frameworks, and strategies. Discourse from government officials and other political parties shows endemic harmful stereotyping of women. The campaigns attracted enough attention to push government officials to publicly denounce violence against women, and perhaps make a small token gesture to introduce a new, non-binding policy or programme, but with little to no impact on the epidemics of violence and femicide, and long-term lack of commitment to actually affecting change.

Law enforcement

Law enforcement in Afghanistan was one of the main concerns of the campaign, particularly given that there were police on site when Farkhunda was murdered and that the perpetrators' sentences were commuted or acquitted altogether due to the rushed trials. Some improvements had been seen in the years leading up the campaign.[103] However, the same reports also found that many cases never made it to the official judicial process with many referrals still being made to traditional resolution mechanisms, a trend which continued for many years.[104] A 2012 shadow report also pointed to informal dispute resolution as problematic to women's access to justice.[105] It was reported that only 7 per cent of cases of violence under EVAW go through a judicial process.[106] In the 2013, UNAMA found that while EVAW is being used for more registration of reported incidents, it is not being used in more cases for indictment.[107] Taken together, this all indicates that the courts themselves might have been showing improvements in prosecutions, which is a significant step for Afghanistan, but that local barriers still existed which kept cases out of the system.

One of the most negative outcomes from this campaign was the prosecution of the perpetrators, where 11 police officers were sentenced to one year in prison, eight individuals were sentenced to 16 years, and four

---

[103] Special Inspector General for Afghanistan Reconstruction, 'Report to the United States Congress' (2012) 123; Special Inspector General for Afghanistan Reconstruction (n 24).

[104] Special Inspector General for Afghanistan Reconstruction (n 24) 121.

[105] Afghan Women's Network (n 66) paras 23–25.

[106] Akbar (n 5).

[107] United Nations Assistance Mission in Afghanistan, 'A Way to Go: An Update on Implementation of the Law on Elimination of Violence against Women in Afghanistan' (n 22) 3–4.

were sentenced to death, including the caretaker who started the mob and a young man who was seen on tape throwing stones.[108] The police officers were released on bail after an appeal, and four were acquitted. All continue to work for the government.[109] On appeal, three of the men sentenced to death had their sentences commuted to 20 years in prison, and the youth had his sentence commuted to ten years.[110] The appeal trial was notably held behind closed doors.[111] Human Rights Watch identified vast problems with these court cases: 'At every stage of this case the Afghan criminal justice system failed to adequately investigate, hold to account or appropriately punish those responsible. The trials of those originally accused were conducted in haste and riddled with procedural errors, with many defendants lacking legal counsel.'[112]

The Afghan Women's Network also raised concerns about the trials.[113] More generally, the network comments that: 'Kabul City as the country capital is becoming day by day worse for women's social protection, these kinds of events without prosecution, arresting of the perpetrators and failure to implement justice become cause of the constraints against women's movement as their active presence in all fields.'[114] The network, through a study, found that the lack of prosecutions has led to a culture of impunity and weak governance.[115] This was reiterated in a 2015 shadow report.[116] Other sources indicate that the lack of repercussions has emboldened men to harass women more often.[117] Most agree that the negative attention brought to the country through social media pressured the situation, leading to rushed trials which were then overturned, increasing the feeling of impunity.[118] All

---

[108] Kargar (n 1).

[109] Alissa J Rubin, 'Flawed Justice After a Mob Killed an Afghan Woman' (*The New York Times*, 26 December 2015) https://www.nytimes.com/2015/12/27/world/asia/flawed-justice-after-a-mob-killed-an-afghan-woman.html, accessed 29 November 2023.

[110] Human Rights Watch, 'Dispatches: Afghanistan's Legal System Fails Farkhunda, Again' (Human Rights Watch, 9 March 2016) https://www.hrw.org/news/2016/03/09/dispatc hes-afghanistans-legal-system-fails-farkhunda-again, accessed 16 November 2023; Kargar (n 1); Rubin (n 109); Akbar (n 5).

[111] Rubin (n 109).

[112] Human Rights Watch (n 110).

[113] 'It was further mentioned Civil society expected the Supreme Court to mete justice, but even after eight months, the unfair practices of the legal system and violations of law in connection the case of Martyr Farkhunda has not resulted in any fair outcome.' Afghan Women's Network, 'Afghan Women's Network Annual Report 2015: "Steps Toward Quality"' (2015) 20.

[114] Ibid, 22.

[115] Ibid, 23.

[116] Ibid, 17.

[117] Akbar (n 5).

[118] Ibid; Rubin (n 109).

of this made the situation *worse* for women and girls in Afghanistan. This is certainly the case now in 2023.

The picture was somewhat similar in Turkey. Although prosecutions and convictions were not as rare, mitigating factors to reduce sentences are common. Very little is reported on the role of the courts prior to Özgecan's murder, other than the low prosecution rates and the high use of mitigating factors for reduced sentences. The three men accused of involvement in the murder – the driver, his father, and his friend – were all found guilty and sentenced to aggravated life imprisonment.[119] The minibus driver was later killed in prison. President Erdoğan stated that he would personally follow the case and that 'violence against women is the bleeding wound of our country'.[120] It is possible that his investment in this particular case and not others led to heavy prosecution here but not systematically for other cases of violence against women.[121] Activists identified that courts were continuing to use good behaviour and provocation as mitigating factors; this still continues in 2023.[122]

---

[119] 'Özgecan Aslan's Murderers Sentenced to Aggravated Life Imprisonment' (*Bianet – Bagimsiz Iletisim Agi*, 3 December 2015) https://www.bianet.org/english/women/169 845-ozgecan-aslan-s-murderers-sentenced-to-aggravated-life-imprisonment, accessed 17 November 2023; 'Turkish Court Jails Three to Life for College Girl's Brutal Murder' (*Hürriyet Daily News*, 4 December 2015) http://www.hurriyetdailynews.com/turk ish-court-jails-three-to-life-for-college-girls-brutal-murder.aspx?pageID=238&nID= 92051&NewsCatID=509, accessed 17 November 2023.

[120] 'Violence against Women Is Turkey's "Bleeding Wound" – Erdogan' (*Reuters*, 16 February 2015) http://www.reuters.com/article/us-turkey-women-violence-idUSKBN0LK1OH2 0150216, accessed 22 July 2024; 'Turkish President Erdoğan Slams Women Protesting Özgecan's Murder by Dancing' (*Hürriyet Daily News*, 17 February 2015) http://www. hurriyetdailynews.com/turkish-president-erdogan-slams-women-protesting-ozgecans-murder-by-dancing-.aspx?pageID=238&nID=78423&NewsCatID=338, accessed 17 November 2023; 'Davutoğlu'ndan Bakanlar Kurulu Sonrası Flaş Açıklamalar' (*Sabah*, 16 February 2015) http://www.sabah.com.tr/gundem/2015/02/16/davutoglundan-bakan lar-kurulu-sonrasi-flas-aciklamalar, accessed 17 November 2023; 'Turkey's Introduction of Chemical Castration for Sex Offenders Prompts Mixed Reaction' (*Hürriyet Daily News*, 27 July 2016) http://www.hurriyetdailynews.com/turkeys-introduction-of-chemi cal-castration-for-sex-offenders-prompts-mixed-reaction.aspx?pageID=238&nID=102 147&NewsCatID=509, accessed 17 November 2023.

[121] 'Life Sentence Requested for Three Suspects in Özgecan Murder' (*Hürriyet Daily News*, 9 September 2015) http://www.hurriyetdailynews.com/life-sentence-requested-for-three-suspects-in-ozgecan-murder------.aspx?pageID=238&nID=88257&NewsCatID= 509, accessed 17 November 2023.

[122] US State Department (n 87); Nazlan Ertan, 'Violence against Women in Turkey Increases Both in Number and Brutality' (*Hürriyet Daily News*, 30 November 2015) http://www. hurriyetdailynews.com/violence-against-women-in-turkey-increases-both-in-number-and-brutality.aspx?pageID=238&nID=91880&NewsCatID=569, accessed 22 July 2024; 'Abated Sentence for Man Who Stabbed Wife to Death in Southeast' (*Hürriyet Daily News*,

Statistics showed a slight decrease in the percentage of gender-based violence cases benefiting from mitigating factors after the campaign, from roughly 24 per cent in 2015 to 22 per cent in 2016. It seems that specifically for homicide, it may have reduced from 45 per cent in 2014 to 28 per cent across 2015–2016, but the statistics are difficult to pinpoint.[123] The number of reported cases was much higher in the later years, indicating that the raw number of mitigations is likely similar. It is also worth noting that cases involving a man and a woman in a pre-existing relationship are not eligible for aggravated sentences. In 2015, this excluded 67 out of 284 cases from potentially aggravated sentences.[124] Gülsüm Kav from the We Will Stop Femicide Platform said in July 2017:

> This year we have monitored 108 court cases in the first three months, half of which ended with reduced sentences due to good behavior. Recently we also see long trial periods. Any late arrival of justice is itself a form of injustice. What's more, we have also started seeing more postponements of sentences, especially in cases of sexual violence.[125]

In 2022, We Will Stop Femicide reported 334 femicides and 245 suspicious deaths, representing a continued increase, aggravated by the withdrawal from the Istanbul Convention.[126]

In Kenya, the courts have been attempting to deal with sexual and gender-based violence cases more positively in a victim-centred approach, although progress is slow.[127] This effort pre-dates the campaign. In a case in 2013, the Supreme Court found in favour of the petitioners, opining that the police failed to investigate claims of sexual violence adequately and thus violated fundamental freedoms and rights.[128] This was seen as a landmark

---

11 January 2016) http://www.hurriyetdailynews.com/abated-sentence-for-man-who-stabbed-wife-to-death-in-southeast.aspx?pageID=238&nID=93694&NewsCatID=509, accessed 17 November 2023; Ayşegül Usta, 'Court Lessens Attacker's Sentence despite "no-Show" in Court' (*Hürriyet Daily News*, 27 November 2015) http://www.hurriyetdailynews.com/court-lessens-attackers-sentence-despite-no-show-in-court.aspx?pageID=238&nID=91762&NewsCatID=509, accessed 17 November 2023; Karakas (n 47); AI Monitor (n 48).

[123] Bianet (n 79).

[124] Ibid.

[125] Barçin Yinanç, 'Turkey Should Stick to Istanbul Convention on Violence against Women' (*Hürriyet Daily News*, 31 July 2017) http://www.hurriyetdailynews.com/turkey-should-stick-to-istanbul-convention-on-violence-against-women.aspx?pageID=238&nID=116127&NewsCatID=339, accessed 17 November 2023.

[126] We Will Stop Femicide, 'We Will Stop Femicides Platform 2022 Annual Report' (2022) https://kadincinayetlerinidurduracagiz.net/veriler/3041/we-will-stop-femicides-platform-2022-annual-report, accessed 7 November 2023.

[127] Aura (n 50).

[128] Ibid.

case for gender-based violence, underscoring the unacceptable and indeed illegal nature of the lack of action taken by the police. However, this was a Supreme Court case and the approach of the lower courts is still patchy. Some statistics indicate that conviction rates in some areas are as low as 24 per cent.[129] Research also shows that the Sexual Offences Act is used primarily to prosecute cases of defilement (underage sex), and not to tackle more violent crimes.[130]

One of the cornerstones of this campaign was the problematic requirement for victims to file a complaint at the police station. This was a major barrier for many women in Kenya. In the case that sparked #mydressmychoice, the victim did not file a complaint and therefore the police claimed, in the beginning, that they could not take any action.[131] However, once the campaign climaxed, as many as 200 men were arrested. The BBC reported that 'mass arrests are often carried out by police in Kenya when they are under public pressure. It leads to the arrest of many innocent people who are later released'.[132] The government also set up an 'anti-stripping squad' in the police unit in Nairobi. They also arrested five men specifically linked to the initial incident.[133] Impunity is another major challenge in Kenya. A statement

---

[129] Victoria Kioko, 'Sexual Offences on the Rise in Kenya' (*Capital News*, 27 June 2014) https://www.capitalfm.co.ke/news/2014/06/sexual-offences-on-the-rise-in-kenya/, accessed 8 January 2019.

[130] Agency for Cooperation and Research in Development (n 51) 24.

[131] 'My Dress, My Choice Protest Sparks a Lot of Questions' (*SEWA News Stream*, 23 November 2014) https://www.sewa.news/2014/11/kandeh-mariama-seray-my-dress-my-choice.html; Sophie Wilkinson, 'The #MyDressMyChoice Campaign Is the Only Positive Thing about the Video of a Woman Stripped for Wearing a Miniskirt Going Viral' (*The Debrief*, 19 November 2014) https://web.archive.org/web/20170615104 627/http://www.thedebrief.co.uk/news/opinion/the-mydressmychoice-campaign-is-the-only-positive-thing-about-the-video-of-a-woman-stripped-for-wearing-a-minisk irt-going-viral-20141125515, accessed 16 November 2023; Regev (n 12).

[132] Phumlani Pikoli, '#MyDressMyChoice Campaign Yields Results' (*Eyewitness News*, November 2014) https://web.archive.org/web/20151011164258/http://ewn.co.za/2014/11/19/MyDressMyChoice-campaign, accessed 16 November 2023; 'Kenya Arrests after Women "Stripped"' (*BBC News*, 18 November 2014) http://www.bbc.co.uk/news/world-africa-30093816, accessed 29 November 2023.

[133] Fred Indimuli, '"Anti Stripping Squad" Arrests 5 in Kayole Swoop' (*Mpasho News*, 27 November 2014) https://mpasho.co.ke/anti-stripping-squad-arrests-5-kayole-swoop/, accessed 16 November 2023; 'Kenya "Anti Stripping Squad" Formed' (*AGR NEWS*, 26 November 2014) https://agrfm.wordpress.com/2014/11/26/kenya-anti-stripp ing-squad-formed/, accessed 16 November 2023; Pkemoi Ngenoh, 'Anti-Stripping Squad: We Will Hunt You Down Perverts!' (*Standard Digital News*, 28 November 2014) https://web.archive.org/web/20150719040924/http://www.sde.co.ke/thena irobian/article/2000142730/anti-stripping-squad-we-will-hunt-you-down-perverts, accessed 16 November 2023.

endorsed by many Kenyan women's rights groups in March 2015 outlined several incidents of violence, many involving MPs or the police, who are often protected from prosecution.[134]

Since the campaign, the courts still vary in their treatment of gender-based violence cases. For example, in 2016, a judge overturned a 20-year sentence for a man who 'defiled' a young girl, finding that the girl had acted like an adult (sneaking into a man's house to engage in sexual activity) and therefore should be treated as an adult.[135] Women's groups publicly denounced the ruling as a setback for women and efforts to end gender-based violence.[136] Little has changed in the judicial system in Kenya in its treatment of gender-based violence. It seems that for every landmark decision taking a step forward, another decision takes things a step back.

Across all three of the status quo campaigns, we therefore see similar patterns of poor handling of gender-based violence in law enforcement, particularly in the courts. In #farkhunda, the rushed trials have 'emboldened' criminals and contributed to an increase in the perception of impunity. For #sendeanlat, although some improvement may have been seen in the short term, for the most part mitigating factors of good behaviour and provocation are still widely used to reduce sentences for gender-based violence and femicide. In Kenya with #mydressmychoice, much variation is seen in the treatment of cases of gender-based violence, with some very positive and progressive examples alongside some very negative and regressive rulings.

---

[134] 'KHRC – Joint Press Statement by Kenyan Women & Civil Society Organizations on the Sexual Offences Against Women', https://web.archive.org/web/20181020142019/http://www.khrc.or.ke/2015-03-04-10-37-01/press-releases/375-joint-press-statement-by-kenyan-women-civil-society-organizations-on-the-sexual-offences-against-women.html, accessed 16 November 2023. The 2017 general elections saw continued widespread sexual violence with what appears to be little prosecution or law enforcement. Although not directly linked to public strippings, this is a good indicator of the government's treatment of gender-based violence. 'It will be difficult to end the cycles of election-related sexual abuses—and more generally rape and other gender-based violence—until the government creates an environment in which victims are willing to come forward and it properly investigates and prosecutes complaints.' Human Rights Watch, 'Election-Related Sexual Violence in Kenya' (Human Rights Watch, 7 September 2017) https://www.hrw.org/news/2017/09/07/election-related-sexual-violence-kenya, accessed 16 November 2023.

[135] 'Kenya Rape Verdict World's "Worst Ever"' (*The East African*, 9 June 2017) http://www.theeastafrican.co.ke/news/Kenyan-judge-juma-chitembwe-shamed-for-worst-ruling/2558-3962770-kdwy1dz/index.html, accessed 16 November 2023.

[136] Ibid; Plan International (lead organization), 'Shadow Report in Response to the Eighth Periodic State Report by Kenya to CEDAW' (2017) 6.

UN dialogue

Early UN reports from and to Afghanistan paint a complex picture, with clear impacts of war and religious tensions. Dialogue from the early 1990s was similar to other Islamic countries, with the treaty bodies raising concerns about situations on the ground, in particular for women and girls, and the government reporting on laws and systems, but not their implementation.[137] In 1995, there was a complete change of tone to reflect the horrors of the war and the decimation of infrastructure to support and protect women and girls.[138] State reports often said that the situation for women and girls could not be improved until the conflict ended.[139] By 1998, a UN Resolution was passed specifically addressing the rights of women and girls.[140] Reports also continued to illustrate the tension between the Taliban interpretation of Islam and the perception of threat from Western interference.[141]

In 2006, the Special Rapporteur on Violence Against Women brought attention to a specific case which illustrated the realities for women in Afghanistan. A woman was allegedly murdered for 'her adoption of a Western attitude, her open interaction with her male colleagues on television and her choice of western music'.[142] Although the Special Rapporteur on Violence Against Women sent three communications to the state on this matter, there were no replies.

In 2011, Afghanistan had its first reporting dialogue with the Committee on the Elimination of Discrimination Against Women. Several pages of the

---

[137] Committee on Economic, Social and Cultural Rights, 'Initial Reports Submitted by States Parties: Addendum' (1991) UN Doc E/1990/5/Add.8; Committee on Economic, Social and Cultural Rights, 'Report on the Sixth Session' (1992) UN Doc E/1992/23; Human Rights Committee, 'Second Periodic Reports of States Parties' (1992) UN Doc CCPR/C/57/Add.5.

[138] 'The extremist forces had as their main tenets the total negation of all human values granted to women, the closing of schools for women in the areas under their control and the prohibition of access by women to jobs within the Government. Propaganda had been disseminated in the form of false documents claiming to represent the government position on the rights of women. Despite pressure from extremist forces, the resistance and will of the Government to encourage the continued participation of women in the affairs of State had been unshakeable.' Human Rights Committee, 'Summary Record of the First Part of the 1462nd Meeting' (1995) UN Doc CCPR/C/SR.1462 paras 7–8.

[139] Human Rights Council, 'Report of the Special Rapporteur on Violence against Women, Its Causes and Consequences: Mission to Pakistan and Afghanistan' (2000) UN Doc E/CN.4/2000/68/Add.4 para 39.

[140] Economic and Social Council, 'Situation of Women and Girls in Afghanistan' (1998) Resolution 1998/9.

[141] Human Rights Council (n 139) para 78.

[142] Human Rights Council, 'Report of the Special Rapporteur on Violence against Women, Its Causes and Consequences, Yakin Ertürk Addendum Communications to and from Governments' (2006) UN Doc E/CN.4/2006/61/Add.1 para 3.

state report dealt specifically with violence against women. The government acknowledged that violence targeting women 'even on the street' was a problem and they were seeking to address it in amendments to EVAW.[143] The 2013 report on the situation, yet again, raised concerns that the efforts made by the government were not actually reducing the risk or incidence of violence.[144] Of note, the report also stated: '[t]hose cases ... [that] *receive public attention due to their egregious nature* represent the tip of the iceberg of incidents of violence against women throughout the country' (emphasis added).[145] Generally, the UN dialogue becomes extremely repetitive. The same issues and concerns are raised, and the same responses are given.[146] It seems Farkhunda's case and the attention it received did not lead to any change in approach or discourse, but rather served to highlight the ongoing problems seen in these reports for over a decade before her murder.

Turkey, on the other hand, was actively involved in the UN human rights system. As is true across all the status quo campaigns, concerns about violence against women were present in the UN dialogue both before and after the campaign with little perceptible change in approach, discourse, or content. Violence against women was first raised in the 1996 Committee on the Elimination of Discrimination Against Women state report; the hearing on this report noted that violence against women in the private domain was an issue.[147] The state party indicated that new legislation specifically addressing violence against women was necessary.[148] The Committee raised concerns about the growing fundamentalist movement and Turkey's continued reservations to the Convention, noting specifically the 'growing climate of violence against women and girls'[149] and that there were 'very serious attitudinal and behavioural patterns in Turkey, among both men and women'.[150]

The next CEDAW cycle took place in 2003. The state reported new domestic violence legislation, the lifting of CEDAW reservations, and the

---

[143] Committee on the Elimination of Discrimination Against Women, 'Summary Record of the 1132nd Meeting' (2013) UN Doc CEDAW/C/SR.1132 para 15.

[144] Human Rights Council, 'Report of the United Nations High Commissioner for Human Rights on Situation of Human Rights in Afghanistan' (2013) UN Doc A/HRC/22/37 paras 37–38.

[145] Ibid, 39, emphasis added.

[146] See, for example, Human Rights Council, 'Working Group Summary Report Afghanistan' (2013) UN Doc A/HRC/WG.6/12/AFG/3.

[147] Committee on the Elimination of Discrimination Against Women, 'Summary Record of the 318th Meeting' (1998) UN Doc CEDAW/C/SR.318 para 18.

[148] Ibid, 43.

[149] Committee on the Elimination of Discrimination Against Women, 'Summary Record of the 319th Meeting' (1998) UN Doc CEDAW/C/SR.319 para 11.

[150] Ibid, 28.

ratification of the Optional Protocol. The report contained a whole section on violence against women, which shows how the issue had become more and more prominent. Interestingly, one of the barriers identified by the state to addressing violence against women was the 'provocative role the media continues to display in covering acts of violence'.[151]

In 2009, a case was decided by the European Court of Human Rights, *Opuz v. Turkey*.[152] The court found that the failings of the criminal justice system 'undermined the deterrent effect' and that the state authorities did not do enough to protect the applicant from harm. The Committee on the Elimination of Discrimination Against Women then raised the *Opuz* case, inquiring about specific measures taken to implement the decision. The state responded that they 'did not fully agree with the decision of the Court, as Turkey's legal framework was well developed and a great deal of work had gone into reforming legislation'.[153]

In 2014, Turkey submitted its 7th periodic report to CEDAW. Notably, this was the first time Turkey clearly used the term 'femicide' in a state report to the UN.[154] This reporting cycle concluded after the campaign began. After Özgecan's murder, CEDAW raised serious concerns about the 'judicial leniency' and the use of good behaviour and provocation as mitigating factors.[155] The state defensively responded that:

> Article 29 of the Criminal Code stipulated that unjust provocation could not be considered as a mitigating factor in cases of honour killings, rape, or sexual assault. The determination of a defendant's good conduct as a mitigating factor, which was entirely at the discretion of the judge, was based on his or her record and behaviour and on the expected impact of the punishment on his or her future life.[156]

---

[151] Committee on the Elimination of Discrimination Against Women, 'Combined Fourth and Fifth Periodic Reports of States Parties Turkey' (2003) UN Doc CEDAW/C/TUR/4-5 para 14.

[152] *Opuz v Turkey* [2009] 33401/2 (European Court of Human Rights).

[153] Committee on the Elimination of Discrimination Against Women, 'Summary Record of the 937th Meeting' (2010) UN Doc CEDAW/C/SR.937 para 61. The ECtHR has heard several cases on violence against women in Turkey, uniformly finding in favour of the petitioners: (2013) *Izci v. Turkey* (42606/05); (2015) *Durmaz v. Turkey* (3621/07); (2016) *Civek v Turkey* (55354/11); (2016) *Halime Kilic v Turkey* (63034/11); (2016) *MG v. Turkey* (646/10). All events in question took place before the campaign, even though some decisions were handed down after the start of the campaign.

[154] Committee on the Elimination of Discrimination Against Women, 'Consideration of Reports Submitted by States Turkey' (2014) UN Doc CEDAW/C/TUR/7 para 37.

[155] Committee on the Elimination of Discrimination Against Women, 'Summary Record of the 1416th Meeting' (2016) UN Doc CEDAW/C/SR.1416 paras 4–5.

[156] Ibid, 7.

The concluding observations take a noticeably different approach to the issue of violence against women, placing far more emphasis on Turkey's shortcomings and problems.[157]

The final campaign to explore is #mydressmychoice. Again, the overall picture is much the same before the campaign as after the campaign, with little to no perceptible differences uncovered through analysing the dialogue with the UN human rights mechanisms. As early as 1981, the Human Rights Committee raised concerns about the status of women in Kenya.[158] Concerns were raised again in 1993 by the Committee on Economic, Social and Cultural Rights.[159] In the 2000 CEDAW cycle, the Committee specifically raised concerns over the implementation of the domestic violence law.[160]

The 2007 Committee on Economic, Social and Cultural Rights list of issues was very forthright in highlighting the problem of violence against women.[161] The government did reply to the question with information on the Sexual Offences Act, the Domestic Violence Bill, the associated task force, and educational and training efforts. The paragraphs were verbatim from the state replies to the Committee on the Elimination of Discrimination Against Women the same year. The 2010 cycle was almost identical, with the Committee asking for information and the state deflecting on why the bills had not yet been passed into law.[162]

After #mydressmychoice began, the state submitted a report to Committee on Economic, Social and Cultural Rights writing: '[T]he

---

[157] Committee on the Elimination of Discrimination Against Women, 'Concluding Observations on the Seventh Periodic Report of Turkey' (2016) UN Doc CEDAW/C/TUR/CO/7. The Committee stated that 'protection orders are rarely implemented and are insufficiently monitored, with such failure often resulting in prolonged gender-based violence against women or the killing of the women concerned' and that 'lenient judgments are given to perpetrators of sexual violence, including those found guilty of the rape of girls, and reduced sentences are imposed owing to the perpetrator's "good behaviour" during trial' (paragraph 32).

[158] Human Rights Committee, 'Summary Record of the 272nd Meeting' (1981) UN Doc CCPR/C/SR.272 para 5.

[159] Committee on Economic, Social and Cultural Rights, 'Concluding Observations Kenya' (1993) UN Doc E/C.12/1993/6.

[160] Committee on the Elimination of Discrimination Against Women, 'Summary Record of the 592nd Meeting' (2003) UN Doc CEDAW/C/SR.592 para 17.

[161] Committee on Economic, Social and Cultural Rights, 'List of Issues Kenya' (2007) UN Doc E/C.12/KEN/Q/1 para 22.

[162] Committee on the Elimination of Discrimination Against Women, 'List of Issues Kenya' (2010) UN Doc CEDAW/C/KEN/Q/7 paras 11–12; Committee on the Elimination of Discrimination Against Women, 'Responses to the List of Issues and Questions with Regard to the Consideration of the Seventh Periodic Report Kenya' (2010) UN Doc CEDAW/C/KEN/Q/7/Add.1 paras 31–34. Similar concerns were raised in the CCPR dialogue.

government acknowledges that there is still a lot that needs to be done as the enforcement of this [violence against women] act is still very slow.'[163] Similar dialogue occurred in the 2016 and 2017 Committee on the Elimination of Discrimination Against Women reports.[164] The reports and dialogue therefore show absolutely no change after the campaign took off.

All three of these campaigns show extremely similar patterns in their interactions with the UN human rights mechanisms before, during, and in the aftermath of the campaigns. Concerns around violence against women were raised both before and after the campaigns, often rooted in implementation and enforcement issues, and often pointing to a lack of political will or ability to address the issue. These patterns of discourse were almost identical before and after the campaign, showing no change.

Twitter characteristics

These campaigns were quite average in many aspects, including overall participation, with #farkhunda at 8,600 Tweets, #sendeanlat at 38,407, and #mydressmychoice at 44,573. Interestingly though, the campaigns showed unusual variation in the number of non-English tweets. #mydressmychoice targeted an English-speaking country and thus the per cent of non-English Tweets is expectedly low (5 per cent). However, #farkhunda showed a similarly low percentage when the target country is not English speaking (9 per cent), exactly the same as #stopstoning. Conversely, #sendeanlat had 76 per cent of Tweets in languages other than English.

---

[163] Committee on Economic, Social and Cultural Rights, 'Replies of Kenya to the List of Issues' (2016) UN Doc E/C.12/KEN/Q/2-5/Add.1 para 92.

[164] Of note, both before and after the campaign, at no point in any of the UN reports to or from the state are public strippings specifically addressed. However, a shadow report in 2017 stated: '[A]cts of gender-based violence can include muggings, which occur daily, public stripping of women, for example on public transport, and there have even been cases of murder. Tradition and religion are often used as excuses for such treatment of women, demoralising them and providing a safeguard for their perpetrators.' Franciscans International, Edmund Rice International and The Office of Justice Peace and Integrity of Creation Franciscans Africa, 'Civil Society Responses to the List of Issues in Relation to the Eighth Report of Kenya to CEDAW' (2017) para 13. Although lengthy, the report gives a very accurate and comprehensive view of gender-based violence in Kenya, from a domestic voice: 'In Kenya, as in many other countries, victims of gender-based violence, particularly sexual violence, suffer from stigma and discrimination. As a result, the incidences of gender-based violence remain highly underreported. ... Moreover, it is reported that in some cases the police officers are reluctant to take up such cases, considering them as "private affairs." Even when they do respond, the procedures often take long, which has led to a mistrust of survivors on state institutions' response to resolve cases of gender-based violence.' Ibid, 14–15.

Overall, these hashtag campaigns illustrate many of the theoretical risks in social media campaigning explored in digital feminist activist literature and social media literature in Chapter 2. They all garnered relatively large levels of attention in the immediate aftermath of the spark incidents but were unable to sustain any meaningful levels of attention or engagement. It is likely that this lack of persistence was responsible for the overall lack of legal change in the short and long term. In all campaigns, some effort was made to change laws, but there simply was not enough continued pressure to lead to long term positive or progressive changes. The capricious nature of social media struggled to maintain pressure on the governments long enough to implement meaningful legal change. Equally, this initial considerable attention led to the specific perpetrators in these cases facing charges, but the lack of sustained attention or activity meant that systematic changes have not been realized in any of the three countries. Impunity is thus a very real danger.

Persistence (Tweets per day)

These three campaigns showed very similar persistence behaviours. All three campaigns showed the same characteristics – extreme peaks around the time of the spark incident followed by low numbers of Tweets for the remainder of the campaign. The spark incidents here all garnered enormous attention with initial peaks rising above 10,000 for both #sendeanlat and #mydressmychoice. All three campaigns had a very high percentage of Tweets in peak periods, 53 per cent for #farkhunda, 89 per cent for #sendeanlat, and 71 per cent for #mydressmychoice. Figure 4.1 illustrates this similarity.

As depicted in Figure 4.1, all three campaigns show their highest peaks at the very beginning, with little to no increase across the life of the campaign. #farkhunda showed a few small residual peaks, but not nearly as high as the initial spark incident and interest. These peaks were markedly different from the other campaigns, which showed more peaks spread throughout the lifespan of the campaigns or longer initial peak periods. It is plausible that the initial high level of interest provided the pressure needed to begin some areas of positive change, but the lack of ongoing or continued persistence and interest left the campaigns 'unfinished'. This would explain why these campaigns made positive strides in some areas but lack of progress in others for an overall status quo outcome.

This is also reflected in the percentage of days with more than five Tweets as seen in Table 4.1. Although higher than the two Iranian campaigns, these three campaigns did not see results nearly as high as the more successful campaigns.

STATUS QUO

Figure 4.1: Number of Tweets per day, status quo campaigns

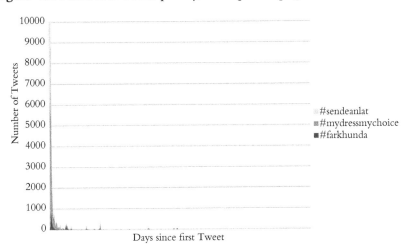

Table 4.1: Number of active days, status quo campaigns

	#farkhunda	#sendeanlat	#mydressmychoice
Number of days Tweets > 0	366	382	487
Number of days Tweets > 5	121	84	119
Number of days Tweets > 100	20	10	29
Percentage of days Tweets = 0	40	42	35
Percentage of days Tweets > 5	20	13	16

More successful campaigns saw at least 25 per cent of campaign days with more than five Tweets, while less successful campaigns were under 5 per cent. Again, this could explain the status quo outcomes. There was enough attention at the very start of the campaign to push some changes through, but not enough sustained attention to carry the campaign on and drive through more long-term, meaningful changes. This differs from the tactical concessions campaigns which saw much more sustained attention through the campaigns and much higher peaks in the beginning.

Engagement (retweets, likes, and replies)

In the engagement metrics, these campaigns showed very different behavioural patterns. #farkhunda showed a high proportion of retweets. At first glance it may seem that this shows a lack of engagement, as simply retweeting something does not take as much effort or involvement as replying or writing original content. However, having explored these campaigns in great detail, retweeting can also be linked to consistent messaging. This may have been one of the more positive aspects of the #farkhunda campaign. #mydressmychoice was also a campaign driven by retweets, though not to same extent as #farkhunda.

#sendeanlat, on the other hand, was a campaign dominated by likes. This in essence shows a lack of engagement as simply 'liking' a Tweet takes the least amount of effort and, arguably, contributes the least to the overall campaign. For every Tweet in the #sendeanlat campaign, there were nearly three likes. In a negative sense, this lack of engagement could again be a reason why the campaign did not progress as far as it could have.

Across all the campaigns, the level of replies during non-peak periods is a statistically significant indicator of positive legal change. These three status quo campaigns showed expected mid-range performance, with more non-peak dialogue than the backsliding campaigns but not as much as the successful campaigns.

Users (profiles of 100 most active users)

Coding the user profiles showed particularly interesting results in this group of campaigns. Nearly 25 per cent of the 100 most active users in #farkhunda were non-domestic individuals. The next largest category was non-domestic activist. Together, the non-domestic individuals and non-domestic activists accounted for 37 per cent of Tweets from the 100 most active users. Also of note, non-domestic news agencies accounted for 40 per cent of the reach of the 100 most active users, significantly more than any other category. This indicates that the domestic voice was not seen nearly as much as the non-domestic voice, particularly when viewed alongside the low percentage of non-English Tweets. This may have been partially down to the algorithms, filter bubbles, and non-neutrality of Twitter discussed in Chapter 2.

This finding is consistent with the perception that foreign media pressured the government into forcing swift, and in the end erroneous, trials, which according to experts has now 'emboldened' criminals. The Afghan government was particularly sensitive to foreign media, as evidenced by US State Department reports and UN dialogue. Given the history and the geopolitical positioning this is not surprising. A campaign driven by foreign voices would, therefore, be associated with reactionary actions and not necessarily long-term meaningful change. On the other hand, #mydressmychoice was the most domestically driven campaign in the whole study, with 72 per cent of the 100 most active users from Kenya. #mydressmychoice, although overall still a status quo campaign, did see more positive legal change than #farkhunda. It is very likely that this difference can be explained, at least in part, by the presence and strength of domestic drive and voice (or lack thereof).

#sendeanlat is the first campaign where we see the counter-narrative in the 100 most active users, with one domestic Tweeting 19 times with a reach of 80, and one non-domestic Tweeting 17 times with a reach of 2,302. Although not particularly large in number, the presence of the counter-narrative in the 100 most active users could have an adverse impact on outcomes. Additionally, the counter-narrative voice in this campaign represented religious conservatives, a barrier to legal change that has been identified in many campaigns. In this sense, it was not *against* the goals of the campaign per se, but equally this was not a voice in favour of women's rights or international human rights norms for gender equality.[165]

Similarly, #mydressmychoice opened the door to a strong counter-narrative around so-called decency laws. Rather than addressing the underlying issues allowing violence against women to run rampant (despite the name #mydressmychoice, the campaign's goals were about preventing violence against women regardless of what women do or don't wear), this counter-narrative focused on what women wear, arguing that women should be dressing 'decently' to end public strippings. In this campaign, three of the 100 most active users represented this perspective, all domestic, generally with a Christian profile. Their views are exemplified in the tweets below.

> If interested in walking half naked then do it to yur bf & NOT to the world, it's embarassin.

> [L]adies should mind thea dressing.

> 2 wrongs don't make a right. But the first wrong is a very bad wrong. Strip them up!

> Decency is absolute and not relative as most of you campaigners of scunty dressing are trying to make us believe.

For these users to be in the top 100 most active users in the entire campaign certainly underscores the harmful distilling down of the issue to what women wear as opposed to the underlying conditions which allow violence against women. These users very much encapsulate what one activist said:

> Tragically, the conversation centred on the hemline of dresses instead of the sex gangs. Women blamed women for the indecent dressing that provoked the strippings. People of stature in the church said that if stripping was the only way to achieve decency, they would support

---

[165] Willis (n 14).

it. … Still more people said that the debate was about decency, and that was all. The Church leadership was silent. … The President was silent. The First Lady was silent.[166]

This kind of activity again underscores the risks inherent in using social media for campaigning. There is no way to control who uses the hashtag or how it is used. Counter-narratives and those seeking to exploit attention can easily co-opt a hashtag, in this case even quickly becoming the most active users, at times distorting, perverting, or even mocking the campaign's original goals to protect women's rights. Across all three campaigns, the user profiles may uncover some of the reasons behind the negative legal outcomes: #farkhunda was heavily driven by non-domestic users from Western countries, while the #sendeanlat and #mydressmychoice opened doors to counter-narratives, conservative voices, and off-topic messaging.

Content analysis (sentiment, personalization, framing, messaging, and norms)

Although sentiment, overall, is not a statistically significant predictor of legal change, #sendeanlat showed the most negative scores out of all the campaigns, meaning that the content of the Tweets, on average, had a more negative tone. One hypothesis for this negative tone could have been the subject matter of femicide, however several other campaigns dealt with femicide, violence, and other harrowing events similar to this spark incident but did not show this level of negativity. Another hypothesis could be that the lack of positive outcomes and campaign stagnation could have had an effect on the Tweets themselves. It is difficult to say if this then perpetuated the lack of progress in the campaign. This too could be evidence of the damage that can be done to a campaign through the non-neutrality of social media platforms. The algorithms, filter bubbles, and 'personalization' which is intended to improve user experience could have perpetuated the negative sentiment in this campaign, which could in turn have contributed to the lack of positive legal changes. In other words, if the Tweets became more negative with the government's lack of implementing change, but negative Tweets hold a campaign back, then perhaps the cycle was self-fulfilling. In order to investigate further, a plot over time can be helpful (see Figure 4.2).

Here we see the sentiment score over time. Points below 0.5 are negative, and those above are positive, representing an average score per day plotted over time. Looking at the sentiment over time, it appears that there was a

---

[166] Meshack Yobby, 'Women, Gangs, and Silence' (26 November 2014) http://forum.ngecke nya.org/chat/women-gangs-and-silence, accessed 1 January 2019.

Figure 4.2: Sentiment over time, #sendeanlat

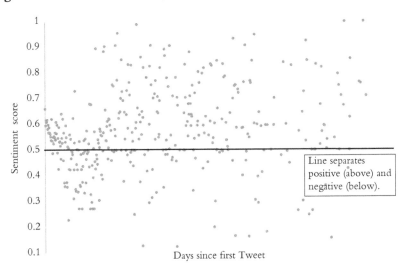

cluster of negative Tweets towards the beginning of the campaign with a few scattered very negative days throughout. On the whole, the somewhat chaotic nature of the positive and negative scores does not show any sort of definitive pattern. It is therefore not possible to conclude whether the negative Tweets influenced the lack of legal outcomes, equally it is not possible to conclude that they did not.

#farkhunda showed more consistent framing, with messaging staying constant and uniform across the event-based time periods (this echoes the high proportion of retweets). Due to the nature of the campaign, #sendeanlat had just two event-based time periods. Again, there were more consistent messages than variable, although the variable framing in the non-peak period did send a coherent and clear message. #mydressmychoice had fewer consistent messages than variable, though the variable content across different event-based time periods was very similar. Figures 4.3, 4.4, and 4.5 visually represent the number of times each word was used in a Tweet.

There was very consistent framing and messaging present in #farkhunda, whereas #sendeanlat and #mydressmychoice showed far less consistency. #farkhunda also showed significant focus on the court case and the legal system. #sendeanlat, while still focusing on Özgecan Aslan throughout the campaign, was far less specific. The other consistently used words could have been part of any campaign. #mydressmychoice was more akin to #letwomengotostadium, with a factual focus on the issue in the campaign, namely public strippings of women by men. Interestingly, the words 'should' and 'dress/dresses/dressed' both appear in the consistent messaging. This may

Figure 4.3: Consistently used words, #farkhunda

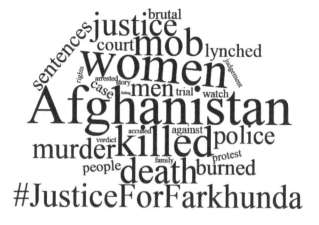

Figure 4.4: Consistently used words, #sendeanlat

Figure 4.5: Consistently used words, #mydressmychoice

be, to some extent, representing the strong counter-narrative which used the hashtag to advocate for women dressing more conservatively.

The variable framing and messaging in these three campaigns show differences. #farkhunda stayed quite reflective of the trials and sentencing, a core part of the overall goals of the campaign. #sendeanlat did not tend to show a clear focus or messaging, although emotional words in the non-peak period were very prevalent. #mydressmychoice remained focused on the incident with very factual words, with the exception of the potential prevalence of the counter-narrative. This inconsistency and variation may have contributed to the lack of change; without clear, consistent, on point framing and messaging, the campaigns were not likely to achieve the desired change.

Finally, looking at the presence of international norms in these campaigns (statistically significant), as expected there is a very average representation across all three campaigns, ranging from 54 per cent to 72 per cent of international norms present. Interestingly, these campaigns showed the lowest rates of Tweets with international norms, with only 23 per cent, 24 per cent, and 29 per cent, respectively. This means that even though the international norms were mentioned, they were not mentioned very often. This may have contributed to the lack of change seen in these campaigns. Perhaps had the international norms been used *more* the campaigns would have seen higher success levels.

Conclusion

These campaigns most exemplify the chaotic and unmanaged risks of social media, though each campaign showed different aspects of the spiral model critique theories. All three campaigns showed a marked lack of persistence, with very high peaks around spark events but very little continued or sustained attention or dialogue. #sendeanlat in particular showed a lack of engagement. #farkhunda lacked in domestic voices, while #sendeanlat and #mydressmychoice opened doors for counter-narratives, manifesting many of the digital feminist activist concerns around enhanced hostility to these kinds of campaigns. These characteristics combined show very little incentive for the governments to make or implement meaningful changes. This is then represented in the legal outcomes, where these campaigns, overall, left women and girls in much the same situations as they were before the campaigns started.

5

Tactical Concessions: #delhigangrape and #niunamenos

The next set of campaigns showed very similar outcomes as well as Twitter campaign behaviours. Both climaxed in close proximity to domestic, democratic elections with the possibility of regime change, and in both cases the government in power implemented legislative change extremely quickly (the 'tactical' concessions as specified in the theoretical spiral model). The legislative changes were generally seen as responses to the public attention driven by social media and indeed, on paper, met many of the goals of the campaigns regarding the letter of the law. However, likely due to the speed with which the changes were made and the governments' lack of long-term attention to the issues, little to no change has been seen on the ground. Metrics of institutionalization, in particular in India, underscore the short-term, reactionary nature of the changes.

#delhigangrape campaign overview

On 16 December 2012, a young woman and a male companion boarded a minibus in Delhi. The bus driver and a group of men beat the man unconscious and raped the woman. The victims were left by the side of the road and it took several hours for someone to find and help them. The woman died two weeks later, on 29 December, after being transferred to a hospital in Singapore. Her death sparked a massive outcry about violence against women in India and the lack of protections afforded to them. Large-scale protests took place in India and around the world in solidarity.[1]

---

[1] Niharika Mandhana and Anjani Trivedi, 'Indians Outraged Over Rape on Moving Bus in New Delhi' (*The New York Times – India Ink*, 18 December 2012) https://india. blogs.nytimes.com/2012/12/18/outrage-in-delhi-after-latest-gang-rape-case/, accessed

The hashtag campaign sought better legal protections and law enforcement for violence against women and sexual violence. Some felt that the campaign was successful in raising awareness domestically.[2] However, awareness-raising is usually not enough, and most felt that much more needed to be done to protect women and girls.[3] This case also brought the impact of class-based discrimination in sexual violence to the forefront, demonstrating some of the identity politics work in fourth wave and digital feminism.[4] The hashtag campaign is best summed up by this quote:

> The fierce debate in the weeks after the attack – setting conservatives who blamed westernisation against liberals blaming reactionary sexist and patriarchal attitudes – has faded. A package of laws increasing punishments for sexual assault and redefining a range of offences may do some good, campaigners concede, if enforcement is simultaneously improved, but dozens of men accused of rape remain members of local and national parliamentary assemblies. ... It is a few weeks of outrage against hundreds of years of tradition.[5]

#niunamenos campaign overview

Ni Una Menos ('Not One Less') began as a small collective of activists a few months before the hashtag took off, in response to high levels of femicide in Argentina. A few months later, in 2015, a 14-year-old girl was killed by her boyfriend and his mother when they discovered she was pregnant and

---

29 November 2023; Nita Bhalla, 'Key Events in the Delhi Gang Rape Case' (news.trust. org, 10 September 2013) http://news.trust.org/item/20130909143244-h09lu/, accessed 16 November 2023.

[2] Gabriel Dominguez and Srinivas Mazumdaru, 'What Has Changed?' (16 December 2013) http://www.dw.com/en/a-year-after-the-delhi-gang-rape-what-has-changed/a-17293325 accessed 16 November 2023.

[3] Ibid.

[4] 'Of every 10 women raped in India, nine are afraid to speak up against their perpetrators or do not have access to the social media.' Jasmine Bala, 'Behind the Curtain: On Unreported Rapes in India' (9 March 2013) https://web.archive.org/web/20181220193421/https://www.girlsglobe.org/2013/03/09/behind-the-curtain-on-unreported-rapes-in-india/, accessed 16 November 2023; Soutik Biswas, 'Does the Delhi Gang Rape Sentence Bring Closure?' (*BBC News*, 13 September 2013) http://www.bbc.co.uk/news/world-asia-india-24059601, accessed 29 November 2023.

[5] Jason Burke, 'Delhi Rape: How India's Other Half Lives' (*The Guardian*, 10 September 2013) http://www.theguardian.com/world/2013/sep/10/delhi-gang-rape-india-women, accessed 29 November 2023. See also Justin Rowlatt, 'Viewpoints: Has Delhi Rape Case Changed India?' (*BBC News*, 10 September 2013) http://www.bbc.co.uk/news/world-asia-india-24012424, accessed 29 November 2023.

wanted to keep the baby.[6] The first Tweet, notably from a journalist, turned the collective into a hashtag campaign in response to this murder.[7] The Tweet was shared by other journalists and together they decided to hold the first protest under the banner of #niunamenos; it is thought that celebrity participation in the campaign contributed to the large scale of participation.[8] The campaign developed five clear legal demands.[9] There were then well attended protests in June 2015, June 2016, the 'Black Wednesday' protest and strike in October 2016, and June 2017. The June 2015 protest saw an estimated 200,000 women in Buenos Aires alone,[10] though some estimate it higher.[11] In general, many of the campaign's initial legislative goals were met, and fairly quickly. However, long-term implementation is severely lacking.[12]

---

[6] Meaghan Beatley, 'Meet the Argentine Women Behind Ni Una Menos, the Feminist Collective Angela Davis Cites as Inspiration' (*Remezcla*, 9 March 2017) http://remez cla.com/features/culture/ni-una-menos-collective-argentina-founders/, accessed 17 November 2023.

[7] Uki Goñi, 'Argentine Women Call Out Machismo' (*The New York Times*, 15 June 2015) https://www.nytimes.com/2015/06/16/opinion/argentine-women-call-out-machismo.html, accessed 29 November 2023; Jamie Ballard, 'Battle Cry of #NiUnaMenos Echoes Through Latin America' (*Huffington Post*, 22 June 2015) https://www.huffing tonpost.com/jamie-ballard/battle-cry-of-niunamenos-_b_7631972.html, accessed 17 November 2023; Muireann O'Dwyer, '#NiUnaMenos; Standing up to Femicides and "Machismo" in Argentina' (*Gender and Politics*, 3 February 2016) https://genderandpoli ticsucd.wordpress.com/2016/02/03/niunamenos-standing-up-to-femicides-and-machi smo-in-argentina/, accessed 17 November 2023.

[8] Goñi (n 7); 'Femicide in Argentina' (*Women Across Frontiers Magazine*, 22 November 2015) http://wafmag.org/2015/11/femicide-in-argentina/, accessed 17 November 2023; Ezequiel Adamovsky, '"Ni Una Menos": Feminism and Politics in Argentina' (*teleSUR*, 6 July 2015) https://web.archive.org/web/20170807171158/https://www.telesurtv.net/ english/opinion/Ni-una-menos-Feminism-and-Politics-in-Argentina-20150706-0011. html, accessed 17 November 2023.

[9] (1) Implement the National Plan of Action for the Prevention, Assistance and Eradication of Violence against Women, as established in the Law 26,485; (2) ensure victims' access to justice; (3) develop a Unique Official Register of violence victims; (4) guarantee and deepen a program of Comprehensive Sex Education at all educational levels for a life free of discrimination and gender-based 'machista') violence; (5) guarantee the protection of the victims of violence. '#NiUnaMenos: Not One Less' (*Vital Voices*, 1 July 2015) https:// www.vitalvoices.org/2015/07/niunamenos-not-one-less/, accessed 17 November 2023; Irene, '#niunamenos: A Combination of Offline and Online Feminist Activism' (*Decoding Digital Activism*, 4 October 2017) http://wpmu.mah.se/nmict172group6/2017/10/04/ niunamenos-feminist-activism/, accessed 17 November 2023.

[10] Goñi (n 7).

[11] 'Femicide in Argentina' (n 8).

[12] Some legislative results were achieved as a consequence, but there is still a lot that needs to be done. Judge Elena Highton de Nolasco launched the Femicide Registration Unit for the Supreme Court. Following this, the national government, through the Human Rights Committee, formalized the unit, as well as the Fiscal Specialised Unit on Violence against Women (UFEM). However big this progress may seem, between the first and second

Context

Although the outcomes of these campaigns were very similar, the context is not. This finding continues to underscore earlier chapters where context shows to be less important than one might hypothesize.

Gender indices for these countries are particularly interesting, with Argentina showing very positive rankings. These indices indicate that women enjoy a fairly equal status in Argentina, at least compared to the other countries in this study. India, on the other hand, showed very poor gender indices. The baseline for women in these two countries was therefore quite different. Perhaps reflecting the picture on the ground, India reported the highest number of civil society organizations (CSOs) working on women's rights in the study, with 560. This was significantly higher than the other countries, with the next highest being Kenya at 115. There is clearly a vibrant, active, and internationally connected women's rights movement in India with this number of officially registered CSOs. Argentina had only 40. Data is not available to indicate the size or operating incomes of these CSOs, therefore it is possible that 560 small CSOs in India have the same potential impact as 40 large CSOs in Argentina. However, even if this is true, the sheer difference in numbers does indicate that the situation for women and girls is likely different in the two countries.

Engagement with international human rights mechanisms is quite different as well. Argentina showed the most formal engagement out of all countries in the study, with 13 treaties ratified, including the Convention on the Elimination of all Forms of Discrimination Against Women (CEDAW) and the Optional Protocols. India had ratified eight treaties, also including CEDAW, but without the Optional Protocol and with three reservations. As will be seen later in this chapter, India's engagement with international human rights mechanisms for women is not ideal. Again, based on context alone, one would expect very different outcomes in these two countries.

The most interesting finding in these two campaigns was the proximity to potential regime change, something not particularly prevalent in social media activism literature. #niunamenos peaked approximately six months before a presidential election. The election also included senate and local government seats. General elections of this nature take place every four years in Argentina (senate and local have mid-term elections every two years). As it turned out, there was a change in ruling party in the October 2015

#NiUnaMenos protests (2015–2016) 275 women died as victims of gender violence. Andrés Del Río, '#NiUnaMenos: Against Femicide in Latin America' (*openDemocracy*, 7 November 2016) https://www.opendemocracy.net/democraciaabierta/andr-s-del-r-o/niunamenos-against-femicide-in-latin-america, accessed 17 November 2023.

election, just months after the largest peaks in the campaign. The role of the elections in the campaign was made clear by one activist: '#NiUnaMenos presented a series of five pledges for fighting violence against women, asking each of the candidates to sign their names to them. Crucially, they did it over Twitter and copied each Tweet onto their website ... several candidates used the slogan '#NiUnaMenos' directly in their campaign ads.'[13]

Similarly, in India, the spark incident took place 16 months before an election, again closer in time than other campaigns in the study. Elections in India take place every five years. As with Argentina, there was a change in ruling party as a result of the election following the campaign. It can therefore begin to be seen that, perhaps, campaigns which peak in relatively close proximity to elections may force ruling governments to implement reactionary, tactical concession changes as a strategic choice for re-election, but without any political will to address the issue long-term.

Legal outcomes

#delhigangrape and #niunamenos showed strikingly similar legal changes. These are the first campaigns to show more positive than status quo or negative change, reporting very positive legislative outcomes in particular. However, as introduced earlier in this chapter, this legislative change has not translated into meaningful institutionalization, more so for India. Law enforcement in both countries, particularly in prosecutions and convictions, is very poor, reflecting that the positive change in the law is not being implemented properly. Lack of implementation can lead to perceptions of impunity from potential and actual perpetrators. Additionally, as the governments have technically already addressed the campaigns' primary goals through legislative change, there is little incentive for continued work or change from the state. In this way, these campaigns can be seen as missed opportunities, where more work could have been done had the change not happened so quickly or reactively.

Legislative change

Sexual violence and rape in India were not a new phenomenon.[14] Some groups proffered statistics that in India there was one rape every hour, with

---

[13] Ciara Nugent, 'Four Months From #NiUnaMenos: Has Anything Changed?' (*The Argentina Independent*, 5 October 2015) https://web.archive.org/web/20170704235054/http://www.argentinaindependent.com/currentaffairs/four-months-from-niunamenos-has-anything-changed/, accessed 8 November 2023.

[14] 'India Faces Rape Debate' (*BBC News*, 24 November 2002) http://news.bbc.co.uk/1/hi/world/south_asia/2508929.stm, accessed 29 November 2023.

socially vulnerable women and girls more at risk. A report by the BBC written after the #delhigangrape spark incident details the many similarly horrific stories of rape, violence, and murder in India, occurring before #delhigangrape, which were 'forgotten'.[15] Legislative reform had been at the forefront of activism for years, continually pointing to ongoing problems of low conviction rates, lack of political will, and problems with frontline unresponsiveness as obstacles to change.[16]

Some changes before #delhigangrape had been achieved. After the rape of a 16-year-old tribal girl in a police station, in 1983 the law was amended to say that if the victim says she does not consent, the court will believe her.[17] An incident in 2009 led to 47 days of protests in Kashmir.[18] The Attorney General at the time stated that simply a change in the law would not have an impact, as the rape culture was so ingrained in society.[19] Disappointingly, an incident in 2010 which made headlines led to legislative changes not dissimilar to #delhigangrape. The changes were intended to protect women using public transportation.[20]

Many women's groups found the legislative actions taken by the government to be lacking. Activists felt that the reforms tackled superficial issues and not underlying social issues, which they predicted would not lead to meaningful change, reflecting some of the social media literature.[21] Even the report commissioned in the aftermath of the #delhigangrape found

---

[15] 'On most days, Indian newspapers report shocking new atrocities – a 10-month-old raped by a neighbour in Delhi; an 18-month-old raped and abandoned on the streets in Calcutta; a 14-year-old raped and murdered in a police station in Uttar Pradesh; a husband facilitating his own wife's gang rape in Howrah; a 65-year-old grandmother raped in Kharagpur. But in a country where a rape is reported every 21 minutes, even these most horrific of crimes soon get forgotten – except by the victims and their families. They are left to fight their long lonely battles for justice which, more often than not, is denied to them.' Justin Rowlatt, 'The Rapes That India Forgot' (*BBC News*, 5 January 2013) http://www.bbc.co.uk/news/world-asia-india-20907755, accessed 29 November 2023.

[16] 'India Faces Rape Debate' (n 14); Gethin Chamberlain, 'Five Years after the Gang-Rape and Murder of Jyoti Singh, What Has Changed for Women in India?' (*The Guardian*, 3 December 2017) http://www.theguardian.com/society/2017/dec/03/five-years-after-gang-murder-jyoti-singh-how-has-delhi-changed, accessed 29 November 2023.

[17] Rowlatt (n 15).

[18] Ibid.

[19] Ibid.

[20] 'Delhi Police Move to Protect Women Workers after Rapes' (*BBC News*, 10 December 2010) http://www.bbc.co.uk/news/mobile/world-south-asia-11966664, accessed 29 November 2023.

[21] Working Group on Human Rights in India and the UN, 'Human Rights in India: Status Report 2012' (2012) 119–120.

shortcomings in the government's previous legislative efforts, with many promises left unfulfilled and policies left unimplemented.[22]

After the #delhigangrape incident, the government appointed a legal commission, under Justice Verma (a former chief justice), to review laws on sex crimes and make recommendations. The commission was given just 30 days to complete its work, which included a national public consultation. Over 70,000 responses were received.[23] The resulting report was published at the end of January 2013, only one month after her death. The committee identified 'failure of governance' as the root cause for the high incidence of sexual violence, blaming the government and the police for their 'apathy'.[24] The report called for broadening legal definitions, establishing special courts with women judges, allowing faster appeals, as well as more accountability and uniform forensic protocols.[25]

The Indian government took several steps in the aftermath of the protests, notably setting up fast-track courts for cases of sexual violence and reforming other areas of concern in criminal law relating to rape and other sexual offences.[26] After these initial legislative changes were made, activists continued to lobby for changes to the way juveniles are treated in the Indian criminal justice system. The main perpetrator in this case was just shy of his 18th birthday, meaning he was treated as a juvenile and received a far more lenient sentence than the others. This caused outrage in the campaign.[27] In December 2015, the government passed the Juvenile Justice Bill, which meant that 16-year-olds involved in particularly serious or heinous crimes would be tried as adults.[28] This may have been a more positive legal outcome of the campaign, whereby the government took time and effort in debating and drafting the changes. It is notable that the more long-term meaningful

---

[22] Justice JS Verma, Justice Leila Seth, and Gopal Subramanium, 'Report on the Committee on Amendments to Criminal Law' (2013) iii.

[23] Human Rights Watch, '"Everyone Blames Me" Barriers to Justice and Support Services for Sexual Assault Survivors in India' (2017) 68.

[24] Chamberlain (n 16).

[25] 'India Urged to Reform Rape Trials' (*BBC News*, 23 January 2013) http://www.bbc. co.uk/news/world-asia-india-21156283, accessed 29 November 2023; Chamberlain (n 16); Verma et al (n 22) 416.

[26] Aviva Shen, 'One Year After Horrific New Delhi Gang Rape, India Still Struggles With Rape Culture' (Think Progress, 29 December 2013) https://thinkprogress.org/one-year-after-horrific-new-delhi-gang-rape-india-still-struggles-with-rape-culture-5d0d0f1ff404/ , accessed 16 November 2023.

[27] Dominguez and Mazumdaru (n 2).

[28] 'Rajya Sabha Passes Juvenile Justice Bill, Nirbhaya's Mother "Satisfied"' (*Times of India*, 22 December 2015) https://timesofindia.indiatimes.com/india/Rajya-Sabha-passes-Juvenile-Justice-Bill-Nirbhayas-mother-satisfied/articleshow/50285328.cms, accessed 16 November 2023.

change seen in India is not specifically related to violence against women. Although this is an important outcome for the Indian criminal justice system, it will not specifically benefit women and girls.

Since the sexual violence legislative changes were passed, many have highlighted the shortcomings of the government's actions. Some campaigners feel that while the laws have changed and more rapes were being reported, investigated, and perhaps prosecuted, nothing has been done to prevent them from happening in the first place.[29] The United Nations (UN) criticized India for not addressing the underlying societal causes of violence against women and sexual violence.[30] Activists were concerned from the start about the use of the death penalty in sexual crimes: 'if sentences are thought of as too harsh by the judges, the already high acquittal rate in cases of sexual violence will rise further'.[31] Human Rights Watch found that there were still serious issues with poor police response and stigma, poor access to sensitive medical care, and lack of access to effective legal assistance, including continued delays even with the fast-track courts.[32] It appears that the public pressure of the campaign pushed the government to commission the report far too quickly and implement arguably superficial legislative changes. In the strictest regard, the campaign was successful in lobbying for changes in the law, the goals of which were indeed met. However it can be seen now that the changes were made too quickly to allow for any sort of meaningful implementation. The evidence also suggests that the changes were specifically made prior to the elections, perhaps as a tactic by the ruling party to try to ensure re-election.

In the decade since the campaign, little to nothing has changed.[33] Reports continue to highlight problems in corruption, police failures, horrific 'tests' to assess the validity of claims, social pressures, and class distinctions.[34]

A nearly identical picture comes through in Argentina. The government had taken legislative steps to address violence against women, passing the

---

[29] Chamberlain (n 16).

[30] Shen (n 26).

[31] 'Explaining India's New Anti-Rape Laws' (*BBC News*, 28 March 2013) http://www.bbc.co.uk/news/world-asia-india-21950197, accessed 29 November 2023.

[32] Human Rights Watch (n 23).

[33] Joe Wallen, 'Ten Years on from Fatal Gang Rape, India's Women Are Haunted by a Sexual Violence Epidemic' (*The Telegraph*, 21 December 2022) https://www.telegraph.co.uk/global-health/women-and-girls/ten-years-fatal-gang-rape-indias-women-haunted-sexual-violence/, accessed 8 November 2023; Severyna Magill, 'Indian Women's Struggle against Sexual Violence Has Had Little Support from the Men in Power' (*The Conversation*, 27 July 2023) http://theconversation.com/indian-womens-struggle-against-sexual-violence-has-had-little-support-from-the-men-in-power-210318, accessed 16 November 2023.

[34] Equality Now, 'Sexual Violence in India', https://www.equalitynow.org/learn_more_sexual_violence_in_india/, accessed 8 November 2023.

first gender violence law in 1994,[35] which was broadened and improved a few years later (Law 26.485).[36] In 2012, the government passed a law specifically addressing femicide.[37] As seen in India, however, women's groups in Argentina noted that the laws alone did not have the desired impact.[38] Before #niunamenos, only eight of the 45 articles in Law 26.485 had been properly or fully implemented.[39]

Shortcomings in the law were noted as a lack of education on the issue of violence against women, no national hotline, not enough shelters, no free legal assistance, and a lack of appropriate budget.[40] One of the focal points of #niunamenos was the inaction in establishing the official register to collect information on femicides. Activists agreed that having access to such data would reveal the magnitude of the problem and provide an important evidence base for future work. The lack of such data also indicated that the relevant government agencies were not fulfilling their responsibilities.[41]

#niunamenos sought to address these shortcomings. Within days of the protests which erupted from #niunamenos, the government announced

---

[35] Ley No. 24.417: Proteccion Contra la Violencia Familiar 1994.

[36] Ley No. 26.485: Ley de protección integral para prevenir, sancionar y erradicar la violencia contra las mujeres en los ámbitos en que desarrollen sus relaciones interpersonales 2009; O'Dwyer (n 7).

[37] O'Dwyer (n 7); Graciela Rodriguez-Ferrand, 'Argentina: Criminal Code Amendment to Include Femicide' (*Global Legal Monitor*, 3 May 2012) https://web.archive.org/web/20161223034606///www.loc.gov/law/foreign-news/article/argentina-criminal-code-amendment-to-include-femicide/, accessed 17 November 2023; 'El Femicidio Fue Aprobado En Diputados y Está Cerca de Ser Ley' (19 April 2012) https://www.clarin.com/sociedad/femicidio-aprobado-diputados-cerca-ley_0_r1xDWS3vQx.html, accessed 1 January 2019.

[38] O'Dwyer (n 7).

[39] Elisabeth Jay Friedman and Constanza Tabbush, '#NiUnaMenos: Not One Woman Less, Not One More Death!' (NACLA, 1 November 2016) https://nacla.org/news/2016/11/01/niunamenos-not-one-woman-less-not-one-more-death, accessed 17 November 2023; Teresa Sofia Buscaglia, 'Casi No Se Aplica La Ley Contra Los Femicidios' (*La Nacion*, 7 June 2015) https://web.archive.org/web/20170728203313/http://www.lanacion.com.ar/1799664-casi-no-se-aplica-la-ley-contra-los-femicidios, accessed 17 November 2023. 'In April 2009, law 26.485 on Violence Against Women was enacted. When the law was promulgated, several active feminist groups took it as a very good start. Three years later, one can say that law 26,485 is a great legal tool with no use. The law itself is complete, though extremely long, not fully regulated, and most importantly, very difficult to implement.' Soledad Vega, 'Women's Rights: An Unfinished Business' (*The Argentina Independent*, 29 March 2013) https://web.archive.org/web/20170926112835/http://www.argentinaindependent.com/socialissues/development/womens-rights-an-unfinished-business/, accessed 17 November 2023.

[40] Vega (n 39).

[41] 'Femicide in Argentina' (n 8).

steps to realize the implementation of Law 26.485.[42] The first aspect to be addressed was the data collection issue and the establishment of the federal registry. When announcing the registry, the vice president of the Federal Supreme Court of Argentina, Elena Highton de Nolasco, cited jurisdictional problems as the reason for the lack of previous progress and shifted blame to the provinces.[43] The government then claimed that the large-scale protest driven by social media forced *the provinces* to change their perspective and agree to the registry.[44] Shortly thereafter, Argentina's attorney general, Alejandra Gils Carbó, also set up a special prosecution unit for violence against women and confirmed the enactment of the registry.[45] The registry's first report was published just months later in September, corroborating the work previously done by women's groups illustrating the magnitude of the problem. Some provinces took action to improve legislation as well.[46] In October following the first wave of protests, the National Women's Council also released an Action Plan, another demand of the campaign, including the establishment of a national hotline.[47] Again, it is important to note that all of these changes were made before the pending national and regional elections.

Sadly, even with the establishment of a registry, a national action plan, a hotline, a special prosecution unit, and local legislative efforts, little change is seen in the incidence of femicide. As will be seen later in this chapter, there has been a particular lack of impact in the courts. These changes were seemingly implemented in a 'knee jerk' fashion in reaction to the combination of public pressure in the sheer scale of the campaign and the pending elections. The changes were not accompanied by any meaningful institutionalization or efforts to address underlying, root causes of violence against women in Argentina.

Since the campaign, further legislative action has been taken, including a law requiring training on gender issues for anyone working in the civil service, a new Ministry of Women, Gender, and Diversity, several national educational campaigns, and legislative efforts to address gun violence towards women from security personnel.[48] While visibility of violence may

---

[42] '60% of Femicides Committed by Partners' (*Buenos Aires Herald*, 12 June 2016) https://web.archive.org/web/20160612092324/http://www.buenosairesherald.com/article/215488/, accessed 17 November 2023.

[43] 'Femicide in Argentina' (n 8).

[44] 'The demonstration was extremely useful for us since so many of the jurisdictions that hadn't signed the agreements to be part of the registry finally agreed to sign up on June 4' (Mariana Gras, president of the Council).

[45] 'Femicide in Argentina' (n 8).

[46] Ibid.

[47] Ibid.

[48] Natalie Alcoba and Charis McGowan, '#NiUnaMenos Five Years on: Latin America as Deadly as Ever for Women, Say Activists' (*The Guardian*, 4 June 2020)

have improved, rates of femicide are higher now than in 2015.[49] Similar to Kenya, the country experienced a harrowing increase of domestic violence and femicide during COVID-19 lockdowns.[50]

Institutionalization

For many years before #delhigangrape, the Indian government had not prioritized the elimination of violence against women, generally seen as paying lip service when incidents were reported in the media but not following up with action or investment.[51]

> In a 2010 survey, nearly 80% of women in New Delhi reported being worried about their safety, and a quick glance at any paper in the morning will offer some insight as to why. Let's take last Thursday. On April 26, the Times of India covered the following stories: an alleged rape by a Delhi cop, two separate cases of naked and mutilated female corpses being dumped in different parts of the city, and a husband who murdered his wife whom he suspected of infidelity.[52]

With the government not being seen to take the issue seriously, neither did the general public. Polls showed that most men in Delhi thought that harassing women on the street in public was acceptable behaviour

---

https://www.theguardian.com/global-development/2020/jun/04/niunamenos-five-years-on-latin-america-as-deadly-as-ever-for-women-say-activists, accessed 8 November 2023; Lucía Leszinsky and Emma Dewick, '#NiUnaMenos Six Years on: Triumphs and New Demands of Argentina's Feminist Movement' (*Global Voices*, 22 June 2021) https://globalvoices.org/2021/06/22/niunamenos-six-years-on-triumphs-and-new-demands-of-argentinas-feminist-movement/, accessed 8 November 2023; Nayla Santisteban, 'The Women, Police, and Insecurity Agenda: Argentina's Response to Surging Femicide and Domestic...' (*Medium*, 14 August 2023) https://smallarmssurvey.medium.com/the-women-police-and-insecurity-agenda-argentinas-response-to-surging-femicide-and-domestic-1431a425faa3, accessed 17 November 2023.

[49] 'Number of Femicide Victims in Argentina 2022' (*Statista*) https://www.statista.com/statistics/1102274/number-femicide-victims-argentina/, accessed 17 November 2023.

[50] Karen Naundorf and Sarah Pabst, 'Argentina Recorded More Than 250 Femicides in 2020, One Every 35 Hours' (*Washington Post*, 2 December 2021) https://pulitzercenter.org/stories/argentina-recorded-more-250-femicides-2020-one-every-35-hours, accessed 17 November 2023; Santisteban (n 48).

[51] Debolina Dutta and Oishik Sircar, 'India's Winter of Discontent: Some Feminist Dilemmas in the Wake of a Rape' (2013) 39 Feminist Studies 293; Burke (n 5).

[52] Krista Mahr, 'New Delhi's Women Problem: What Does It Take to Make a City, and Society, Safe?' (*Time*, 2 May 2012) http://world.time.com/2012/05/02/new-delhis-women-problem-what-does-it-take-to-make-a-city-and-society-safe/, accessed 16 November 2023.

and that many police felt the victims of sexual violence were to blame.[53] Local politicians equally gave little importance to the issue.[54] Interestingly, the government's first reaction when #delhigangrape social media led to widespread protests was to crack down on the protesters themselves, assumingly to shut down the criticism of the government which allowed this violent act against a woman to occur.[55] It took a whole week before the government's reaction became sympathetic.[56] This capricious approach did not sit well with the public, being 'dismissed as too little, too late'.[57] It was this environment which spurred the government to set up the commission.[58]

With elections in the near future, it was not long before the opposition party took up the issue, asking what the current government had done to protect women and calling for stricter laws.[59] Many politicians joined in the public dialogue, pointing fingers, issuing blame, inciting anger, and calling for change.[60] One of India's most high ranking police officers joined in, notably on Twitter, blaming a failure of governance.[61] Judges in turn blamed the police for letting the perpetrators slip through.[62]

Public discourse ranged from defensive to aggressive, with some voices even exposing deep-seated misogyny.[63] This continued for quite some time. Nearly a year later, a government official publicly stated 'if you can't prevent rape, enjoy it', reigniting the Twitter debate about attitudes towards rape in India, in particular the culture of victim-blaming.[64] Language and attitudes

---

[53] Burke (n 5); 'Student "Gang-Raped on Delhi Bus"' (*BBC News*, 17 December 2012) http://www.bbc.co.uk/news/world-asia-india-20753075, accessed 29 November 2023.

[54] Burke (n 5).

[55] Gardiner Harris, '5 in New Delhi Rape Case Face Murder Charges' (*The New York Times*, 3 January 2013) https://www.nytimes.com/2013/01/04/world/asia/murder-char ges-filed-against-5-men-in-india-gang-rape.html, accessed 29 November 2023.

[56] Burke (n 5).

[57] Ibid.

[58] 'Delhi Gang Rape: Parliamentary Panel Summons Union Home Secretary, Delhi Police Chief' (*Times of India*, 21 December 2012) https://timesofindia.indiatimes.com/india/ Delhi-gang-rape-Parliamentary-panel-summons-Union-home-secretary-Delhi-police-chief/articleshow/17707153.cms, accessed 16 November 2023.

[59] 'Parliament Uproar over Delhi Rape' (*BBC News*, 18 December 2012) http://www.bbc. co.uk/news/world-asia-india-20765869, accessed 29 November 2023.

[60] Ibid.

[61] Mandhana and Trivedi (n 1).

[62] 'Delhi Gang-Rape: What Was the Police Doing, Asks Angry High Court' (NDTV, 19 December 2012) https://www.ndtv.com/cheat-sheet/delhi-gang-rape-what-was-the-pol ice-doing-asks-angry-high-court-507939, accessed 16 November 2023.

[63] Chamberlain (n 16).

[64] Miriam Berger, 'India's Top Police Official: "If You Can't Prevent Rape, Enjoy It"' (*BuzzFeed*, 13 November 2013) https://www.buzzfeed.com/miriamberger/indias-top-police-official-if-you-cant-prevent-rape-enjoy-it, accessed 16 November 2023.

expressed by those in power continued to show a lack of understanding of the seriousness of the epidemic of violence against women in India.[65] Another high profile case occurred in 2014, when two girls aged 12 and 14 were raped and hanged in a rural area on their way to use a field for a toilet. It was alleged that the police ridiculed and ignored the family when they reported trouble, apparently due to caste discrimination.[66] In 2017, a Thomson Reuters research poll found that Delhi was seen as the 'world's worst megacity for sexual violence against women', though some saw this as more of a perception than a reality.[67] Regardless, this evidence does not show that the government worked towards meaningful institutionalization of women's rights or to implement changes in the laws after the hashtag campaign.[68]

The situation in Argentina is similar – all the right discourse in all the right places, but the truth of a lack of meaningful institutionalization emerges when looking a bit deeper. Even the president at the time of #niunamenos, back when he was a governor, was quoted as saying: 'Deep inside, all women like to hear a piropo (catcall), even women who say they don't. I don't believe them. There can't be anything nicer than being told how pretty you are, even if it comes along with vulgarity, like being told what a nice ass you have.'[69] This statement is very illustrative of the South American 'machismo' or 'machista' culture.[70] Street harassment is common, even socially

---

[65] Shen (n 26).

[66] 'The Village Where Cousins Were Raped and Hanged' (*BBC News*, 30 May 2014) http://www.bbc.co.uk/news/world-asia-27622236, accessed 29 November 2023.

[67] Nita Bhalla and Karla Mendes, 'Delhi, Sao Paulo Seen as Worst Megacities for Sex Attacks on Women' (*Reuters*, 16 October 2017) https://www.reuters.com/article/world/exclusive-delhi-sao-paulo-seen-as-worst-megacities-for-sex-attacks-on-women-poll-idUSL4N1M14XB/, accessed 16 November 2023.

[68] Although for an unrelated cause, in April 2017, the governments in Jammu and Kashmir banned 22 social media sites, including Twitter, to curb protest. The governments 'felt that continued misuse of social networking sites and instant messaging services is likely to be detrimental to the interests of peace and tranquillity in the state'. 'J&K Government Bans 22 Social Networking Sites Citing Their Misuse' (*Times of India*, 26 April 2017) https://timesofindia.indiatimes.com/india/jk-government-bans-22-social-networking-sites-citing-their-misuse/articleshow/58382769.cms, accessed 16 November 2023. This adds yet another dimension to the evidence of the lack of institutionalization of international human rights norms.

[69] Goñi (n 7); Adamovsky (n 8); Teresa Jusino, 'Feminism Around the World: #NiUnaMenos Protest in Argentina Highlights Epidemic of Violence Against Women' (*The Mary Sue*, 28 October 2016) https://www.themarysue.com/feminism-around-the-world-argentina-ni-una-menos/, accessed 17 November 2023.

[70] O'Dwyer (n 7); Del Río (n 12); Sarah Gordon, 'NiUnaMenos: How the Brutal Gang Rape and Murder of a Schoolgirl United the Furious Women of Latin America' (*The Telegraph*, 21 October 2016) http://www.telegraph.co.uk/women/life/niunamenos-how-a-schoolgirls-brutal-gang-rape-and-murder-united/, accessed 29 November 2023.

acceptable as an expression of masculinity to some.[71] Argentina is identified as a deeply patriarchal country, 'plagued with sexist stereotypes'.[72] Almost identical to India, for some time women's groups have raised concerns about institutionalized apathy to violence against women, particularly through police victim-blaming and a lack of convictions in the courts.[73]

Publicly, government officials seemed to address this perceived apathy in the aftermath of the #niunamenos protests. Many politicians attended the protests for photo opportunities, using the images in their election campaigns.[74] Although to some this was political opportunism, to many it was an important step forward in accountability and agenda setting.[75] There was some evidence that the hashtag campaign influenced local elections, in a positive way (a known misogynist lost his seat).[76] Frontline workers noted that more women used shelters and national helplines.[77] A new national action plan specifically addressing violence against women was announced, continuing to address the goals of the campaign, particularly in terms of education and increases to available services.[78] Additionally, the government 'elevated' the National Women's Council within the government to give the agency more autonomy.[79]

Notably, many female legislators introduced bills to protect women from violence in the months following the campaign (Dirección de Información Parlamentaria, Honorable Cámera de Diputados de la Nación, República Argentina).[80] Some experts posit that perhaps there was success because there are quota systems in place in Argentina, and although the female politicians had not made much change prior to the movement, the protests may have enabled the female politicians already in post to take more drastic action.[81]

---

[71] Goñi (n 7).

[72] Vega (n 39).

[73] US State Department, 'Country Reports on Human Rights Practices for 2015' (2015) 13.

[74] Adamovsky (n 8).

[75] Nugent (n 13).

[76] Adamovsky (n 8).

[77] Jusino (n 69); '#NiUnaMenos: Not One Less' (n 9); Nugent (n 13).

[78] 'Argentina Has New Gender Violence Plan' (*BBC News*, 27 July 2016) http://www.bbc.co.uk/news/world-latin-america-36901113, accessed 29 November 2023; US State Department, 'Country Reports on Human Rights Practices for 2016' (2016) https://www.state.gov/j/drl/rls/hrrpt/humanrightsreport/index.htm#wrapper, accessed 13 April 2017.

[79] Karla Zabludovsky, 'This Woman Devoted Her Life To Keeping Women Safe. And Then A Man Killed Her' (*BuzzFeed*, 29 October 2017) https://www.buzzfeed.com/karlazabludovsky/these-women-tried-to-take-hashtag-activism-into-the-streets, accessed 17 November 2023.

[80] Madeline Gannon, 'At What Cost? Discrepancies between Women's Legislative Representation and Effective Policy to Protect Women from Violence in Argentina' (2016) 33 SIGMA Journal of Political and International Studies 81, 82.

[81] Ibid.

It seems, however, that for every positive and perhaps meaningful action the government took to institutionalize a commitment to women, there was an equal negative action. In one instance, the government was accused of being 'incompetent' when they publicly announced the location of three new safe houses for victims of domestic violence.[82] The fact that the protests continued alone gives credence to the lack of political will and investment in women. Femicides themselves have likely increased in the years since the campaign.[83] In short, 'activists in Argentina fear that, for all the efforts they made, for all the noise they created, women's rights have barely inched forward – with new laws largely ignored, few safe havens for victims of abuse, and a justice system that remains dominated by men'.[84]

Law enforcement

The Verma Report was very clear in its findings about the role of the courts in allowing the epidemic of violence against women in India prior to the #delhigangrape case and campaign.[85] Myriad cases of failures in the justice system for victims of gender-based violence existed before the #delhigangrape incidents.[86] The case of the perpetrators of the #delhigangrape caught and held the attention of the public. As explored later in this chapter, many of the peak days in the campaign related to milestones in the progression of the legal case. On 3 January 2013, murder charges were filed against the five alleged perpetrators as well as charges of destruction of evidence and attempted murder of her male companion. The sixth suspect was treated as a juvenile.[87] The case was referred to the new fast-track courts, set up in

---

[82] Princess Weekes, '#NiUnaMenos: Fighting Femicide In Argentina' (*The Mary Sue*, 30 October 2017) https://www.themarysue.com/niunamenos-fighting-femicide-in-argent ina/, accessed 17 November 2023; Zabludovsky (n 79).

[83] 'Argentina: Paro Contra Feminicidios y Maltrato a Las Mujeres', http://www.dw.com/ es/argentina-paro-contra-feminicidios-y-maltrato-a-las-mujeres/a-36094088, accessed 17 November 2023.

[84] Zabludovsky (n 79).

[85] '[F]ull justice continues to elude the victim of sexual harassment and sexual assault even after two decades (after a landmark case). … The mindset of the judiciary also needs to be improved by their education in gender sensitivity. The women's tragedy is to face the compounding of gender and social injustice contrary to the constitutional promise to "secure a social order in which justice, social, economic and political, shall inform all the institutions of national life", and the State's obligation "to eliminate inequalities in status, facilities and opportunities, not only amongst individuals but also amongst groups of people"'. Verma et al (n 22) 15.

[86] Verma et al (n 22).

[87] Harris (n 55).

just days in response to the protests.[88] One of the accused died in jail, in a questionable suicide.[89] The four remaining men were found guilty.[90] They were given the death penalty in September 2013.[91] A frontline worker aptly described the situation:

> This decision will have a positive effect on patriarchal and reactionary societal attitudes because they only understand the language of fear. However, the full effect of this verdict will be felt only when it fast-tracks all other pending rape trials in the country and other rape victims get their justice too.[92]

Others were not as positive about the sentence, finding that while authorities needed to take action on this case given the public attention driven by social media, the death penalty is also a violation of international human rights norms: 'authorities must avoid using the death penalty as a quick-fix solution'.[93]

The death penalties were upheld upon appeal in March 2014.[94] However, the following day two of the sentences were put on hold for another

---

[88] '5 Special Fast Track Courts by January 3' (*Hindustan Times*, 25 September 2013) https://web.archive.org/web/20130925062509/http://www.hindustantimes.com/India-news/NewDelhi/5-special-fast-track-courts-by-January-3/Article1-982169.aspx, accessed 16 November 2023.

[89] Dominguez and Mazumdaru (n 2); 'Delhi Rape Accused Is Found Dead' (*BBC News*, 11 March 2013) http://www.bbc.co.uk/news/world-asia-21737748, accessed 29 November 2023; Rahul Bedi, 'India Gang-Rape: Accused Ram Singh "Commits Suicide"' (*The Telegraph*, 11 March 2013) http://www.telegraph.co.uk/news/worldnews/asia/india/9921621/India-gang-rape-accused-Ram-Singh-commits-suicide.html, accessed 29 November 2023; Niharika Mandhana and Heather Timmons, 'Suspect in India Gang Rape Found Dead in Jail' (*The New York Times*, 10 March 2013) india.blogs.nytimes.com/2013/03/10/suspect-in-india-gang-rape-found-dead-in-jail/, accessed 29 November 2023.

[90] 'Anger and Calls for Justice in Delhi' (*BBC News*, 10 September 2013) http://www.bbc.co.uk/news/world-asia-india-24031909, accessed 29 November 2023.

[91] *State v Ram Singh and another* (ASJ (Special Fast Track Court), Saket Courts, New Delhi); Nilanjana Bhowmick, 'Death Sentences Handed Down in India's Delhi Gang Rape Case' (*Time*, 13 September 2013) http://world.time.com/2013/09/13/death-sentences-handed-down-in-indias-delhi-gang-rape-case/, accessed 29 November 2023; 'Delhi Gang-Rape: Four Men Sentenced to Death' (NDTV, 13 September 2013) https://www.ndtv.com/india-news/delhi-gang-rape-four-men-sentenced-to-death-732920, accessed 16 November 2023.

[92] Bhowmick (n 91).

[93] 'Death Penalties for Delhi Gang Rape' (*BBC News*, 13 September 2013) http://www.bbc.co.uk/news/world-asia-india-24078339, accessed 29 November 2023.

[94] *Vinay Sharma and Anr v State* [2014] High Court of Delhi 1398/2013. '[T]he shocking incident left an indelible scar on the social order and became a burning societal issue. An enraged and infuriated society took to the streets to avenge the affront inflicted upon it. Social abhorrence could not have been more manifest nor the national shock at the

appeal.[95] The sentences were again upheld in May 2017, seen as an unusual move by the court given that a high percentage of death sentences are overturned or commuted.[96] A study at the time had exposed that death sentences in India are often handed down but rarely carried out.[97] As is necessary for the death penalty in India, the judges found this to be the 'rarest of rare cases'.[98] In upholding the sentences, the judge opined:

> I hope that this gruesome incident in the capital and death of this young woman will be an eye-opener for a mass movement 'to end violence against women' and 'respect for women and her dignity' and sensitizing public at large on gender justice. ... The battle for gender justice can be won only with strict implementation of legislative provisions, sensitization of public, taking other pro-active steps at all levels for combating violence against women and ensuring widespread attitudinal changes and comprehensive change in the existing mind set.[99]

Many believe that because this level of punishment is not doled out equally for all sexual assault cases, it will not serve as a deterrent. Rather, it was the public outrage sparked by the social media attention and expressed in both online and offline activities which led to these extreme sentences, not the

---

incident more perceptible. It would be no exaggeration or hyperbole to state that the shocking incident had ramifications which crossed the national borders into international terrain' (para 397). '[W]e are of the considered view that the instant case without a shadow of doubt falls in the category of the rarest of rare cases where culpability has assumed the proportion of extreme depravity' (para 398). The opinion also stated 'the appetite for sex, the hunger for violence, the position of the empowered and the attitude of perversity, to say the least, are bound to shock the collective conscience which knows not what to do. It is manifest that the wanton lust, the servility to absolutely unchained carnal desire and slavery to the loathsome beastility of passion ruled the mindset of the appellants to commit a crime which can summon with immediacy "tsunami" of shock in the mind of the collective and destroy the civilised marrows of the milieu in entirety' (para 356).

[95] 'Delhi Gang Rape: Death Penalty for Two Men Put on Hold' (*BBC News*, 15 March 2014) http://www.bbc.co.uk/news/world-asia-india-26593587, accessed 29 November 2023.

[96] Ellen Barry, 'In Rare Move, Death Sentence in Delhi Gang Rape Case Is Upheld' (*The New York Times*, 5 May 2017) https://www.nytimes.com/2017/05/05/world/asia/death-sentence-delhi-gang-rape.html, accessed 29 November 2023; 'Delhi Gang Rapists' Death Penalty Upheld' (*BBC News*, 5 May 2017) http://www.bbc.co.uk/news/world-asia-india-39814910, accessed 29 November 2023.

[97] Hari Kumar and Ellen Barry, 'Death Sentences in India Usually End in Question Marks, Study Finds' (*The New York Times*, 7 May 2016) https://www.nytimes.com/2016/05/07/world/asia/india-death-sentences-executions.html, accessed 29 November 2023.

[98] *Mukesh & Anr v State for NCT of Delhi & Others* [2017] Supreme Court of India 607–608 [146].

[99] Ibid, 19.

nature of the crime itself.[100] A young woman who lived near the families of the perpetrators was quoted as saying that 'the court should not give special preference to this case and must decide like it does in other cases. They should be punished within the law'.[101] Another local woman felt instead that all rapists should be given the death penalty, including the rich and famous.[102] Some even felt that there would have been more protests if the perpetrators had *not* been given the death penalty.[103]

All four men were hanged in January 2020.[104]

Other high-profile cases have been decided since, with varying results. Those cases where the government 'feared' public backlash led to harsh penalties, while those which garnered less attention were given softer sentences.[105] The role of the courts is highly questionable, appearing to hand down death penalties when the media is involved, but releasing other perpetrators when it does not gain any attention.

Indian crime statistics are publicly available, and, according to the official reports, the crime statistics on sexual violence paint a very telling picture.[106] By 2016, conviction rates remained between 25 and 30 per cent for rape and around 20 per cent for sexual harassment. As expected, there were minor improvements in the year immediately following the campaign, but as the echo of the campaign dwindled, so did the attention to violence against women. Conviction rates of merely 25 per cent for cases of rape are extremely low. It is also interesting to note that in 2013, one-third of cases were labelled as false charges. This could possibly indicate that police do not take cases of rape seriously (as stated by activists and victims over the years). Additionally, despite the establishment of fast-track courts, the number of

---

[100] Barry (n 96).

[101] 'Anger and Calls for Justice in Delhi' (n 90).

[102] Ibid.

[103] 'Understanding India's Rape Crisis' (*The Harvard Gazette*, 20 September 2013) https://news.harvard.edu/gazette/story/2013/09/understanding-indias-rape-crisis/, accessed 16 November 2023.

[104] 'Nirbhaya Case: Four Indian Men Executed for 2012 Delhi Bus Rape and Murder' (*BBC News*, 20 March 2020) https://www.bbc.com/news/world-asia-india-51969961, accessed 29 November 2023.

[105] Amy Kazmin and Kiran Stacey, 'Violence Erupts in India after Guru Is Convicted of Rape' (*Financial Times*, 25 August 2017) https://www.ft.com/content/9f04b77c-896f-11e7-bf50-e1c239b45787, accessed 16 November 2023; 'Rapist Indian Guru Jailed for 20 Years' (*BBC News*, 28 August 2017) http://www.bbc.co.uk/news/world-asia-india-41070764, accessed 29 November 2023; Michael Safi, ' "A Feeble No May Mean Yes": Indian Court Overturns Rape Conviction' (*The Guardian*, 26 September 2017) http://www.theguardian.com/world/2017/sep/26/a-feeble-no-may-mean-yes-indian-court-overturns-conviction, accessed 29 November 2023.

[106] 'National Crime Records Bureau', http://ncrb.gov.in/, accessed 2 January 2019.

backlog cases does not seem to have changed much over the past decade. At the end of 2016, in the aftermath of the campaign, 133,373 rape cases were still pending. Over 30,000 sexual harassment cases were pending.

The one positive to take from these statistics has nothing to do with law and order, but rather women themselves. There was a marked increase in the number of rapes reported after the campaign which has been maintained since. Given all the evidence, it is highly likely that this number is much more representative than the lower number reported before the campaign, indicating that women are more empowered to come forward and report the crime, demonstrating some of the positive aspects of digital feminist activism literature.

The combination of attention paid only to high profile cases with the persistently low and unchanging conviction rates shows that the situation is worse in India following the campaign. A chance was created to make real improvements, but these were never realized.

In Argentina, again there is a nearly identical picture, with persistently low conviction rates before and after the campaign. In many cases of femicide, again both before and after the campaign, the victims had already sought the protection of the state.[107] There were, and continue to be, many reports of incidents of violence when there was already a court restraining or protection order in place.[108] This is also not dissimilar to the situation around femicide in Turkey discussed in Chapter 4.

According to the Argentinian Attorney General's office, in 2010, complaints were filed in only three out of every ten suspected rape cases, and only one of those three was then prosecuted.[109] Prior to the campaign there were also reports of judicial leniency and acceptance of the machismo culture. One judge cited 'violent emotion' as a mitigating circumstance in one femicide case which led to a reduced sentence for the perpetrator.[110] Public outcry over that particular case did lead the government to pass legislation

---

[107] Sol Amaya and Marthe Rubio, 'El Mapa de Los Femicidios En La Argentina' (*La Nacion*, 20 May 2015) https://web.archive.org/web/20170821064237/http://www.lanacion.com. ar/1794148-el-mapa-de-los-femicidios-en-la-argentina, accessed 17 November 2023; Naundorf and Pabst (n 50).

[108] 'Femicide in Argentina' (n 8); 'Argentines Protest Violence against Women' (*Al Jazeera America*, 4 June 2015) https://web.archive.org/web/20221021125212/http://america. aljazeera.com/articles/2015/6/4/Thousands-of-Argentines-rally-against-femicide.html, accessed 17 November 2023.

[109] US State Department, 'Country Reports on Human Rights Practices for 2010' (2010) 20.

[110] Meaghan Beatley, 'How One Woman's Murder Made Argentina Rethink the Idea of "Crimes of Passion"' (*The New Statesman*, 27 April 2017) https://www.newstatesman. com/culture/observations/2017/04/how-one-woman-s-murder-made-argentina-reth ink-idea-crimes-passion, accessed 17 November 2023.

Table 5.1: Conviction rates of femicides, Argentina, 2014–2016

Year	Total victims	Convictions	%	Previous complaints	%
2014	225	27	13	30	13
2015	235	7	3	46	20
2016	254	22	9	60	24

Source: Registro Nacional de Femicidios de la Justicia Argentina, 'Datos Estadisticos Del Poder Judicial Sobre: Femicidios'

imposing stricter sentences. The change, however, did not have the desired deterrent effect as femicides continued to increase.[111]

After the campaign, these patterns continued. In 2015, Human Rights Watch found that out of a reported 235 femicides, there were only seven convictions.[112] Compiled statistics from the federal registry (set up in response to the campaign) are shown in Table 5.1.[113]

The statistics in Table 5.1 show that conviction rates *decreased* after the campaign – and continue to do so. These statistics also show the relatively high percentage of femicides where a previous complaint has been recorded. This also confirms that femicides increased, from 225 in 2014 to 254 in 2016. One journalist summed up the situation: 'However big this progress [the legislative achievements] may seem, between the first and second #NiUnaMenos protests (2015–2016) 275 women died as victims of gender violence.'[114] Human Rights Watch reported that in 2020, there were 251 femicides reported with only four convictions – a 2 per cent conviction rate.[115]

Conviction rates in both countries are therefore shockingly low, hovering around 25 per cent for sexual violence in India and 10 per cent, perhaps even lower now, for femicide in Argentina. These rates are consistent both before and after the hashtag campaigns. With the legislative changes introduced, one would expect to see any meaningful change work its way to the courts with a resulting positive change in conviction rates by

---

[111] Ibid.

[112] Human Rights Watch, 'World Report 2017: Rights Trends in Argentina' (2017) https://www.hrw.org/world-report/2017/country-chapters/argentina, accessed 2 January 2019.

[113] Registro Nacional de Femicidios de la Justicia Argentina, 'Datos Estadisticos Del Poder Judicial Sobre: Femicidios'.

[114] Del Río (n 12); see also Magdalena Medley, '5 Things I Learned at Argentina's #NiUnaMenos March against Femicide' (Amnesty International USA, 14 July 2016) https://www.amnestyusa.org/5-things-i-learned-at-argentinas-niunamenos-march-against-femicide/, accessed 17 November 2023.

[115] Human Rights Watch, 'Argentina: Events of 2021', *World Report 2022* (2021) https://www.hrw.org/world-report/2022/country-chapters/argentina, accessed 8 November 2023.

now. Given the time that has passed since the legislative changes in both countries, it is reasonable to expect to see improvements in the judicial system based on theories of legal change. However, this research indicates that the speed of the legislative changes was not an indication of meaningful state commitment and political will to address violence against women, but rather a reactionary tactical concession to appease the public's visible anger driven by social media, most likely related to pending elections, reflecting one of the main theoretical critiques of the spiral model (lack of progression from tactical concessions to institutionalization and rule-consistent behaviour).

UN dialogue

The final area to explore evidencing legal change is the catalogue of reports with UN human rights treaty bodies. This dialogue, when examined closely, provides a wealth of information about the true situation for women and girls on the ground. It also provides an in-depth insight into the government's perspective, uncovering truths about commitment and investment in women. In this legal aspect, India and Argentina actually differed greatly in their relationship with the UN human rights mechanisms. India showed rather surprising aggression, defensiveness, and at times outright rejection of engagement with international human rights mechanisms. Argentina, on the other hand, exhibited what could be an honest recognition of the problem of violence against women with evidence of some meaningful commitment to change. This area is the primary reason Argentina overall scored better than India in legal outcomes.

In early UN reports to and from India, there is a clear focus on marriage and women's roles as mothers. Although it seems some small steps were being taken towards liberalization, the overall rhetoric fell squarely within traditional gender roles.[116] When pushed on the government's supposed commitment to improve the status of women,[117] India responded that 'the macho image did not exist in India, where women were traditionally accorded a high degree of respect'.[118] The Human Rights Committee raised similar concerns in the early 1990s as well.[119] There, India claimed that

---

[116] Committee on Economic, Social and Cultural Rights, 'Implementation of the International Covenant on Economic, Social, and Cultural Rights. State Report from India' (1983) UN Doc E/1980/6/Add.34.

[117] Committee on Economic, Social and Cultural Rights, 'Summary Record of the 6th Meeting' (1984) UN Doc E/1984/WG.1/SR.6 para 50.

[118] Committee on Economic, Social and Cultural Rights, 'Summary Record of the 8th Meeting' (1984) UN Doc E/1984/WG.1/SR.8 para 37.

[119] Human Rights Committee, 'Report of the Human Rights Committee' (1991) UN Doc Supplement No. 40 (A/46/40) paras 272–273.

the 'difficulty in reaching the goal of equality was more a social than a law enforcement problem'.[120]

In 2001, the Special Rapporteur on Violence Against Women had several communications with the government of India regarding allegations of rape, many of which dealt with police or armed forces.[121] The government stated that six out of the ten cases raised were false or unsubstantiated accusations. This indicates a rather dismissive state attitude towards the work of the Special Rapporteur on Violence Against Women and the issues raised in her communications. Similarly, in 2002 the Special Rapporteur communicated with the government on 11 cases dealing with serious allegations of rape and violence, many of which involved police inaction, intimidation, and death threats.[122] India did not respond to any communications on allegations of cases of violence against women from the Special Rapporteur in 2006.[123] In 2007 the government only replied to one allegation, and claimed that after their investigation they could not substantiate the claim.[124] In 2008, the government replied to a 2007 allegation, again finding that it was fabricated.[125] Two additional allegations from 2008 led the government to ask for more information; according to the state's response one was being investigated, three had no response, and the government found another to be false.[126] In 2009, the Special Rapporteur received an allegation of serious government threats to a woman who had given a statement to the Human Rights Committee about the situation of violence against women and girls in India. The government denied this.[127] A further two responses were sent

---

[120] Ibid, 304.

[121] Human Rights Council, 'Report of the Special Rapporteur on Violence against Women, Its Causes and Consequences Addendum Communications to and from Governments' (2001) UN Doc E/CN.4/2001/73/Add.1 paras 23–34.

[122] Human Rights Council, 'Report of the Special Rapporteur on Violence against Women, Its Causes and Consequences, Addendum Communications to and from Governments' (2002) UN Doc E/CN.4/2002/83/Add.1 paras 27–39.

[123] Human Rights Council, 'Report of the Special Rapporteur on Violence against Women, Its Causes and Consequences, Yakin Ertürk Addendum Communications to and from Governments' (2007) UN Doc A/HRC/4/34/Add.1 paras 272–297.

[124] Human Rights Council, 'Report of the Special Rapporteur on Violence against Women, Its Causes and Consequences, Yakin Ertürk Addendum Communications to and from Governments' (2008) UN Doc A/HRC/7/6/Add.1 paras 169–191.

[125] Human Rights Council, 'Report of the Special Rapporteur on Violence against Women, Its Causes and Consequences, Yakin Ertürk Addendum Communications to and from Governments' (2009) UN Doc A/HRC/11/6/Add1) para 192.

[126] Ibid, 185–246. .

[127] Human Rights Council, 'Report of the Special Rapporteur on Violence against Women, Its Causes and Consequences, Rashida Manjoo Addendum Communications to and from Governments' (2010) UN Doc A/HRC/14/22/Add.1 paras 152–153.

to previous communications where, unsurprisingly, the government found no basis or were unable to substantiate the claims.[128] This dialogue is very indicative of the state not taking these issues seriously, over quite a lengthy time period.

The next engagement with international human rights mechanisms occurred while the campaign was reaching its climax. In early 2013, the Special Rapporteur on Violence Against Women was invited to undertake a mission to India.[129] This was clearly in response to the spark incident. The Special Rapporteur found that sexual violence was widespread, affecting women's feeling of security particularly in public urban spaces. She also identified shame and stigma as barriers to justice, at times even leading to victim suicide.[130] She then went on to highlight the lack of effective implementation of existing legislation, pointing to the exclusion of women's participation in society as a primary underlying cause of the epidemic of violence.[131] The Special Rapporteur specifically addressed #delhigangrape. She found that:

> The laws that were adopted did not fully reflect the recommendations of the Verma Committee. The opportunity to adopt a holistic approach to violence against women, including addressing the root causes and consequences of such violence, was lost. ... Serious concerns were expressed with regard to the insensitive and taunting attitude of some members of Parliament with regard to the Criminal Law (Amendment) Act. The Special Rapporteur regrets that some political leaders are not fully committed to the process of legal and social change as regards women's human rights.[132]

The Special Rapporteur continued to draw attention to gaps in legislation, lack of redress, lack of holistic approach, and patriarchal norms as root causes of violence against women which were not being adequately addressed by the state.[133]

Amnesty International also submitted a report in response to the Special Rapporteur's mission, clearly supporting her findings and agreeing that

---

[128] Ibid, 154–158.

[129] Human Rights Council, 'Report of the Special Rapporteur on Violence against Women, Its Causes and Consequences, Rashida Manjoo Addendum Mission to India' (2014) UN Doc A/HRC/26/38/Add.1.

[130] Ibid, 12.

[131] Ibid, 45.

[132] Ibid, 49–51.

[133] Ibid, 75–76.

the legislative reforms were not enough.[134] The state's response provides significant insight into the lack of institutionalization of women's rights norms and the resistance to engage with international human rights mechanisms and, although lengthy, is critical to this study:

> India is constrained to make certain observations on the Report of the Special Rapporteur as there are too many instances in the Report that leads a conclusion that the Report lacks full objectivity and exhibits a tendency to over-simplify the issues at hand. *It is rather difficult to comprehend the reasons for the Special Rapporteur, who despite her learned experience, has taken rather a simplistic approach while drawing conclusions, and thereafter present them as her findings. The proclivity for making unsubstantiated yet sweeping generalizations is very high in the Report, which tends to point to either a lack of understanding of issues or a high degree of prejudice playing a predominant role while arriving at such conclusions.* We do not agree with the labeling of 'violence against women in India as systematic,' as noted in Paragraph 8. Such a sweeping remark smacks of a highly prejudiced state of mind. It also fails to recognize that India, the world's largest democracy, values and respects the rule of law as one of its major strengths.[135]

The government then asked for specific evidence for 14 statements made by the Special Rapporteur.[136] Having read several hundred UN periodic reports for this study, this statement was by far the most openly antagonistic, dismissive, and disappointing of all the reports. For the state to so blatantly defend the government's rejection of the magnitude of these issues, after the campaign, goes quite some way to affirming the significant lack of institutionalization across the country.

Argentina, on the other hand, showed an improvement in dialogue. The state, at least in words, seemed to recognize the problems with femicide and violence against women, and, to some extent at least, was open to discussing the human rights implications with the international mechanisms. There was evidence of more willingness to change after the campaign than before.

---

[134] Amnesty International, 'Written Statement Submitted by Amnesty International, a Non-Governmental Organization in Special Consultative Status' (2013) UN Doc A/HRC/23/NGO/102 2.

[135] Human Rights Council, 'Report of the Special Rapporteur on Violence against Women, Its Causes and Consequences, Rashida Manjoo Addendum Mission to India: Comments by the State on the Report of the Special Rapporteur' (2014) UN Doc A/HRC/26/38/Add.4 paras 2–3, emphasis added.

[136] Ibid, 12.

Concerns in Argentina first began to emerge with the 1999 Committee on Economic, Social and Cultural Rights session, where the committee felt that perhaps there were 'inadequate mechanisms' and 'slowness of justice' for women.[137] In its concluding observations, the committee also highlighted the increase in incidents of violence against women, particularly domestic violence. During the 1999–2000 reporting cycle with the Human Rights Committee, there was some back and forth about national and provincial legislation on domestic violence and violence against women. However, the committee still raised this as an area of concern in its concluding observations.[138] It is also important to note that as far back as 1999, concerns were being raised over the lack of data collection, which became one of the focal points of #niunamenos.

Nearly 10 pages of the 2002 CEDAW state report were dedicated to the work and programmes of the government in reducing domestic violence and violence against women, though mostly covering training, awareness raising, plans for the future, and interagency working. Of note, the government still talked about the need to collect better statistics and the pilot domestic violence register.[139] In the follow-up CEDAW session, the committee stated 'the follow-up report was rather disappointing with respect to Argentina's efforts to eliminate violence against women', raising concerns over proper investigation of complaints and issues with persistently low conviction rates and barriers to accessing justice for victims.[140] These concerns then featured highly in the 2008 Universal Periodic Review cycle for Argentina, in both the compilation report and the stakeholder report.[141]

In its 2015 report to CEDAW, just months before #niunamenos, the government stated: 'Argentina joins the eight Latin American countries that have incorporated the concept of femicide into their legislation. Article 80 of the Argentine Penal Code, on homicide, includes femicide as an aggravating factor, carrying a sentence of life imprisonment.'[142] CEDAW's next list of issues in 2016 (after the campaign), once again, inquire about data

---

[137] Committee on Economic, Social and Cultural Rights, 'Summary Record of the 35th Meeting' (1999) UN Doc E/C.12/1999/SR.35 para 42.

[138] Human Rights Committee, 'Concluding Observations Argentina' (2000) UN Doc CCPR/CO/70/ARG.

[139] Committee on the Elimination of Discrimination Against Women, 'Fifth Periodic Reports of States Parties: Argentina' (2002) UN Doc CEDAW/C/ARG/5.

[140] Committee on the Elimination of Discrimination Against Women, 'Summary Record of the 660th Meeting' (2004) UN Doc CEDAW/C/SR.660 para 8.

[141] Human Rights Council, 'Compilation Report Argentina' (2008) UN Doc A/HRC/WG.6/1/ARG/2 para 31; Human Rights Council, 'Summary Report Argentina' (2008) UN Doc A/HRC/WG.6/1/ARG/3.

[142] Committee on the Elimination of Discrimination Against Women, 'Seventh Periodic Reports of States Parties Argentina' (2015) UN Doc CEDAW/C/ARG/7 2–3.

collection.[143] Finally, the state was able to provide official, federal statistics.[144] In session, the government said:

> After a string of demonstrations across the country in which Argentinians had, for the third time in two years, expressed their outrage at femicide, the Government had taken note of the strength of public feeling and had for the first time placed the elimination of gender-based violence at the top of the political agenda.[145]

The exchange which followed shows that the campaign, made so visible through the social media attention, did present enough pressure on the government to force action.[146] This dialogue is also quite positive, certainly compared to India. The Argentinian government at the very least speaks about the issue with importance and priority. However, the evidence presented earlier in this chapter does show that the government's actions have not had any impact on the ground for women or in the courts with convictions. In fact, this lack of impact was raised as an area of concern in the next Human Rights Committee reporting cycle, even using the word 'deplore' to describe the lack of implementation of existing legislation.[147]

The Special Rapporteur on Violence against Women visited Argentina in 2016 and found that 'machismo culture' was a key reason for persistent gender-based violence, and that 'systems to prevent attacks were not fully

---

[143] Committee on the Elimination of Discrimination Against Women, 'Replies by the Government of Argentina to the List of Issues' (2016) UN Doc CEDAW/C/ARG/Q/7/Add.1 para 9.

[144] Ibid, 49.

[145] Committee on the Elimination of Discrimination Against Women, 'Summary Record of the 1443rd Meeting' (2016) UN Doc CEDAW/C/SR.1443 para 2.

[146] The committee responded: '[W]hile the information provided about the State party's efforts to combat gender stereotypes through education was very helpful, she would like to hear more about the issue of femicide and the role of the communication media. She had been particularly struck by the extraordinary #NiUnaMenos ("Not One Woman Less") social movement sweeping Argentina and Latin America as a whole. Thousands of women had been protesting against macho behaviour and gender-based violence and in favour of greater equality and autonomy for women. She wondered to what extent the National Women's Council envisaged aligning itself with that movement so that more far-reaching, more continuous campaigns against deep-rooted stereotypes and cultural attitudes might be launched' (ibid, 63). The government replied with 'while the #NiUnaMenos movement had initially emerged from online social networks, it was now an intrinsic part of Argentine culture: all of society was engaged in the fight to end femicide' (ibid, 66).

[147] Human Rights Committee, 'Concluding Observations on the Fifth Periodic Report of Argentina' (2016) UN Doc CCPR/C/ARG/CO/5 paras 9–10.

functional'.[148] She went on to point out that the data, while helpful in understanding the scope of the problem, showed that very little had changed for women in Argentina, particularly the low conviction rates.[149]

Therefore, the impact of the actions of both the Indian and the Argentinian government were very similar. In fact, neither country has seen a meaningful improvement in reducing violence against women, despite legislative changes introduced in response to the campaigns. India's engagement with the international human rights mechanisms was far less positive than that of Argentina. The language displayed in the reports showed India's hostility towards the international mechanisms, while Argentina, at least on the surface, appeared to have a much more engaged and open approach.

Twitter characteristics

#niunamenos was the largest campaign in the study, with 410,858 Tweets analysed, 63 per cent of which were non-English. #delhigangrape was the second largest campaign with 144,867 Tweets analysed, with 7 per cent non-English (as expected from an English-speaking country). These two campaigns showed very large peaks on many occasions, indicating a huge public following. The significant public attention of these campaigns, combined in some part with the proximity of elections and related political interest, seemed to push the governments to engage in tactical concessions in the form the legislative change far too quickly, with little to no chance of long-term, meaningful change. This reflects one of the core critiques of the spiral model, the lack of progression, where countries mapped along the spiral have gotten 'stuck' at tactical concessions without moving fully to rule-consistent behaviour. This was manifested in these campaigns, and likely exacerbated by the use of social media.

Persistence (Tweets per day)

These campaigns showed incredibly similar patterns of persistence, highlighting the large and sustained online public attention on the campaigns. Although this led to increased public pressure on the governments, this pressure in some ways had a potentially negative impact, contributing

---

[148] 'UN Special Rapporteur Challenges Argentina to Step up Protection of Women in "Machismo Culture"' (21 November 2016) https://www.ohchr.org/fr/newsevents/pages/displaynews.aspx?newsid=20903&langid=e, accessed 2 January 2019.

[149] Human Rights Council, 'Report of the Special Rapporteur on Violence against Women, Its Causes and Consequences, on Her Mission to Argentina' (2017) UN Doc A/HRC/35/30/Add.3 paras 10–11.

to tactical concessions but losing potency to continue campaigning for institutionalization and rule-consistent behaviour.

These two campaigns showed the highest averages of Tweets per day, with 100 for #delhigangrape and 589 for #niunamenos. The two campaigns also showed the most peak days and peak periods. #delhigangrape had 12 peak days over seven peak periods, with 28 days having over 1,000 Tweets, and #niunamenos had 87 peak days over 21 peak periods, with 101 days with more than 1,000 Tweets. The longest peak period in #delhigangrape was 22 days, 34 in #niunamenos. These numbers are far higher than other campaigns, and again paint a clear picture of the height of the public attention and pressure.

Figure 5.1 visualizes the persistence of the campaigns over the active period (roughly 600 days). The backlash campaigns did not show nearly the same heights or lengths of peaks, and the status quo campaigns showed huge peaks but only in the immediate aftermath of the spark incident. These tactical concessions campaigns show far more persistence, with higher and more consistent peaks, longer peak periods, and peaks further into the lifespan of the campaigns. However, as we see, this persistence may have been *too* much, in that the online pressure which then triggered offline protests may have forced governments into premature action.

Engagement (retweets, likes, replies)

Engagement metrics show fewer similarities between these two campaigns than measures of persistence. #niunamenos was a campaign very much driven

Figure 5.1: Number of Tweets per day, #delhigangrape and #niunamenos

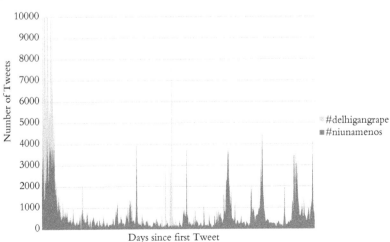

by retweets and likes. Throughout the life of the campaign, the ratio of retweets to Tweets was 3.07, meaning that for every Tweet in the campaign there were at least three retweets (on average). Although in some campaigns this might indicate a lack of engagement, in #niunamenos it appears that this very high level of retweeting resulted in consistent messaging. Particularly around the times of protests and rallies, similar images and notices about the upcoming protests were shared and retweeted many times. Surprisingly, however, #niunamenos also showed a very high ratio of likes to Tweets, second only to #letwomengotostadium. This tends to indicate a low level of engagement, that is, simply clicking 'like' to a Tweet involves the least effort and the lowest level of participation. Perhaps this is one of the campaign behaviours that contributed to less positive outcomes, particularly in the areas of institutionalization and law enforcement. More online dialogue tends to be associated with better outcomes, and a high proportion of likes shows a negative directionality in the correlation to legal outcomes (explained fully in Chapter 7). In other words, more likes lead to less positive outcomes. #delhigangrape showed a more evenly distributed behavioural pattern of engagement, driven by retweets (and therefore consistent messaging) but not with such stark differences.

Interestingly, this behaviour in #niunamenos differed from peak to non-peak periods. One of the strongest statistical correlations in this study is the reply to Tweet ratio specifically during non-peak periods, showing the importance of ongoing and consistent levels of dialogue and engagement. For #niunamenos, the reply to Tweet ratio during non-peak periods was much more in line with the other campaigns. The campaign with the most positive ratio of replies to Tweets was #delhigangrape. Here we see a point of similarity between the two campaigns, showing a positive and consistent level of conversation during non-peak time periods.

Users (profiles of the 100 most active users)

#delhigangrape and #niunamenos were again very similar in user profiles. As the two largest campaigns, it is not surprising that these campaigns attracted a larger number of unique users. In total, 46,487 users participated in the #delhigangrape campaign, with 185,883 unique users in #niunamenos. Users in #delhigangrape Tweeted on average three times, with users in #niunamenos Tweeting twice. Overall, nearly 40 million Twitter users were reached by the active campaigners in #delhigangrape and 11.2 million in #niunamenos. This reach was considerably more than the other campaigns, again underscoring the online public pressure on the governments to take visible action quickly.

Both campaigns showed a high proportion of domestic users driving the campaign, and of those users most were individuals or news agencies. Out of the 100 most active users in #delhigangrape, domestic individuals, non-domestic individuals, and domestic news agencies drove the campaign. #niunamenos was also driven by domestic individuals and news agencies, but this was followed by domestic organizations. These campaigns therefore showed a fair amount of interest from domestic news agencies. In both campaigns, the domestic news agencies Tweeted enough times to be in this top 100 category. What is also interesting is the reach of the domestic news agencies. In India, the combined number of followers of the domestic news agencies accounted for 94 per cent of the reach of these top 100. In raw numbers, these active domestic news agencies reached over 37 million Twitter users. Again, it is very likely that this reach and public pressure was part of the motivation for the government's reactionary legislative change.

As indicated earlier in this chapter, #niunamenos also attracted the attention of government officials and politicians. Although the numbers are fairly small, it should be noted that this means that, in raw numbers, four out of the most 100 active users in this campaign were involved in politics. That is actually quite meaningful, given that this metric explores the *most active* users out of over 185,000 users. The only other campaign showing a similar level of political involvement was #stopstoning where European Union ministers became active in the campaign. Proximity to election is likely the reason there is more political activity in #niunamenos than the other campaigns. As evidenced earlier, targeting politicians and candidates was a specific campaign strategy.

Content analysis

Here the two tactical concessions campaigns differ. Looking at sentiment, #delhigangrape was dominated by positive Tweets with very little polarity. Conversely, #niunamenos was a far more negative campaign, second only to #sendeanlat, showing large variation in sentiment over time. In other words, #niunamenos was a far more volatile campaign as opposed to the generally positive sentiment in #delhigangrape.

Figure 5.2 plots the number of Tweets per day against the average positivity score. For #niunamenos, there were clear patterns in the sentiment, indicating a potential relationship to peak events. The sentiment appears to become more positive when peak events occurs, particularly later in the campaign. The baseline is a slightly positive sentiment, ranging around 0.6 (0.5 being neutral). However, around peak times the sentiment becomes more positive, ranging from 0.7 to 0.8. This is particularly evident in the final two peak periods, which relate to two large protests. Tweets became much more positive in the days just before, during, and after the protests. The campaign was clearly buoyed by the face-to-face activism of the protests, the

Figure 5.2: Positivity and peaks, #niunamenos

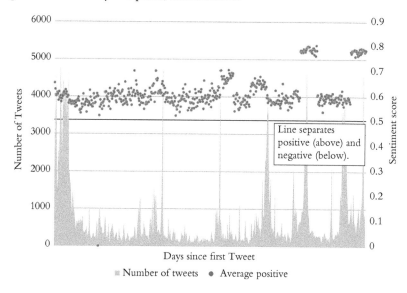

excitement of the protest drawing closer, and reporting the large numbers of people attending the protests. This certainly presents an interesting dimension when looked at through the lens of social media literature, which finds that online activism is stronger when there are offline ties as well. This clustering pattern was more distinct in #niunamenos than in other campaigns as can be seen in Figure 5.3.

Conversely, the pattern in #delhigangrape is steadier and consistently positive. The sentiment does not appear to be as affected by peak events as it was in #niunamenos. The average sentiment over the life of this campaign is 0.75. As peaks in #delhigangrape tend to occur around milestones in the court cases it follows that there would be less positive sentiment. On the contrary, peak events in #niunamenos are almost always around the organization of protests. It also follows that, as seen earlier, Tweets about protests would be more positive than Tweets about prosecution and sentencing of perpetrators. The campaigns, in terms of sentiment, are almost mirror images of each other.

Normatively, these campaigns showed very intriguing, but somewhat different, findings. #delhigangrape Tweets showed both high levels of consistency with, on average, more consistent organic framing present in each time period than variable, as well as extremely clear messaging. The variable content paints an incredibly clear picture of the campaign's focus and mood in almost all time periods. #niunamenos, on the other hand, had less consistent and less focused framing and messaging, despite the high proportion of retweets around the time of protests. The analysis of the

Figure 5.3: Positivity and peaks, #delhigangrape

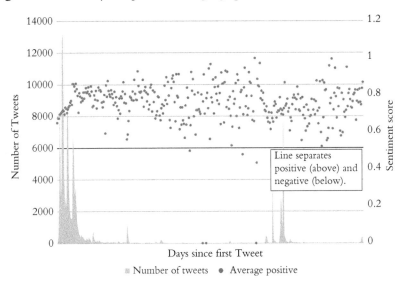

Tweets seem to confirm some of the other evidence which indicated that the #niunamenos campaign lost focus over time.

#delhigangrape showed another notable finding in the presence of a high number of legal words. This campaign manifested and kept a focus on the law, the cases, and the overall involvement of the judicial system far more than any other campaign. This appears to be a connection to the tactical concession outcome for this campaign. The campaign clearly demanded a change in the law, so the government reacted with an immediate change in the law. Forty-five per cent of the consistent words and 18 per cent of the variable words were of a legal nature. This did not appear to be the case in #niunamenos, where the emerging frames and messages, both consistent and variable, did not have a clear legal focus.

These visualizations of consistent words show in detail the overall focus of the campaigns (see Figures 5.4 and 5.5). #delhigangrape Tweets consistently used words and ideas relating to justice. Words such as 'victim', 'case', 'government', 'justice', 'accused', 'sentence', and 'law' remained prevalent throughout the lifespan of the campaign. In #niunamenos, the one focus which remained clear was the organization of marches and protests, with words such as 'march', the prevalence of the dates of the big marches, and words like 'join'.

Overall, the Tweets in #delhigangrape show clear, focused messaging. There was a consistent emphasis on justice, the judicial system, and the law, with many consistent messages of a legal nature and much of the organic content showing reactions to milestones in the cases. #niunamenos had

Figure 5.4: Consistently used words, #delhigangrape

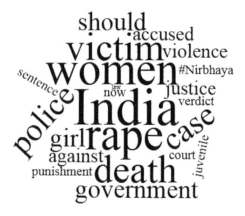

Figure 5.5: Consistently used words, #niunamenos

Notes: An unusual finding was a trend where #niunamenos was connected to the Argentinian version of *Big Brother*. Across several months, Tweets were consistently referencing an incident in the *Big Brother* house which many felt was exemplary of the epidemic of violence against women and machismo in Argentina. Although *Big Brother* is a reality television show, this shows an interesting 'pop culture' connection between social media users and reality television audiences. This kind of pop culture reference was not prevalent in the other campaigns.

a much more varied approach, with fewer consistent messages sending a coherent message and much less focus in the variable organic content. #niunamenos did lose its campaign focus over time, which may have contributed to the tactical concessions outcome with less long-term implementation. It is perhaps surprising then that the clear legal focus of #delhigangrape did not lead to more positive long-term outcomes. Even though #delhigangrape was generally persistent, there was a tail-off of Tweets over the life of the campaign. Perhaps had the campaign maintained a higher level of participation and visibility over a longer period of time, the focused nature of the Tweets themselves could have had a greater impact on the implementation of legal changes. The lack of visibility in the later months of the campaign may have rendered the consistent messaging less impactful.

These campaigns both showed a good presence of international norms, with 84 per cent of international norms analysed present in #delhigangrape and 87 per cent in #niunamenos. #niunamenos also showed the highest percentage of consistent and organic norms which are also international norms at 10 per cent. Inclusion of international norms is linked to campaign success.

Conclusion

These two campaigns exemplified the theoretical critique of the spiral model discussed in Chapter 2 which points to a problematic lack of progression through the model, with both countries engaging in tactical concessions but with little to no movement towards the spiral model theorized rule-consistent behaviour, echoing concerns in the feminist and slactivist literature on hashtag campaigns. It appears that the large public attention, driven by domestic users, in close proximity to potential regime change, could run the risk of stalling the process. Both campaigns showed extremely positive persistence parameters and very similar users driving the campaigns. Differences were seen in the engagement metrics and content analysis, which may have impacted in some of the differences in the components of legal change.

6

Possible Success: #women2drive

One campaign showed potentially positive results and can, tentatively, be categorized as a possible success. It is a complex story as the campaign did so much for women in Saudi and was considered a milestone success, but in the years since the government has cracked down on activism and activists who use social media in particular.[1] However some do still see the change as a watershed moment which has paved the way for other opportunities for women in Saudi.[2] This may just underscore the power of the campaign and how it forced the government to change. The campaign may therefore provide critical insight into what an 'ideal' hashtag campaign might look like from a feminist perspective.

#women2drive campaign overview

For decades, Saudi Arabia has enforced a ban on women driving. In modern times, Saudi was the only country to enforce such a ban. Beginning in 1990, women activists began to protest the ban by driving themselves.[3] The

---

[1] Time Magazine, 'After Lifting the Driving Ban, Saudi Arabia's War on Women Is Only Getting Worse' (*Time*, 10 April 2019) https://time.com/5567330/saudi-arabia-women-rights-drive/, accessed 17 November 2023.

[2] 'Roadblocks Still in Place for Saudi Women after Five Years of Driving' (*France 24*, 7 July 2023) https://www.france24.com/en/live-news/20230707-after-five-years-of-driv ing-roadblocks-remain-for-saudi-women-1, accessed 17 November 2023.

[3] 'Saudi Women Rejoice at End of Driving Ban' (*BBC News*, 27 September 2017) http:// www.bbc.co.uk/news/world-middle-east-41411799, accessed 29 November 2023; Human Rights Watch, 'Saudi Arabia: As Women's Driving Ban Ends, Provide Parity' (27 September 2017) https://www.hrw.org/news/2017/09/27/saudi-arabia-womens-driv ing-ban-ends-provide-parity, accessed 17 November 2023; Daily Mail, 'Saudi Women Protest Driving Ban in 1990' (*Daily Mail*, 27 September 2017) http://www.dailymail. co.uk/wires/ap/article-4924266/Saudi-women-protest-driving-ban-1990.html, accessed 17 November 2023.

first major driving protest resulted in the arrest of 47 women.[4] In 2011, a prominent Saudi activist, Manal al-Sharif, filmed herself driving and used social media (YouTube) to share, leading to her arrest and detention. The hashtag campaign went 'viral'. Driving protests first took place annually on 17 June and then on 26 October, with the 2013 October protest seeing the largest turnout.[5] Some activists point out that it was in the middle of the Arab Spring, giving a unique opportunity to reignite the protest movement.[6] In September 2017, the new King of Saudi announced that the ban would be lifted, starting in June 2018.

Many activists are said to have 'met' over Twitter through the hashtag campaign.[7] Nearly all media articles about #women2drive focus on Tweets.[8] '[Twitter] has proved to be a potent tool in many respects and is a constant reminder to the Government of the importance of public engagement, especially in relation to social and economic policies'[9] and 'social networking

---

4   Alexandra Johnson, 'Saudi Women Gain the Right to Drive' (Center for Security Policy, 2 October 2017) https://www.centerforsecuritypolicy.org/2017/10/02/saudi-women-gain-the-right-to-drive/, accessed 17 November 2023.

5   Human Rights Watch (n 3); 'Dozens of Saudi Arabian Women Drive Cars on Day of Protest against Ban' (*The Guardian*, 26 October 2013) http://www.theguardian.com/world/2013/oct/26/saudi-arabia-woman-driving-car-ban, accessed 29 November 2023.

6   Lan Anh Vu, 'How I Got There: Manal al-Sharif' (*Huffington Post*, 4 November 2016) https://www.huffingtonpost.com/lan-anh-vu/how-i-got-there-manal-als_b_12650 652.html, accessed 29 November 2023; Jason Burke, 'Saudi Arabia Women Test Driving Ban' (*The Guardian*, 17 June 2011) http://www.theguardian.com/world/2011/jun/17/saudi-arabia-women-drivers-protest, accessed 29 November 2023; Neil MacFarquhar, 'Saudis Arrest Woman Leading Right-to-Drive Campaign' (*The New York Times*, 23 May 2011) https://www.nytimes.com/2011/05/24/world/middleeast/24saudi.html, accessed 29 November 2023.

7   Laura Stampler, 'Saudia Arabian Women Launch Campaign For Right To Drive: But Will It Make A Difference?' (*HuffPost UK*, 17 June 2011) http://www.huffingtonpost.com/2011/06/17/saudi-arabia-women-drive_n_878884.html, accessed 29 November 2023; 'Saudi Authorities Detain Six Women for Driving' (*ArabianBusiness.com*, 10 June 2011) http://www.arabianbusiness.com/saudi-authorities-detain-six-women-for-driving-404597.html, accessed 17 November 2023.

8   See, for example, Robert Mackey, 'Saudi Women Drive, Despite Ban, and Find Some Support on the Kingdom's Roads' (*The New York Times*, 10 October 2013) //thelede.blogs.nytimes.com/2013/10/10/saudi-women-drive-despite-ban-and-find-some-support-on-the-kingdoms-roads/, accessed 29 November 2023; Team Position, 'Social Media Fuels #Women2Drive Campaign' (29 June 2011) https://web.archive.org/web/20160511185 001/https://blogs.position2.com/social-media-fuels-women2drive-campaign, accessed 17 November 2023.

9   'End of Mission Statement Special Rapporteur on Extreme Poverty and Human Rights, Professor Philip Alston on His Visit to Saudi Arabia' (OHCHR, 19 January 2017) http://www.ohchr.org/EN/NewsEvents/Pages/DisplayNews.aspx?NewsID=21094, accessed 17 November 2023.

sites such as Twitter and Facebook have been key for the women drivers, providing support networks and, crucially, publicity outside the kingdom'.[10]

The domestic activists driving this campaign publicly noted the importance of foreign pressure, in particular from the United States.[11] Many reports on the hashtag campaign focus on the role of US foreign policy.[12] Notably, at one point, Hillary Clinton stated that the United States was not actively involved in the campaign given Saudi's 'suspicion of foreign influence, especially Western influence', but she did note that the United States engaged in 'quiet diplomacy' on the issue.[13] Manal al-Sharif claims that it was pressure from Hillary Clinton and international non-governmental organizations, fuelled by social media, which led to her release.[14] Leaked cables indicate that the United States did put some pressure on Saudi officials to lift the ban.[15] Of note, the lifting of the ban was announced via state television in Saudi as well as a media event in Washington, DC.[16] This clearly indicates a desire to speak to and engage with Western influences.[17]

---

[10] Burke (n 6).

[11] Katherine Zoepf, 'What Overturning the Ban on Female Drivers Means for Saudi Arabia and the World' (*The New Yorker*, 12 October 2017) https://www.newyorker.com/news/news-desk/what-overturning-the-ban-on-female-drivers-means-for-saudi-arabia-and-the-world, accessed 13 February 2018.

[12] 'Hillary Clinton Backs Saudi Women Defying Driving Ban' (GulfNews.Com, 12 October 2013) http://gulfnews.com/news/gulf/saudi-arabia/hillary-clinton-backs-saudi-women-defying-driving-ban-1.1242231, accessed 17 November 2023.

[13] 'Clinton Adds Her Voice in Support of Saudi Women' (*The New York Times*, 22 June 2011) http://www.nytimes.com/2011/06/22/world/middleeast/22clinton.html, accessed 29 November 2023.

[14] Vu (n 6); 'Saudi Women Defy Ban to Take Driver's Seat' (*Al Jazeera*, 17 June 2011) http://www.aljazeera.com/video/middleeast/2011/06/201161713200141723.html, accessed 29 November 2023; John D Sutter, 'The Woman Who Defied Saudi's Driving Ban and Put It on YouTube' (*CNN*, 12 June 2012) https://edition.cnn.com/2012/06/10/world/meast/sharif-saudi-women-drive/index.html, accessed 29 November 2023; 'Freedom House Shows Solidarity with Saudi #Women2Drive Campaign' (25 October 2013) https://web.archive.org/web/20170423034810/https://freedomhouse.org/article/freedom-house-shows-solidarity-saudi-women2drive-campaign, accessed 17 November 2023.

[15] David Leigh, 'US Put Pressure on Saudi Arabia to Let Women Drive, Leaked Cables Reveal' (*The Guardian*, 27 May 2011) http://www.theguardian.com/world/2011/may/27/us-pressurised-saudis-let-women-drive, accessed 29 November 2023; 'Is This the Year Saudi Women Drive?' (Saudi Arabia Riyadh 2009) Wikileaks Public Library of US Diplomacy 09RIYADH357_a, https://wikileaks.org/plusd/cables/09RIYADH357_a.html, accessed 23 July 2024.

[16] Ben Hubbard, 'Saudi Arabia Agrees to Let Women Drive' (*The New York Times*, 26 September 2017) https://www.nytimes.com/2017/09/26/world/middleeast/saudi-arabia-women-drive.html, accessed 29 November 2023.

[17] Zoepf (n 11).

Al-Sharif in an interview two years after the ban was lifted said: 'Social media was the place where we could talk, where we could discuss – it was our virtual parliament.'[18]

Context

While the general measures of context in this study show that Saudi is neither the best nor the worst place for women and activism, some context which is not captured in the basic metrics is important to this campaign. As introduced earlier, #women2drive particularly and specifically used Twitter to reach and include Westerners as a strategic pressure point. A similar strategy was adopted around the 1990 protests: 'the drivers had intentionally looked to attract attention from the high number of foreign journalists who were in the kingdom covering the buildup to the first Gulf War'.[19] It seems that the first attempt to campaign with such a strategy did not work. Social media, however, opened a new door. This campaign was therefore more strategically driven from the outset, manifesting the positivism around digital feminist activism discussed in Chapter 2.

Many think that the legal changes resulting from this campaign are also part of a wider programme of modernization by the new, young, modern king who came to power in 2015 and, more importantly, the crown prince who came into power in 2017 just months before the ban was lifted.[20] That the campaign spanned regime change may indeed be important to its success. Given a whole range of changes that could have been made, activists agree that the social media attention this particular campaign garnered was a primary reason the crown prince chose to make *this* reform. Saudi women activists celebrated the move and largely attributed the lifting of the ban to the protest efforts over the years and the hashtag campaign.[21]

---

[18] Time Magazine (n 1).

[19] Zoepf (n 11).

[20] Katie Paul and Stephen Kalin, 'Saudi Women Can Drive at Last but Some Say Price Is Silence' (*Reuters*, February 2017) https://web.archive.org/web/20180709125334/https://uk.reuters.com/article/uk-saudi-women-driving-politics/saudi-women-can-drive-at-last-but-some-say-price-is-silence-idUKKCN1C71TJ, accessed 17 November 2023; Rothna Begum, 'Opinion: Give Saudi Women the Right to Drive' (*CNN*, 24 October 2013) https://edition.cnn.com/2013/10/24/opinion/begum-saudi-women-driving/index.html, accessed 17 November 2023.

[21] Chris Bell and Lina Shaikhouni, 'Saudi Women Driving Reform: "We Did It"' (*BBC News*, 27 September 2017) http://www.bbc.co.uk/news/blogs-trending-41412237, accessed 29 November 2023.

Legal outcomes

This campaign showed the most positive successes, not just in the change in legislation, as this was also seen in the tactical concession's campaigns, but also in institutionalization and dialogue with United Nations (UN) human rights mechanisms. #women2drive showed poor outcomes in law enforcement, particularly as women activists continue to be arrested, detained, and charged for unrelated activities. Additionally, guardianship laws remain in place which call into question the true status of women in the country.

Legislative change

Since 1957, women had been legally banned from driving, unable to obtain a licence and risking arrest for being caught driving. Women relied on male guardians or chauffeurs for transportation.[22] Although it is technically a royal decree and more recently a fatwa (not a law per se), several administrative laws brought it into force, such as traffic laws which did not allow the issuing of licences to women.[23] The original rationale behind the introduction of the ban was of a religious, cultural, and social nature. One piece of evidence stated that 'the grand mufti claimed that allowing women to drive would result in public mixing of women, put women into dangerous situations because they could be alone in cars, and therefore result in social chaos'.[24] Activists also refer to it as a 'societal norm'.[25] Some commentators are of the view that the ban came less from the royal family and more as a means to appease hard-line clerics over the years.[26] Again, this is a story that was seen across several of the legal issues in this study – religious leaders versus elected politicians.

---

[22] Johnson (n 4).

[23] Hubbard (n 16); Harriet Alexander, 'Saudi Arabia to Allow Women to Drive in Major Milestone for Country' (*The Telegraph*, 26 September 2017) http://www.telegraph.co.uk/news/2017/09/26/saudi-arabia-allow-women-drive/, accessed 17 November 2023.

[24] Elizabeth Flock, 'Saudi Arabian Women Banned from Driving Because of Fatwa against Gender "Mixing"' (*The Washington Post*, 6 June 2011) https://www.washingtonpost.com/blogs/blogpost/post/fatwa-against-gender-mixing-prevents-saudi-women-from-driving-according-to-wikileaks-cable/2011/06/06/AGVVTDKH_blog.html?utm_term=.b836f08b6f24, accessed 29 November 2023.

[25] Vu (n 6).

[26] Jane Kinninmont, 'End of Saudi Women Driving Ban Reflects Deep Changes in Society' (*BBC News*, 27 September 2017) http://www.bbc.co.uk/news/world-middle-east-41412022, accessed 29 November 2023; 'Saudi Women Rejoice at End of Driving Ban' (n 3); 'Dozens of Saudi Arabian Women Drive Cars on Day of Protest against Ban' (n 5); Burke (n 6).

Protests against the ban started in 1990.[27] After the 1990 protest, rather than lifting or easing the ban, the religious conservatives expressed backlash and in fact strengthened the ban with a religious fatwa. In response, the government then issued a decree to solidify the ban.[28]

In 2008, a similar protest effort emerged from women but with much less following and much less success. The activists had been encouraged by what they thought was a softening of the government.[29] In November 2007, the foreign minister told the press that he thought women should be allowed to drive and that the ban was a social, not political, issue for 'the people to decide'.[30] Yet no progress was made. In 2010, reports again emerged that the ban might be lifted.[31] The #women2drive hashtag rose to international prominence in 2011.

Discussions around lifting the ban started in November 2014, after a full three years of online campaigning driving offline activities. Many felt that the conversation started because of the 'feminist cyber-activism'.[32] At the time, the contemplation over lifting the ban was limited to women over the age of 30, only during the day, and with a male guardian.[33] Some local news outlets even outright denied that discussions were taking place.[34]

Interestingly, just a year earlier, Prince Saud told local media outlets that the Saudi community 'is not convinced about women driving' and 'women driving is not a religious issue as much as it is an issue that relates to the community itself that either accepts it or refuses it'.[35] This very much

---

[27] 'Saudi Women Rejoice at End of Driving Ban' (n 3); Human Rights Watch (n 3); Daily Mail (n 3).

[28] Begum (n 20).

[29] Faiza Saleh Ambah, 'Saudi Women See a Brighter Road on Rights' (*Washington Post*, 31 January 2008) http://www.washingtonpost.com/wp-dyn/content/article/2008/01/30/AR2008013003805.html, accessed 29 November 2023.

[30] Ibid.

[31] Fahad Faruqui, 'Saudi Women Get in the Driver's Seat' (*The Guardian*, 5 May 2010) https://www.theguardian.com/commentisfree/2010/may/05/saudi-women-drivers-seat, accessed 29 November 2023.

[32] Huda Mohsin, 'Cyberactivism: The Case of the Women2Drive Movement in Saudi Arabia' (F come) https://web.archive.org/web/20160608122432/http://www.fcome.org/portfolio-view/cyberactivism-the-case-of-the-women2drive-movement-in-saudi-arabia/, accessed 17 November 2023.

[33] 'Saudi Activists Call for the Release of Women Detained for Driving' (*The New York Times*, 9 December 2014) https://www.nytimes.com/2014/12/09/world/middleeast/saudi-activists-call-for-the-release-of-women-detained-for-driving.html, accessed 29 November 2023.

[34] Ibid.

[35] Jess Staufenberg, 'Saudi Arabia Is "not Ready" for Women Drivers, Says Deputy Crown Prince' (*The Independent*, 28 April 2016) http://www.independent.co.uk/news/world/middle-east/saudi-arabia-is-not-ready-for-women-drivers-says-deputy-crown-prince-mohammed-bin-salman-a7004611.html, accessed 29 November 2023.

reflects the discourse from before the campaign. This indicates that, if the government truly thought of this as a social issue for the people to decide, then the social media campaign in particular would be well positioned to see success, demonstrating some of the more positive theories around the effectiveness of hashtag campaigns.

In September 2017, the new king announced that the ban would be lifted and women could apply for driving licences from June 2018.[36] Although some sceptics see it as a concession used by the Saudi government to divert attention away from other human rights abuses,[37] it is more generally felt that the strength of the campaign likely led to the decision to lift the ban as part of the larger programme of modernization and moving away from the stronghold of the hard-line conservative clerics.[38] In other words, had it not been for #women2drive and the social media pressure and attention, perhaps other issues would have benefited from the programme of modernization.[39] Saudi women activists celebrated the move and largely attributed the lifting of the ban to the protest efforts over the years and the hashtag campaign.[40] 'Brave women's driving activists were the tip of the iceberg.'[41] One female activist called it a 'great victory', while another said things would 'never be the same again'.[42]

In the years since the initial study, further legislative change has been implemented – some positive and some not. For example, the laws around dress codes for women have been dropped, dramatically changing women's

---

[36] Johnson (n 4); Hubbard (n 16); 'Saudi Arabia to Allow Women to Drive' (*Al Jazeera*, 27 September 2017) http://www.aljazeera.com/news/2017/09/saudi-arabia-women-drive-170926190857109.html, accessed 29 November 2023; Human Rights Watch (n 3).

[37] Human Rights Watch (n 3); Zoepf (n 11); Human Rights Watch, 'Human Rights Abuses Stemming from Male Guardianship and Sex Segregation in Saudi Arabia' (2008) https://www.hrw.org/report/2008/04/19/perpetual-minors/human-rights-abuses-stemming-male-guardianship-and-sex, accessed 15 February 2018; Human Rights Watch, 'Saudi Arabia: Repression Overshadows Women's Reforms' (2018) https://www.hrw.org/news/2018/01/18/saudi-arabia-repression-overshadows-womens-reforms, accessed 15 February 2018; ' "Battle of the Sexes": Saudi Men React to Women Driving' (*Dhaka Tribune*, 4 October 2017) https://web.archive.org/web/20171006172747/http://www.dhakatrib une.com/world/middle-east/2017/10/04/saudi-men-react-women-driving/, accessed 17 November 2023.

[38] Kinninmont (n 26); 'Saudi Arabia to Allow Women to Drive' (n 36); Ben Hubbard, 'Saudi Arabia's Driving Ban and the Pioneering Women Who Got It Lifted' (*The Independent*, 18 October 2017) http://www.independent.co.uk/news/world/middle-east/saudi-ara bia-driving-ban-women-protestors-who-lifted-fought-against-sexist-law-a7993306.html, accessed 29 November 2023.

[39] Kinninmont (n 26).

[40] Bell and Shaikhouni (n 21).

[41] Kinninmont (n 26).

[42] 'Saudi Women Rejoice at End of Driving Ban' (n 3).

place in the public sphere.[43] Harassment laws have also been reformed to better protect women in public.[44]

Institutionalization

Discourse from those in power in Saudi Arabia had indicated for many years a lack of institutionalization of women's rights norms, with religious clerics being particularly outspoken and derogatory towards women.[45] However, in more recent years the split between hard-line conservatives and those looking to move towards a more liberal way of life became apparent. In 2005, in an interview with American reporter Barbara Walters, King Abdullah said: 'I believe strongly in the rights of women, my mother is a woman, my sister is a woman, my daughter is a woman, my wife is a woman. I believe the day will come when women drive.'[46] Four years later in 2009, Saudi royal Prince Waleed made statements that seemed to indicate the ban would be overturned. However, shortly thereafter when King Abdullah appointed a woman to a governmental position of power and opened a mixed-sex university, there was significant backlash.[47] Quotes from clerics included denouncing 'the King's teaching of deviant ideas such as evolution', 'mixing with women ... [would] open the field for them to undertake jobs for which they were not created', and that women had 'abandoned their basic duties such as housekeeping, bringing up children ... and replaced this by beautifying themselves and wantonness'.[48] This tension continued into and throughout the campaign, and is still palpable now that the ban has been lifted. Yet it appears that, while before the campaign the religious conservatives had the dominant discourse, now the pendulum has swung and the more liberal, arguably Western, voices have more of a say, perhaps influenced by the voice of society on social media. This campaign then tends to query the theoretical critiques of the spiral model, demonstrating that strategically managed

---

[43] Hanaa Almoaibed, 'License to Drive Change: The Status of Saudi Women under Vision 2030' (2023) https://blogs.lse.ac.uk/mec/2023/01/10/license-to-drive-change-the-status-of-saudi-women-under-vision-2030/, accessed 9 November 2023.

[44] Alison Pittaway, 'Four Years of Women Drivers in Saudi, What Has Changed?' (*Global Fleet*, 30 March 2022) https://www.globalfleet.com/en/taxation-and-legislation/global/features/four-years-women-drivers-saudi-what-has-changed, accessed 9 November 2023.

[45] Hubbard (n 38).

[46] 'One Day Women Will Drive, Saudi King Says' (*ABC News*, 14 October 2005) http://www.abc.net.au/news/2005-10-14/one-day-women-will-drive-saudi-king-says/2124474, accessed 29 November 2023; see also Begum (n 20).

[47] Flock (n 24).

[48] Ibid.

social media campaigns *can* potentially lead to legal change as specified by the model.

Before the 26 October 2013 driving protest, the government made it clear that protests would not be tolerated.[49] Specifically referring to the protests organized over social networks, the government said that demonstrations of such nature were legally prohibited in the Kingdom.[50] Amnesty International responded and called upon the government to allow the public protests.[51] After the 26 October 2013 driving protest, the #women2drive website was shut down in Saudi Arabia, but an online petition fuelled by the hashtag still managed to collect somewhere between 14,000 and 16,000 signatures.[52]

After a loosening on women's ability to sit on the Shura Council (the country's legislative assembly), three women on the council just before the October 2013 driving protest publicly stated that women should be allowed to drive.[53] The Council, however, rejected this, claiming that since only three members of the Shura brought the proposal it was considered an individual recommendation which is not part of the Council's remit. The same year, after another major driving protest, clerics organized a counter-protest outside the royal palace.[54] One hundred and fifty clerics gathered to protest *against* women driving.[55] 'We came here for many issues, most

---

[49] 'Saudi Arabia Issues Warning against Women's Driving Campaign' (*Foreign Policy*, 25 October 2013) https://foreignpolicy.com/2013/10/25/saudi-arabia-issues-warning-against-womens-driving-campaign/, accessed 14 February 2018; 'Kingdom of Saudi Arabia – Statement on Female Driving Protest' (Genius) https://genius.com/Kingdom-of-saudi-arabia-statement-on-female-driving-protest-annotated, accessed 17 November 2023; Mohammed Jamjoom, 'Saudi Arabia Issues Warning to Women Drivers, Protesters' (*CNN*, 24 October 2013) https://www.cnn.com/2013/10/24/world/meast/saudi-ara bia-women-drivers/index.html, accessed 29 November 2023.

[50] Mohammed Jamjoom, 'Saudi Government Says Laws Will Be Enforced on "Female Driving" Day' (*CNN*, 23 October 2013) https://edition.cnn.com/2013/10/23/world/meast/saudi-arabia-women-drivers/index.html, accessed 29 November 2023.

[51] 'Saudi Arabia Must Not Thwart Campaign for Women Drivers' (Amnesty, 24 October 2013) https://www.amnesty.org/en/latest/news/2013/10/saudi-arabia-must-not-thw art-campaign-women-drivers/, accessed 17 November 2023.

[52] Jasmine Bager, 'Forbidden to Drive: A Saudi Woman On Life Inside the Kingdom' (*Time*, 25 October 2013) http://ideas.time.com/2013/10/25/forbidden-to-drive-a-saudi-woman-on-life-inside-the-kingdom/, accessed 14 February 2018.

[53] '3 Saudi Shura Council Women Urge Female Drive Ban Lifted' (*Daily Nation*, 8 October 2013) https://www.nation.co.ke/lifestyle/women/3-Saudi-Shura-Council-women-urge-female-drive-ban-lifted/1950830-2024144-12mi5dsz/index.html, accessed 17 November 2023.

[54] Alexander (n 23).

[55] 'Saudi Clerics Protest Outside King's Palace, Blame US for Women Driving' (*Mehr News Agency*, 23 October 2013) https://en.mehrnews.com/news/56993/Saudi-clerics-prot est-outside-king-s-palace-blame-US-for-women, accessed 29 November 2023.

importantly to combat Westernization and particularly women', claimed one cleric, notably (ironically?) using YouTube to convey his message.[56] Another cleric accused the campaign of being driven by the United States as the protest was advertised with a Western date and not an Islamic one.[57] One cleric went so far as to state that driving would harm women's ovaries and would lead to birth defects.[58] As late as 2017, a cleric was quoted as saying that women have only 'half the brains of men', adding that the figure drops to one quarter 'when they go to market', claiming that allowing them to drive would therefore be unsafe.[59] However, this time the cleric was suspended from preaching and all religious activity after his comments.[60] Unsurprisingly, Twitter users reacted to his statement, using an Arabic hashtag 'Al-Hijri-women-quarter-brain'.[61]

The royal family and the government began showing signs of change as the campaign progressed. In 2016, Prince Alwaleed bin Talal released a lengthy statement titled 'it is high time that Saudi women started driving their cars'.[62] He likened the ban to restrictions on access to education or employment, both of which are rights which Saudi women already had. He detailed several factors, including financial, economic, social, religious, and political.[63] Bin Talal's wife, Princess Ameerah Al-Taweel, was also outspoken about women's rights, stating in a US interview that she saw nothing in religion that forbid women from driving.[64] Both the Council of Senior Scholars (the

---

[56] 'Saudi Clerics Protest Women Driving at the Royal Court' (Riyadh Bureau) https://riyadhbureau.wordpress.com/tag/royal-court/, accessed 17 November 2023.

[57] 'Saudi Clerics Protest Outside King's Palace, Blame US for Women Driving' (n 55).

[58] 'Driving Damages Women's Ovaries: Saudi Cleric' (*Al Akhbar English*, 29 September 2013) https://web.archive.org/web/20171019231115/http://english.al-akhbar.com/content/driving-damages-womens-ovaries-saudi-cleric, accessed 17 November 2023; 'Cleric Says Driving Risk to Ovaries' (*BBC News*, 29 September 2013) http://www.bbc.co.uk/news/world-middle-east-24323934, accessed 29 November 2023.

[59] Manal Al-Sharif, 'Opinion: I Can't Wait to Drive in Saudi Arabia Again' (*The New York Times*, 27 September 2017) https://www.nytimes.com/2017/09/27/opinion/saudi-arabia-women-driving-.html, accessed 29 November 2023.

[60] Nadia Khomami, 'Saudi Cleric Banned for Saying Women's Brains "a Quarter the Size" of Men's' (*The Guardian*, 23 September 2017) http://www.theguardian.com/world/2017/sep/23/saudi-cleric-saad-al-hijri-banned-woman-driving-cars-quarter-brain, accessed 29 November 2023.

[61] Ibid.

[62] 'It's High Time That Saudi Woman Started Driving Their Cars' (*Alwaleed*, 24 November 2016) https://web.archive.org/web/20161231043133/http://www.alwaleed.com.sa/news-and-media/news/driving/, accessed 17 November 2023.

[63] Ibid.

[64] 'Saudi Princess Lobbies For Women's Right To Drive' (NPR.org, 14 July 2011) https://www.npr.org/2011/07/14/137840538/saudi-princess-lobbies-for-womens-right-to-drive, accessed 17 November 2023.

top clerical body) and the head of the morality police eventually agreed that allowing women to drive could be done in accordance with *Shari'a* law and that driving per se was not a religious violation.[65]

The delay between announcing the lifting of the ban and the implementation was seen to be to make it easier to adjust for the clerics.[66] This delay is, however, a major difference between the tactical concessions campaigns and this potential success campaign, as it indicates the regime's intention to properly implement the change over time, rather than a reactionary and hasty legislative move to quell waves of public outrage.

Unfortunately, the move towards institutionalization is far from complete. Some rumours circulated after the ban was lifted, claiming that the government had contacted activists telling them to keep silent, to downplay the role of activism in the lifting of the ban.[67] This was denied by the government.[68] The longer-term picture is complex. The public and economic sphere is positive, with over 174,000 driving licences having been issued to women, seven women-only driving schools, a Saudi woman Formula E racer, and an extraordinary growth of women in employment, now making up over 30 per cent of the workforce.[69] Moves have been made to 'dismantle' the guardianship system.[70] In July 2022, two women secured key roles in the government.[71] Notably, women have significant reproductive rights in Saudi.[72] However, the private sphere seems to remain a place of discrimination against women, with a recent strengthening of the private guardianship laws.[73] The government claims, publicly, that the new

---

[65] Hubbard (n 16); 'Saudi Arabia to Allow Women to Drive' (n 36); see also ' "Battle of the Sexes": Saudi Men React to Women Driving' (n 37); Human Rights Watch (n 3); 'Saudi Women Driving Ban Not Part of Sharia-Morality Police Chief' (*Reuters*, 19 September 2013) https://www.reuters.com/article/us-saudi-women-driving/saudi-women-driv ing-ban-not-part-of-sharia-morality-police-chief-idUSBRE98I0LJ20130919, accessed 23 July 2024.

[66] Kinninmont (n 26).

[67] Hubbard (n 38); see also Paul and Kalin (n 20); Hubbard (n 38).

[68] Paul and Kalin (n 20).

[69] Alison (n 44); ibid.

[70] Human Rights Watch, 'Saudi Arabia: Important Advances for Saudi Women' (Human Rights Watch, 2019) https://www.hrw.org/news/2019/08/02/saudi-arabia-important-advances-saudi-women, accessed 9 November 2023.

[71] Alison (n 44).

[72] The New Arab, 'Greater Abortion Access in Saudi Arabia than in US States' (*The New Arab*, 25 June 2022) https://www.newarab.com/news/greater-abortion-access-saudi-ara bia-us-states, accessed 17 November 2023.

[73] Human Rights Watch, 'Saudi Arabia: Law Enshrines Male Guardianship' (Human Rights Watch, 2023) https://www.hrw.org/news/2023/03/08/saudi-arabia-law-enshrines-male-guardianship, accessed 9 November 2023.

Personal Status Law is progressive for women, but in reality it represents a step backwards in the private sphere.[74]

Law enforcement

As soon as women began the driving protests many years ago, there were arrests, detentions, and confiscation of passports.[75] Forty-seven women were arrested at the 1990 driving protest. They were not released from custody until their male guardians signed statements confirming that the women would not drive again.[76] This practice continued for years throughout the country. In 2010, American female drivers were hired to drive the Saudi royal family on a visit in Minnesota in the United States. The women were fired from that job for being female.[77] Notably, the drivers brought a case of discrimination in the United States, and won, but damages from the Saudis have not emerged.[78]

Arrests carried on once the hashtag campaign took off.[79] The first major protest drive from the hashtag campaign took place in 2011, leading to the documenting of 70 women who once again had to sign statements that they would not drive again.[80] Most famously, after Manal al-Sharif filmed herself driving and posted it on YouTube, she was arrested and detained for more than a week.[81] According to Amnesty International, she was only released when she pledged to not participate in any further driving protests. The official headline after the arrest was to underscore that driving was illegal for women.[82] Some women when arrested for driving as part of the protests were asked not only to sign a statement that they would not drive again,

---

[74]   Ibid.

[75]   Johnson (n 4); Hubbard (n 38).

[76]   Human Rights Watch (n 3); see also Hubbard (n 38).

[77]   'Driving Out Oppression' (*Gender Justice*) https://www.genderjustice.us/work/driving-out-oppression/, accessed 17 November 2023.

[78]   Ibid.

[79]   Sabria Jawhar, 'Saudi Religious Police Clamp Down on Rural Women Drivers' (*Huffington Post*, 18 March 2010) https://www.huffingtonpost.com/sabria-jawhar/saudi-religious-pol ice-cl_b_320071.html, accessed 29 November 2023; 'Five Saudi Women Drivers Arrested, Says Activist' (*The Guardian*, 29 June 2011) http://www.theguardian.com/world/2011/ jun/29/saudi-women-drivers-arrested-jiddah, accessed 29 November 2023.

[80]   Alexander (n 23); Johnson (n 4); Begum (n 20).

[81]   Robert Mackey, 'A Saudi Activist, in Her Own Words' (*The Lede – The New York Times*, 31 May 2011) https://thelede.blogs.nytimes.com/2011/05/31/a-saudi-activist-in-her-own-words/, accessed 17 November 2023.

[82]   Stampler (n 7).

but also that they would not film themselves or any other women driving.[83] Prominent activist Wajiha Howeidar stated in response: 'Usually, they just make you sign a paper that you will not do it again and let you go. They don't want anybody to think that they can get away with something like that. It is a clear message that you cannot organize anything on Facebook.'[84] Then, in September 2011, between the 17 June and 26 October driving protests, a woman was sentenced to ten lashes, the first time this kind of legal punishment was used against women for driving.[85] Many found the sentence surprising, given that it came just one day after the announcement that women would have the right to vote and run in the next general election.[86] At the time, activists saw the sentencing as evidence of the power of the hard-line conservatives over the courts and the police in Saudi.[87] Human Rights Watch officials stated that the courts were being used 'to send a message that they won't tolerate any attempt to alleviate the dismal status of women's rights in the kingdom'.[88] Her sentence was eventually overturned by the king.[89]

In 2014, an activist was arrested attempting to drive into Saudi from the United Arab Emirates.[90] She used Twitter to keep followers updated as she attempted to cross.[91] She was arrested and detained for 73 days, alongside another activist who came to help her.[92] Their initial detention

---

[83] Mohammed Jamjoom, 'Saudi Blogger Detained, but Hopeful about Push to Let Women Drive' (CNN, 11 October 2013) https://www.cnn.com/2013/10/11/world/meast/saudi-arabia-women-drivers/index.html, accessed 29 November 2023.

[84] MacFarquhar (n 6).

[85] 'Saudi Woman to Get 10 Lashes for Driving a Car' (CBS News, 27 September 2011) https://www.cbsnews.com/news/saudi-woman-to-get-10-lashes-for-driving-a-car/, accessed 29 November 2023; see also 'Saudi Woman "Spared Lashing" in Driving Case' (Al Jazeera, 28 September 2011) http://www.aljazeera.com/news/middleeast/2011/09/201192820341050915.html, accessed 29 November 2023.

[86] 'Saudi Woman "Spared Lashing" in Driving Case' (n 85).

[87] Ibid.

[88] Human Rights Watch, 'Saudi Arabia: Activists Convicted for Answering Call for Help' (Human Rights Watch, 17 June 2013) https://www.hrw.org/news/2013/06/17/saudi-arabia-activists-convicted-answering-call-help, accessed 17 November 2023.

[89] 'Saudi Woman's Lashing "Revoked"' (BBC News, 29 September 2011) http://www.bbc.co.uk/news/world-middle-east-15102190, accessed 29 November 2023.

[90] 'Saudi Woman "Arrested" for Driving' (Al Jazeera, 5 December 2014) http://www.aljazeera.com/news/middleeast/2014/12/saudi-woman-arrested-driving-2014121165739368209.html, accessed 29 November 2023.

[91] 'Saudi Woman Driving Blog "Arrest"' (BBC News, 3 December 2014) http://www.bbc.co.uk/news/blogs-trending-30316837, accessed 29 November 2023.

[92] Hubbard (n 16); 'Saudi Woman Driving Blog "Arrest"' (n 91).

was then extended by 25 days.[93] This was the longest detention for driving in recent years.[94] She was released only when she signed a statement that she would never speak out 'in videos' again; she claims she negotiated this specific wording so that she could continue to use Twitter to campaign for women's rights in Saudi.[95] Notably, she also announced her release on Twitter.[96]

Since the lifting of the ban, but before it came into effect, there was only one report of a woman being 'penalized', though not arrested, for driving.[97] However in the years since the ban, activists have been targeted for arrest and detention.[98] According to Human Rights Watch, while most are released, some remain in detention or have been convicted.[99] This remains the preferred tool of repression of the government – while public-facing laws and policies are progressive and introduce important changes, the voice of civil society and activism (feminist activism in particular) is continually silenced.

UN dialogue

Saudi Arabia is party to several international treaties, though notably not the Convention on Civil and Political Rights (CCPR) or the Convention on Economic, Social, and Cultural Rights (CESCR), ratifying the Convention on the Elimination of all Forms of Discrimination Against Women (CEDAW) in 2000. As expected, Saudi submitted a reservation of the primacy of Islamic law. The first CEDAW report was submitted in 2007, where the state claimed that 'generally, there is no discrimination against women in the laws of the Kingdom'.[100] The report is filled with references

---

[93] 'Saudi Arabia Extends Detention of Women Driving Activists: Amnesty' (*The Express Tribune*, 9 December 2014) https://tribune.com.pk/story/804221/saudi-arabia-extends-detention-of-women-driving-activists-amnesty/, accessed 17 November 2023.

[94] Ibid.

[95] Roula Khalaf, 'Loujain Alhathloul on How Saudi Women Won the Right to Drive' (*Financial Times*, 7 December 2017) https://www.ft.com/content/b4186c36-da18-11e7-a039-c64b1c09b482, accessed 17 November 2023.

[96] Robert Mackey, 'Saudi Women Free After 73 Days in Jail for Driving' (*The New York Times*, 12 February 2015) https://www.nytimes.com/2015/02/13/world/middleeast/saudi-women-free-after-73-days-in-jail-for-driving.html, accessed 29 November 2023.

[97] 'Saudi Woman Penalised for Driving Car before Ban Is Lifted' (*The Guardian*, 9 October 2017) https://www.theguardian.com/world/2017/oct/09/saudi-arabia-woman-penalised-driving-car-before-ban-lifted, accessed 29 November 2023.

[98] Human Rights Watch (n 70); Time Magazine (n 1); 'Roadblocks Still in Place for Saudi Women after Five Years of Driving' (n 2).

[99] Human Rights Watch (n 70).

[100] Committee on the Elimination of Discrimination Against Women, 'Combined Initial and Second Periodic Reports of States Parties Saudi Arabia' (2007) UN Doc CEDAW/C/SAU/2.

to and framing of rights in Islam. The word Islam or Islamic is used 46 times in the report. In response, the committee specifically addressed the lack of discussion of the driving ban.[101] The driving ban was brought up in session as well.[102] The government responded:

> In the early days of Islam, women had ridden donkeys and camels; the question of their right to drive cars was not covered by sharia or secular law, but rather by traditional mentalities that influenced decision makers. ... When those attitudes changed ... women would be able to drive ... the Government needed to study the issue and to deal with it quietly so that the people would not think that the nation's sovereignty was being threatened.[103]

The committee included the issue in concluding observations.[104] This discourse seems to indicate a willingness to change, but in a way that could be properly institutionalized over time. This reads as a positive indication of the government's approach to the issue, especially when compared to other state reports from countries such as Iran and India.

After the campaign, there was some movement in the dialogue with the UN, particularly around the time the announcement was made that the ban would be lifted. Although again not a complete shift, positive change can be detected. However, it did take time. After the election of Saudi to the Human Rights Council in 2013, there was much controversy. In 2015, Amnesty International submitted a statement to the Human Rights Council on Saudi's participation as a member.[105] In a second report it specifically referred to the campaign.[106]

Shifts, however, were reported by Special Rapporteur Philip Alston after his 2017 mission to Saudi. After pointing out areas of progress and problems,

---

[101] Committee on the Elimination of Discrimination Against Women, 'List of Issues Saudi Arabia' (2007) UN Doc CEDAW/C/SAU/Q/2 para 7.

[102] Committee on the Elimination of Discrimination Against Women, 'Summary Record of the 816th Meeting' (2008) UN Doc CEDAW/C/SR.816 para 70.

[103] Ibid, 78.

[104] Committee on the Elimination of Discrimination Against Women, 'Concluding Comments Saudi Arabia' (2008) UN Doc CEDAW/C/SAU/CO/2 para 15.

[105] Amnesty International, 'Written Statement Submitted by Amnesty International, a Non-Governmental Organization in Special Consultative Status' (2015) UN Doc A/HRC/28/NGO/19.

[106] Amnesty International, 'Saudi Arabia: Is This What Is to Be Expected of a UN Human Rights Council Member (Part 2)?' (21 May 2015). 'Women who supported the Women2Drive campaign, launched in 2011 to challenge the prohibition on women driving vehicles, faced harassment and intimidation by the authorities, and were threatened with arrest and detention. Some were arrested but released after a short period.'

he went on to state: 'As in almost every country today, societal change is driven by both external and internal factors, and Saudi Arabia is now an integral and deeply connected part of the global system.'[107] Upon the lifting of the ban, Alston commented:

> In January, I praised Vision 2030, the country's change agenda, as an ambitious and deeply transformative plan that could be a catalyst for women's rights. The end of the driving ban is of crucial importance for Vision 2030 because it unlocks the economic potential of women in the Kingdom, especially those women living in poverty.[108]

The work recently undertaken by Alston shows a possible change in the dialogue and engagement with international human rights mechanisms. There are still concerns, but the general discourse and agendas seem to cautiously indicate some positive progress.

Twitter characteristics

#women2drive was the third largest campaign with 88,100 Tweets analysed. Thirty-eight per cent of those were in a language other than English, which is fairly representative of the target audience given the strategy outlined earlier.

Persistence (Tweets per day)

This was the second longest running campaign, shorter only than #stopstoning. In total, 2,033 days were analysed. What this campaign exhibited was not necessarily the highest or the most peaks, but the most

---

[107] 'End of Mission Statement Special Rapporteur on Extreme Poverty and Human Rights, Professor Philip Alston on His Visit to Saudi Arabia' (n 9); Human Rights Council, 'Report of the Special Rapporteur on Extreme Poverty and Human Rights on His Mission to Saudi Arabia' (2017) UN Doc A/HRC/35/26/Add.3. 'Most officials suggest that the Government is not opposed to abolishing the ban on driving or eliminating many of the guardianship restrictions, but they quickly add that important elements in society remain opposed. However, the Government cannot just remove itself from those debates. It has obligations to respect and promote the human rights of women, as acknowledged in the context of the universal periodic review, and it should seek to educate and inform the general public, especially in relation to any traditional and community practices that seek to deny basic rights to any group. It is also important to note that when systematic surveys of public opinion have been undertaken, a clear majority has in fact favoured letting women drive' (para 49)

[108] OHCHR, 'End to Saudi Driving Ban for Women Should Be Just the First Step' (28 September 2017) http://www.ohchr.org/EN/NewsEvents/Pages/DisplayNews. aspx?NewsID=22179&LangID=E, accessed 17 November 2023.

Figure 6.1: Number of Tweets per day up to 1,000, #women2drive

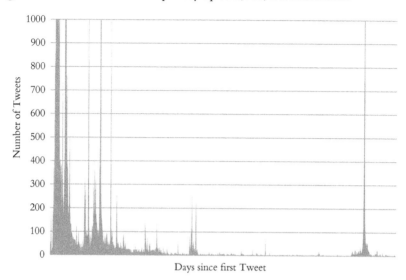

sustained and consistent activity. Sixty-one per cent of the total days in the campaign showed at least one Tweet. #women2drive also showed the second highest percentage of days with more than five Tweets at 26 per cent (#niunamenos was significantly higher at 84 per cent). Notably, a comparatively small percentage of Tweets were in peaks – 32 per cent.

As compared to other campaigns, Figure 6.1 shows a high level of persistence, with mid to high peaks continuing long into the campaign. The kinds of events which correlate to the peaks change over time as well. The first driving protests resulted in peaks, followed by the arrest of an activist for driving. The next peak was the lashing sentence for another activist. Another large-scale driving protest resulted in a peak two years into the campaign. This study did not collect any data after November 2016 which pre-dated the announcement of the lifting of the ban and the changes to the law. It is very much expected that there would be large peaks at that time.

Looking at the Tweets over time in more detail (up to 200 Tweets in Figure 6.2 as opposed to 1,000 in Figure 6.1), it becomes very clear that this campaign was extremely persistent, with very consistent, albeit low levels, of Tweeting throughout the campaign. This is one aspect of this campaign that is markedly different from the others. The other campaigns did not show the same levels of consistency. Although this campaign did not show many extreme metrics in persistence, it was a very low-level persistent campaign, which could be one of the reasons behind its success. This campaign overcame the lack of progression theoretical critique of the

Figure 6.2: Number of Tweets per day up to 200, #women2drive

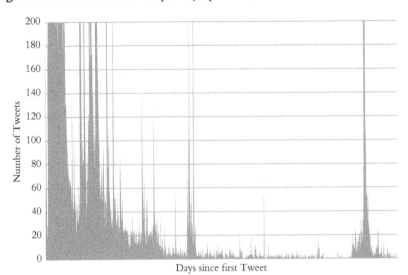

spiral model, proving that social media campaigns *can* exert long-term and sustained pressure on decision makers.

Engagement (retweets, likes, and replies)

As might be hypothesized based on the level of consistency seen here, #women2drive showed very high levels of uniform engagement across the campaign. #women2drive had the lowest like to Tweet ratio, indicating that very few individuals participating in the online campaign simply clicked 'like' to engage. More individuals retweeted than other engagement metrics, which again shows consistent messaging. The ratios of replies, retweets, and likes to Tweets were extremely similar in peak and non-peak periods, showing very little variation. One could say that this campaign was 'slow and steady' to win the race.

Users (profiles of the 100 most active users)

As seen earlier in this chapter, attracting foreign users was a strategic cornerstone of this campaign. This strategy, given the political context of Saudi Arabia, may have contributed to some of the campaign's success. Also, as noted earlier, #women2drive was a very *consistent* campaign. This is reflected in some of the user metrics as well. #women2drive was one of only two campaigns with more unique users in non-peak periods than in peak periods. This is a good indication of the stability of #women2drive, where the campaign itself was less volatile around peak periods. Having more unique users in non-peak periods shows the ongoing nature of the campaign, attracting continued, if lower levels, of attention throughout the campaign. This was not just a campaign which gained participants during high coverage events, but rather individuals show continued and ongoing interest in the campaign by participating outside of peak, viral events. Adding to these campaign characteristics, #women2drive showed the second highest average Tweets per user at 3.81 (#letwomengotostadium was top with 4.28). Those who were involved in this campaign were very involved, Tweeting on average almost four times.

One of the most prominent activists in #women2drive was Manal al-Sharif. She herself accounted for 15 per cent of the Tweets from the 100 most active users. She sent out a total of 290 Tweets, placing her in the top ten of the most active. This is an important finding in this campaign, showing that while there was a strategic choice to appeal to foreigners, the campaign was still primarily driven by domestic activists who had the knowledge and experience to accurately represent the situation of women living in Saudi Arabia. The most active user is a Saudi individual who Tweeted 1,802 times in this campaign. Interestingly, the second most prolific user in #women2drive self-labelled as a 'Saudi-American', living in the United States but Tweeting in both English and Arabic.

Overall, 44 per cent of the 100 most active users were from Saudi Arabia, accounting for 48 per cent of the Tweets from the most active users. Having a strong domestic individual voice is statistically significant for positive legal outcomes. Non-domestic users had more reach, however, accounting for 61 per cent. This is line with the strategic goals of the campaign, where it seems that Saudi women themselves were steering the campaign but achieving a global reach to increase foreign pressure.

Figure 6.3 shows the percentage share of users, campaign Tweets, and reach of the top 100 most active accounts, disaggregated across domestic and non-domestic locations. #women2drive was clearly a campaign driven by activists and individuals, both domestic and non-domestic. There were a small number of counter-narrative accounts in the top 100, primarily from religious individuals who did not approve of women driving. What is interesting to note here is where the percentage share differs from users to Tweets to reach. For example, while domestic activists make up 2 per cent of the users, they account for 15 per cent of the reach. Equally, domestic individuals are 30 per cent of the users, 38 per cent of the Tweets, and 13 per cent of the reach, indicating that they are more active but with fewer followers. Also of note is that foreign independent journalists take 3 per cent of the users but 33 per cent of the reach. Overall, this chart shows that domestic users are very active but, generally, foreign users have more followers and thus more reach (with the exception of the domestic activists).

Figure 6.3: Profiles of the 100 most active users, #women2drive

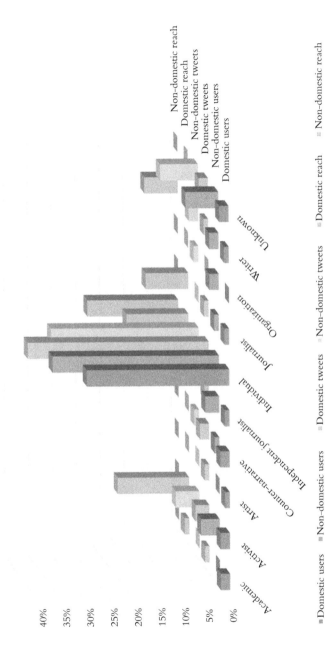

Figure 6.4: Positivity over time, #women2drive

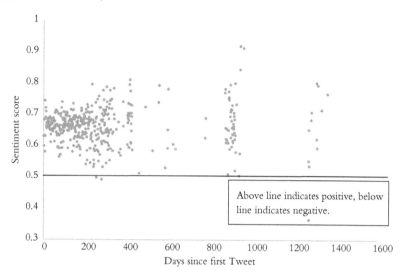

Content analysis (sentiment, personalization, framing, messaging, and norms)

#women2drive was a generally positive campaign (see Figure 6.4). In the beginning of the campaign, there was a very consistent picture painted with the sentiment scores. Unlike most of the other campaigns, there was very little variation or volatility in the sentiment. Over the life of the campaign, for days with at least ten Tweets, the standard deviation in average positivity score was only 0.06, demonstrating again the consistency in this campaign.

As the campaign progressed, however, spikes in positive sentiment were seen. Interestingly, the spikes in positivity do not correspond to peak events. The highest positive days surrounded praise for a Human Rights Watch video about the campaign and women driving in Saudi Arabia (December 2013). Another extremely positive day was on the first anniversary of #women2drive where a Twibbon campaign was launched (22 June 2012). Another small peak in positivity occurred when two more activists were arrested for driving (December 2014). While this may not seem like a particularly 'positive' event, the sentiment of activism and purpose was high on these days, which resulted in a higher positive sentiment.

Overall, as seen in many other Twitter variables, this campaign showed great consistency in the normative analysis. #women2drive had the highest proportion of consistent organic messaging compared to variable organic messaging of any of the campaigns studied; 37 per cent of the words analysed were consistent. Although this clearly is not a majority, it is higher than any other campaign, where the percentages ranged from 16 per cent to 33 per cent. Similarly, #women2drive also showed the highest ratio of average number of consistent words to variable words per event-based time period. Also contributing to its success is likely the presence of international norms, with 86 per cent of the international norms analysed mentioned over the course of the campaign.

The consistent frames and messages appear to stay focused on the campaign itself, with continued reference to activist and campaign leader Manal al-Sharif (see Figure 6.5), uniform use of words such as 'rights' and 'support', and references to Twibbons and the campaign itself. Although perhaps outdated now, at the time of the campaign, Twibbons (a combination of Twitter + Ribbon, as in wearing a specific coloured ribbon to participate in a campaign) were a popular tool. There was also a clear and consistent focus on the issue, with derivatives of the word 'drive' in nearly 30 per cent of all Tweets, as well words such as 'ban' and 'car' appearing consistently throughout the lifespan of the campaign. It is also interesting to note that God was mentioned in 5 per cent of all Tweets across the campaign. Spot-checking shows that this comes from both activists *and* counter-narratives, both using religion as a point of persuasion. The analysis of this campaign has time and time again pointed to the consistency as a positive force behind its success. This framing and messaging continue to underscore that point.

There are some interesting findings in the analysis of variable content. The most intriguing result, perhaps of any campaign, was the emergence of the word 'Clinton' in the middle of the campaign. Hillary Clinton was the foreign secretary at the time and, as seen earlier in this chapter, was very involved in 'quiet diplomacy' on the matter. It is extremely interesting that her name emerged in the 100 most words used in that specific time period, being mentioned 294 times, or in 3 per cent of all Tweets in the time period. That Clinton's name emerged so clearly is a fascinating outcome – both in

Figure 6.5: Consistently used words, #women2drive

the representation of the strategic campaign choices in the Tweets and in the prevalence of her role in the Twitter campaign. It was also very interesting to see a shift in focus to the royal family after the campaign took off. This was true in English and Arabic, again underscoring the strategic drive of the campaign to tap into transnational networks as well as domestic to exert pressure, going some way to prove the theory of the spiral model of human rights change.

Conclusion

#women2drive was a fascinating campaign. Although all the campaigns were deeply rooted in Twitter, this campaign used social media more as a strategic choice, tapping into both domestic and non-domestic pressures. It was a campaign steered by domestic activists, but the non-domestic attention and participation was strong, the backbone of the theory of the spiral model of human rights change and digital feminist activism. The Twitter characteristics again and again exhibited clear consistency, with long-term persistence, uniformity in engagement, and maintained focus in the content of Tweets. This persistence and consistency are likely associated with the high levels of success, particularly in the parameters of institutionalization and UN dialogue, setting it apart from the partially successful campaigns #delhigangrape and #niunamenos. While the overall situation for women and girls in Saudi remains challenging with the continued enforcement of guardianship laws in the private sector and the targeted arrests and detentions of feminist activists in the public sector, the campaign itself demonstrated that change can happen for women and girls.

7

Aggregate Analysis and Conclusions

This chapter draws the analyses from each campaign detailed in the previous chapters to explore overall findings.

Campaign 'groupings' based on outcomes

An initial important finding in this research was the general 'grouping' of campaigns by outcome, based on the three theoretical frames (spiral model theory of legal change, media effects and social media theories, and digital feminist activism theories). Campaigns primarily fell into four different categories: negative outcomes (government backlash – critique of the spiral model), status quo (no overall change, critiques of social media activism), tactical concessions (legislative change but lacking institutionalization based on the spiral model), and possible success (some indication of overall positive legal change and positive social media behaviours). In the following section, broad conclusions are drawn about the different categories of potential outcomes.

Backlash campaigns: lack of domestic drive

At first, it may seem that the common characteristic of the backlash campaigns was simply the target country: Iran. However, this assumption failed when tested further. First and foremost, there were important differences in legal outcomes between the two Iranian campaigns themselves. Although they both overall showed negative outcomes, the gradient and degree were different. This indicates that something other than simply context in the target country was likely influencing outcomes. Second, context variables across all of the campaigns in the study were collected specifically to ensure that the domestic situation could be tested as a control factor. In this case, the context variables in Iran were not different from context variables in other target countries. This indicates, at least to some extent, that it was not solely the target country of Iran that pre-determined the negative legal outcomes. Although this may have *contributed* to the outcomes, it was not a *sufficient* factor to explain all of the differences. In particular, countries such as Afghanistan, Turkey, India, and Saudi Arabia had some similar domestic characteristics. A wide variety of context variables were examined in order to ensure that it was not down to researcher choice. Therefore, other factors are likely at play. In other words, while the target country of course matters in a pre-determined way, characteristics in the Twitter campaigns themselves can still influence the outcome, making it worse or better.

Twitter behaviours across #stopstoning and #letwomengotostadium were fairly similar but did show enough differences to tentatively draw some conclusions. Both showed high levels of non-domestic involvement with low levels of domestic drive, lacked in persistence and engagement, and lacked focus on international women's rights norms. It is likely the combination of these factors led to the similarly regressive outcomes. However, these behaviours were seen to a *greater* degree in #stopstoning, particularly the lack of domestic drive and voice in the campaign. Government responses were driven primarily from hard-line religious conservatives expressing deep hostility towards 'Western' propaganda, in line with Hemmings' 'colonial violence' theories.[1] It also appeared that law enforcement was used as a tool to reassert domestic power and prominence over foreign influences, adversely affecting the lives of women and girls in Iran. These campaigns are a stark example of the theories of potential dangers of social media driven advocacy campaigns and the very real potential for destructive domestic government backlash and regression.

This interestingly demonstrates both sides of the digital feminist activism debate. Some campaigns were able to harness the power of social media and succeed in challenging norms, but only those that were domestically driven. This finding aligns with Fraser, Ahmed, Travers, and (to some extent) Hemmings, while *also* demonstrating the pitfalls extolled by scholars such as boyd, Lang, and Ott. We can also align these findings in the anticolonial literature with such clear resistance to 'Western' influence and control.[2]

---

[1] Clare Hemmings, 'Resisting Popular Feminisms: Gender, Sexuality and the Lure of the Modern' (2018) 25 Gender, Place & Culture 963.

[2] Julian Go, 'Thinking against Empire: Anticolonial Thought as Social Theory' (2023) 74 The British Journal of Sociology 279; Walter D Mignolo, 'Prophets Facing Sidewise: The Geopolitics of Knowledge and the Colonial Difference' (2005) 19 Social Epistemology 111; Walter D Mignolo, 'Coloniality and Globalization: A Decolonial Take' (2021) 18 Globalizations 720; Walter D Mignolo and Fábio Santino Bussmann, 'Coloniality and the State: Race, Nation and Dependency' (2023) 40 Theory, Culture & Society 3; Veeran Naicker, 'The Problem of Epistemological Critique in Contemporary Decolonial Theory' (2023) 49 Social Dynamics 220; Sujata Patel, 'Anti-Colonial Thought and Global Social

Status quo campaigns: lack of persistence

Three campaigns showed no meaningful overall legal change – #farkhunda, #sendeanlat, and #mydressmychoice. These campaigns may have shown some aspects of positive legal change, but there were equally some negative aspects. As seen with the backlash campaigns, the geopolitical and socioeconomic contexts of the countries in this category (Afghanistan, Turkey, and Kenya) were markedly different and thus not likely a sufficient explanation for the similarity in lack of legal changes. This group also underscores how a country can have a relatively decent baseline status for women and girls but not necessarily be primed for meaningful change.

The three campaigns did, however, show remarkable similarities in aspects of the Twitter behaviours. All three campaigns showed almost identical timelines with very large peaks around the initial viral spread of the campaign but little to no activity in the long term. All three spark incidents – Farkhunda's mob murder video, the death of Özgecan, and the video of the public stripping in Nairobi – gathered enormous social media attention in the immediate aftermath. Peaks of more than 10,000 Tweets per day were recorded for #sendeanlat and #mydressmychoice. This attention however quickly waned, with these three campaigns showing very little activity after the reaction to the initial incident faded. It is likely that this initial interest contributed to some of the positive legal outcomes, but that the lack of sustained interest left the campaigns 'unfinished' with no pressure to implement meaningful long-term change.

Campaigns which showed higher levels of success showed far more persistence in the level of Twitter activity. This tends to indicate that campaigns which show high levels of attention that quickly fade are less likely to lead to long-term change. Although this may seem like an obvious conclusion given social media theory, this study now provides empirical evidence for what many may have assumed.

Tactical concession campaigns: extremely high level of domestic attention in close proximity to election

These two campaigns – #delhigangrape and #niunamenos – appeared to gather extreme levels of attention around the spark incident, primarily from domestic users, *and* began fairly close to elections and potential regime change. They were the largest campaigns in the study at 144,867 and 410,858 Tweets, respectively. Legal outcomes showed quick, reactionary

---

Theory' (2023) 8 Frontiers in Sociology, https://www.frontiersin.org/articles/10.3389/fsoc.2023.1143776, accessed 13 November 2023.

tactical concessions but lacked in moving to institutionalization or rule-consistent behaviour, exhibiting the theoretical critiques of the spiral model of human rights change relating to lack of progression and some critiques in the social media and slactivist literature. In Argentina, the campaign peaked approximately six months before national elections, where a change in ruling party occurred. #delhigangrape peaked 16 months before a national election that also saw a change in the ruling party. Candidates in #niunamenos openly used the hashtag in their campaigning.[3]

The evidence suggests that these kinds of high-profile online campaigns could push governments to implement changes in reaction to the mass negative public attention fuelled by social media rather than a more considered long-term decision. Both campaigns scored high in legislative change but low in law enforcement, showing the wide gap between legislating and implementation and enforcement. Although they were the only two campaigns in this study which showed this relationship, it was quite strong and striking how similar the two were. The mass online public attention brought about the large-scale 'naming and shaming' and reputational damage on which the theoretical spiral model relies. However, as some scholarly critiques of the spiral model warned, this push to tactical concessions did not then translate to long-term efforts to move towards institutionalization and rule-consistent behaviour. This can be seen as a missed opportunity, perhaps even closing doors to future advocacy work. If the government feels that they have 'done their bit' and addressed the campaign's concerns through the legislative changes, then continuing advocacy work could be hampered or seriously impeded.

Potential success campaign: consistency across all Twitter behaviours

One campaign in the study appeared to be associated with a tentative level of success. #women2drive, after years of online advocacy and campaigning, finally saw the Saudi government change the law to allow women to drive in July 2018.[4] This campaign did not see perfect outcomes, however, as there

---

[3] Ciara Nugent, 'Four Months From #NiUnaMenos: Has Anything Changed?' (*The Argentina Independent*, 5 October 2015) https://web.archive.org/web/20170704235054/http://www.argentinaindependent.com/currentaffairs/four-months-from-niunamenos-has-anything-changed/, accessed 8 November 2023.

[4] Alexandra Johnson, 'Saudi Women Gain the Right to Drive' (Center for Security Policy, 2 October 2017) https://www.centerforsecuritypolicy.org/2017/10/02/saudi-women-gain-the-right-to-drive/, accessed 17 November 2023; 'Saudi Arabia Agrees to Let Women Drive' (*The New York Times*, 26 September 2017) https://www.nytimes.com/2017/09/26/world/middleeast/saudi-arabia-women-drive.html, accessed 29 November 2023; 'Saudi Arabia to Allow Women to Drive' (*Al Jazeera*, 27 September 2017) http://www.aljazeera.com/news/2017/09/saudi-arabia-women-drive-170926190857109.html, accessed 29 November 2023; Human Rights Watch, 'Saudi Arabia: As Women's Driving

are still issues around institutionalization and law enforcement, particularly around the lack of change to guardianship laws and the continued arrests of activists.[5] However, the campaign *does* show association with success and the potential to have opened doors to other law reforms and therefore it is worthwhile to identify the key characteristics that may have led to the positive legal changes.

On the whole, this campaign showed a much higher level of consistency across all theoretically grounded variables than the other campaigns. It did not show the fluctuation in peaks and troughs of the other campaigns, and the framing, messaging, and norms tended to be both internationally driven and consistent. The driving users remained domestic but there was a well-executed strategic choice to ensure that the campaign tapped into foreign pressure, particularly from the United States.[6] This pattern of consistency, domestic drive, and strategically selected foreign pressure appears to have combined to see positive legal outcomes, demonstrating the optimistic theories of legal change, social media activism, and digital feminist activism. Although international actors were potentially central to its success, this was not at the expense of the domestic drive. The critiques of the spiral model were less prominent, if present at all, in this campaign.

However, returning to the analytical lens of digital feminist activism, there is another aspect of this campaign to consider. This is a campaign which closely aligns with both Western ideals (what's more Western than driving an oil-guzzling car?) and capitalist economic drivers – both which can be antagonistic to feminist ideology.

Statistical analysis

Given the in-depth analysis of the legal changes and Twitter characteristics for each campaign and outcome group, this chapter now sets out to explore any overarching findings, beginning to build simple statistical models to understand in more detail the role of Twitter in legal change and to answer the

---

Ban Ends, Provide Parity' (27 September 2017) https://www.hrw.org/news/2017/09/27/saudi-arabia-womens-driving-ban-ends-provide-parity, accessed 17 November 2023.

[5] Jane Kinninmont, 'End of Saudi Women Driving Ban Reflects Deep Changes in Society' (*BBC News*, 27 September 2017) http://www.bbc.co.uk/news/world-middle-east-41412 022, accessed 29 November 2023; see also ' "Battle of the Sexes": Saudi Men React to Women Driving' (*Dhaka Tribune*, 4 October 2017) https://web.archive.org/web/201 71006172747/http://www.dhakatribune.com/world/middle-east/2017/10/04/saudi-men-react-women-driving/, accessed 17 November 2023.

[6] Katherine Zoepf, 'What Overturning the Ban on Female Drivers Means for Saudi Arabia and the World' (*The New Yorker*, 12 October 2017) https://www.newyorker.com/news/news-desk/what-overturning-the-ban-on-female-drivers-means-for-saudi-arabia-and-the-world, accessed 13 February 2018.

overarching research questions. To frame the work presented in this chapter, Table 7.1 builds upon the theoretical framework set out in Chapter 2. This shows the various statistical tests that have been performed to investigate the overarching research questions and to identify patterns and trends in hashtag campaigns on Twitter which could help to understand legal outcomes. The research questions in this book, to reiterate, are:

- Can international campaigns originating in and driven by a hashtag on Twitter contribute to domestic legal change in women's rights?
- If so, which campaign behaviours are associated with change?

It is also critical to reiterate the selection criteria for the campaigns in the study:

- international attention;
- more than 1,000 Tweets;
- seeking specific domestic legal change in the area of women's rights;
- originating in, and continuing to be driven by, a hashtag on Twitter.

Returning now to the research map, the next elements to add are the statistical tests chosen to analyse each independent variable (see Table 7.1). This chapter will work through these tests sequentially, culminating in testing the aggregated model and presenting tentative conclusions.

Lack of focus on domestic actors

A key critique of the spiral model is its overemphasis on foreign (Western) actors and its lack of focus on domestic actors.[7] Social media is statistically dominated by the Global North and is constructed in a way that favours

---

[7] Alison Brysk, 'Communicative Action and Human Rights in Colombia: When Words Fail' (2009) Colombia Internacional 36; Anthony Tirado Chase, 'The State and Human Rights: Governance and Sustainable Human Development in Yemen' (2003) International Journal of Politics, Culture, and Society 213; Isabelle Cheng and Lara Momesso, 'Look, the World Is Watching How We Treat Migrants! The Making of the Anti-Trafficking Legislation during the Ma Administration' (2017) 46 Journal of Current Chinese Affairs 61; Umit Cizre, 'The Truth and Fiction About (Turkey's) Human Rights Politics' (2001) 3 Human Rights Review 55; Xinyuan Dai, 'The "Compliance Gap" and the Efficacy of International Human Rights Institutions' in Thomas Risse-Kappen and Stephen C Ropp (eds), *The Persistent Power of Human Rights: From Commitment to Compliance* (Cambridge University Press, 2013); Man-ho Heo, 'Mongolia's Political Change and Human Rights in Five-Phase Spiral Model: Implications for North Korea: Mongolia's Political Change and HR' (2014) 29 Pacific Focus 413; Andreas Laursen, 'Israel's Supreme Court and International Human Rights Law: The Judgement on "Moderate Physical Pressure"' (2000) 69 Nordic Journal of International Law 413; Alejandro Anaya Muñoz, 'Transnational and Domestic Processes in the Definition of Human Rights Policies in Mexico' (2009) 31

Table 7.1: Overview of statistical tests

Theoretical grounding	Independent variable(s)	Null hypothesis (that which this research sets out disprove)	Test
Spiral model lack of focus on domestic actors/ overemphasis on Western approaches; social media is elite-driven and non-neutral; campaigns may be dominated and/or driven by elite international actors, drawing from digital feminist activism critiques	Twitter profiles of 100 most prolific users in each campaign	Campaigns dominated by foreign actors will be more successful	Mapping exercise of campaign drivers Correlate domestic and non-domestic user variables to outcomes
Potential government backlash; lack of message tempering due to organic nature of medium; Hemmings' 'colonial violence' approach to feminist activism	Content analysis	Consistency of messaging in Tweets will not affect campaign outcomes	Correlate consistency variables to outcomes Compare to correlations of organic content
Lack of long-term progression; 'fickleness' and speed of social media	Persistence (Tweets per day)	Persistence of Tweets in Twitter-driven campaigns do not affect campaign outcomes	Correlate persistence variables to outcomes
Ignores domestic capacity issues; lack of knowledge of domestic context; colonial concerns from feminist literature	Context (various indicators of domestic political context and situation for women)	Domestic context has no impact on campaign success	Analysis of variance (ANOVA) test based on domestic political capacity scores
Ignores material or nuanced incentives; does not present enough incentive for change to domestic government	Engagement (reply, retweet, and like data)	Campaigns driven by 'likes' will have the same impact as campaigns driven by replies (replies used as a proxy for engagement/ investment/risk in campaign, as opposed to a simple click to like)	Correlate likes versus replies to outcomes
Theoretical weaknesses in spiral model and feminist scholarly concerns are amplified in social media driven campaigns	Combined quantified variables	Twitter variables have no relationship to campaign outcomes	Testing composite scores

the elite, however the domestic targets for change in this research are predominantly located in the Global South.[8] The critique of the spiral model is that there is not enough emphasis on domestic actors, and the overemphasis on foreign influence can contribute to unintended and indeed negative domestic outcomes. If this is a risk in a campaign which is not driven by social media, this risk is even more prevalent and concerning in a social media environment, dominated by elite, usually Western, users.[9] This variable is therefore crucial to understanding the impact of international social media campaigns on domestic law. This can also be viewed through the lens of feminist activism scholarship and anticolonial thought, challenging notions of elite, white, Western women imposing their version of feminism in a non-Western context.[10]

The hypothesis in this area is that campaigns which are driven by domestic actors and voices, as opposed to being overshadowed or driven by foreign actors, will be more likely to influence domestic governments to change. If feminist social media campaigns continue to be dominated by Western influences, the hypothesis is that it is very unlikely that they will contribute to long-term meaningful legal change.

As the campaigns progress from least successful through to more successful, the concentration of most active users in the domestic country and surrounding region tends to increase. It is of particular interest that #niunamenos was the first campaign to show no drivers from the United

---

Human Rights Quarterly 35; Rolf Schwarz, 'The Paradox of Sovereignty, Regime Type and Human Rights Compliance' (2004) 8 The International Journal of Human Rights 199; Beth A Simmons, 'From Ratification to Compliance: Quantitative Evidence on the Spiral Model' in Thomas Risse-Kappen and Stephen C Ropp (eds), *The Persistent Power of Human Rights: From Commitment to Compliance* (Cambridge University Press, 2013).

[8] Simon Kemp, 'Global Digital & Social Media Stats: 2015' (*Social Media Today*, 22 January 2015) http://www.socialmediatoday.com/content/global-digital-social-media-stats-2015, accessed 14 March 2016; ITU, 'Key ICT Indicators for Developed and Developing Countries and the World (Totals and Penetration Rates)' (2014) http://www.itu.int/en/ITU-D/Statistics/Documents/facts/ICTFactsFigures2014-e.pdf, accessed 14 March 2016; Maeve Duggan and Aaron Smith, 'Social Media Update 2013' (*Pew Research Center: Internet, Science & Tech*, 30 December 2013) http://www.pewinternet.org/2013/12/30/social-media-update-2013/, accessed 14 March 2016.

[9] 'Digital in 2018: World's Internet Users Pass the 4 Billion Mark' (We Are Social UK, 30 January 2018) https://wearesocial.com/uk/blog/2018/01/global-digital-report-2018, accessed 4 October 2018; Kate Ott, 'Social Media and Feminist Values: Aligned or Maligned?' (2018) 39 Frontiers: A Journal of Women Studies 93.

[10] See, for example, danah boyd, 'Can Social Network Sites Enable Political Action?' (2008) International Journal of Media and Cultural Politics 241; Tarleton Gillespie, 'The Politics of "Platforms"' (2010) 12 New Media & Society 347; Mignolo, 'Prophets Facing Sidewise' (n 2); Hemmings (n 1).

States. Although not a perfect model, there is a general identifiable trend for campaigns with a larger geographic spread of driving users to be associated with less long-term success. Even though #women2drive was strategically designed to utilize foreign pressures, there is still a strong concentration of Saudi users *driving* the campaign – the most active users. On the contrary, #stopstoning and #farkhunda showed a large geographic spread of most active users.

Another interesting point may be a diaspora effect, whereby domestic nationals are currently located in non-domestic locations.[11] This could show as 'foreign' influence when in fact it is more closely linked to the domestic interests. However the users still do not have any domestic power as they do not currently reside in the target country, under the target government. Therefore they cannot be classified as true domestic voices either. While it is not possible to specifically identify a possible diaspora effect given the availability of information on Twitter profiles, this may indicate this phenomenon in #sendeanlat (many users in Germany) and #delhigangrape (many users in the UK) in particular.

To explore this theory further, correlations between some of the key user variables against outcome variables were run.[12] The significant results are presented in Table 7.2. In other words, the relationships with R closer to 1.00 and a p-value <0.01 indicate that the independent variable explains a statistically significant amount of variation in the dependent variable. As the independent variable moves up or down (ordinally) the dependent variable will likely do the same. The higher the R, the stronger the relationship, and the lower the p-value, the more statistically significant.

As it is not logical that the number of Tweets from domestic users and the number of Tweets from non-domestic users can both be significant, there is likely a confounding factor at play, possibly the overall number of Tweets in the campaign. In other words, it is not whether the Tweets are domestic or non-domestic that is showing significance, but just the raw number of Tweets influencing the relationship. This is underscored by the correlation shown between the percentage of campaign Tweets which are from non-domestic users to changes in legislation. Partial correlations, which control for other variables, are necessary to exclude the possible confounding factor of total

---

[11] Response from Dr Sebastian Peyer to Reilly Dempsey Willis, 'Evaluating the Impact of Global Twitter Campaigns on Domestic Women's Rights: Statistical Modelling and Analysis' (Research Seminar, University of East Anglia School of Law, 6 June 2018).

[12] Pearson correlations measure the relationship between two variables, looking at both strength and directionality. In the simplest terms, changes in one variable will result in changes to the other. A value of 1 means a perfect linear relationship, a value of 0 means there is no relationship at all, and a value of -1 is a perfect negative relationship.

Table 7.2: Summary of significant relationships, user profiles

	Strong correlation (0.01)	Correlation (0.05)
Of the 100 most active users in the campaign, the number clearly identified as being domestic		Overall legal change
Number of Tweets in the campaign sent by the most active users who clearly identified as being domestic	Legislative change^	Overall legal change^
Number of Tweets in the campaign sent by the most active users who identified as being non-domestic	Overall legal change^, legislative change	
Per cent of Tweets sent by the most active users from those who identified as being non-domestic		Overall legal change
Of the 100 most active users in the campaign, the per cent who clearly identified as being domestic individuals	Law enforcement	
Per cent of Tweets sent by the most active users from those who clearly identified as being domestic individuals		Law enforcement

Note: ^ Relationships which change when running partial correlations.

number of Tweets. Running this test shows that there is, actually, no strong relationship between the number of Tweets sent by domestic campaign drivers ($R=0.807$, $p=0.028$), but there remains a significant correlation between the number of Tweets sent by non-domestic campaign drivers and changes in legislative change ($R=0.900$, $p=0.006$).

The initial significance between domestic campaign Tweets and overall legal change is removed completely when controlling for total number of Tweets ($R=0.642$, $p=0.120$). The strong correlation between non-domestic campaign Tweets and overall legal change is also weakened in the partial correlation. However, the strong relationship between non-domestic campaign Tweets and legislative change remains. This is contrary to the hypothesis and in fact *upholds*, in part, the theoretical role of international actors in the spiral model and some of the more optimist digital feminist activist literature. This may indicate that some level of online foreign pressure is indeed necessary to push a government to change the law. This was certainly seen in #women2drive and these statistics further prove the relationship.

This is tempered to some extent by the relationship between the strength of the voice of domestic individuals and law enforcement. There is a strong statistical relationship between the percentage of campaign drivers who self-identify as domestic individuals and law enforcement (R=0.852, p=0.007) and the percentage of campaign Tweets from drivers sent by domestic individuals (R=0.725, p=0.042). This indicates that the voice of 'ordinary' domestic individuals may have an influence on how seriously law enforcement takes the issue. For example, #delhigangrape and #niunamenos had particular problems in law enforcement outcomes, and these campaigns showed only 27 per cent and 14 per cent domestic drivers respectively. Conversely, #mydressmychoice and #women2drive showed more positive outcomes in law enforcement and reported higher levels of domestic individuals at 32 per cent and 30 per cent respectively. Although the differences may not seem large, the patterns are still informative and statistically significant. The campaigns with the poorest outcomes in law enforcement, #stopstoning and #farkhunda, showed the lowest levels of domestic individuals at 0 per cent and 6 per cent, respectively.

The Saudi campaign on this particular variable is of interest. Campaign analysis showed that foreign pressure, given foreign relations and the domestic political situation, was actively sought. No other campaign visibly or vocally used this strategy.

This could indicate that for *most* campaigns, domestic voices are indeed critical to success, however there may be exceptions where it is both appropriate and necessary to draw upon foreign pressure. As discussed earlier, it could also be the strength and importance of the domestic voices that matters more than the number. In the case of #women2drive, using social media to tap into transnational advocacy networks and specifically American public opinion was a strategic choice, yet the campaign was still very much driven by the domestic activists. Other campaigns which saw success (albeit limited), such as #niunamenos and #delhigangrape, also had domestic drive to the campaign, greater in number but perhaps not in strength. In other words, it is always important to understand what is going on behind the numbers. At the opposite end of the scale, with campaigns such as #stopstoning and #farkhunda, it appears that the foreign involvement was associated with poorer outcomes, seen perhaps through the anticolonial feminist lens.

Therefore there are three important findings in these tests:

1. that there is a relationship between the number of domestic drivers and overall legal change (both in the correlations and the mapping trends);
2. that there is a strong relationship between the number of Tweets sent by non-domestic drivers and legislative change; and
3. that there is a strong relationship between the voice of 'ordinary' domestic individuals and law enforcement.

Taken as a whole, this may show that the spiral model theory holds true for legislative change (that is, Phase 3 tactical concessions), but that more emphasis on domestic voices, influence, and power is needed to see long-term, on-the-ground implementation and societal change. This finding also links to the critique on the lack of progression seen in the spiral model case studies. It may be that the emphasis on foreign influence is also to blame for the lack of long-term progression. Perhaps a more correct assessment would see foreign influence curtailed and limited to early phase legislative work, but a complete shift to domestic pressure to move from tactical concessions towards rule-consistent behaviour.

Again, this aligns with digital feminist activism scholarship which warns of the Westernization of feminism and the potential dangers of using elite, heteronormative, patriarchal platforms.[13] The risk is ever present, but not insurmountable.

Potential government backlash

Theoretical critiques of the spiral model highlight that the model 'ignores' the potential for governments to lash out against what can be interpreted as foreign interference in domestic matters. Critics point out that the model's emphasis on the role and power of foreign actors could have a negative impact on domestic matters if the state reacts to foreign 'meddling'.[14] Taking this a step further to Hemmings' 'colonial violence' work makes this risk with feminist campaigns perhaps even greater.[15] Given the possibility of both *actual* foreign involvement in social media campaigns and the *perception* of overinvolvement from foreigners/Westerners in social media, this risk is potentially greater. The legal and discourse analysis showed on multiple occasions and in multiple countries a distrust of Western influences and Western-driven media. Statistics also show that social media tends to be Western-driven.[16] In a structured, strategically designed, and driven

---

[13] See, for example, boyd (n 10); Gillespie (n 10); Hemmings (n 1).

[14] Brysk (n 7); Omar G Encarnación, 'International Influence, Domestic Activism, and Gay Rights in Argentina' (2013) 128 Political Science Quarterly 687; Ryan Goodman and Derek Jinks, 'How to Influence States: Socialization and International Human Rights Law' (2004) 54 Duke Law Journal 621; Kathryn Sikkink, 'The United States and Torture: Does the Spiral Model Work?' in Thomas Risse-Kappen and Stephen C Ropp (eds), *The Persistent Power of Human Rights: From Commitment to Compliance* (Cambridge University Press, 2013); Anja Jetschke, 'The Power of Human Rights a Decade after: From Euphoria to Contestation?' in Thomas Risse-Kappen and Stephen C Ropp (eds), *The Persistent Power of Human Rights: From Commitment to Compliance* (Cambridge University Press, 2013).

[15] Hemmings (n 1).

[16] 'Digital in 2018: World's Internet Users Pass the 4 Billion Mark' (n 9).

advocacy campaign, messages can be tempered and carefully constructed so as to avoid this impression. Messaging can also be designed to ensure a focus on the domestic aspects, again in the hopes of avoiding potential backlash. Framing and messaging on social media, however, is by definition unstructured and unfiltered.

Additionally, the non-neutrality of Twitter may contribute to the lack of control over messaging as the algorithms working in the background which allow some messages to thrive (elite, heteronormative, patriarchal, Western messaging) and some to become suppressed will contribute to the perception of the campaign.[17] There is little strategic design to what is said, repeated, or reported as social media content is user-defined, even if activists and organizations attempt to steer the campaign. They still cannot control what individuals Tweet or what Twitter promotes. This could indicate that the lack of controlled, consistent messaging on social media may increase the risk of government backlash.

Although difficult to assess, as a proxy for the content of Tweets two tests were run. Each campaign was divided into event-driven time periods (as opposed to peak and non-peak time periods which are defined by the number of Tweets on a given day). For each time period, the 100 most used words were collected and the number of instances of words which relate to international norms on women's rights were counted. From these tests, four distinct areas of interest emerged: the use of pronouns, the content of consistent yet still user-defined framing and messaging, variable framing and messaging which was strong but differed across time periods, and the presence of international norms. The use of pronouns does not relate to the content of messaging and is discussed later in this chapter.

The hypothesis here is that more consistent and 'structured' messaging will lead to less government backlash and therefore more likely to see positive legal change. Campaigns with less consistent messaging and more variable (and potentially volatile or perceived as Western-driven) organic messaging which may stray from the overarching goals are hypothesized to see less success and run a greater risk of alienating government inroads for change.

As shown in Table 7.3, these correlations show a potentially significant relationship between messaging and outcomes. As hypothesized, campaigns which have more variable, erratic, and irregular content, specific to time periods and not the overarching campaign, are correlated to less positive outcomes, while campaigns with consistent messaging which draw heavily from women's rights norms are associated with more positive outcomes.

To explore these relationships further, scatter plots were created and regression equations generated. The presence of organically emerging

---

[17] Ott (n 9).

Table 7.3: Summary of significant relationships, messaging content

	Strong correlation (0.01)	Correlation (0.05)
Per cent of tweets with variable messaging	UN dialogue (negative relationship)	Overall legal change (negative relationship)
Highest per cent of Tweets in a given time period with a given variable word		Law enforcement (negative relationship)
Ratio of consistent to variable words		UN dialogue
Per cent of international women's rights norms present	Overall legal change	Legislative change, UN dialogue

messages in Tweets continues to show a negative relationship with dialogue with UN international human rights mechanisms in particular (see Figure 7.1).

This plot shows the negative relationship between the presence of variable (unstructured and changing) messaging and legal outcomes, looking in more detail at UN dialogue. Of critical importance, UN dialogue is the legal variable that most clearly shows government backlash. In particular in the Iranian campaigns, dialogue with the UN treaty bodies was where state backlash against the campaigns was most clearly evidenced. Although not as strong as the percentage of Tweets, the continued *negative* statistical relationship between the presence of variable framing to law enforcement supports the findings. The presence of variable framing shows the percentage of times that one particular organically emerging word or phrase was used for each campaign. This is another indicator of the strength and visibility of the changing, variable messaging across event-based time periods as opposed to the consistent campaign-driven framing and messaging which are evidenced across the lifespan of the campaign and international norms which reflect a focus on women's rights norms.

This relationship therefore begins to give credence to the hypothesis that less controlled social media messaging is more likely to see a hostile government response, and less likely to be associated with positive legal outcomes. This is underscored by the additional, though less strong, relationship between the ratio of consistent messaging to organic messaging and UN dialogue. The less consistent the campaign Tweets are, the more likely it is to show backlash in UN dialogue, going some way to support theoretical critiques of the spiral model and digital feminist activist literature.

Figure 7.1: Relationship between changing messaging and UN dialogue

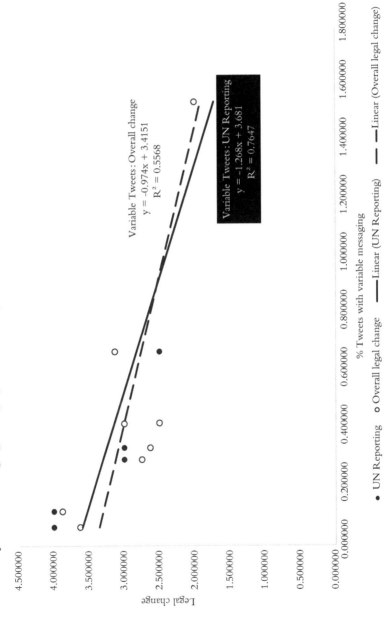

Lack of long-term progression

Some of the case studies used to develop the spiral model, even after years of strategic advocacy work, never progressed to full rule-consistent behaviour and institutionalization of human rights change. Critics of the model point to this risk of lack of long-term progression as a major fault in the model.[18] When used in a social media context, which is quite renowned for being short-term and short-lived, the risk is potentially increased. To explore this further, several variables to measure campaign persistence were examined. Although the clearest indicator of persistence would be the total number of days in the campaign, given the selection criteria for the campaigns in this study total days is not necessarily a comparable variable (that is, campaigns were not selected to be matched in length of time). Additionally, a cut-off date for data collection was practically necessary to complete this research, while some of the campaigns were still in an active phase. However, an initial look at the relationship between the total number of days analysed and the legal outcomes shows that this is not a statistically significant predictor. Figure 7.2 plots the number of Tweets against the number of days of the campaign (log scale for comparability). As can be seen, there is no discernible pattern and certainly no linear relationship to indicate that simply being a 'bigger' campaign means the campaign will see more success.

Therefore, other indicators of a hashtag campaign's persistence need to be explored. The hypothesis here, based on social media theory, is that campaigns which show more persistence will be more likely to see to legal change; in other words, campaigns which are more sensitive to the whims of social media that 'die out' of public interest quicker are far less likely to achieve meaningful success. Given that most hashtags on Twitter trend for a short amount of time, it is very likely that most social media campaigns will lack the persistence necessary for long-term change, particularly given that some critiques of the spiral model point to the lack of persistence of traditional advocacy campaigns which may take several years.

Persistence in these tests is therefore measured not by the simple length of a campaign, but rather the *ongoing activity* in the campaign. More days with more Tweets are therefore defined as persistent, for example, #women2drive. Higher numbers of days with fewer Tweets and completely inactive days (no Tweets) are defined as lacking persistence as was the case with #stopstoning. The number of peaks (numerically defined) are also included as indicators

---

[18] Raed A Alhargan, 'The Impact of the UN Human Rights System and Human Rights INGOs on the Saudi Government with Special Reference to the Spiral Model' (2012) 16 The International Journal of Human Rights 598; Brysk (n 7); Jetschke (n 14); Eran Shor, 'Conflict, Terrorism, and the Socialization of Human Rights Norms: The Spiral Model Revisited' (2008) 55 Social Problems 117.

Figure 7.2: Relationship between total number of days of campaign and overall legal outcomes (log scale)

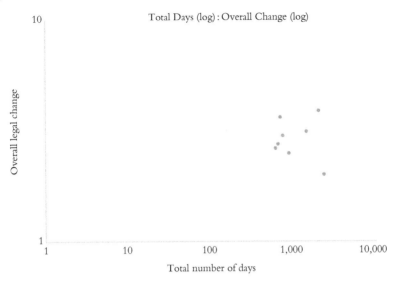

of persistence; in other words, days with a very high number of Tweets. Campaigns which have more peak days over time are also defined as more persistent, and it is hypothesized are more likely to contribute to long-term meaningful change. Fewer peaks are indicative of campaigns which lack persistence – those that grab attention for short periods of time but do not engage users to participate over a longer time span, for example, the status quo campaigns #farkhunda, #sendeanlat, and #mydressmychoice. Based on the critique of the spiral model around lack of progression, the hypothesis follows that social media campaigns with less persistence will see less change, and equally campaigns with more persistence will be associated with more positive change, as seen in Table 7.4.

In order to verify the strength of the relationship between the number of days with more than zero Tweets and the number of days with more than five Tweets, it is necessary to run a partial correlation controlling for the total number of days in the campaign. The partial correlation test confirms that the relationship stands when controlling for total days (see Table 7.5).

Taking these correlations with the negative directionality of the correlations of per cent of days with no Tweets, there is a strong relationship between the number of 'active' days in a campaign to outcomes, regardless of the total length of the campaign. A campaign therefore could be ongoing for years, but with very few days with more than just a handful of, if any, Tweets (that is, #stopstoning), whereas a campaign could be relatively short but with

Table 7.4: Summary of significant relationships, Tweets per day

	Strong correlation (0.01)	**Correlation (0.05)**
Persistence composite score	Overall legal change^	Legislative change^
Number of Tweets in non-peak periods		Legislative change
Number of days with at least one Tweet	Overall legal change	Legislative change, institutionalization
Number of days with at least five Tweets	Overall legal change, legislative change	UN dialogue
Per cent of days with no Tweets		Overall legal change (negative)

Note: ^ Relationships which change when running partial correlations.

Table 7.5: Partial correlations, Tweets per day

Control variables			**Overall legal change**
Total days of campaign	Number of days with at least one Tweet	*Correlation coefficient (R)*	**0.949**
		Significance (p-value)	**0.001**
	Number of days with at least five Tweets	*Correlation coefficient (R)*	**0.931**
		Significance (p-value)	**0.002**

Note: **Bold italics** indicate a statistically significant relationship at p<0.01 level.

mostly very active days (that is, #niunamenos). The latter is much more likely to be associated with success. The status quo campaigns tended to show very high activity levels in the early days but lacked in persistence over the long-term course of the campaign. These campaigns therefore were not statistically likely to see positive change.

It is also important to control for the total number of days in the persistence composite score as well. That partial correlation produces the results shown in Table 7.6.

This shows that the relationship between persistence and overall legal change and legislative change is weakened, though only slightly, when controlling for total number of days of the campaign. The significance level for both shifts to the 0.05 level.

Figure 7.3 shows the strong relationship between active days and outcomes: The theory-based hypothesis that campaigns exhibiting higher levels of persistence would lead to more positive legal change is therefore tentatively supported. The most important component part is the number of active days of the campaign. Campaigns with a high number of inactive days are not

Table 7.6: Summary of significant relationships, Tweets per day, after partial correlations

Control variables			Overall legal change	Legislative change
Total days of campaign	Persistence composite score	*Correlation coefficient (R)*	*0.868*	*0.831*
		Significance (p-value)	*0.011*	*0.020*

Note: *Italics* indicate a statistically significant relationship at p<0.05 level.

likely to be associated with positive legal change. This is a challenging finding for social media campaigns, as they generally tend to come and go quite quickly. In this study alone, the majority of campaigns lacked in persistence.

Domestic capacity issues

The spiral model itself recognizes that the capacity and ability of the domestic government to implement change could be an issue, but some scholars critique the model in that it does not pay *enough* attention to the potential barrier of domestic capacity.[19] This critique holds that governments may have the will to change but lack the practical capacity to initiate and implement change. Measuring capacity is challenging. Only two useful indices, produced by researchers at Harvard, were found for this research. Both measure relative political capacity, one which approximates the ability of governments to appropriate portions of the national output to advance public goals and one which gauges the capacity of governments to mobilize populations under their control. Indices such as these are never perfect and are based on many assumptions, however as a proxy for estimating a government's ability to implement legal change (based on the campaign goals), these indices will suffice. Each campaign was then grouped into low, medium, and high capacity to compare.

The domestic capacity issue could be a potentially major barrier to success in social media campaigns. As opposed to more structured and strategically planned campaigns which can work within the bounds of capacity for change, social media campaigns lack this strategic direction. While some domestic activists participating in social media campaigns may

---

[19] Tanja Borzel and Thomas Risse, 'Human Rights in Areas of Limited Statehood: The New Agenda' in Thomas Risse-Kappen and Stephen C Ropp (eds), *The Persistent Power of Human Rights: From Commitment to Compliance* (Cambridge University Press, 2013); Jack Goldsmith and Stephen D Krasner, 'The Limits of Idealism' (2003) 132 Daedalus 47; Shor (n 18).

HASHTAG ACTIVISM AND WOMEN'S RIGHTS

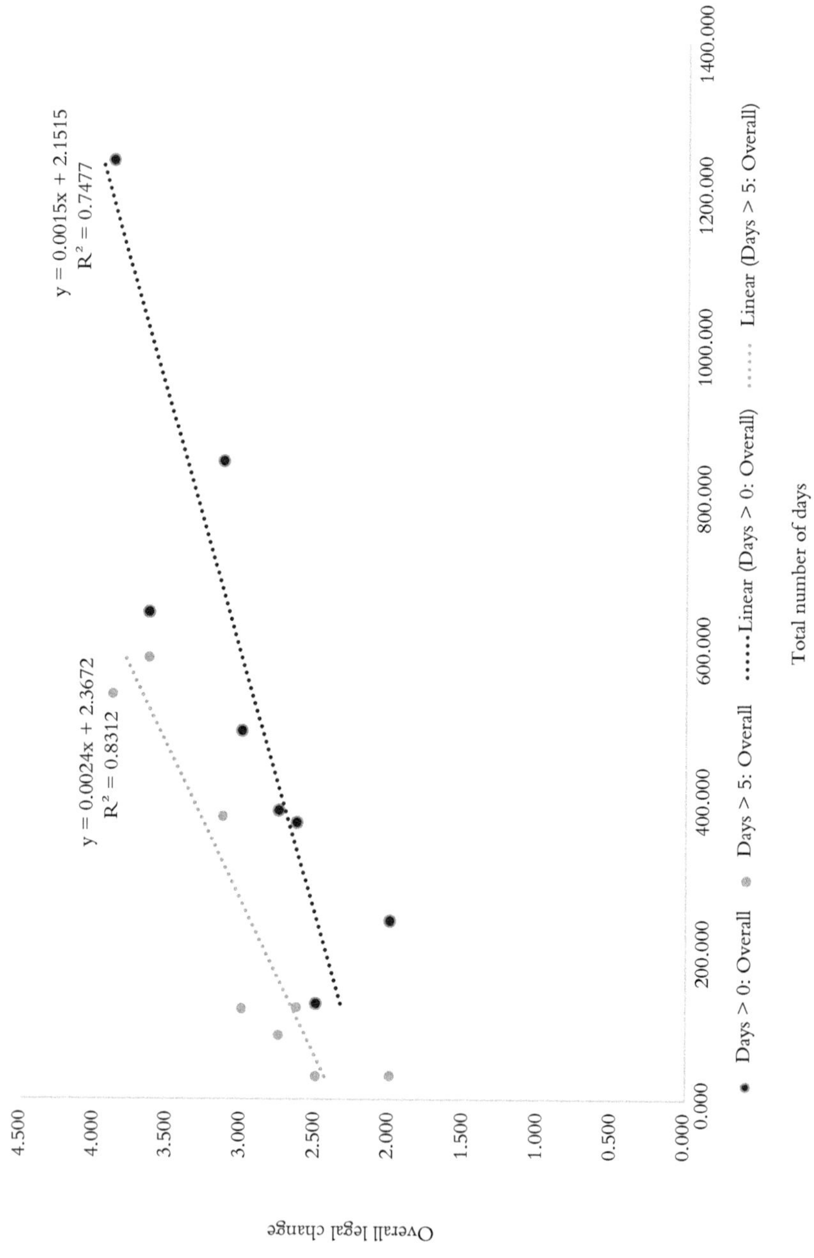

Figure 7.3: Relationship between number of active days and overall legal change

be aware of government capacity issues, it can at least be speculated that most hashtag participants will be relatively unaware of a state's capacity to implement change. In practical terms, this means that it is possible that a hashtag campaign is asking a government to do something that it is not capable of doing.

The primary statistical test to explore this hypothesis is a one-way ANOVA (Analysis of Variance). This tests for statistically significant differences in the dependent variable average for different groups. A statistically significant difference between the groups would indicate that capacity is critical to change. ANOVAs were performed for both capacity measures against the overall legal change score and all its component parts. There were no statistically significant differences between capacity groups across any of the outcomes, although the small number of campaigns in this study does mean that the finding must be interpreted with caution.

Still, this is a particularly interesting, and perhaps tentatively positive, finding for social media campaigns. If these assumptions are correct, then it matters not whether or not a government has political capacity. Campaign success, including institutionalization, does not vary significantly across countries with different domestic capacities. For example, India ranks relatively low in capacity, yet this research shows at least some change resulting from the Twitter-driven hashtag campaign. The government was able to commission a judicial report and pass legislative change relatively quickly once the campaign took hold. Similarly, Saudi Arabia scored quite low on the capacity measures, yet seems to exhibit the most ability to implement and institutionalize change (for better or worse). Perhaps the public nature of social media campaigns somehow *help* a government to overcome capacity issues, at least those relating to mobilization. It is important to note that this may be based on the measures chosen, however it is a challenge across the field finding ways to accurately measure capacity. It is hoped that by using more than one measure, and finding a lack of statistical difference in both, will at least go some way to overcoming this challenge.

However, this does not mean that context does not matter at all. This research also uses the World Justice Project Open Government Index to understand the domestic context. The Open Government Index looks at four indicators of the openness of a government: publicized laws and government data, right to information, civic participation, and complaint mechanisms.[20] The spiral model itself specifies some conditions of the

---

[20] 'WJP Open Government Index 2015' (*World Justice Project*) https://worldjusticeproject. org/our-work/wjp-rule-law-index/wjp-open-government-index-2015, accessed 20 October 2018.

Figure 7.4: Relationship between World Justice Project rankings and overall legal change, excluding Saudi Arabia

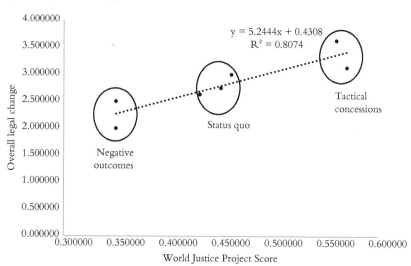

openness of a government as a scope condition for success. While this is a very useful measurement of domestic governments, it must be looked at with significant caution as there is no index available for Saudi Arabia. Although pure conjecture, one could assume that Saudi would not likely rank high on the openness scale but has shown responsiveness to the campaign.

The other campaigns have all been ranked by the World Justice Project, and within this group the variable has proven to be significant (see Figure 7.4).

This scatter plot shows three distinct groupings; these groupings directly map onto the legal outcome groups. This indicates, to some extent, that governments which are more open are more likely to respond to online campaigns. It does not mean that this is the only predictor of success; the level of success within the grouping is still dependent on the other variables discussed in this chapter. However it does appear that the openness of a government is an important factor in social media campaigning. Again this must be interpreted with caution as it excludes Saudi Arabia and the inclusion of Saudi Arabia most likely would change the significance, rendering it less important.

Ignores material or nuanced incentives

Yet another theoretical critique of the spiral model is that is it based almost exclusively on the concept of naming and shaming, using international reputational harm as the primary incentive for governments to change.[21] Critics highlight that, in many cases, material incentives are actually at play in pressuring a state to change. Social media campaigns not only rely solely on naming and shaming but can even fall below that level of incentive as users are not necessarily in a position to put themselves at risk or present any incentive at all for a government to change. Although this is an extension of the critique of the spiral model, it bears exploration. The hypothesis is that campaigns with lower levels of user engagement will be less likely to lead to positive change; the lack of engagement equates to a lack of pressure on the government which is linked to lack of incentives. In other words, if the online campaign participants are not properly engaged with the issue and the campaign, then there is no compulsion for the government to implement change; essentially even *less so* than traditional campaigns on which the spiral model was developed and on which the critique rests.

To test this hypothesis, several engagement metrics were explored to determine both the level and type of engagement linked to each campaign. Replies are deemed the highest level of engagement; users are engaged in dialogue and debate on the issue, taking the time and effort to write original thoughts and responses in conversation with other campaign users. Replying is also the best proxy for a user putting themselves at any sort of risk, which is usually a necessary component for a protest-driven campaign.[22] By putting their own thoughts, words, images, and responses in the public sphere, users take a much more risky and active part in the campaign. A campaign with more replies is therefore categorized as showing higher levels of engagement, and therefore more likely to contribute to positive legal change. Likes are seen as the least engaged form of Twitter campaigning. Users show their support and participation by simply clicking like, showing the least level of risk, time, effort, and participation – otherwise defined as 'slactivism'.[23] This

---

[21] Goldsmith and Krasner (n 19); Jérôme Y Bachelard, 'The Anglo-Leasing Corruption Scandal in Kenya: The Politics of International and Domestic Pressures and Counter-Pressures' (2010) 37 Review of African Political Economy 187; Ronald R Krebs and Patrick Thaddeus Jackson, 'Twisting Tongues and Twisting Arms: The Power of Political Rhetoric' (2007) 13 European Journal of International Relations 35; Robyn Linde, 'Statelessness and Roma Communities in the Czech Republic: Competing Theories of State Compliance' (2006) 13 International Journal on Minority & Group Rights 341; Jack Snyder and Leslie Vinjamuri, 'Trials and Errors: Principle and Pragmatism in Strategies of International Justice' (2003) 28 International Security 5.

[22] Donatella Della Porta and Mario Diani, *Social Movements: An Introduction* (second edition, Blackwell Publishing, 2006); Malcolm Gladwell, 'Small Change' (*The New Yorker*, 10 April 2010) http://www.newyorker.com/magazine/2010/10/04/small-change-malc olm-gladwell, accessed 14 March 2016.

[23] Henrik Serup Christensen, 'Political Activities on the Internet: Slacktivism or Political Participation by Other Means?' (2011) 16 First Monday, http://firstmonday.org/ojs/ index.php/fm/article/view/3336, accessed 7 July 2016; Cerise L Glenn, 'Activism

Table 7.7: Summary of significant relationships, engagement metrics

	Strong correlation (0.01)	Correlation (0.05)
Ratio of total number of replies to total number of Tweets	Legislative change	
Ratio of total number of likes to total number of Tweets		Institutionalization (negative)
Ratio of total number of replies to total number of Tweets during non-peak periods	Overall legal change, legislative change	
Ratio of total number of likes to total number of Tweets during non-peak periods		Institutionalization (negative)
Total number of replies in non-peak periods		Legislative change^

Note: ^ Relationship which changes when running partial correlation.

type of engagement brings the least incentives to domestic governments to change. The final type of engagement is retweeting. While this may not show a high level of engagement, it shows more ownership and participation than liking a Tweet. In a different vein, a campaign driven by retweets may in fact show consistent messaging, which could also lead to positive legal outcomes. Therefore, it is expected that replies would be associated with the most success, retweets somewhere in the middle, and likes the least amount of legal change.

Again, starting from a series of correlations the following variables emerged as potentially significant (see Table 7.7).

---

or "Slacktivism?": Digital Media and Organizing for Social Change' (2015) 29 Communication Teacher 81; Kirk Kristofferson, Katherine White, and John Peloza, 'The Nature of Slacktivism: How the Social Observability of an Initial Act of Token Support Affects Subsequent Prosocial Action' (2014) 40 Journal of Consumer Research 1149; YH Lee and G Hsieh, 'Does Slacktivism Hurt Activism? The Effects of Moral Balancing and Consistency in Online Activism' (2013) https://www.researchgate.net/publ ication/259823361_Does_slacktivism_hurt_activism_The_effects_of_moral_balancing_ and_consistency_in_online_activism#:~:text=We%20also%20found%20that%20parti cipants,decision%20on%20subsequent%20civic%20actions.&text=Content%20may%20 be%20subject%20to%20copyright, accessed 23 July 2024; Stephanie Vie, 'In Defense of "Slacktivism": The Human Rights Campaign Facebook Logo as Digital Activism' (2014) 19 First Monday, http://journals.uic.edu/ojs/index.php/fm/article/view/4961, accessed 7 July 2016.

Initially, these results seem to support the hypothesis – replies look to be positively associated with legal change, while likes seems to be negatively associated (less likely to lead to positive change). It also appears that, closely linked to persistence metrics, having that dialogue and debate continue in non-peak periods is also potentially important for positive change. It is necessary to run a partial correlation on the non-peak total replies, as again this significance could simply be reflecting the overall number of Tweets in the campaign. Controlling for total Tweets, the significance is no longer present ($R=0.484$, $p=0.271$). This eliminates this variable from having any statistical significance.

There are no other identified potential confounders for the remaining significant variables. It appears that campaigns with high levels of dialogue and debate are linked to more positive outcomes, and in particular legislative change. Producing a scatter plot further clarifies the relationships (see Figure 7.5).

The role of dialogue, debate, and indeed user engagement in non-peak periods appears to be even more important than that during the campaign overall. This relates to the spiral model critique in that it shows the highest level of engagement and therefore, by extension, risk to the user and incentive to the government.

Equally, looking at the relationship of likes to campaign outcomes, a similar finding can be seen (see Figure 7.6).

Although a weaker relationship, the trend can still be identified. Campaigns with more likes, and therefore the least level of engagement, risk, and incentive, are correlated with less positive change in the institutionalization of legal change. The incentives for the state to work towards institutionalization simply are not present in campaigns where the users are less engaged.

Overall models

The final piece of analysis attempts to put all the variables and hypotheses together into composite models. The first test to explore a composite, aggregated view of the research is to look at the relationship between the overall legal change and an overall composite campaign score. The overall campaign composite score in essence distils down over 500 potential parameters of interest into one summary number. It is an average of four composite scores: users, engagement, persistence, and content. Context and sentiment are excluded as these are not continuous, ordinal scales on which to build a linear regression. The composite scores include a selection of parameters chosen as the most illustrative of the variable. Therefore, a higher score indicates:

Figure 7.5: Relationship between replies and legal outcomes

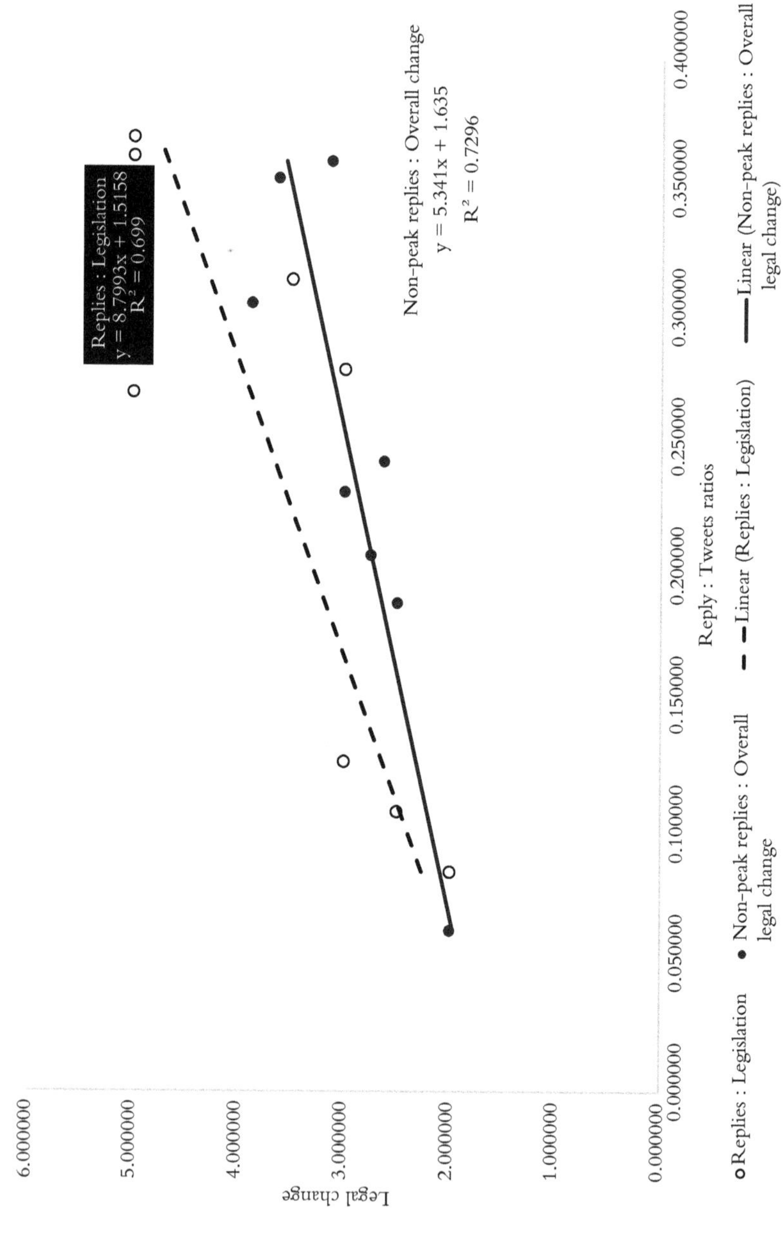

Figure 7.6: Relationship between likes and institutionalization

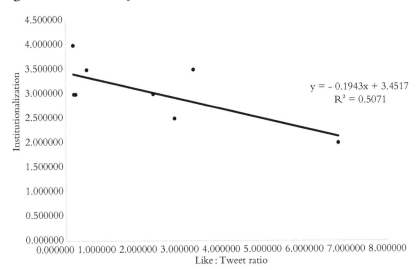

1. a more domestically driven campaign;
2. with high levels of ongoing dialogue and debate from users;
3. with high levels of activity in both peak and non-peak periods; and
4. consistent messaging which draws down from international norms on women's rights.

Table 7.8 shows that the overall composite score does show a statistically significant relationship with the overall legal change, and in particular with changes in legislation and to a lesser but still important extent, institutionalization. Running a partial correlation controlling for the total number of days of the campaign (which could play a part in the persistence component), the relationship remains significant with overall legal change at the 0.01 level (R=0.907, p=0.005), while the relationship remains but slightly weaker for legislative change (R=0.851, p=0.015) and institutionalization (R=0.784, p=0.037).

Looking at a simple linear regression between the overall composite campaign score and the overall legal change may show some summary insight. It is important to note that aggregated models do tend to lose some of the nuances of more complex or disaggregated models but can be useful as a simple way to summarize a large amount of information. At this stage, it is also worth noting that the outcome variable is normally distributed (analysed with a histogram and P-P plot).

Figure 7.7 shows that there does appear to be a linear relationship between the overall composite score and the overall legal change. As this is a relatively small sample size (N=8), any extrapolation of these findings

Table 7.8: Correlation between overall campaign score and legal change

		Overall legal change	Legislative change	Institutionalization	Law enforcement	UN dialogue
Overall hashtag campaign composite score	Correlation coefficient (R)	**0.907****	**0.850****	*0.732**	0.444	0.594
	Significance (p-value)	**0.002**	**0.008**	*0.039*	0.271	0.121

Note: *Italics* indicate a statistically significant relationship at p<0.05 level and ***bold italics*** indicate a p<0.01 level.

Figure 7.7: Relationship between overall campaign score and overall legal change

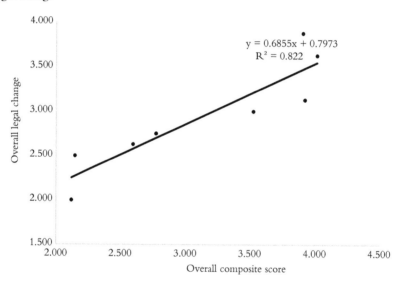

to the entire 'population' of campaigns meeting the selection criteria must be thought of with (extreme!) caution. Additionally, the variance appears to show heteroscedasticity, meaning that the spread of outcomes is larger at the successful end of the range and less varied at the unsuccessful end (although a preliminary test using a weighted estimate regression which corrects for this kind of variation returned the same results). Future work may need to make adjustments to overcome these potential biases. However, we can apply this model with confidence to *this* data, and therefore draw some tentative conclusions about next steps to develop models which may apply outside of the data set.

The full analysis shows that this is a statistically significant relationship (R= 0.907, R^2=0.822, R^2Adj=0.792, p=0.002). This means that 82 per cent of the changes in the overall legal score are explained by the Twitter-driven hashtag campaign's composite score, or 79 per cent in the model adjusted for the small sample size. This also means that 18 per cent (or 21 per cent) of the variance is due to other factors. However, explaining 82 per cent of the variance is a fairly good fit. Examining the output further, the model produces a B value of 0.686. This means that for each increase of 1 in the overall campaign composite, it is likely that the legal change will improve by 0.686. Again, this is a statistically significant result. It can therefore be concluded, albeit tentatively, that there is a meaningful relationship between the characteristics of the hashtag campaign and the legal outcome. Although it would have been desirable to look at the relationship while controlling for the World Justice Project index, without a value for #women2drive this runs the risk of presenting false results. At this stage, it will just be said that openness of a government may be a scope condition for success, but without full data it cannot be explored further.

Ideal Twitter campaign behaviours

This research has provided strong evidence of Twitter campaign behaviours that are associated with positive legal outcomes. The ultimate aim from a research impact perspective is to understand if there is a 'package' of elements which, taken together, are more likely to contribute to positive legal change for women and girls. The 'package' of elements for an ideal feminist hashtag campaign are variables which are drawn from the critiques of the spiral model and overcome some of the potential risks of campaigning in social media. Keeping in mind the overall scores of legal change, not a single campaign reached a level of perfect change, nor even breaching the 4th bracket.[24] The best campaign came in at 3.88 out of a possible 5.00. While this still shows a range of outcomes, it is not necessarily a range of successful outcomes, but rather a range of *less than* successful outcomes. Even #women2drive, with its success in lifting the ban on women driving, has major issues around the continuation of guardianship laws and the role of the courts in arbitrary arrests and detentions of women activists.

The ideal feminist hashtag campaign would be steered in the direction presented in Table 7.9, as much as possible (with full understanding that the organic, user-driven, and non-neutral nature of social media in and of itself presents challenges).

The future of the hashtag

Having identified ideal campaign behaviours, it is now critical to look to the future of hashtag campaigns and existing platforms, in particular Twitter/X. While the future of Twitter is important, it is equally important

---

[24] 5.00 being perfect change and 1.00 representing total regression.

Table 7.9: Ideal campaign behaviours

Variable	Indicators of success
Context	Target governments which are considered more 'open' It may also be advisable to avoid social media campaigning in close proximity to elections and potential regime change
Size of campaign	Try to ensure that the campaign is big enough to exert pressure (as in #women2drive), but not so big that it pushes the government into reactionary change (as evidenced by #delhigangrape and #niunamenos)
Persistence	Avoid days with no Tweets and aim for at least five Tweets per day. Equally, huge peak days with more than 10,000 Tweets may have a 'tactical concession' effect. Slow and steady campaigns are linked to more positive outcomes, as seen in #women2drive
Users	While the campaign needs to be domestically driven, there *also* needs to be a baseline level of foreign pressure, most importantly to move towards legislative change. Falling below the baseline of foreign pressure, particularly without domestic groundswell, runs the risk of government backlash, as seen in #stopstoning. The voice of ordinary domestic individuals (as opposed to activists or organizations) is important
Engagement	Higher levels of replies, particularly in non-peak periods, show higher levels of engagement and are linked to more positive outcomes. Retweeting indicates consistent messaging and has some positive effects. Campaigns with high proportions of likes without the dialogue of replies or the consistent messaging of retweets are likely to lead to less positive outcomes
Sentiment	Negative sentiment is linked with more *positive* outcomes in law enforcement. Go on – be angry!
Framing, messaging, and norms	The consistent presence of international norms around women's rights is one of the most important elements of a campaign's success. Volatile and changing framing and messaging is linked with government backlash, particularly evident in dialogue with UN treaty bodies

Note: Campaigns which target more 'open' governments may be associated with better outcomes, however this finding must be qualified as it does not include Saudi Arabia. Given that #women2drive saw the highest level of legal success, but that it might be speculated that Saudi Arabia would not have scored positively in the World Justice Project scores, the overall relationship may very well change with the inclusion of Saudi.

to note that this study was not necessarily tied to Twitter itself. This was more about hashtag organizing and, at the time, the accessibility and quality of Twitter data.[25] The study could equally have been conducted

---

[25] See, for example, Sheila Dang, 'Exclusive: Elon Musk's X Restructuring Curtails Disinformation Research, Spurs Legal Fears' (*Reuters*, 6 November 2023) https://www.reuters.com/technology/elon-musks-x-restructuring-curtails-disinformation-research-spurs-legal-fears-2023-11-06/, accessed 15 November 2023; Justine Calma, 'Scientists

using Facebook data or any other text-based social media site where we see hashtags. Twitter was an obvious design choice given the data available and the relatively short length of text, as well as some researcher preference for Twitter as a more open space, but the findings will be applicable across all media.[26] Indeed, it may be preferable to look to new and emerging social media sites as there is some indication that the quality of conversation on Twitter has declined since becoming X, possibly due in part to Musk's new algorithms (which of course were already problematic for feminist activism).[27] Traffic to the site showed a decline in the year since the takeover as well.[28]

That being said, understanding the future of Twitter is not unimportant or irrelevant either. With Elon Musk's takeover of Twitter, the immediate attitude towards research was hostile at best. In 2023, there were reports of many significant large-scale studies being cancelled in response to Musk's new policies which remove free academic access to the Application Programming Interface (API) and instead charge exorbitant amounts for the same data.[29] According to the news site *The Verge*, '[we were] unable to verify that news with Twitter, which now routinely responds to inquiries from reporters with a poop emoji'.[30] However, it is to be noted that manual data collection, as done in this study, is still available.

Beyond the availability of data, however, is also Musk's attitude towards information sharing and transparency. Reports had emerged that Musk was

---

Say They Can't Rely on Twitter Anymore' (*The Verge*, 31 May 2023) https://www.theverge.com/2023/5/31/23739084/twitter-elon-musk-api-policy-chilling-academic-research, accessed 15 November 2023. 'Before Musk bought Twitter for $44 billion, a large proportion of studies about social media had been related to Twitter, because the platform was a valuable source of information about politics and current events. Its data was easily accessible.'

[26] Calma (n 25).

[27] Kate Conger, 'How Elon Musk Changed the Meaning of Twitter for Users' (*The New York Times*, 27 October 2023) https://www.nytimes.com/2023/10/27/technology/elon-musk-twitter-year.html, accessed 15 November 2023; Mary-Ann Russon, 'Elon Musk's New Twitter Algorithm Changes Are "Amplifying Anger", Say Researchers' (*Evening Standard*, 30 May 2023) https://www.standard.co.uk/news/tech/elon-musk-twitter-algorithm-cyberbullying-discrimination-cornell-uc-berkeley-b1084490.html, accessed 15 November 2023.

[28] Conger (n 27).

[29] Dang (n 25); Calma (n 25); Mark Scott, 'Twitter's Plan to Charge Researchers for Data Access Puts It in EU Crosshairs' (*Politico*, 22 March 2023) https://www.politico.eu/article/twitter-elon-musk-plan-to-charge-researchers-for-data-access-puts-it-in-eu-crosshairs/, accessed 15 November 2023; Mark Scott, 'Elon Musk Goes to War with Researchers' (*Politico*, 7 February 2023) https://www.politico.eu/article/elon-musk-twitter-goes-to-war-with-researchers-api/, accessed 15 November 2023.

[30] Calma (n 25).

intending to pursue legal action against researchers who documented an increase in hate speech on Twitter (X) since Musk's takeover.[31] Researchers fear that this will have a chilling effect on researchers, adding another barrier to the now unattainable cost of data.[32]

Whether it is called Twitter, X, Blue Sky, or any other platform, social media and hashtag campaigning will still persist. There is nothing in this study that suggests that feminist activists should stop using social media tools. What this study shows is that there are ways in which activists could perhaps harness the power of social media in more meaningful ways, at least when it comes to international campaigns targeting domestic legal change for women's rights. The study also cannot compare the legal outcomes given the existence of the Twitter-driven hashtag campaigns to what might have happened if the campaigns had not started to trend or go 'viral'. It could be that the situation would be worse for women and girls if the issues had never made it into the public social media conscious at all. What this study aims to provide is, rather, empirical insight into how campaigns can be more successful once they 'take off', and how, to whatever extent possible, to avoid the campaign behaviours which bring an element of risk for women and girls. Although social media is by definition chaotic, unpredictable, and elite user-driven, there may be ways for activists and even organizations to creatively work to avoid these risky social media behaviours that potentially lead to negative outcomes. Some of these efforts may already be underway, but it is hoped that the level of comparative, empirical evidence in this book will help to inform advocacy in the future. Conversely, if it proves impossible to 'control' hashtag campaigns, then this research may serve as a caution to activists over the potential for unanticipated and unintentional negative outcomes.

Final thoughts: are social media campaigns really making laws better for women and girls?

In short, this research has shown that international Twitter-driven hashtag campaigns *can* and *do* have relationships with domestic legal change for women and girls. This research provides crucial evidence-based insight for activists, academics, and campaigners around the world working to improve the lives of women and girls. The data shows that there are certain campaign behaviours which are associated with more positive legal

---

[31] 'Musk Threatens to Sue Researchers Documenting the Rise in Hateful Tweets' (*PBS NewsHour*, 31 July 2023) https://www.pbs.org/newshour/economy/musk-threatens-to-sue-researchers-documenting-the-rise-in-hateful-tweets, accessed 15 November 2023.

[32] Ibid.

outcomes and characteristics which are linked to negative legal outcomes. Campaigns which are domestically driven, with a high level of foreign attention, showing persistence, engagement, and consistency, are more likely to lead to positive legal outcomes. Conversely, campaigns which lack in domestic drive, can be seen as 'foreign meddling' or 'colonial violence', and fail to achieve persistence, engagement, or consistency, are more likely to lead to negative outcomes. It is hoped that these findings can help campaigning in the future to, at the very least, attempt to avoid social media campaigns that could lead to more harm than good. This research has also contributed to scholarship on digital feminist activism, aligning with both those who conceptualize social spaces as potential opportunities[33] and those who share deep concerns about online spaces.[34]

---

[33] Carrie Rentschler, '#Safetytipsforladies: Feminist Twitter Takedowns of Victim Blaming' (2015) 15 Feminist Media Studies 353; Carrie A Rentschler, 'Distributed Activism: Domestic Violence and Feminist Media Infrastructure in the Fax Age' (2015) 8 Communication, Culture & Critique 182; Carrie A Rentschler, '#MeToo and Student Activism against Sexual Violence' (2018) 11 Communication Culture & Critique 503; Nancy Fraser, 'Rethinking the Public Sphere: A Contribution to the Critique of Actually Existing Democracy' (1990) Social Text 56; Sara Ahmed (ed), *Thinking through Feminism* (Routledge, 2000); Sara Ahmed, *Living a Feminist Life* (Duke University Press, 2017); Clare Hemmings, 'Affective Solidarity: Feminist Reflexivity and Political Transformation' (2012) 13 Feminist Theory 147; Ott (n 9); Ann Travers, 'Parallel Subaltern Feminist Counterpublics in Cyberspace' (2003) 46 Sociological Perspectives 223.

[34] danah boyd, *It's Complicated: The Social Lives of Networked Teens* (Yale University Press, 2014); boyd (n 10); Joan Donovan and danah boyd, 'Stop the Presses? Moving From Strategic Silence to Strategic Amplification in a Networked Media Ecosystem' (2019) American Behavioral Scientist 000276421987822; Gail Lewis and Clare Hemmings, '"Where Might We Go If We Dare": Moving beyond the "Thick, Suffocating Fog of Whiteness" in Feminism' (2019) 20 Feminist Theory 405; Gillespie (n 10); Heather Lang, '#MeToo: A Case Study in Re-Embodying Information' (2019) Computers and Composition, https://linkinghub.elsevier.com/retrieve/pii/S8755461519300222, accessed 23 August 2019; Kaitlynn Mendes, Jessica Ringrose, and Jessalynn Keller, *Digital Feminist Activism: Girls and Women Fight Back Against Rape Culture* (Oxford University Press, 2019) https://www-oxfordscholarship-com.uea.idm.oclc.org/view/10.1093/oso/9780190697846.001.0001/oso-9780190697846, accessed 10 February 2020; Kaitlynn Mendes, Jessica Ringrose, and Jessalynn Keller, '#MeToo and the Promise and Pitfalls of Challenging Rape Culture through Digital Feminist Activism' (2018) 25 European Journal of Women's Studies 236; Kaitlynn Mendes, Jessalynn Keller, and Jessica Ringrose, 'Digitized Narratives of Sexual Violence: Making Sexual Violence Felt and Known through Digital Disclosures' (2019) 21 New Media & Society 1290.

APPENDIX

Design Challenges and Technological Solutions

Collection of Tweets

The process of finding historical Twitter data was extremely complex. At the time of writing the initial research proposal, historical Tweets were freely available via various online tools. However, Twitter changed the terms and conditions for accessing historical Tweets (defined as more than two weeks old) during the initial phases of the research. This therefore meant that the data needed for the study was going to be difficult to obtain.

Quotes were gathered for the monetized services available for purchasing bulk sets of Twitter data. This was deemed to be far outside the research budget and this option was therefore null. Web scraping was explored, however this option clearly violates the Twitter terms and conditions and was rejected on this basis. The final option was to collect the Tweets manually. This entailed using Twitter's advanced search function and copying and pasting Tweets. This is fully in line with Twitter's terms and conditions.[1] Although time- and labour-intensive, this method of data collection was chosen as the best possible option for collecting the data.

This is an important note as, with the 2023 developments in Twitter (X)'s approach to research, manual data collection may be a solution to the emerging challenges.[2]

---

[1] Twitter, 'Developer Agreement and Policy', https://developer.twitter.com/en/develo per-terms/agreement-and-policy.html, accessed 15 September 2018; 'Archiving Tweets: Reckoning with Twitter's Policy' (*Insight News Lab*), http://newslab.insight-cen tre.org/tweetarchivingchallenges/, accessed 15 September 2018.

[2] Justine Calma, 'Scientists Say They Can't Rely on Twitter Anymore' (*The Verge*, 31 May 2023) https://www.theverge.com/2023/5/31/23739084/twitter-elon-musk-api-policy-chilling-academic-research, accessed 15 November 2023; Heidi Ledford, 'How Musk's Takeover Might Change Twitter: What Researchers Think' (2022) 611 Nature 436; Mark

In the end, this became an incredibly important process within the study. Having the opportunity to scroll through all of the Tweets and thus become intimately familiar with each campaign positively influenced the end result analysis. The process of manual collection meant that for each campaign, significant time was spent developing an understanding of campaign drivers, ebbs and flows of Tweets and information, images which appeared perhaps hundreds of times, Tweets which were retweeted regularly, the issues, topics, and even emotions which dominated different epochs, and an overall general impression of what was really *happening* in each campaign.

The process for collecting the Tweets manually was as follows. First, the researcher used the Twitter advanced search function to search by hashtag, over a given time period based on the campaign timelines. Google Chrome was used consistently, from two different work station PCs. The Tweets were first loaded under the 'Latest' tab. In most cases, with well-defined time periods (that is, perhaps 24 hours for peaks, or one week for quieter times), all Tweets were able to be loaded into one batch using scrolling. When reaching the end of the available Tweets, they were copied and pasted into a plain text format and saved as individual files. The process was repeated using the 'Top' tab to ensure that the highest number of Tweets were collected and that any collection errors would be rectified through the dual process.

Difficulties arose when there were more than roughly 8,000 Tweets during one 24-hour period. The smallest possible search is one calendar day and the Tweets are always loaded in reverse time order (the most recent first). While attempting to load more than approximately 8,000 Tweets in the same page, Chrome would 'crash' and the Tweets that had been loading via scrolling were lost; it was not possible to cut down or reorder the search parameters to avoid the crash or collect the Tweets differently. After extensive trial and error, it was determined that the source of the limitation was the memory available in the browser. By monitoring the memory usage in Chrome while loading Tweets, it was possible to anticipate a potential crash and save progress. Then more Tweets could be loaded onto the page, saving every time approximately 100 additional Tweets had been loaded, until Chrome crashed. This meant that there were a small number of incomplete days where it was not possible to access the full range of Tweets over approximately 8,000 (less than 1 per cent of total days in most campaigns, 5 per cent in

---

Scott, 'Elon Musk Goes to War with Researchers' (*Politico*, 7 February 2023) https://www.politico.eu/article/elon-musk-twitter-goes-to-war-with-researchers-api/, accessed 15 November 2023; Mark Scott, 'Twitter's Plan to Charge Researchers for Data Access Puts It in EU Crosshairs' (*Politico*, 22 March 2023) https://www.politico.eu/article/twitter-elon-musk-plan-to-charge-researchers-for-data-access-puts-it-in-eu-crosshairs/, accessed 15 November 2023.

#niunamenos – see the next paragraph). It also meant that for some of these very high activity days, it was not feasible to repeat the process using both 'Latest' and 'Top' tabs.

Additionally, the initial data collection phase took place from December 2016 to March 2017. In the initial phase, the hashtag #niunamas was used to collect data on the Argentinian campaign. However, during the legal data collection and analysis, it was determined that the more widely used hashtag was #niunamenos. Therefore, in December 2017 and January 2018, data collection on this hashtag was undertaken. It appeared that either Google Chrome or Twitter had changed memory allocations and fewer Tweets per day were accessible. Chrome crashed at approximately 4,000 Tweets. This explains the higher number of incomplete days in the #niunamenos campaign. However, as this campaign was also the largest by quite some margin, there were still ample Tweets available for analysis and it was decided that the campaign could therefore still be included in the study.[3] In total, it took approximately five months to collect the Tweets manually.

Cleaning the Twitter data

Once the Tweets for all campaigns were collected and saved in plain text formats, technical assistance was provided in programmatically writing a simple script to format the data and remove duplicates.[4] Given that Tweets were collected via Latest and Top tabs, removing the duplicates was important. The Tweets were then in tab-delineated format (.csv) and could easily be imported into Excel. Simple descriptive statistics were generated during this process as well, including the most 100 used words, the most 100 used hashtags, word length (that is, number of two letter words used, number of four letter words used, and so on), Tweet length (that is, number of 140 character Tweets, and so on), 100 most prolific users, numbers of retweets, replies, and likes, and Tweets per day. The data was then disaggregated over peak and non-peak time periods, determined by the number of Tweets

---

[3]   Additionally, if the Latest tab could not be fully loaded, it would be the earlier Tweets that would be missing. This could have meant that for those days Tweets from a specific time of day would consistently be missing. However, as many days were complete and a third of the incomplete days were able to be gathered via Latest and Top tabs, it was determined any gaps in specific time periods on the incomplete days gathered via Latest only would be overcome. As it took several hours to load just one day of Tweets, practical realities were taken into consideration.

[4]   Dr David Willis, a research associate and clinical scientist in UEA's Medical School at the time, with senior expertise in computer programming and data analysis, provided this assistance. As a matter of disclosure, he is also the researcher's husband.

per day (the bar for peak was set for each campaign based on the average number of Tweets per day).

A small set of Tweets generated unreadable content only. Something was lost in translation in the process of copying and pasting. These were therefore included in the persistence, engagement, and user analysis, but were excluded from the sentiment and content analysis. As a small percentage of total Tweets, this was deemed an acceptable level of loss (<1 per cent in most campaigns, 2 per cent in #farkhunda, and 4 per cent in #sendeanlat).

Quality assurance was undertaken by spot-checking various randomly selected data points against the original text files and against live data on Twitter.com. This process provided all the data needed to continue to analysis.

Initial analysis of Twitter data

Once the data was collected and cleaned, analysis could begin. When looking at persistence across the campaigns, various parameters were derived from the basic data. The clearest parameter was simply the number of Tweets each day, which was used to generate timelines and overall peaks for the campaigns. In more detail, this data was also broken down to look at the standard deviation of Tweets per day and the mean Tweets per day. These provide information about the variability of the campaign's popularity. Additional information on peaks was also produced, such as the number of peak periods, the number of individual peaks, the number of Tweets on peak days, and the breakdown of the campaign across peak and non-peak periods. The data was explored to look at the number of days with no Tweets, with five or more Tweets, with ten or more Tweets, and with 1,000 or more Tweets. Where possible, these figures were converted into percentages for comparability. Some of this data was explored but not included in statistical tests given the issue with incomplete days explained earlier. For example, even though the highest peak for #niunamenos was 4,809, this is not comparable to the other campaigns given the differences in maximum Tweets collected per day. Equally, although the highest peak for #delhigangrape is 13,136, for #sendeanlat is 12,993, and for #women2drive is 12,055, these are not accurate representations of the peaks themselves but rather the ability to load as many Tweets as possible given the browser memory constraints. Therefore raw numbers in this vein are interesting, but not comparable.

The engagement metrics are drawn from the number of times each Tweet in the data set was retweeted, replied to, or liked. These numbers were then tallied up and used to generate ratios to compare the incidence of the different kinds of engagement to the total number of Tweets and to each other. The process was then repeated for peak versus non-peak periods. This was done in order to characterize the kind of engagements most prominent in each campaign.

From manually accessing the profile pages of the 100 most prolific users in each campaign, information was collected to measure their campaign activity, reach (number of followers), overall activity (number of Tweets ever sent), location, and profile category. Note that these profiles reflect the current number of followers and Tweets, and thus are a proxy for what the profile may have looked like at the time of the campaign.

Profile categories were inductively coded, using a free coding method which was then standardized and used as a code book for recoding the profiles.[5] Users were categorized into the following profile codes: academic, activist, artist, business, counter-narrative, entertainment industry, government party, independent journalist, individual, official journalist, news agency, organization, individual politician, sales/product account, trending topics, writer, or unknown. The code was determined based on what the users wrote themselves in their profile description. Therefore, to be coded as an activist, this word must have been used in their self-written profile. To be considered an independent journalist, the user self-identified as a journalist but was clear that they were not associated with an official outlet. News agencies were the official Twitter accounts for local, national, or international news outlets. Individuals were Twitter users who did not self-identify as a specific category and clearly identified as unaffiliated users. Unknown were profiles that had been left blank or were otherwise nonsensical. The profiles were also used to identify locations. As these also are generated by the users themselves, the location was not always accurate or included. If a location was listed but unknown to the researcher, Google Maps was used to pinpoint a country. Locations were coded as domestic or non-domestic, as it was clear whether a user was in the target country, but when the location was unclear it was more accurate to label the user as 'non-domestic' as opposed to 'foreign' as they may not have been foreign, but equally could not clearly be classed as domestic. These groups could then be 'sliced and diced' to look at relationships across the different metrics as percentages.

Content analysis started with basic information, such as most used word length, most used Tweet length, and total hashtags (apart from the campaign hashtag) used. Sentiment analysis was performed programmatically with Python, using TextBlob to generate positivity, negativity, polarity, and subjectivity scores.[6] The process also has a built-in system for translation, using Google Translate.

---

[5]   Alan Bryman, *Social Research Methods* (fifth edition, Oxford University Press, 2016).

[6]   TextBlob, 'TextBlob: Simplified Text Processing', https://textblob.readthedocs.io/en/dev/, accessed 18 September 2018. TextBlob uses the natural language processing (NLP)

APPENDIX

Significant time, effort, and creativity went into the problem of translation. How could a study that critiques the spiral model for its overemphasis on Western actors and underemphasis on domestic voices be valid if Tweets in the native language were not analysed? Equally, how could a small study like this access the resources necessary to translate several hundred thousand Tweets? This was an extraordinarily difficult barrier to overcome in the research design and much time was spent thinking, testing, and exploring options.

First, it is important to note that translation only affected one area of independent variables (content). Persistence, engagement, and users could be analysed without large-scale translation. The exploration of consistent, variable, and international norms, alongside the sentiment analysis, were the areas which necessitated translation. Equally, some of the campaigns targeted English-speaking countries; again, translation was not a concern in these campaigns.

The initial, and unsatisfying, decision was that translation was simply too expensive and complicated. Only English Tweets would be included in the content analysis. However, upon further reflection, this just seemed unacceptable given the nature and overall aims of the study. After extensive problem-solving thoughts, a novel approach was devised. As the normative analysis was only looking at sets of most commonly used words or phrases, only these needed to be translated, which could easily be done via Google Translate. In other words, the 100 most commonly used words or phrases could be collected from Tweets in any language, and the short sets of results could then be translated into English. There was no need to translate the entire set of Tweets, just the emerging norms. Equally, the presence of international norms was distilled down into a list of roughly 100 key words and phrases. This list could be translated via Google Translate into any number of languages and searches undertaken accordingly.

The initial study design did not include sentiment analysis. However, once all the Tweets were collected it was decided that adding in the sentiment analysis would be a fairly straightforward endeavour that would not add too much time to the data collection. Once this was in place, it was then discovered that a fairly simple programmatic add-on for sentiment analysis included translation. Therefore, in the end, it was actually possible to translate discrete sets of Tweets (see Table A.1).

---

through the 'Natural Language Toolkit' (NLTK) and the pattern.en module to classify the Tweets. The process removes 'stopwords' such as I, am, you, are, and so on and then classifies words based on their part of speech (adjective, noun, adverb, and so on). Only those parts of speech which can be classified as positive or negative are passed through to the sentiment analysis. The TextBlob sentiment analysis uses a Naïve Bayes Classification system on a known dataset to score the Tweets.

195

HASHTAG ACTIVISM AND WOMEN'S RIGHTS

Table A.1: Overview of translated Tweets

Campaign	% non-English	Language translated to English
#stopstoning	1	No translation
#letwomengotostadium	60	Persian
#farkhunda	9	No translation
#sendeanlat	76	Turkish
#mydressmychoice	5	No translation
#delhigangrape	7	No translation
#niunamenos	63	Spanish
#women2drive	38	Arabic

The translated Tweets were analysed for sentiment. Spot-checks were undertaken to ensure that, to the extent possible, the sentiment score was reflective of the Tweets. This was particularly undertaken for days which showed either extremely positive or extremely negative average scores. Various parameters were generated using these scores, looking at the differences between peak and non-peak periods, weighted scores (based on the number of Tweets), highest and lowest scores, and differences.

The final piece of initial Twitter analysis was to explore framing and messaging and to proxy the presence of norms in Tweets. This process took two forms: one inductive and one deductive. The inductive process used a script to programmatically search for the 100 most used words across a set of event-based epochs (time periods). The deductive process used a pre-defined set of 93 words to measure the presence of international norms in each campaign. The list was derived from a survey of international instruments and reports on women's rights and violence against women, utilizing both United Nations and non-governmental organization documents to have a rounded approach.

From the list of most 100 used words from each epoch, words which could not be used to interpret a norm or message were removed (that is, and, are, were, the, and so on) The remaining list of inductive words were then divided into those that appeared in three or more epochs and those that appeared in less than three epochs. This showed the difference between organically emerging but consistent framing and messaging (more than three epochs) and organically emerging but variable and short-lived framing and messaging (less than three). This process emerged through the initial cleaning and analysis of the data and was then applied to all campaigns. Finally, each epoch was scanned for the number of times each of the deductive international norm key words were used. Inductive frames were also matched against deductive international norms to see how many of the most used words were also representative of international norms. Frames, messages, and norms which were legal in nature were also identified to see how much of a legal focus was taken on by the campaign users.

Collection and analysis of legal data

The collection of legal evidence was much more straightforward. Additionally, collection and analysis were undertaken simultaneously for each campaign, rather than bulk collection followed by bulk analysis (as done for the Twitter data). This approach was adopted as it was a cyclical and snowballing process of collection, analysis, further collection and cross-referencing, analysis, and so on. While the collection process was unique and specific for each campaign, a few general principles were applied. The collection began with a simple internet search of the hashtag. This provided the starting point for research. Amnesty International and Human Rights Watch materials were searched for all campaigns, as well as the BBC and *New York Times*. Where possible, non-governmental organizations actively supporting the campaigns were identified and their websites were thoroughly searched for any and all relevant reports, statistics, or press releases. Government websites were searched for relevant materials, including crime statistics. Case law was accessed where possible, after identification of relevant cases. An extensive process of cross-referencing was undertaken to ensure that a wide range of materials were sourced. Once the initial round was completed, analysis began. Tables were created to collect information and quotes, and to help identify gaps in evidence. The collection process was then repeated to fill gaps and follow up on additional referenced sources or involved non-governmental organizations. This carried on until the table was as complete as possible. Each campaign generated a table of 10–15 pages of analysis to ensure a comparable level of information gathered for each. The quantification was done as an ongoing process during the analysis, reviewed regularly and ultimately when all campaigns were completed to ensure consistency and comparability.

Statistical analysis

The issue of correlation versus causation is ripe in any study of this nature. Robinson highlights this point when exploring the CNN effect: 'the difficulty [is in] measuring exactly the precise impact which media has on policy ... and the significance each attaches to policy certainty (and uncertainty) in determining media influence'.[7] Similar challenges are

---

[7] Piers Robinson, 'The CNN Effect: Can the News Media Drive Foreign Policy?' (1999)

discussed across many areas of media effect studies.[8] As with the media effects literature, it is not possible to show direct causation in this kind of research, but it is possible to ensure the study design is rigorous enough to allow for correlations and indirect relationships to be shown.[9] In this case, the correlations are between the campaigns and the legal outcomes:

> Correlation can also be underscored by timelines, quotes, and government activities. For example, in some cases there were spikes in Tweets followed by government action (#delhigangrape). In other cases, the government specifically referred to the hashtag campaign when discussing legislative changes (#stopstoning). Government officials implementing change even referred to the hashtag itself, announcing changes on Twitter (#niunamenos). The campaigners themselves used Twitter as the platform to engage officials in some instances. In #niunamenos, candidates in upcoming elections were asked to sign a pledge to implement the campaign demands and, critically to Tweet this pledge out.[10]

It is this kind of evidence which supports the finding of relationships between the campaigns and the legal outcomes are valid.

All of the parameters collected and cleaned were collated into one 'master data set' spreadsheet. Here it was possible to compare the campaigns side-by-side, identify key characteristics (very high or very low scores in any given parameter), and begin to gain an overview into overall trends or patterns. From this exercise and the in-depth legal analysis, it became clear that the campaigns fell into broad groupings based on legal outcomes.[11]

---

    25 Review of International Studies 301, 304.

[8] Elizabeth M Perse and Jennifer L Lambe (eds), *Media Effects and Society* (second edition, Routledge, 2017).

[9] Robinson (n 7) 305.

[10] Reilly Dempsey Willis, 'Exploring the Relationship between Global Twitter Campaigns and Domestic Law: Methodological Challenges and Solutions' (2021) 30 Information & Communications Technology Law 3.

[11] #stopstoning and #letwomengotostadium showed many signs of government backlash, and scored at 2.5 or less (1.0 being the worst and 5.0 being the best) in legal outcomes. Not one of the components showed any positive change above 3.0 and but did show more than two parameters at 2.0 or less. Although both targeted Iran, the campaigns were different enough to see that this grouping was based on the legal outcomes more than the context. #farkhunda, #sendeanlat, and #mydressmychoice all broadly showed no overall legal change, categorized as status quo. Each of the campaigns had two or more parameters that scored 3.0 or greater, and no campaign scored less than 2.5 in more than one category. Although #farkhunda showed a particularly negative score in law enforcement, this was balanced out by some positive change in legislation, placing this campaign in the status quo grouping. #farkhunda was a borderline campaign, but the positive change in legislation set it apart from the two Iranian campaigns which

APPENDIX

As an initial test of the hypotheses, simple correlations were run between all parameters and the overall legal outcomes. To explore further, coefficients of determination (R^2) were produced to identify parameters with a strong linear relationship with the overall legal change. These were initially done quite simply in Excel in the master data set. These tests provided excellent insight into which parameters may be of interest overall, and which parameters, while important to explore in each campaign, may have less of a linear and therefore predictive relationship with legal outcomes. SPSS was used to run more extensive tests. The information contained in the master data set, including all of the parameters, the composite scores, and the initial associative tests were then used to analyse the results.

---

showed no positive change. #delhigangrape and #niunamenos showed extremely similar legal results, with full marks in legislative change but poorer scores in law enforcement. They also showed a lack of progress in institutionalization (at 3.0 and 3.5 respectively). These campaigns showed very clear signs of tactical concessions but lacked long term implementation or institutionalization. Finally, #women2drive stood apart from the other campaigns as showing the most positive signs of change, particularly in institutionalization.

References

Abbasgholizadeh M, ' "To Do Something We Are Unable to Do in Iran": Cyberspace, the Public Sphere, and the Iranian Women's Movement' (2014) 39 Signs 831

Adamovsky E, ' "Ni Una Menos": Feminism and Politics in Argentina' (*teleSUR*, 6 July 2015) https://web.archive.org/web/20170807171158/https://www.telesurtv.net/english/opinion/Ni-una-menos-Feminism-and-Politics-in-Argentina-20150706-0011.html, accessed 17 November 2023

The Advocates for Human Rights, 'Turkey CEDAW Alternative Report DV Femicide' (2022) https://www.theadvocatesforhumanrights.org/Res/FINAL%20Turkey%20CEDAW%20Alternative%20Report%20DV%20Femicide.pdf, accessed 7 November 2023

Afghan Women's Network, 'Afghan Women's Network Annual Report 2015: "Steps Toward Quality" ' (2015)

Afghan Women's Network, 'Afghanistan CEDAW Shadow (NGO) Report' (2012)

Afghan Women's Network, 'Beijing+20 Afghanistan Civil Society Progress Report' (2015)

Agence France-Presse, 'Three Men Get Life Sentence for Murder and Attempted Rape of Student in Turkey' (*The Guardian*, 4 December 2015) https://www.theguardian.com/world/2015/dec/04/three-men-life-sentence-murder-student-turkey-ozgecan-aslan, accessed 29 November 2023

Agency for Cooperation and Research in Development, 'Making the Law Count: Kenya: An Audit of Legal Practice on Sexual Violence' (2009)

Ahmed S, 'Beyond Humanism and Postmodernism: Theorizing a Feminist Practice' (1996) 11 Hypatia 71

Ahmed S, 'Deconstruction and Law's Other: Towards a Feminist Theory of Embodied Legal Rights' (1995) 4 Social & Legal Studies 55

Ahmed S, *Living a Feminist Life* (Duke University Press, 2017)

Ahmed S (ed), *Thinking through Feminism* (Routledge, 2000)

Ahmed Y, 'Political Discourse Analysis: A Decolonial Approach' (2021) 18 Critical Discourse Studies 139

REFERENCES

AI Monitor, 'Fury in Turkey as Convicted Wife Killer Murders Third Victim' (6 January 2023) https://www.al-monitor.com/originals/2023/01/fury-turkey-convicted-wife-killer-murders-third-victim, accessed 17 November 2023

Akbar N 'A Year Later, Still No Justice for Farkhunda' (*Foreign Policy*, 1 April 2016) https://foreignpolicy.com/2016/04/01/a-year-later-still-no-justice-for-farkhunda/, accessed 16 November 2023

Akyol M, 'The Monsters among Us' (*Hürriyet Daily News*, 18 February 2015) http://www.hurriyetdailynews.com/the-monsters-among-us.aspx?pageID=449&nID=78486&NewsCatID=411, accessed 17 November 2023

Alcoba N and McGowan C, '#NiUnaMenos Five Years on: Latin America as Deadly as Ever for Women, Say Activists' (*The Guardian*, 4 June 2020) https://www.theguardian.com/global-development/2020/jun/04/niunamenos-five-years-on-latin-america-as-deadly-as-ever-for-women-say-activists, accessed 8 November 2023

Alexander H, 'Saudi Arabia to Allow Women to Drive in Major Milestone for Country' (*The Telegraph*, 26 September 2017) http://www.telegraph.co.uk/news/2017/09/26/saudi-arabia-allow-women-drive/, accessed 17 November 2023

Alfred C, 'Women In Turkey Share Devastating Stories Of Sexual Harassment In #Sendeanlat Twitter Campaign' (*Huffington Post*, 17 February 2015) http://www.huffingtonpost.com/2015/02/17/turkey-sendeanlat-twitter-campaign_n_6699702.html, accessed 29 November 2023

Alhargan RA, 'The Impact of the UN Human Rights System and Human Rights INGOs on the Saudi Government with Special Reference to the Spiral Model' (2012) 16 The International Journal of Human Rights 598

Alison P, 'Four Years of Women Drivers in Saudi, What Has Changed?' (*Global Fleet*, 30 March 2022) https://www.globalfleet.com/en/taxation-and-legislation/global/features/four-years-women-drivers-saudi-what-has-changed, accessed 9 November 2023

Almoaibed H, 'License to Drive Change: The Status of Saudi Women under Vision 2030' (2023) https://blogs.lse.ac.uk/mec/2023/01/10/license-to-drive-change-the-status-of-saudi-women-under-vision-2030/, accessed 9 November 2023

Al-Sharif M, 'Opinion: I Can't Wait to Drive in Saudi Arabia Again' (*The New York Times*, 27 September 2017) https://www.nytimes.com/2017/09/27/opinion/saudi-arabia-women-driving-.html, accessed 29 November 2023

Altaher N, 'Iranian Woman Denied Soccer Stadium Access Dies after Setting Herself on Fire' (*CNN*, 10 September 2019) https://edition.cnn.com/2019/09/10/football/iran-football-women-sahar-khodayari-spt-intl/index.html, accessed 12 December 2019

Amaya S and Rubio M, 'El Mapa de Los Femicidios En La Argentina' (*La Nacion*, 20 May 2015) https://web.archive.org/web/20170821064237/ http://www.lanacion.com.ar/1794148-el-mapa-de-los-femicidios-en-la-argentina, accessed 17 November 2023

Ambah FS, 'Saudi Women See a Brighter Road on Rights' (*Washington Post*, 31 January 2008) http://www.washingtonpost.com/wp-dyn/content/article/2008/01/30/AR2008013003805.html, accessed 29 November 2023

Amnesty International, 'Action Appeal' (2010)

Amnesty International, 'Afghanistan Women Still under Attack – a Systematic Failure to Protect' (2005)

Amnesty International, 'Back-Tracking, Compromises, and Failed Pledges – Human Rights Sidelined in Afghanistan. Amnesty International Submission to the UN Universal Periodic Review' (2014)

Amnesty International, 'Death Penalty/Stoning: Mokarrameh Ebrahimi' (9 July 2007)

Amnesty International, 'Fears Grow for Iran Stoning Case Lawyer and Son' (3 November 2010)

Amnesty International, 'Iran End Executions by Stoning' (2008) MDE 13/001/2008

Amnesty International, 'Iran Executions by Stoning' (2010) MDE 13/095/2010

Amnesty International, 'Iran Must End Harassment of Stoning Case Lawyer' (28 July 2010)

Amnesty International, 'Iran: New Executions Demonstrate Need for Unequivocal Legal Ban of Stoning' (2009)

Amnesty International, 'Iran Stoning Sentence Suspension Not Enough' (8 September 2010)

Amnesty International, 'Saudi Arabia: Is This What Is to Be Expected of a UN Human Rights Council Member (Part 2)?' (21 May 2015)

Amnesty International, 'Stoning: Global Summary' (2010)

Amnesty International, 'Strengthening the Rule of Law and Protection of Human Rights, Including Women's Rights, Is Key to Any Development Plan for Afghanistan: Open Letter to Participants in the International Donors Conference on Afghanistan in Tokyo' (2012)

Amnesty International, 'Too Many Missed Opportunities: Human Rights in Afghanistan under the Karzai Administration' (2014)

Amnesty International, 'UNAMA Mandate Extension a Clear Reminder to Prioritise Human Rights in Afghanistan' (2015)

Amnesty International, 'Written Statement Submitted by Amnesty International, a Non-Governmental Organization in Special Consultative Status' (2013) UN Doc A/HRC/23/NGO/102

REFERENCES

Amnesty International, 'Written Statement Submitted by Amnesty International, a Non-Governmental Organization in Special Consultative Status' (2015) UN Doc A/HRC/28/NGO/19

Arruzza C, Bhattacharya T, and Fraser N, *Feminism for the 99 Percent: A Manifesto* (Verso, 2019)

ArtMattersInfo, 'Kenyan Universities Call for "Decent" Dressing and Grooming' (ArtMatters.Info, 18 November 2015) http://artmatters.info/2015/11/kenyan-universities-call-for-decent-dressing-and-grooming/, accessed 16 November 2023

Asquith C, 'Ozgecan Aslan and Violence Against Women in Turkey' (*The New York Times*, 23 February 2015) https://www.nytimes.com/2015/02/24/opinion/ozgecan-aslan-and-violence-against-women-in-turkey.html, accessed 29 November 2023

Asquith C and Jones S, 'Turkish Women Rising' (*Ms. Magazine Blog*, 23 March 2017) http://msmagazine.com/blog/2017/03/23/turkish-women-rising/, accessed 17 November 2023

Atuhaire P, 'Mini-Skirts and Morals in Uganda' (*BBC News*, 9 July 2017) http://www.bbc.co.uk/news/world-africa-40507843, accessed 29 November 2023

Auger GA, 'Fostering Democracy through Social Media: Evaluating Diametrically Opposed Nonprofit Advocacy Organizations' Use of Facebook, Twitter, and YouTube' (2013) 39 Public Relations Review 369

Aura R, 'Kenya Law: Situational Analysis and the Legal Framework on Sexual and Gender-Based Violence in Kenya: Challenges and Opportunities' (Kenya Law) http://kenyalaw.org/kl/index.php?id=4512, accessed 6 November 2023

Babacan N, 'Erdoğan's Remarks on Gender Equality Stir Fury' (*Hürriyet Daily News*, 26 November 2014) http://www.hurriyetdailynews.com/erdogans-remarks-on-gender-equality-stir-fury-.aspx?pageID=238&nID=74820&NewsCatID=338, accessed 17 November 2023

Bachelard JY, 'The Anglo-Leasing Corruption Scandal in Kenya: The Politics of International and Domestic Pressures and Counter-Pressures' (2010) 37 Review of African Political Economy 187

Bager J, 'Forbidden to Drive: A Saudi Woman On Life Inside the Kingdom' (*Time*, 25 October 2013) http://ideas.time.com/2013/10/25/forbidden-to-drive-a-saudi-woman-on-life-inside-the-kingdom/, accessed 14 February 2018

Bakardjieva M, 'Do Clouds Have Politics? Collective Actors in Social Media Land' (2015) 18 Information, Communication & Society 983

Bal AS, Archer-Brown C, Robson K, and Hall DE, 'Do Good, Goes Bad, Gets Ugly: Kony 2012' (2013) 13 Journal of Public Affairs 202

Bala J, 'Behind the Curtain: On Unreported Rapes in India' (9 March 2013) https://web.archive.org/web/20181220193421/https://www.girlsglobe. org/2013/03/09/behind-the-curtain-on-unreported-rapes-in-india/, accessed 16 November 2023

Ballard J, 'Battle Cry of #NiUnaMenos Echoes Through Latin America' (*Huffington Post*, 22 June 2015) https://www.huffingtonpost.com/ jamie-ballard/battle-cry-of-niunamenos-_b_7631972.html, accessed 17 November 2023

Barry E, 'In Rare Move, Death Sentence in Delhi Gang Rape Case Is Upheld' (*The New York Times*, 5 May 2017) https://www.nytimes.com/ 2017/05/05/world/asia/death-sentence-delhi-gang-rape.html, accessed 29 November 2023

Beatley M, 'How One Woman's Murder Made Argentina Rethink the Idea of "Crimes of Passion"' (*The New Statesman*, 27 April 2017) https:// www.newstatesman.com/culture/observations/2017/04/how-one- woman-s-murder-made-argentina-rethink-idea-crimes-passion, accessed 17 November 2023

Beatley M, 'Meet the Argentine Women Behind Ni Una Menos, the Feminist Collective Angela Davis Cites as Inspiration' (*Remezcla*, 9 March 2017) http://remezcla.com/features/culture/ni-una-menos-collective- argentina-founders/, accessed 17 November 2023

Beckley P, '#Mydressmychoice v #Nudityisnotmychoice' (*Go Woman Africa*, 18 November 2014) https://web.archive.org/web/20190219025838/ http://gowomanafrica.com/mydressmychoice-vs-nudityisnotmychoice/, accessed 16 November 2023

Bedi R, 'India Gang-Rape: Accused Ram Singh "Commits Suicide"' (*The Telegraph*, 11 March 2013) http://www.telegraph.co.uk/news/worldnews/ asia/india/9921621/India-gang-rape-accused-Ram-Singh-commits-suic ide.html, accessed 29 November 2023

Bell C and Shaikhouni L, 'Saudi Women Driving Reform: "We Did It"' (*BBC News*, 27 September 2017) http://www.bbc.co.uk/news/blogs-trend ing-41412237, accessed 29 November 2023

Berger M, 'India's Top Police Official: "If You Can't Prevent Rape, Enjoy It"' (*BuzzFeed*, 13 November 2013) https://www.buzzfeed.com/miriamber ger/indias-top-police-official-if-you-cant-prevent-rape-enjoy-it, accessed 16 November 2023

Bhalla N, 'Key Events in the Delhi Gang Rape Case' (news.trust.org, 10 September 2013) http://news.trust.org/item/20130909143244-h09lu/, accessed 16 November 2023

Bhalla N and Mendes K, 'Delhi, Sao Paulo Seen as Worst Megacities for Sex Attacks on Women' (*Reuters*, 16 October 2017) https://www.reuters.com/ article/world/exclusive-delhi-sao-paulo-seen-as-worst-megacities-for-sex- attacks-on-women-poll-idUSL4N1M14XB/, accessed 16 November 2023

REFERENCES

Bhowmick N, 'Death Sentences Handed Down in India's Delhi Gang Rape Case' (*Time*, 13 September 2013) http://world.time.com/2013/09/13/death-sentences-handed-down-in-indias-delhi-gang-rape-case/, accessed 29 November 2023

Bianet, 'BİANET (Independent Communication Network) Shadow Report to GREVIO' (2017)

Biswas S, 'Does the Delhi Gang Rape Sentence Bring Closure?' (*BBC News*, 13 September 2013) http://www.bbc.co.uk/news/world-asia-india-24059601, accessed 29 November 2023

Blank G, 'The Digital Divide Among Twitter Users and Its Implications for Social Research' (2017) 35 Social Science Computer Review 679

Boehner J, *President Ashraf Ghani of Afghanistan's Address to a Joint Meeting of Congress*, https://www.youtube.com/watch?v=cgqc7MO9zl0, accessed 22 July 2024

Boniadi N, 'One Year On, Iranian Women Are Still Fighting' (*TIME*, 14 September 2023) https://time.com/6313431/iran-women-defiant-amini-anniversary/, accessed 17 November 2023

Borch C, 'Crowds, Race, Colonialism: On Resuscitating Classical Crowd Theory' (2023) 90 Social Research: An International Quarterly 245

Borzel T and Risse T, 'Human Rights in Areas of Limited Statehood: The New Agenda' in T Risse-Kappen and SC Ropp (eds), *The Persistent Power of Human Rights: From Commitment to Compliance* (Cambridge University Press, 2013)

boyd d, 'Can Social Network Sites Enable Political Action?' (2008) International Journal of Media and Cultural Politics 241

boyd d, *It's Complicated: The Social Lives of Networked Teens* (Yale University Press, 2014)

Bryman A, *Social Research Methods* (fifth edition, Oxford University Press, 2016)

Brysk A, 'Changing Hearts and Minds' in T Risse, SC Ropp, and K Sikkink (eds), *The Persistent Power of Human Rights* (Cambridge University Press, 2013)

Brysk A, 'Communicative Action and Human Rights in Colombia: When Words Fail' (2009) Colombia Internacional 36

Burke J, 'Delhi Rape: How India's Other Half Lives' (*The Guardian*, 10 September 2013) http://www.theguardian.com/world/2013/sep/10/delhi-gang-rape-india-women, accessed 29 November 2023

Burke J, 'Saudi Arabia Women Test Driving Ban' (*The Guardian*, 17 June 2011) http://www.theguardian.com/world/2011/jun/17/saudi-arabia-women-drivers-protest, accessed 29 November 2023

Buscaglia TS, 'Casi No Se Aplica La Ley Contra Los Femicidios' (*La Nacion*, 7 June 2015) https://web.archive.org/web/20170728203313/http://www.lanacion.com.ar/1799664-casi-no-se-aplica-la-ley-contra-los-femicidios, accessed 17 November 2023

Butler N, 'Exclusive: FIVB "Hopeful" Ban on Women Attending Volleyball Matches in Iran Will Be Lifted by February' (*Inside the Games*, 27 November 2015) http://www.insidethegames.biz/articles/1032038/exclusive-fivb-hopeful-ban-on-women-attending-volleyball-matches-in-iran-will-be-lifted-by-february, accessed 16 November 2023

Calma J, 'Scientists Say They Can't Rely on Twitter Anymore' (*The Verge*, 31 May 2023) https://www.theverge.com/2023/5/31/23739084/twitter-elon-musk-api-policy-chilling-academic-research, accessed 15 November 2023

Cammaerts B, 'Protest Logics and the Mediation Opportunity Structure' (2012) 27 European Journal of Communication 117

Castells M, 'Communication, Power and Counter-Power in the Network Society' (2007) 1 International Journal of Communication (19328036) 238

Castells M, *Networks of Outrage and Hope: Social Movements in the Internet Age* (second edition, Polity Press, 2015)

Chamberlain G, 'Five Years after the Gang-Rape and Murder of Jyoti Singh, What Has Changed for Women in India?' (*The Guardian*, 3 December 2017) http://www.theguardian.com/society/2017/dec/03/five-years-after-gang-murder-jyoti-singh-how-has-delhi-changed, accessed 29 November 2023

Chase AT, 'The State and Human Rights: Governance and Sustainable Human Development in Yemen' (2003) International Journal of Politics, Culture, and Society 213

Cheng I and Momesso L, 'Look, the World Is Watching How We Treat Migrants! The Making of the Anti-Trafficking Legislation during the Ma Administration' (2017) 46 Journal of Current Chinese Affairs 61

Christensen HS, 'Political Activities on the Internet: Slacktivism or Political Participation by Other Means?' (2011) 16 First Monday http://firstmonday.org/ojs/index.php/fm/article/view/3336, accessed 7 July 2016

Cizre U, 'The Truth and Fiction About (Turkey's) Human Rights Politics' (2001) 3 Human Rights Review 55

Comments of the Human Rights Committee 1993 (CCPR/C/79/Add25)

Committee on Economic, Social and Cultural Rights, 'Concluding Observations Kenya' (1993) UN Doc E/C.12/1993/6

Committee on Economic, Social and Cultural Rights, 'Implementation of the International Covenant on Economic, Social, and Cultural Rights. State Report from India' (1983) UN Doc E/1980/6/Add.34

Committee on Economic, Social and Cultural Rights, 'Initial Reports Submitted by States Parties: Addendum' (1991) UN Doc E/1990/5/Add.8

REFERENCES

Committee on Economic, Social and Cultural Rights, 'List of Issues Kenya' (2007) UN Doc E/C.12/KEN/Q/1

Committee on Economic, Social and Cultural Rights, 'Replies of the Islamic Republic of Iran to the List of Issues' (2013) UN Doc E/C.12/IRN/Q/2/Add.1

Committee on Economic, Social and Cultural Rights, 'Replies of Kenya to the List of Issues' (2016) UN Doc E/C.12/KEN/Q/2-5/Add.1

Committee on Economic, Social and Cultural Rights, 'Report on the Sixth Session' (1992) UN Doc E/1992/23

Committee on Economic, Social and Cultural Rights, 'Second Periodic Report Submitted by States Parties Islamic Republic of Iran' (2011) UN Doc E/C.12/IRN/2

Committee on Economic, Social and Cultural Rights, 'Summary Record of the 6th Meeting' (1984) UN Doc E/1984/WG.1/SR.6

Committee on Economic, Social and Cultural Rights, 'Summary Record of the 8th Meeting' (1984) UN Doc E/l984/WG.l/SR.8

Committee on Economic, Social and Cultural Rights, 'Summary Record of the 35th Meeting' (1999) UN Doc E/C.12/1999/SR.35

Committee on the Elimination of Discrimination Against Women, 'Combined Fourth and Fifth Periodic Reports of States Parties Turkey' (2003) UN Doc CEDAW/C/TUR/4-5

Committee on the Elimination of Discrimination Against Women, 'Combined Initial and Second Periodic Reports of States Parties Saudi Arabia' (2007) UN Doc CEDAW/C/SAU/2

Committee on the Elimination of Discrimination Against Women, 'Concluding Comments Saudi Arabia' (2008) UN Doc CEDAW/C/SAU/CO/2

Committee on the Elimination of Discrimination Against Women, 'Concluding Observations on the Seventh Periodic Report of Turkey' (2016) UN Doc CEDAW/C/TUR/CO/7

Committee on the Elimination of Discrimination Against Women, 'Consideration of Reports Submitted by States Turkey' (2014) UN Doc CEDAW/C/TUR/7

Committee on the Elimination of Discrimination Against Women, 'Fifth Periodic Reports of States Parties: Argentina' (2002) UN Doc CEDAW/C/ARG/5

Committee on the Elimination of Discrimination Against Women, 'List of Issues Kenya' (2010) UN Doc CEDAW/C/KEN/Q/7

Committee on the Elimination of Discrimination Against Women, 'List of Issues Saudi Arabia' (2007) UN Doc CEDAW/C/SAU/Q/2

Committee on the Elimination of Discrimination Against Women, 'Replies by the Government of Argentina to the List of Issues' (2016) UN Doc CEDAW/C/ARG/Q/7/Add.1

Committee on the Elimination of Discrimination Against Women, 'Responses to the List of Issues and Questions with Regard to the Consideration of the Seventh Periodic Report Kenya' (2010) UN Doc CEDAW/C/KEN/Q/7/Add.1

Committee on the Elimination of Discrimination Against Women, 'Seventh Periodic Reports of States Parties Argentina' (2015) UN Doc CEDAW/C/ARG/7

Committee on the Elimination of Discrimination Against Women, 'Summary Record of the 318th Meeting' (1998) UN Doc CEDAW/C/SR.318

Committee on the Elimination of Discrimination Against Women, 'Summary Record of the 319th Meeting' (1998) UN Doc CEDAW/C/SR.319

Committee on the Elimination of Discrimination Against Women, 'Summary Record of the 592nd Meeting' (2003) UN Doc CEDAW/C/SR.592

Committee on the Elimination of Discrimination Against Women, 'Summary Record of the 660th Meeting' (2004) UN Doc CEDAW/C/SR.660

Committee on the Elimination of Discrimination Against Women, 'Summary Record of the 816th Meeting' (2008) UN Doc CEDAW/C/SR.816

Committee on the Elimination of Discrimination Against Women, 'Summary Record of the 937th Meeting' (2010) UN Doc CEDAW/C/SR.937

Committee on the Elimination of Discrimination Against Women, 'Summary Record of the 1132nd Meeting' (2013) UN Doc CEDAW/C/SR.1132

Committee on the Elimination of Discrimination Against Women, 'Summary Record of the 1416th Meeting' (2016) UN Doc CEDAW/C/SR.1416

Committee on the Elimination of Discrimination Against Women, 'Summary Record of the 1443rd Meeting' (2016) UN Doc CEDAW/C/SR.1443

Committee on the Elimination of Racial Discrimination, 'Summary Record of the 2016th Meeting' (2011) UN Doc CERD/C/SR.2016

Committee on the Elimination of Racial Discrimination, 'Summary Record of the 2017th Meeting' (2010) UN Doc CERD/C/SR/2017

Committee on the Rights of the Child, 'Concluding Observations on the Combined Third and Fourth Periodic Reports of the Islamic Republic of Iran' (2016) UN Doc CRC/C/IRN/CO/3-4

REFERENCES

Conger K, 'How Elon Musk Changed the Meaning of Twitter for Users' (*The New York Times*, 27 October 2023) https://www.nytimes.com/2023/10/27/technology/elon-musk-twitter-year.html, accessed 15 November 2023

Cummings B, 'Kenyans Protest after Woman Is Beaten and Stripped in Public' (*The Guardian*, 17 November 2014) http://www.theguardian.com/world/2014/nov/17/kenya-mydressmychoice-protest-woman-stripped, accessed 29 November 2023

Dagoula C, 'Mapping Political Discussions on Twitter: Where the Elites Remain Elites' (2019) 7 Media and Communication 225

Dai X, 'The "Compliance Gap" and the Efficacy of International Human Rights Institutions' in T Risse-Kappen and SC Ropp (eds), *The Persistent Power of Human Rights: From Commitment to Compliance* (Cambridge University Press 2013)

Daily Mail, 'Saudi Women Protest Driving Ban in 1990' (*Daily Mail*, 27 September 2017) http://www.dailymail.co.uk/wires/ap/article-4924266/Saudi-women-protest-driving-ban-1990.html, accessed 17 November 2023

Dang S, 'Exclusive: Elon Musk's X Restructuring Curtails Disinformation Research, Spurs Legal Fears' (*Reuters*, 6 November 2023) https://www.reuters.com/technology/elon-musks-x-restructuring-curtails-disinformation-research-spurs-legal-fears-2023-11-06/, accessed 15 November 2023

Davidson H, 'Rape and Murder of Young Woman Sparks Mass Twitter Protest in Turkey' (*The Guardian*, 17 February 2015) http://www.theguardian.com/world/2015/feb/17/turkish-woman-ozgecan-aslans-sparks-anti-violence-campaign-sendeanlat, accessed 29 November 2023

Della Porta D and Diani M, *Social Movements: An Introduction* (second edition, Blackwell Publishing, 2006)

Del Río A, '#NiUnaMenos: Against Femicide in Latin America' (*openDemocracy*, 7 November 2016) https://www.opendemocracy.net/democraciaabierta/andr-s-del-r-o/niunamenos-against-femicide-in-latin-america, accessed 17 November 2023

Dominguez G and Mazumdaru S, 'What Has Changed?' (16 December 2013) http://www.dw.com/en/a-year-after-the-delhi-gang-rape-what-has-changed/a-17293325, accessed 16 November 2023

Donovan J and boyd d 'Stop the Presses? Moving From Strategic Silence to Strategic Amplification in a Networked Media Ecosystem' (2019) American Behavioral Scientist 000276421987822

Dorsey J, '#Bluegirl: Iranian Football Fan Who Set Herself on Fire Indicted FIFA & Iran' (*Global Village Space*, 13 September 2019) https://www.globalvillagespace.com/bluegirl-iranian-football-fan-who-set-herself-on-fire-indicted-fifa-iran/, accessed 6 November 2023

Dorsey JM, 'Bowing To Pressure: Iran Grants Women Spectators Access To Sporting Event' (*Huffington Post*, 19 February 2017) http://www.huf fingtonpost.com/entry/bowing-to-pressure-iran-grants-women-spectat ors-access_us_58a92da2e4b0fa149f9ac73d, accessed 16 November 2023

Duggan M and Smith A, 'Social Media Update 2013' (*Pew Research Center: Internet, Science & Tech*, 30 December 2013) http://www.pewinter net.org/2013/12/30/social-media-update-2013/, accessed 14 March 2016

Dutta D and Sircar O, 'India's Winter of Discontent: Some Feminist Dilemmas in the Wake of a Rape' (2013) 39 Feminist Studies 293

Economic and Social Council, 'Situation of Women and Girls in Afghanistan' (1998) Resolution 1998/9

Eileraas K, 'Sex(t)Ing Revolution, Femen-Izing the Public Square: Aliaa Magda Elmahdy, Nude Protest, and Transnational Feminist Body Politics' (2014) 40 Signs 40

Encarnación OG, 'International Influence, Domestic Activism, and Gay Rights in Argentina' (2013) 128 Political Science Quarterly 687

Equality Now, 'Kenya Just Committed to Ending Gender Based Violence in Five Years. Here's How They Plan to Do It' (*Equality Now*, 10 August 2021) https://www.equalitynow.org/news_and_insights/kenya_just_ committed_to_ending_gbv_in_5_years_here_s_how_they_plan_to_do_ it/, accessed 16 November 2023

Equality Now, 'Sexual Violence in India', https://www.equalitynow.org/ learn_more_sexual_violence_in_india/, accessed 8 November 2023

Ertan N, 'Violence against Women in Turkey Increases Both in Number and Brutality' (*Hürriyet Daily News*, 30 November 2015) http://www.hurriy etdailynews.com/violence-against-women-in-turkey-increases-both-in- number-and-brutality.aspx?pageID=238&nID=91880&NewsCatID=569, accessed 22 July 2024

Extra-Legal Executions in Iran, 'Capital Offenses in the Islamic Republic of Iran: Submission to the UPR' (2009)

Faruqui F, 'Saudi Women Get in the Driver's Seat' (*The Guardian*, 5 May 2010) https://www.theguardian.com/commentisfree/2010/may/05/saudi- women-drivers-seat, accessed 29 November 2023

Feldman E, 'Violence against Women in Turkey: Erdogan Takes a Surprising Stand' (*Mashable*, 19 February 2015) http://mashable.com/2015/02/19/ erdogan-violence-against-women/, accessed 17 November 2023

Fisher C, 'Legislation Is Not Enough: Turkey Fails to Enforce Its Violence Against Women Laws' (*Global Rights for Women*, 10 April 2015) https:// web.archive.org/web/20170329062905/http://globalrightsforwomen.org/ 2015/04/10/legislation-is-not-enough-turkey-fails-to-enforce-its-viole nce-against-women-laws/, accessed 17 November 2023

REFERENCES

Flock E, 'Saudi Arabian Women Banned from Driving Because of Fatwa against Gender "Mixing"' (*The Washington Post*, 6 June 2011) https://www.washingtonpost.com/blogs/blogpost/post/fatwa-against-gender-mixing-prevents-saudi-women-from-driving-according-to-wikileaks-cable/2011/06/06/AGVVTDKH_blog.html?utm_term=.b836f08b6f24, accessed 29 November 2023

France24, 'Turkey Drops Bid to Close Leading Women's Rights Group' (*France 24*, 13 September 2023) https://www.france24.com/en/live-news/20230913-turkey-drops-bid-to-close-leading-anti-femicide-group, accessed 17 November 2023

Franciscans International, Edmund Rice International and The Office of Justice Peace and Integrity of Creation Franciscans Africa, 'Civil Society Responses to the List of Issues in Relation to the Eighth Report of Kenya to CEDAW' (2017)

Fraser N, 'Rethinking the Public Sphere: A Contribution to the Critique of Actually Existing Democracy' (1990) Social Text 56

Frenkel S, 'Iranian Authorities Block Access to Social Media Tools' (*The New York Times*, 3 January 2018) https://www.nytimes.com/2018/01/02/technology/iran-protests-social-media.html, accessed 28 December 2018

Friedman EJ and Tabbush C, '#NiUnaMenos: Not One Woman Less, Not One More Death!' (NACLA, 1 November 2016) https://nacla.org/news/2016/11/01/niunamenos-not-one-woman-less-not-one-more-death, accessed 17 November 2023

Gallo M and Cagatay S, 'Fighting for Women's Rights in Turkey' (*International Viewpoint*, 21 February 2015) http://www.internationalviewpoint.org/spip.php?article3891, accessed 17 November 2023

Gannon M, 'At What Cost? Discrepancies between Women's Legislative Representation and Effective Policy to Protect Women from Violence in Argentina' (2016) 33 SIGMA Journal of Political and International Studies 81

Gerbaudo P, *Tweets and the Streets: Social Media and Contemporary Activism* (Pluto Press, 2012)

Gerbaudo P and Treré E, 'In Search of the "We" of Social Media Activism: Introduction to the Special Issue on Social Media and Protest Identities' (2015) 18 Information, Communication & Society 865

Gilboa E, 'The CNN Effect: The Search for a Communication Theory of International Relations' (2005) 22 Political Communication 27

Gillen, N 'Iran Continues to Get Away with Discriminatory Policy towards Female Spectators' (*Inside the Games*, 17 October 2020) https://www.insidethegames.biz/articles/1099687/iran-get-away-with-gender-discrimination, accessed 6 November 2023

Gillespie T, 'The Politics of "Platforms"' (2010) 12 New Media & Society 347

Girit S, 'Özgecan'ın Ölümü Kadına Yönelik Şiddette Milat Olur Mu?' (*BBC Türkçe*, 20 February 2015) http://www.bbc.com/turkce/haberler/2015/02/150220_ozgecan_aslan, accessed 29 November 2023

Gladwell M, 'Small Change' (*The New Yorker*, 10 April 2010) http://www.newyorker.com/magazine/2010/10/04/small-change-malcolm-gladwell, accessed 14 March 2016

Gladwell M and Shirky C, 'From Innovation to Revolution: Do Social Media Make Protests Possible?' (2011) 90 Foreign Affairs 153

Glenn CL, 'Activism or "Slacktivism?": Digital Media and Organizing for Social Change' (2015) 29 Communication Teacher 81

Go J, 'Thinking against Empire: Anticolonial Thought as Social Theory' (2023) 74 The British Journal of Sociology 279

Goldsmith J and Krasner SD, 'The Limits of Idealism' (2003) 132 Daedalus 47

Goñi U, 'Argentine Women Call Out Machismo' (*The New York Times*, 15 June 2015) https://www.nytimes.com/2015/06/16/opinion/argentine-women-call-out-machismo.html, accessed 29 November 2023

Goodale M and Engle-Merry S (eds), *The Practice of Human Rights* (Cambridge University Press, 2007)

Goodman R and Jinks D, 'How to Influence States: Socialization and International Human Rights Law' (2004) 54 Duke Law Journal 621

Good Practices in Legislation on Violence against Women in Turkey and Problems of Implementation 2008 (EGM/GPLVAW/2008/EP13)

Gordon S, 'NiUnaMenos: How the Brutal Gang Rape and Murder of a Schoolgirl United the Furious Women of Latin America' (*The Telegraph*, 21 October 2016) http://www.telegraph.co.uk/women/life/niunamenos-how-a-schoolgirls-brutal-gang-rape-and-murder-united/, accessed 29 November 2023

Gossman P, 'I Thought Our Life Might Get Better' (Human Rights Watch, 2021) https://www.hrw.org/report/2021/08/05/i-thought-our-life-might-get-better/implementing-afghanistans-elimination, accessed 7 November 2023

Habib M, 'New Afghan Law Targets Sexual Harassment' (Institute for War and Peace Reporting, 8 March 2017) https://web.archive.org/web/20170823165516/https://iwpr.net/global-voices/new-afghan-law-targets-sexual-harassment, accessed 16 November 2023

Harris G, '5 in New Delhi Rape Case Face Murder Charges' (*The New York Times*, 3 January 2013) https://www.nytimes.com/2013/01/04/world/asia/murder-charges-filed-against-5-men-in-india-gang-rape.html, accessed 29 November 2023

Hemmings C, 'Affective Solidarity: Feminist Reflexivity and Political Transformation' (2012) 13 Feminist Theory 147

REFERENCES

Hemmings C, '"But I Thought We'd Already Won That Argument!": "Anti-Gender" Mobilizations, Affect, and Temporality' (2022) 48 Feminist Studies 594

Hemmings C, 'Resisting Popular Feminisms: Gender, Sexuality and the Lure of the Modern' (2018) 25 Gender, Place & Culture 963

Heo M, 'Mongolia's Political Change and Human Rights in Five-Phase Spiral Model: Implications for North Korea: Mongolia's Political Change and HR' (2014) 29 Pacific Focus 413

Hoffman M, 'Protests Across Turkey Denounce Violence Against Women After Student's Brutal Murder' (*VICE News*, 15 February 2015) https://news.vice.com/article/protests-across-turkey-denounce-violence-agai nst-women-after-students-brutal-murder, accessed 17 November 2023

Hogg J, 'Fight against Domestic Violence Stalls in "Patriarchal" Turkey' (*Hürriyet Daily News*, 23 July 2014) http://www.hurriyetdailynews.com/fight-against-domestic-violence-stalls-in-patriarchal-turkey.aspx?pageID=238&nID=69455&NewsCatID=339, accessed 17 November 2023

Hosseinkhah M, 'The Execution of Women in Iranian Criminal Law: An Examination of the Impact of Gender on Laws Concerning Capital Punishment in the New Islamic Penal Code' (IHR, 2012)

Hubbard B, 'Saudi Arabia Agrees to Let Women Drive' (*The New York Times*, 26 September 2017) https://www.nytimes.com/2017/09/26/world/mid dleeast/saudi-arabia-women-drive.html, accessed 29 November 2023

Hubbard B, 'Saudi Arabia's Driving Ban and the Pioneering Women Who Got It Lifted' (*The Independent*, 18 October 2017) http://www.independ ent.co.uk/news/world/middle-east/saudi-arabia-driving-ban-women-pro testors-who-lifted-fought-against-sexist-law-a7993306.html, accessed 29 November 2023

Human Rights Center, 'Sexual Offences Act: Implementation Workshop' (2012)

Human Rights Committee, 'Concluding Observations Argentina' (2000) UN Doc CCPR/CO/70/ARG

Human Rights Committee, 'Concluding Observations on the Fifth Periodic Report of Argentina' (2016) UN Doc CCPR/C/ARG/CO/5

Human Rights Committee, 'Report of the Human Rights Committee' (1991) UN Doc Supplement No. 40 (A/46/40)

Human Rights Committee, 'Second Periodic Reports of States Parties' (1992) UN Doc CCPR/C/57/Add.5

Human Rights Committee, 'Summary Record of the 272nd Meeting' (1981) UN Doc CCPR/C/SR.272

Human Rights Committee, 'Summary Record of the First Part of the 1462nd Meeting' (1995) UN Doc CCPR/C/SR.1462

Human Rights Committee, 'Third Periodic Reports of States Parties: Iran' (2010) UN Doc CCPR/C/IRRN/3

Human Rights Council, 'Compilation Report Argentina' (2008) UN Doc A/HRC/WG.6/1/ARG/2

Human Rights Council, 'Report of the Special Rapporteur on Extreme Poverty and Human Rights on His Mission to Saudi Arabia' (2017) UN Doc A/HRC/35/26/Add.3

Human Rights Council, 'Report of the Special Rapporteur on the Situation of Human Rights in the Islamic Republic of Iran' (2011) UN Doc A/66/374

Human Rights Council, 'Report of the Special Rapporteur on the Situation of Human Rights in the Islamic Republic of Iran' (2014) UN Doc A/HRC/25/61

Human Rights Council, 'Report of the Special Rapporteur on the Situation of Human Rights in the Islamic Republic of Iran' (2015) UN Doc A/HRC/28/70

Human Rights Council, 'Report of the Special Rapporteur on the Situation of Human Rights in the Islamic Republic of Iran' (2016) UN Doc A/HRC/31/69

Human Rights Council, 'Report of the Special Rapporteur on Violence against Women, Its Causes and Consequences Addendum Communications to and from Governments' (2001) UN Doc E/CN.4/2001/73/Add.1

Human Rights Council, 'Report of the Special Rapporteur on Violence against Women, Its Causes and Consequences, Addendum Communications to and from Governments' (2002) UN Doc E/CN.4/2002/83/Add.1

Human Rights Council, 'Report of the Special Rapporteur on Violence against Women, Its Causes and Consequences, on Her Mission to Argentina' (2017) UN Doc A/HRC/35/30/Add.3

Human Rights Council, 'Report of the Special Rapporteur on Violence against Women, Its Causes and Consequences: Mission to the Islamic Republic of Iran' (2006) UN Doc E/CN.4/2006/61/Add.3

Human Rights Council, 'Report of the Special Rapporteur on Violence against Women, Its Causes and Consequences: Mission to Pakistan and Afghanistan' (2000) UN Doc E/CN.4/2000/68/Add.4

Human Rights Council, 'Report of the Special Rapporteur on Violence against Women, Its Causes and Consequences, Rashida Manjoo Addendum Communications to and from Governments' (2010) UN Doc A/HRC/14/22/Add.1

Human Rights Council, 'Report of the Special Rapporteur on Violence against Women, Its Causes and Consequences, Rashida Manjoo Addendum Mission to India' (2014) UN Doc A/HRC/26/38/Add.1

Human Rights Council, 'Report of the Special Rapporteur on Violence against Women, Its Causes and Consequences, Rashida Manjoo Addendum Mission to India: Comments by the State on the Report of the Special Rapporteur' (2014) UN Doc A/HRC/26/38/Add.4

REFERENCES

Human Rights Council, 'Report of the Special Rapporteur on Violence against Women, Its Causes and Consequences, Yakin Ertürk Addendum Communications to and from Governments' (2006) UN Doc E/CN.4/2006/61/Add.1

Human Rights Council, 'Report of the Special Rapporteur on Violence against Women, Its Causes and Consequences, Yakin Ertürk Addendum Communications to and from Governments' (2007) UN Doc A/HRC/4/34/Add.1

Human Rights Council, 'Report of the Special Rapporteur on Violence against Women, Its Causes and Consequences, Yakin Ertürk Addendum Communications to and from Governments' (2008) UN Doc A/HRC/7/6/Add.1

Human Rights Council, 'Report of the Special Rapporteur on Violence against Women, Its Causes and Consequences, Yakin Ertürk Addendum Communications to and from Governments' (2009) UN Doc A/HRC/11/6/Add.1

Human Rights Council, 'Report of the United Nations High Commissioner for Human Rights on Situation of Human Rights in Afghanistan' (2013) UN Doc A/HRC/22/37

Human Rights Council, 'Report of the Working Group on the Universal Periodic Review: Islamic Republic of Iran' (2014) UN Doc A/HRC/28/12

Human Rights Council, 'Resolution Adopted by the Human Rights Council' (2011) UN Doc A/HRC/RES/16/9

Human Rights Council, 'Summary Report Argentina' (2008) UN Doc A/HRC/WG.6/1/ARG/3

Human Rights Council, 'Universal Periodic Review National Report Iran' (2014) UN Doc HRC/WG.6/20/IRN/1

Human Rights Council, 'Working Group Summary Report Afghanistan' (2013) UN Doc A/HRC/WG.6/12/AFG/3

Human Rights Watch, 'Argentina: Events of 2021', *World Report 2022* (2021) https://www.hrw.org/world-report/2022/country-chapters/argentina, accessed 8 November 2023

Human Rights Watch, 'Dispatches: Afghanistan's Legal System Fails Farkhunda, Again' (Human Rights Watch, 9 March 2016) https://www.hrw.org/news/2016/03/09/dispatches-afghanistans-legal-system-fails-farkhunda-again, accessed 16 November 2023

Human Rights Watch, 'Election-Related Sexual Violence in Kenya' (Human Rights Watch, 7 September 2017) https://www.hrw.org/news/2017/09/07/election-related-sexual-violence-kenya, accessed 16 November 2023

Human Rights Watch, '"Everyone Blames Me" Barriers to Justice and Support Services for Sexual Assault Survivors in India' (2017)

Human Rights Watch, 'Ghoncheh Ghavami: The Shifting Goal Posts of Iran's Hardliners' (Human Rights Watch, 21 October 2014) https://www.hrw.org/news/2014/10/21/ghoncheh-ghavami-shifting-goal-posts-irans-hardliners, accessed 16 November 2023

Human Rights Watch, '"He Loves You, He Beats You": Family Violence in Turkey and Access to Protection' (2011)

Human Rights Watch, 'Human Rights Abuses Stemming from Male Guardianship and Sex Segregation in Saudi Arabia' (2008) https://www.hrw.org/report/2008/04/19/perpetual-minors/human-rights-abuses-stemming-male-guardianship-and-sex, accessed 15 February 2018

Human Rights Watch, '"I Had to Run Away" The Imprisonment of Women and Girls for "Moral Crimes" in Afghanistan' (2012)

Human Rights Watch, 'Interview: How Turkey's Failure to Protect Women Can Cost Them Their Lives' (Human Rights Watch, 2022) https://www.hrw.org/news/2022/05/26/interview-how-turkeys-failure-protect-women-can-cost-them-their-lives, accessed 7 November 2023

Human Rights Watch, 'Iran: Mass Arrests of Women's Rights Defenders' (Human Rights Watch, 19 August 2023) https://www.hrw.org/news/2023/08/19/iran-mass-arrests-womens-rights-defenders, accessed 8 November 2023

Human Rights Watch, 'Iran: Proposed Penal Code Retains Stoning' (3 June 2013)

Human Rights Watch, 'Iran: UPR Submission' (2014)

Human Rights Watch, 'Iran: Volleyball Federation Should Penalize Ban on Women' (Human Rights Watch, 2 July 2015) https://www.hrw.org/news/2015/07/02/iran-volleyball-federation-should-penalize-ban-women, accessed 16 November 2023

Human Rights Watch, 'Kenya: Survivors of Gender-Based Violence Lack Help' (21 September 2021) https://www.hrw.org/news/2021/09/21/kenya-survivors-gender-based-violence-lack-help, accessed 7 November 2023

Human Rights Watch, 'Saudi Arabia: Activists Convicted for Answering Call for Help' (Human Rights Watch, 17 June 2013) https://www.hrw.org/news/2013/06/17/saudi-arabia-activists-convicted-answering-call-help, accessed 17 November 2023

Human Rights Watch, 'Saudi Arabia: As Women's Driving Ban Ends, Provide Parity' (27 September 2017) https://www.hrw.org/news/2017/09/27/saudi-arabia-womens-driving-ban-ends-provide-parity, accessed 17 November 2023

Human Rights Watch, 'Saudi Arabia: Important Advances for Saudi Women' (Human Rights Watch, 2019) https://www.hrw.org/news/2019/08/02/saudi-arabia-important-advances-saudi-women, accessed 9 November 2023

REFERENCES

Human Rights Watch, 'Saudi Arabia: Law Enshrines Male Guardianship' (Human Rights Watch, 2023) https://www.hrw.org/news/2023/03/08/saudi-arabia-law-enshrines-male-guardianship, accessed 9 November 2023

Human Rights Watch, 'Saudi Arabia: Repression Overshadows Women's Reforms' (2018) https://www.hrw.org/news/2018/01/18/saudi-arabia-repression-overshadows-womens-reforms, accessed 15 February 2018

Human Rights Watch, 'The "Ten-Dollar Talib" and Women's Rights Afghan Women and the Risks of Reintegration and Reconciliation' (2010)

Human Rights Watch, 'Turkey: Backward Step for Women's Rights' (Human Rights Watch, 2011) https://www.hrw.org/news/2011/06/09/turkey-backward-step-womens-rights, accessed 17 November 2023

Human Rights Watch, 'World Report 2017: Rights Trends in Argentina' (2017) https://www.hrw.org/world-report/2017/country-chapters/argentina, accessed 2 January 2019

Hundle AK, 'Uganda's Colonial-Style Dress Code' (*Al Jazeera*, 14 August 2017) http://www.aljazeera.com/indepth/opinion/2017/08/uganda-colonial-style-dress-code-170808072148083.html, accessed 16 November 2023

Igunza E, 'Stripping Videos Outrage Kenyans' (*BBC News*, 26 November 2014) http://www.bbc.co.uk/news/world-africa-30217462, accessed 29 November 2023

Indimuli F, '"Anti Stripping Squad" Arrests 5 in Kayole Swoop' (*Mpasho News*, 27 November 2014) https://mpasho.co.ke/anti-stripping-squad-arrests-5-kayole-swoop/, accessed 16 November 2023

International Federation for Human Rights (FIDH), 'Iran/Death Penality: A State Terror Policy' (2009)

International Telecommunication Union, 'Measuring Digital Development: Facts and Figures 2022' (2022) https://www.itu.int/hub/publication/d-ind-ict_mdd-2022/, accessed 9 November 2023

Iran Human Rights Documentation Center, 'Annual Death Penalty Report 2012' (2012)

Iran Human Rights Documentation Center, 'At Least 7 Stonings Implemented by the Iranian Authorities in the Past 4 Years. 14 More Sentenced to Stoning' (21 August 2010) https://iranhr.net/en/articles/603/, accessed 17 November 2023

Iran Human Rights Documentation Center, 'Death Penalty Annual Report 2022' (2022) https://iranhr.net/media/files/Rapport_iran_2022_PirQr2V.pdf, accessed 6 November 2023

Irene, '#niunamenos: A Combination of Offline and Online Feminist Activism' (*Decoding Digital Activism*, 4 October 2017) http://wpmu.mah.se/nmict172group6/2017/10/04/niunamenos-feminist-activism/, accessed 17 November 2023

Islamic Republic of Afghanistan, 'Progress Report on Women's Status and Empowerment and National Action Plan (NAP 1325)' (2016)

ITU, 'Key ICT Indicators for Developed and Developing Countries and the World (Totals and Penetration Rates)' (2014) http://www.itu.int/en/ITU-D/Statistics/Documents/facts/ICTFactsFigures2014-e.pdf, accessed 14 March 2016

Jamjoom M, 'Saudi Arabia Issues Warning to Women Drivers, Protesters' (*CNN*, 24 October 2013) https://www.cnn.com/2013/10/24/world/meast/saudi-arabia-women-drivers/index.html, accessed 29 November 2023

Jamjoom M, 'Saudi Blogger Detained, but Hopeful about Push to Let Women Drive' (*CNN*, 11 October 2013) https://www.cnn.com/2013/10/11/world/meast/saudi-arabia-women-drivers/index.html, accessed 29 November 2023

Jamjoom M, 'Saudi Government Says Laws Will Be Enforced on "Female Driving" Day' (*CNN*, 23 October 2013) https://edition.cnn.com/2013/10/23/world/meast/saudi-arabia-women-drivers/index.html, accessed 29 November 2023

Jawhar S 'Saudi Religious Police Clamp Down on Rural Women Drivers' (*Huffington Post*, 18 March 2010) https://www.huffingtonpost.com/sabria-jawhar/saudi-religious-police-cl_b_320071.html, accessed 29 November 2023

Jetschke A, 'The Power of Human Rights a Decade after: From Euphoria to Contestation?' in T Risse-Kappen and SC Ropp (eds), *The Persistent Power of Human Rights: From Commitment to Compliance* (Cambridge University Press, 2013)

Jetschke A and Liese A, 'The Spiral Model: How Does It Score After Ten Years?', *Workshop: The Power of Human Rights – Ten Years After* (2009)

Johnson A, 'Saudi Women Gain the Right to Drive' (Center for Security Policy, 2 October 2017) https://www.centerforsecuritypolicy.org/2017/10/02/saudi-women-gain-the-right-to-drive/, accessed 17 November 2023

Joseph S, 'Social Media, Political Change, and Human Rights' (2012) 35 Boston College International and Comparative Law Review 145

Jusino T, 'Feminism Around the World: #NiUnaMenos Protest in Argentina Highlights Epidemic of Violence Against Women' (*The Mary Sue*, 28 October 2016) https://www.themarysue.com/feminism-around-the-world-argentina-ni-una-menos/, accessed 17 November 2023

Justice for Iran, 'Gender Discrimination at Its Worst: An Overview of the Discriminatory Laws of the Islamic Republic of Iran in Family Life: Submission to the United Nations Working Group on Discrimination against Women in Law and in Practice' (2014)

REFERENCES

Justice for Iran, 'Mapping Stoning in Muslim Context' (The Global Campaign to Stop Violence against Women in the Name of Culture, 2012)

Kaba M, Smith A, Adelman L, and Gay R, 'Where Twitter and Feminism Meet' (*The Nation*, 17 April 2014) https://www.thenation.com/article/archive/where-twitter-and-feminism-meet/, accessed 13 November 2023

Karakas B, 'Turkey Faces up to Femicide' (*dw.com*, 19 June 2022) https://www.dw.com/en/turkeys-femicide-problem-all-eyes-on-court-verdicts/a-62165754, accessed 17 November 2023

Kargar Z, 'Farkhunda: The Making of a Martyr' (*BBC News*, 11 August 2015) http://www.bbc.co.uk/news/magazine-33810338, accessed 29 November 2023

Kazmin A and Stacey K, 'Violence Erupts in India after Guru Is Convicted of Rape' (*Financial Times*, 25 August 2017) https://www.ft.com/content/9f04b77c-896f-11e7-bf50-e1c239b45787, accessed 16 November 2023

Keck ME and Sikkink K, *Activists beyond Borders: Advocacy Networks in International Politics* (Cornell University Press, 1998)

Kelland Z, '#MyDressMyChoice – Protests in Kenya after a Woman Is Publicly Stripped' (*Global Citizen*, 20 November 2014) https://www.globalcitizen.org/es/content/mydressmychoice-protests-in-kenya-after-a-woman-is/, accessed 16 November 2023

Kemp S, 'Global Digital & Social Media Stats: 2015' (*Social Media Today*, 2015) http://www.socialmediatoday.com/content/global-digital-social-media-stats-2015, accessed 14 March 2016

Khalaf R, 'Loujain Alhathloul on How Saudi Women Won the Right to Drive' (*Financial Times*, 7 December 2017) https://www.ft.com/content/b4186c36-da18-11e7-a039-c64b1c09b482, accessed 17 November 2023

Khomami N, 'Saudi Cleric Banned for Saying Women's Brains "a Quarter the Size" of Men's' (*The Guardian*, 23 September 2017) http://www.theguardian.com/world/2017/sep/23/saudi-cleric-saad-al-hijri-banned-woman-driving-cars-quarter-brain, accessed 29 November 2023

Kinninmont J, 'End of Saudi Women Driving Ban Reflects Deep Changes in Society' (*BBC News*, 27 September 2017) http://www.bbc.co.uk/news/world-middle-east-41412022, accessed 29 November 2023

Kioko V, 'Sexual Offences on the Rise in Kenya' (*Capital News*, 27 June 2014) https://www.capitalfm.co.ke/news/2014/06/sexual-offences-on-the-rise-in-kenya/, accessed 8 January 2019

Kiruga M, 'Understanding Africa's "Fashion Gestapo": Miniskirts, Maxi Skirts Make-up and Long Beards' (*MG Africa*, 5 December 2014) https://web.archive.org/web/20180401162426/http://mgafrica.com/article/2014-12-04-understanding-africas-fashion-police/, accessed 16 November 2023

Kosha A, 'Farkhunda, Victim of a Society of Oppressors and the Oppressed' (*Radio Salam Watandar*, 17 March 2016) https://web.archive.org/web/201 70218014541/http://salamwatandar.com/english/Article.aspx?a=19458, accessed 16 November 2023

Krebs RR and Jackson PT, 'Twisting Tongues and Twisting Arms: The Power of Political Rhetoric' (2007) 13 European Journal of International Relations 35

Kristofferson K, White K, and Peloza J, 'The Nature of Slacktivism: How the Social Observability of an Initial Act of Token Support Affects Subsequent Prosocial Action' (2014) 40 Journal of Consumer Research 1149

Kumar H and Barry E, 'Death Sentences in India Usually End in Question Marks, Study Finds' (*The New York Times*, 7 May 2016) https://www.nyti mes.com/2016/05/07/world/asia/india-death-sentences-executions.html, accessed 29 November 2023

Lang H, '#MeToo: A Case Study in Re-Embodying Information' (2019) Computers and Composition, https://linkinghub.elsevier.com/retrieve/ pii/S8755461519300222, accessed 23 August 2019

Laursen A, 'Israel's Supreme Court and International Human Rights Law: The Judgement on "Moderate Physical Pressure"' (2000) 69 Nordic Journal of International Law 413

Ledford H, 'How Musk's Takeover Might Change Twitter: What Researchers Think' (2022) 611 Nature 436

Lee YH and Hsieh G, 'Does Slacktivism Hurt Activism?: The Effects of Moral Balancing and Consistency in Online Activism' (2013) http://search. ebscohost.com/login.aspx?direct=true&db=edselc&AN=edselc.2-52.0-84878002162&authtype=sso&custid=s8993828&site=eds-live&scope=site,

Leigh D, 'US Put Pressure on Saudi Arabia to Let Women Drive, Leaked Cables Reveal' (*The Guardian*, 27 May 2011) http://www.theguard ian.com/world/2011/may/27/us-pressurised-saudis-let-women-drive, accessed 29 November 2023

Leszinsky L and Dewick E, '#NiUnaMenos Six Years on: Triumphs and New Demands of Argentina's Feminist Movement' (*Global Voices*, 22 June 2021) https://globalvoices.org/2021/06/22/niunamenos-six-years-on-triumphs-and-new-demands-of-argentinas-feminist-movement/, accessed 8 November 2023

Lewis G and Hemmings C, '"Where Might We Go If We Dare": Moving beyond the "Thick, Suffocating Fog of Whiteness" in Feminism' (2019) 20 Feminist Theory 405

Lewis K, Gray K, and Meierhenrich J, 'The Structure of Online Activism' (2014) Sociological Science 1

Linde R, 'Statelessness and Roma Communities in the Czech Republic: Competing Theories of State Compliance' (2006) 13 International Journal on Minority & Group Rights 341

REFERENCES

Livingston S, 'The CNN Effect Reconsidered (Again): Problematizing ICT and Global Governance in the CNN Effect Research Agenda' (2011) 4 Media, War & Conflict 20

Locke A, Lawthom R, and Lyons A, 'Social Media Platforms as Complex and Contradictory Spaces for Feminisms: Visibility, Opportunity, Power, Resistance and Activism' (2018) 28 Feminism & Psychology 3

Loft P, '2022 Iran Protests: Human Rights and International Response' (26 May 2023) https://commonslibrary.parliament.uk/research-briefings/cbp-9679/, accessed 8 November 2023

Loft P, 'Mahsa Amini Protests in Iran 2022' (7 October 2022) https://commonslibrary.parliament.uk/mahsa-amini-protests-in-iran-2022/, accessed 8 November 2023

Loft P, 'One-Year Anniversary of the Mahsa Amini Protests in Iran' (14 September 2023) https://commonslibrary.parliament.uk/one-year-anniversary-of-the-mahsa-amini-protests-in-iran/, accessed 8 November 2023

Loken M, '#BringBackOurGirls and the Invisibility of Imperialism' (2014) 14 Feminist Media Studies 1100

MacFarquhar N, 'Saudis Arrest Woman Leading Right-to-Drive Campaign' (*The New York Times*, 23 May 2011) https://www.nytimes.com/2011/05/24/world/middleeast/24saudi.html, accessed 29 November 2023

Mackey R, 'A Saudi Activist, in Her Own Words' (*The Lede – The New York Times*, 31 May 2011) https://thelede.blogs.nytimes.com/2011/05/31/a-saudi-activist-in-her-own-words/, accessed 17 November 2023

Mackey R, 'Saudi Women Free After 73 Days in Jail for Driving' (*The New York Times*, 12 February 2015) https://www.nytimes.com/2015/02/13/world/middleeast/saudi-women-free-after-73-days-in-jail-for-driving.html, accessed 29 November 2023Mackey R, 'Saudi Women Drive, Despite Ban, and Find Some Support on the Kingdom's Roads' (*The New York Times*, 10 October 2013) //thelede.blogs.nytimes.com/2013/10/10/saudi-women-drive-despite-ban-and-find-some-support-on-the-kingdoms-roads/, accessed 29 November 2023

Magill S, 'Indian Women's Struggle against Sexual Violence Has Had Little Support from the Men in Power' (*The Conversation*, 27 July 2023) http://theconversation.com/indian-womens-struggle-against-sexual-violence-has-had-little-support-from-the-men-in-power-210318, accessed 16 November 2023

Mahr K, 'New Delhi's Women Problem: What Does It Take to Make a City, and Society, Safe?' (*Time*, 2 May 2012) http://world.time.com/2012/05/02/new-delhis-women-problem-what-does-it-take-to-make-a-city-and-society-safe/, accessed 16 November 2023

Mandhana N and Timmons H, 'Suspect in India Gang Rape Found Dead in Jail' (*The New York Times*, 10 March 2013) //india.blogs.nytimes.com/2013/03/10/suspect-in-india-gang-rape-found-dead-in-jail/, accessed 29 November 2023

Mandhana N and Trivedi A, 'Indians Outraged Over Rape on Moving Bus in New Delhi' (*The New York Times – India Ink*, 18 December 2012) https://india.blogs.nytimes.com/2012/12/18/outrage-in-delhi-after-lat est-gang-rape-case/, accessed 29 November 2023

Mangera D, 'Kenyan Politician Wants to Ban Miniskirts and Tight Trousers' (Index on Censorship, 12 March 2014) https://www.indexoncensorship. org/2014/03/kenya-county-wants-ban-miniskirts-tight-trousers/, accessed 16 November 2023

McCombs ME, Shaw DL, and Weaver DH, 'New Directions in Agenda-Setting Theory and Research' (2014) 17 Mass Communication and Society 781

McCormick T, Lee H, and Spiro E, 'Using Twitter for Demographic and Social Science Research: Tools for Data Collection and Processing' (2017) 46 Sociological Methods & Research, https://journals-sagepub-com.uos. idm.oclc.org/doi/full/10.1177/0049124115605339?casa_token=K4lvY 7ipluQAAAAA%3AwF-Z75tcF63ueaY5HCM1SiXzOg97GfSHs_59I tqA5FTt3Lzi-TQfPwa6xjXd-qA1_QO_QZ_upls5, accessed 26 April 2024

Medley M, '5 Things I Learned at Argentina's #NiUnaMenos March against Femicide' (Amnesty International USA, 14 July 2016) https://www.amn estyusa.org/5-things-i-learned-at-argentinas-niunamenos-march-against-femicide/, accessed 17 November 2023

Meier BM and Kim Y, 'Human Rights Accountability Through Treaty Bodies: Examining Human Rights Treaty Monitoring for Water and Sanitation' (2015) 26 Duke Journal of Comparative and International Law 139

Mendes K, Keller J, and Ringrose J, 'Digitized Narratives of Sexual Violence: Making Sexual Violence Felt and Known through Digital Disclosures' (2019) 21 New Media & Society 1290

Mendes K, Keller J, and Ringrose J, *Digital Feminist Activism: Girls and Women Fight Back Against Rape Culture* (Oxford University Press, 2019) https://www-oxfordscholarship-com.uea.idm.oclc.org/view/10.1093/oso/9780190697846.001.0001/oso-9780190697846, accessed 10 February 2020

Mendes K, Ringrose J, and Keller J, '#MeToo and the Promise and Pitfalls of Challenging Rape Culture through Digital Feminist Activism' (2018) 25 European Journal of Women's Studies 236

Mignolo WD, 'Coloniality and Globalization: A Decolonial Take' (2021) 18 Globalizations 720

REFERENCES

Mignolo WD, 'Prophets Facing Sidewise: The Geopolitics of Knowledge and the Colonial Difference' (2005) 19 Social Epistemology 111

Mignolo WD and Bussmann FS, 'Coloniality and the State: Race, Nation and Dependency' (2023) 40 Theory, Culture & Society 3

Milan S, 'From Social Movements to Cloud Protesting: The Evolution of Collective Identity' (2015) 18 Information, Communication & Society 887

Mohsin H, 'Cyberactivism: The Case of the Women2Drive Movement in Saudi Arabia' (F come) https://web.archive.org/web/20160608122432/http://www.fcome.org/portfolio-view/cyberactivism-the-case-of-the-women2drive-movement-in-saudi-arabia/, accessed 17 November 2023

Morovoz E, 'The Internet' (2010) 179 Foreign Policy 40

Morovoz E, *The Net Delusion: How Not to Liberate the World* (Allen Lane, 2011)

Moshenberg D, '#MyDressMyChoice' (*African Is a Country*, 14 November 2014) http://africasacountry.com/2014/11/mydressmychoice/, accessed 16 November 2023

Mouri L, 'My Share, Half of Azadi: Let Iranian Women Go to Stadium' (*Huffington Post*, 19 June 2014) http://www.huffingtonpost.com/leila-mouri/my-share-half-of-azadi-le_b_5508962.html, accessed 16 November 2023

Mukesh & Anr v State for NCT of Delhi & Others [2017] Supreme Court of India 607–608

Muñoz AA, 'Transnational and Domestic Processes in the Definition of Human Rights Policies in Mexico' (2009) 31 Human Rights Quarterly 35

Mutua MW, 'Savages, Victims, and Saviors: The Metaphor of Human Rights' (2001) 42 Harvard International Law Journal 201

Naghibi N, 'Diasporic Disclosures: Social Networking, NEDA, and the 2009 Iranian Presidential Elections' (2011) 34 Biography 56

Naicker V, 'The Problem of Epistemological Critique in Contemporary Decolonial Theory' (2023) 49 Social Dynamics 220

National Council of Resistance of Iran, 'CEDAW: Why the Iranian Regime Does Not Join CEDAW? A Study by the Women's Committee of the National Council of Resistance of Iran' (2016)

National Council of Resistance of Iran, 'Iranian Regime's 20-Year Conduct since Beijing Platform for Action and Accountability to International Community' (2015)

National Council of Resistance of Iran, 'Women in Pursuit of Justice: Arbitrary Trends and Illegal Proceedings Victimizing Female Political Prisoners in Iran' (2017)

Naundorf K and Pabst S, 'Argentina Recorded More Than 250 Femicides in 2020, One Every 35 Hours' (*Washington Post*, 2 December 2021) https://pulitzercenter.org/stories/argentina-recorded-more-250-femicides-2020-one-every-35-hours, accessed 17 November 2023

Nayyeri M, 'Gender Inequality and Discrimination: The Case of Iranian Women' (Iranian Human Rights Documentation Center, 2013)

Nayyeri M, 'The Question of "Stoning to Death" in the New Penal Code of the IRI' (IHR, 2012)

Neumayer E, 'Do International Human Rights Treaties Improve Respect for Human Rights?' (2005) 49 Journal of Conflict Resolution 925

The New Arab, 'Greater Abortion Access in Saudi Arabia than in US States' (*The New Arab*, 25 June 2022) https://www.newarab.com/news/greater-abortion-access-saudi-arabia-us-states, accessed 17 November 2023

Ngenoh P, 'Anti-Stripping Squad: We Will Hunt You Down Perverts!' (*Standard Digital News*, 28 November 2014) https://web.archive.org/web/20150719040924/http://www.sde.co.ke/thenairobian/article/2000142730/anti-stripping-squad-we-will-hunt-you-down-perverts, accessed 16 November 2023

Njuguna S, 'County Staff Asked to Dress Decently' (*Daily Nation*, 3 September 2017) http://www.nation.co.ke/news/Nakuru--Nyandarua-counties-ask-staff-to-dress-decently/1056-4081652-11cjwvdz/index.html, accessed 16 November 2023

Nnoko-Mewanu J, 'I Had Nowhere to Go' (Human Rights Watch, 2021) https://www.hrw.org/report/2021/09/21/i-had-nowhere-go/violence-against-women-and-girls-during-covid-19-pandemic-kenya, accessed 7 November 2023

Nugent C, 'Four Months From #NiUnaMenos: Has Anything Changed?' (*The Argentina Independent*, 5 October 2015) https://web.archive.org/web/20170704235054/http://www.argentinaindependent.com/current affairs/four-months-from-niunamenos-has-anything-changed/, accessed 8 November 2023

O'Dwyer M, '#NiUnaMenos; Standing up to Femicides and "Machismo" in Argentina' (*Gender and Politics*, 3 February 2016) https://genderandpoliticsucd.wordpress.com/2016/02/03/niunamenos-standing-up-to-femicides-and-machismo-in-argentina/, accessed 17 November 2023

OHCHR, 'End to Saudi Driving Ban for Women Should Be Just the First Step' (28 September 2017) http://www.ohchr.org/EN/NewsEvents/Pages/DisplayNews.aspx?NewsID=22179&LangID=E, accessed 17 November 2023

Opuz v Turkey [2009] 33401/2 (European Court of Human Rights)

Ott K, 'Social Media and Feminist Values: Aligned or Maligned?' (2018) 39 Frontiers: A Journal of Women Studies 93

Ovadia S, 'Exploring the Potential of Twitter as a Research Tool' (2009) 28 Behavioral & Social Sciences Librarian 202

Patel S, 'Anti-Colonial Thought and Global Social Theory' (2023) 8 Frontiers in Sociology, https://www.frontiersin.org/articles/10.3389/fsoc.2023.1143776, accessed 13 November 2023

REFERENCES

Penney J, 'Social Media and Symbolic Action: Exploring Participation in the Facebook Red Equal Sign Profile Picture Campaign' (2015) 20 Journal of Computer-Mediated Communication 52

Perloff RM, 'Mass Media, Social Perception, and the Third-Person Effect' in J Bryant and MB Oliver (eds), *Media Effects: Advances in Theory and Research* (Routledge, 2008)

Perse EM and Lambe JL (eds), *Media Effects and Society* (second edition, Routledge, 2017)

Pikoli P, '#MyDressMyChoice Campaign Yields Results' http://ewn.co.za/2014/11/19/MyDressMyChoice-campaign, accessed 16 November 2023

Pizishkzād Ī and Davis D, *My Uncle Napoleon: A Novel* (first edition, Mage Publishers, 1996)

Plan International (lead organization), 'Shadow Report in Response to the Eigth Periodic State Report by Kenya to CEDAW' (2017)

Poblet M and Kolieb J, 'Responding to Human Rights Abuses in the Digital Era: New Tools, Old Challenges' (2018) 54 Stanford Journal of International Law 259

Psirmoi D, 'MPs Reject Changes to Sex Offences Law' (*The Standard*) https://www.standardmedia.co.ke/article/2001229527/mps-reject-chan ges-to-sex-offences-law, accessed 16 November 2023

Qaane E, 'Harassment of Women in Afghanistan: A Hidden Phenomenon Addressed in Too Many Laws' (Afghanistan Analysts Network, 2 April 2017) https://www.afghanistan-analysts.org/harassment-of-women-in-afghanistan-a-hidden-phenomenon-addressed-in-too-many-laws/, accessed 16 November 2023

Quantara, 'Iran's Stadium Ban on Women: Excluding the People' (9 September 2016) https://en.qantara.de/content/irans-stadium-ban-on-women-excluding-the-people, accessed 16 November 2023

Regevil D, '#MyDressMyChoice: Kenyans Hold Rally to Support Woman Beaten for Wearing Miniskirt' (*dw.com*, 17 November 2014) http://www.dw.com/en/mydressmychoice-kenyans-hold-rally-to-support-woman-bea ten-for-wearing-miniskirt/a-18069645, accessed 11 October 2017

Schnier K, 'Registro Nacional de Femicidios de la Justicia Argentina, Datos Estadisticos Del Poder Judicial Sobre: Femicidios (2016) Qantara

Rentschler C, 'Bystander Intervention, Feminist Hashtag Activism, and the Anti-Carceral Politics of Care' (2017) 17 Feminist Media Studies 565

Rentschler C, 'Distributed Activism: Domestic Violence and Feminist Media Infrastructure in the Fax Age' (2015) 8 Communication, Culture & Critique 182

Rentschler C, '#MeToo and Student Activism against Sexual Violence' (2018) 11 Communication Culture & Critique 503

Rentschler C, '#Safetytipsforladies: Feminist Twitter Takedowns of Victim Blaming' (2015) 15 Feminist Media Studies 353

Report of the Special Rapporteur on violence against women, its causes and consequences, Yakin Ertürk★ Addendum Communications to and from Governments 2009 (A/HRC/11/6/Add1)

Republic of Turkey, 'Report Submitted by Turkey Pursuant to Article 68, Paragraph 1 of the Council of Europe Convention on Preventing and Combating Violence against Women and Domestic Violence (Baseline Report)' (2017)

Risse T, Ropp SC, and Sikkink K (eds), *The Power of Human Rights: International Norms and Domestic Change* (Cambridge University Press, 1999)

Risse-Kappen T, Ropp SC, and Sikkink K (eds), *The Persistent Power of Human Rights: From Commitment to Compliance* (Cambridge University Press, 2013)

Roberts J, 'Turkish Women Launch Twitter Campaign against Sexual Violence' (*Mashable*, 16 February 2015) http://mashable.com/2015/02/16/ozgecan-aslan-sparks-sexual-violence-hashtag/, accessed 17 November 2023

Robinson P, 'The CNN Effect: Can the News Media Drive Foreign Policy?' (1999) 25 Review of International Studies 301

Rodriguez-Ferrand G, 'Argentina: Criminal Code Amendment to Include Femicide' (*Global Legal Monitor*, 3 May 2012) https://web.archive.org/web/20161223034606///www.loc.gov/law/foreign-news/article/argentina-criminal-code-amendment-to-include-femicide/, accessed 17 November 2023

Rowlatt J, 'The Rapes That India Forgot' (*BBC News*, 5 January 2013) http://www.bbc.co.uk/news/world-asia-india-20907755, accessed 29 November 2023

Rowlatt J, 'Viewpoints: Has Delhi Rape Case Changed India?' (*BBC News*, 10 September 2013) http://www.bbc.co.uk/news/world-asia-india-24012424, accessed 29 November 2023

Rubin AJ, 'Flawed Justice After a Mob Killed an Afghan Woman' (*The New York Times*, 26 December 2015) https://www.nytimes.com/2015/12/27/world/asia/flawed-justice-after-a-mob-killed-an-afghan-woman.html, accessed 29 November 2023

Russon M-A, 'Elon Musk's New Twitter Algorithm Changes Are "Amplifying Anger", Say Researchers' (*Evening Standard*, 30 May 2023) https://www.standard.co.uk/news/tech/elon-musk-twitter-algorithm-cyberbullying-discrimination-cornell-uc-berkeley-b1084490.html, accessed 15 November 2023

Safi M, '"A Feeble No May Mean Yes": Indian Court Overturns Rape Conviction' (*The Guardian*, 26 September 2017) http://www.theguardian.com/world/2017/sep/26/a-feeble-no-may-mean-yes-indian-court-overturns-conviction, accessed 29 November 2023

Santisteban N, 'The Women, Police, and Insecurity Agenda: Argentina's Response to Surging Femicide and Domestic…' (*Medium*, 14 August 2023) https://smallarmssurvey.medium.com/the-women-police-and-insecurity-agenda-argentinas-response-to-surging-femicide-and-domestic-1431a425f aa3, accessed 17 November 2023

Santos I, '#MyDressMyChoice: Tackling Gender Discrimination and Violence in Kenya One Tweet at a Time' (World Bank Blogs, 16 March 2015) http://blogs.worldbank.org/developmenttalk/mydressmychoice-tackling-gender-discrimination-and-violence-kenya-one-tweet-time, accessed 16 November 2023

Schwarz E, '@hannah_arendt: An Arendtian Critique of Online Social Networks' (2014) 43 Millennium – Journal of International Studies 165

Schwarz R, 'The Paradox of Sovereignty, Regime Type and Human Rights Compliance' (2004) 8 The International Journal of Human Rights 199

Scott M, 'Elon Musk Goes to War with Researchers' (*Politico*, 7 February 2023) https://www.politico.eu/article/elon-musk-twitter-goes-to-war-with-researchers-api/, accessed 15 November 2023

Scott M, 'Twitter's Plan to Charge Researchers for Data Access Puts It in EU Crosshairs' (*Politico*, 22 March 2023) https://www.politico.eu/article/twitter-elon-musk-plan-to-charge-researchers-for-data-access-puts-it-in-eu-crosshairs/, accessed 15 November 2023

Shaikh T, 'Uganda Bans Miniskirts as MPs Pass Anti-Pornography Bill' (*The Independent*, 19 December 2013) http://www.independent.co.uk/news/world/africa/no-thighs-please-uganda-bans-miniskirts-as-mps-pass-anti-pornography-bill-9016686.html, accessed 29 November 2023

Shen A, 'One Year After Horrific New Delhi Gang Rape, India Still Struggles With Rape Culture' (Think Progress, 29 December 2013) https://thinkprogress.org/one-year-after-horrific-new-delhi-gang-rape-india-still-struggles-with-rape-culture-5d0d0f1ff404/, accessed 16 November 2023

Shirky C, *Here Comes Everybody: How Change Happens When People Come Together* (updated with a new chapter, Penguin Books, 2009)

Shirky C, 'The Political Power of Social Media: Technology, the Public Sphere, and Political Change' (2011) 90 Foreign Affairs 28

Shor E, 'Conflict, Terrorism, and the Socialization of Human Rights Norms: The Spiral Model Revisited' (2008) 55 Social Problems 117

Sikkink K, *A Typology of Relations Between Social Movements and International Institutions* (The American Society of International Law, 2003)

Sikkink K, 'The United States and Torture: Does the Spiral Model Work?' in T Risse-Kappen and SC Ropp (eds), *The Persistent Power of Human Rights: From Commitment to Compliance* (Cambridge University Press, 2013)

Simmons BA, 'From Ratification to Compliance: Quantitative Evidence on the Spiral Model' in T Risse-Kappen and SC Ropp (eds), *The Persistent Power of Human Rights: From Commitment to Compliance* (Cambridge University Press, 2013)

Simmons BA, 'Preface: International Relationships in the Information Age' (2013) 15 International Studies Review 1

Sirat F, 'Violence Against Women: Before and After the Taliban' (OHRH, 15 March 2022) https://ohrh.law.ox.ac.uk/violence-against-women-before-and-after-the-taliban/, accessed 16 November 2023

Sloan L and Quan-Haase A, *The SAGE Handbook of Social Media Research Methods* (SAGE, 2017)

Snyder J and Vinjamuri L, 'Trials and Errors: Principle and Pragmatism in Strategies of International Justice' (2003) 28 International Security 5

Special Inspector General for Afghanistan Reconstruction, 'Report to the United States Congress' (2011)

Special Inspector General for Afghanistan Reconstruction, 'Report to the United States Congress' (2012)

Special Inspector General for Afghanistan Reconstruction, 'Report to the United States Congress' (2013)

Special Inspector General for Afghanistan Reconstruction, 'Report to the United States Congress' (2016)

Stampler L, 'Saudia Arabian Women Launch Campaign For Right To Drive: But Will It Make A Difference?' (*HuffPost UK*, 17 June 2011) http://www.huffingtonpost.com/2011/06/17/saudi-arabia-women-drive_n_878884.html, accessed 29 November 2023

State v Ram Singh and another (ASJ (Special Fast Track Court), Saket Courts, New Delhi)

Staufenberg J 'Saudi Arabia Is "not Ready" for Women Drivers, Says Deputy Crown Prince' (*The Independent*, 28 April 2016) http://www.independent.co.uk/news/world/middle-east/saudi-arabia-is-not-ready-for-women-drivers-says-deputy-crown-prince-mohammed-bin-salman-a7004611.html, accessed 29 November 2023

Stier S, Schünemann WJ, and Steiger S, 'Of Activists and Gatekeepers: Temporal and Structural Properties of Policy Networks on Twitter' (2018) 20 New Media & Society 1910

Sunstein CR, *#Republic: Divided Democracy in the Age of Social Media* (Princeton University Press, 2017)

Sutter JD, 'The Woman Who Defied Saudi's Driving Ban and Put It on YouTube' (*CNN*, 12 June 2012) https://edition.cnn.com/2012/06/10/world/meast/sharif-saudi-women-drive/index.html, accessed 29 November 2023

Tahaoğlu Ç, 'Men Kill 214 Women in 2013' (*Bianet – Bagimsiz Iletisim Agi*, 9 January 2014) http://www.bianet.org/english/women/152706-men-kill-214-women-in-2013, accessed 17 November 2023

REFERENCES

Tahaoğlu Ç, 'Men Kill 281 Women in 2014' (*Bianet – Bagimsiz Iletisim Agi*, 20 January 2015) http://www.bianet.org/english/women/161678-men-kill-281-women-in-2014, accessed 17 November 2023

Tahaoğlu Ç, 'Men Kill over 284 Women in 2015' (*Bianet – Bagimsiz Iletisim Agi*, 16 February 2016) http://www.bianet.org/english/women/172165-men-kill-over-284-women-in-2015, accessed 17 November 2023

Tahaoğlu Ç and Baki B, 'Men Kill At Least 261 Women, Girls in 2016' (*Bianet – Bagimsiz Iletisim Agi*, 3 February 2017) http://www.bianet.org/english/women/183255-men-kill-at-least-261-women-girls-in-2016, accessed 17 November 2023

Tarrow S, *Power in Movement: Social Movements, Collective Action and Politics* (Cambridge University Press, 1994)

Team Position, 'Social Media Fuels #Women2Drive Campaign' (29 June 2011) https://web.archive.org/web/20160511185001/https://blogs.position2.com/social-media-fuels-women2drive-campaign, accessed 17 November 2023

Terman R and Fijabi M, 'Stoning Is Not Our Culture: A Comparative Analysis of Human Rights and Religious Discourses in Iran and Nigeria' (The Global Campaign to Stop Killing and Stoning Women, 2010)

Time Magazine, 'After Lifting the Driving Ban, Saudi Arabia's War on Women Is Only Getting Worse' (*Time*, 10 April 2019) https://time.com/5567330/saudi-arabia-women-rights-drive/, accessed 17 November 2023

Tomlinson H, 'Ashtiani Freed after 9 Years on Death Row' (*The Times*, 2014) https://www.thetimes.co.uk/article/ashtiani-freed-after-9-years-on-death-row-5gk8c3nnds7, accessed 17 November 2023

Tozlu Ç and Göksel A, 'WAVE Violence against Women Country Report Turkey' (2016)

Travers A, 'Parallel Subaltern Feminist Counterpublics in Cyberspace' (2003) 46 Sociological Perspectives 223

United Nations, 'Gender Development Index' (United Nations) https://hdr.undp.org/gender-development-index, accessed 29 November 2023

United Nations Assistance Mission in Afghanistan, 'Justice through the Eyes of Afghan Women: Cases of Violence against Women Addressed through Mediation and Court Adjudication' (2015)

United Nations Assistance Mission in Afghanistan, 'A Long Way to Go: Implementation of the Elimination of Violence against Women Law in Afghanistan' (2011)

United Nations Assistance Mission in Afghanistan, 'In Search of Justice for Crimes of Violence against Women and Girls' (2020) https://unama.unmissions.org/sites/default/files/in_search_of_justice_for_crimes_of_violence_against_women_and_girls.pdf, accessed 7 November 2023

United Nations Assistance Mission in Afghanistan, 'Still a Long Way to Go: Implementation of the Law on Elimination of Violence against Women in Afghanistan' (2012)

United Nations Assistance Mission in Afghanistan, 'A Way to Go: An Update on Implementation of the Law on Elimination of Violence against Women in Afghanistan' (2013)

Uras U, 'Turkey Women Share Harassment Stories after Grim Murder' (*Al Jazeera*, 16 February 2015) http://www.aljazeera.com/news/2015/02/150216101649506.html, accessed 29 November 2023

US State Department, 'Country Reports on Human Rights Practices for 2010' (2010)

US State Department, 'Country Reports on Human Rights Practices for 2015' (2015)

US State Department, 'Country Reports on Human Rights Practices for 2016' (2016) https://www.state.gov/j/drl/rls/hrrpt/humanrightsreport/index.htm#wrapper, accessed 13 April 2017

Usta A, 'Court Lessens Attacker's Sentence despite "no-Show" in Court' (*Hürriyet Daily News*, 27 November 2015) http://www.hurriyetdailynews.com/court-lessens-attackers-sentence-despite-no-show-in-court.aspx?pageID=238&nID=91762&NewsCatID=509, accessed 17 November 2023

Vega S, 'Women's Rights: An Unfinished Business' (*The Argentina Independent*, 29 March 2013) https://web.archive.org/web/20170926112835/http://www.argentinaindependent.com/socialissues/development/womens-rights-an-unfinished-business/, accessed 17 November 2023

Verma JJS, Seth JL, and Subramanium G, 'Report on the Committee on Amendments to Criminal Law' (2013)

The Vice Presidency for Women & Family Affairs, 'National Review on Women's Status in the Islamic Republic of Iran (Beijing+20)' (2015)

Vie S, 'In Defense of "Slacktivism": The Human Rights Campaign Facebook Logo as Digital Activism' (2014) 19 First Monday, http://journals.uic.edu/ojs/index.php/fm/article/view/4961, accessed 7 July 2016

Vinay Sharma and Anr v State [2014] High Court of Delhi 1398/2013

Vu LA, 'How I Got There: Manal al-Sharif' (*Huffington Post*, 4 November 2016) https://www.huffingtonpost.com/lan-anh-vu/how-i-got-there-manal-als_b_12650652.html, accessed 29 November 2023

Wado YD, 'Violence against Women in Kenya: Data Provides a Glimpse into a Grim Situation' (*The Conversation*, 19 October 2021) http://theconversation.com/violence-against-women-in-kenya-data-provides-a-glimpse-into-a-grim-situation-170109, accessed 16 November 2023

Wallen J, 'Ten Years on from Fatal Gang Rape, India's Women Are Haunted by a Sexual Violence Epidemic' (*The Telegraph*, 21 December 2022) https://www.telegraph.co.uk/global-health/women-and-girls/ten-years-fatal-gang-rape-indias-women-haunted-sexual-violence/, accessed 8 November 2023

REFERENCES

Wambua-Soi C, 'My Dress, Whose Choice?' (*Al Jazeera*, 31 December 2014) http://www.aljazeera.com/blogs/africa/2014/11/99751.html accessed 16 November 2023

Wambui R, 'Is your dress really your choice' (*Daily Nation*, 3 March 2017) https://nation.africa/lifestyle/saturday/Is-your-dress-really-your-choice/1216-3835390-c1h5aj/index.html, accessed 16 November 2023

We Are Social, 'Digital 2023' (We Are Social UK, 26 January 2023) https://wearesocial.com/uk/blog/2023/01/digital-2023/, accessed 9 November 2023

Weekes P, '#NiUnaMenos: Fighting Femicide In Argentina' (*The Mary Sue*, 30 October 2017) https://www.themarysue.com/niunamenos-fighting-femicide-in-argentina/, accessed 17 November 2023

Wells M, 'Attacks on Women Continue In Turkey Despite Protests Over Student's Brutal Murder' (*VICE News*, 21 February 2015) https://news.vice.com/article/attacks-on-women-continue-in-turkey-despite-protests-over-students-brutal-murder, accessed 17 November 2023

We Will Stop Femicide, 'We Will Stop Femicides Platform 2022 Annual Report' (2022) https://kadincinayetlerinidurduracagiz.net/veriler/3041/we-will-stop-femicides-platform-2022-annual-report, accessed 7 November 2023

Wilkinson S, 'The #MyDressMyChoice Campaign Is the Only Positive Thing about the Video of a Woman Stripped for Wearing a Miniskirt Going Viral' (*The Debrief*, 19 November 2014) https://web.archive.org/web/20170615104627/http://www.thedebrief.co.uk/news/opinion/the-mydressmychoice-campaign-is-the-only-positive-thing-about-the-video-of-a-woman-stripped-for-wearing-a-miniskirt-going-viral-20141125515, accessed 16 November 2023

Willis RAD, 'Evaluating the Impact of Global Twitter Campaigns on Domestic Women's Rights: Statistical Modelling and Analysis' (Research Seminar, University of East Anglia School of Law, 6 June 2018)

Willis RAD, 'Exploring the Relationship between Global Twitter Campaigns and Domestic Law: Methodological Challenges and Solutions' (2021) 30 Information & Communications Technology Law 3

Willis RAD, 'Habermasian Utopia or Sunstein's Echo Chamber? The "Dark Side" of Hashtag Hijacking and Feminist Activism' (2020) 40 Legal Studies 507

Willis RAD, 'To Tweet or Not to Tweet: How Hashtag Campaigns Open Spaces for Counter-Narratives' (2018) The Society of Legal Scholars Annual Conference at Queen Mary, University of London

Willis RAD, 'Whose Story Is It Anyway? Hashtag Campaigns and Digital Abortion Storytelling' in T Vine and S Richards (eds), *Stories, Storytellers, and Storytelling* (Springer International Publishing, 2022) https://doi.org/10.1007/978-3-031-07234-5_7, accessed 14 November 2023

Willis RAD and Meier BM, 'Framing the Position of Social Media in the Local Institutionalization of International Human Rights Norms' in T Bonacker, J von Heusinger, and K Zimmer (eds), *Localization in Development Aid: How Global Institutions Enter Local Lifeworlds* (Routledge, 2017)

Working Group on Human Rights in India and the UN, 'Human Rights in India: Status Report 2012' (2012)

Yilmaz M, 'Why the Insistence on "Turkish-Style" Rules?' (*Hürriyet Daily News*, 16 July 2016) https://web.archive.org/web/20160716164816/http://www.hurriyetdailynews.com/why-the-insistence-on-turkish-style-rules.aspx?pageID=449&nID=96240&NewsCatID=503, accessed 17 November 2023

Yinanç B, 'Turkey Should Stick to Istanbul Convention on Violence against Women' (*Hürriyet Daily News*, 31 July 2017) http://www.hurriyetdailynews.com/turkey-should-stick-to-istanbul-convention-on-violence-against-women.aspx?pageID=238&nID=116127&NewsCatID=339, accessed 17 November 2023

Yobby M, 'Women, Gangs, and Silence' (26 November 2014) http://forum.ngeckenya.org/chat/women-gangs-and-silence, accessed 1 January 2019

Zaalouni H, 'Annual Report on the Death Penalty in Iran: Alarming Increase in Executions' (WCADP, 18 September 2023) https://worldcoalition.org/2023/09/18/annual-report-iran-2022/, accessed 6 November 2023

Zabludovsky K, 'This Woman Devoted Her Life To Keeping Women Safe. And Then A Man Killed Her' (*BuzzFeed*, 29 October 2017) https://www.buzzfeed.com/karlazabludovsky/these-women-tried-to-take-hashtag-activism-into-the-streets, accessed 17 November 2023

Zimmerman T, '#Intersectionality: The Fourth Wave Feminist Twitter Community' (2017) 38 Atlantis: Critical Studies in Gender, Culture & Social Justice 54

Zoepf K, 'What Overturning the Ban on Female Drivers Means for Saudi Arabia and the World' (*The New Yorker*, 12 October 2017) https://www.newyorker.com/news/news-desk/what-overturning-the-ban-on-female-drivers-means-for-saudi-arabia-and-the-world, accessed 13 February 2018

Articles, author unspecified

'#NiUnaMenos: Not One Less' (*Vital Voices*, 1 July 2015) https://www.vitalvoices.org/2015/07/niunamenos-not-one-less/, accessed 17 November 2023

'3 Saudi Shura Council Women Urge Female Drive Ban Lifted' (*Daily Nation*, 8 October 2013) https://www.nation.co.ke/lifestyle/women/3-Saudi-Shura-Council-women-urge-female-drive-ban-lifted/1950830-2024144-12mi5dsz/index.html, accessed 17 November 2023

REFERENCES

'5 Special Fast Track Courts by January 3' (*Hindustan Times*, 25 September 2013) https://web.archive.org/web/20130925062509/http://www.hindustantimes.com/India-news/NewDelhi/5-special-fast-track-courts-by-January-3/Article1-982169.aspx, accessed 16 November 2023

'60% of Femicides Committed by Partners' (*Buenos Aires Herald*, 12 June 2016) https://web.archive.org/web/20160612092324/http://www.buenosairesherald.com/article/215488/, accessed 17 November 2023

'173 Women Killed in Turkey in First Five Months of 2017: Report' (*Hürriyet Daily News*, 5 June 2017) http://www.hurriyetdailynews.com/173-women-killed-in-turkey-in-first-five-months-of-2017-report.aspx?pageID=238&nID=113936&NewsCatID=509, accessed 17 November 2023

'Abated Sentence for Man Who Stabbed Wife to Death in Southeast' (*Hürriyet Daily News*) http://www.hurriyetdailynews.com/abated-sentence-for-man-who-stabbed-wife-to-death-in-southeast.aspx?pageID=238&nID=93694&NewsCatID=509, accessed 17 November 2023

'Afghanistan: UN Experts Say 20 Years of Progress for Women and Girls' Rights Erased since Taliban Takeover' (OHCHR, 8 March 2023) https://www.ohchr.org/en/press-releases/2023/03/afghanistan-un-experts-say-20-years-progress-women-and-girls-rights-erased, accessed 16 November 2023

'Afghan Woman Lynched by Mob Becomes Rights Symbol' (*CBS News*, 5 April 2015) https://www.cbsnews.com/news/afghan-woman-farkhunda-lynched-mob-rights-symbol/, accessed 29 November 2023

'Anger and Calls for Justice in Delhi' (*BBC News*, 10 September 2013) http://www.bbc.co.uk/news/world-asia-india-24031909, accessed 29 November 2023

'Argentina Has New Gender Violence Plan' (*BBC News*, 27 July 2016) http://www.bbc.co.uk/news/world-latin-america-36901113, accessed 29 November 2023

'Argentina: Paro Contra Feminicidios y Maltrato a Las Mujeres' (*dw.com*, 19 October 2016) http://www.dw.com/es/argentina-paro-contra-feminicidios-y-maltrato-a-las-mujeres/a-36094088, accessed 17 November 2023

'Argentines Protest Violence against Women' (*Aljazeera America*, 4 June 2015) http://america.aljazeera.com/articles/2015/6/4/Thousands-of-Argentines-rally-against-femicide.html, accessed 17 November 2023

'"Battle of the Sexes": Saudi Men React to Women Driving' (*Dhaka Tribune*, 4 October 2017) https://web.archive.org/web/20171006172747/http://www.dhakatribune.com/world/middle-east/2017/10/04/saudi-men-react-women-driving/, accessed 17 November 2023

Morse F, 'Bring Back Our Girls: Boko Haram Should Be Scared of a Hashtag' (*The Independent*, 13 May 2014) http://www.independent.co.uk/voices/comment/the-bring-back-our-girls-campaign-is-working-boko-haram-should-be-scared-of-a-hashtag-9360830.html, accessed 11 December 2018

'Cleric Says Driving Risk to Ovaries' (*BBC News*, 29 September 2013) http://www.bbc.co.uk/news/world-middle-east-24323934, accessed 29 November 2023

'Clinton Adds Her Voice in Support of Saudi Women' (*The New York Times*, 22 June 2011) http://www.nytimes.com/2011/06/22/world/middleeast/22clinton.html, accessed 29 November 2023

'Davutoğlu'ndan Bakanlar Kurulu Sonrası Flaş Açıklamalar' (*Sabah*, 16 February 2015) http://www.sabah.com.tr/gundem/2015/02/16/davutoglundan-bakanlar-kurulu-sonrasi-flas-aciklamalar, accessed 17 November 2023

'Death Penalties for Delhi Gang Rape' (*BBC News*, 13 September 2013) http://www.bbc.co.uk/news/world-asia-india-24078339, accessed 29 November 2023

'Delhi Gang Rape: Death Penalty for Two Men Put on Hold' (*BBC News*, 15 March 2014) http://www.bbc.co.uk/news/world-asia-india-26593587, accessed 29 November 2023

'Delhi Gang-Rape: Four Men Sentenced to Death' (NDTV, 13 September 2013) https://www.ndtv.com/india-news/delhi-gang-rape-four-men-sentenced-to-death-732920, accessed 16 November 2023

'Delhi Gang Rape: Parliamentary Panel Summons Union Home Secretary, Delhi Police Chief' (*Times of India*, 21 December 2012) https://timesofindia.indiatimes.com/india/Delhi-gang-rape-Parliamentary-panel-summons-Union-home-secretary-Delhi-police-chief/articleshow/17707153.cms, accessed 16 November 2023

'Delhi Gang-Rape: What Was the Police Doing, Asks Angry High Court' (NDTV, 19 December 2012) https://www.ndtv.com/cheat-sheet/delhi-gang-rape-what-was-the-police-doing-asks-angry-high-court-507939, accessed 16 November 2023

'Delhi Gang Rapists' Death Penalty Upheld' (*BBC News*, 5 May 2017) http://www.bbc.co.uk/news/world-asia-india-39814910, accessed 29 November 2023

'Delhi Police Move to Protect Women Workers after Rapes' (*BBC News*, 10 December 2010) http://www.bbc.co.uk/news/mobile/world-south-asia-11966664, accessed 29 November 2023

'Delhi Rape Accused Is Found Dead' (*BBC News*, 11 March 2013) http://www.bbc.co.uk/news/world-asia-21737748, accessed 29 November 2023

'Digital in 2018: World's Internet Users Pass the 4 Billion Mark' (We Are Social UK, 30 January 2018) https://wearesocial.com/uk/blog/2018/01/global-digital-report-2018, accessed 4 October 2018

REFERENCES

'Dozens of Saudi Arabian Women Drive Cars on Day of Protest against Ban' (*The Guardian*, 26 October 2013) http://www.theguardian.com/world/2013/oct/26/saudi-arabia-woman-driving-car-ban, accessed 29 November 2023

'Driving Damages Women's Ovaries: Saudi Cleric' (*Al Akhbar English*) https://web.archive.org/web/20171019231115/http://english.al-akhbar.com/content/driving-damages-womens-ovaries-saudi-cleric, accessed 17 November 2023

'Driving Out Oppression' (Gender Justice) https://www.genderjustice.us/work/driving-out-oppression/, accessed 17 November 2023

'El Femicidio Fue Aprobado En Diputados y Está Cerca de Ser Ley' (19 April 2012) https://www.clarin.com/sociedad/femicidio-aprobado-diputados-cerca-ley_0_r1xDWS3vQx.html, accessed 1 January 2019

'Emad Baghi's "The Bloodied Stone"' (Center for Human Rights in Iran, 2 August 2008) https://www.iranhumanrights.org/2008/08/baghibloodiedstone/, accessed 17 November 2023

'End of Mission Statement Special Rapporteur on Extreme Poverty and Human Rights, Professor Philip Alston on His Visit to Saudi Arabia' (OHCHR, 19 January 2017) http://www.ohchr.org/EN/NewsEvents/Pages/DisplayNews.aspx?NewsID=21094, accessed 17 November 2023

'Erdoğan Says Turkey's Main Opposition Leader "Politicizes" Murder of Özgecan' (*Hürriyet Daily News*, 18 February 2015) http://www.hurriyetdailynews.com/erdogan-says-turkeys-main-opposition-leader-politicizes-murder-of-ozgecan.aspx?pageID=238&nID=78483&NewsCatID=338, accessed 17 November 2023

'Erdoğan Urges Muhtars to Protect Women from Violence' (*Hürriyet Daily News*, 11 March 2015) http://www.hurriyetdailynews.com/erdogan-urges-muhtars-to-protect-women-from-violence-.aspx?pageID=238&nID=79480&NewsCatID=338, accessed 17 November 2023

'Explained: How Özgecan's Murder United, Divided Turkey' (*Hürriyet Daily News*, 17 February 2015) http://www.hurriyetdailynews.com/explained-how-ozgecans-murder-united-divided-turkey.aspx?pageID=238&nID=78414&NewsCatID=509, accessed 17 November 2023

'Explaining India's New Anti-Rape Laws' (*BBC News*, 28 March 2013) http://www.bbc.co.uk/news/world-asia-india-21950197, accessed 29 November 2023

'Farkhunda Murder: 4 Sentenced to Death' (*TOLOnews*, 6 May 2015) https://www.tolonews.com/afghanistan/farkhunda-murder-4-sentenced-death, accessed 16 November 2023

'Farkhunda's Murder: A National Tragedy' (*TOLOnews*, 28 March 2015) https://www.tolonews.com/opinion/farkhundas-murder-national-tragedy, accessed 16 November 2023

'Female Iran VP Scolds Hardliners over Volleyball Ban' (*Middle East Eye*, 20 June 2015) http://www.middleeasteye.net/news/female-iran-vp-scolds-hardliners-over-volleyball-ban-411944926, accessed 16 November 2023

'Femicide in Argentina' (*Women Across Frontiers Magazine*, 22 November 2015) http://wafmag.org/2015/11/femicide-in-argentina/, accessed 17 November 2023

'Femicides on the Rise as Watchdog Releases First Quarter Figures' (*Hürriyet Daily News*, 7 April 2016) http://www.hurriyetdailynews.com/femici des-on-the-rise-as-watchdog-releases-first-quarter-figures.aspx?pageID= 238&nID=97398&NewsCatID=339, accessed 17 November 2023

'Five Saudi Women Drivers Arrested, Says Activist' (*The Guardian*, 29 June 2011) http://www.theguardian.com/world/2011/jun/29/saudi-women-drivers-arrested-jiddah, accessed 29 November 2023

'Freedom House Shows Solidarity with Saudi #Women2Drive Campaign' (25 October 2013) https://web.archive.org/web/20170423034810/ https://freedomhouse.org/article/freedom-house-shows-solidarity-saudi-women2drive-campaign, accessed 17 November 2023

'Global Gender Gap Report 2023' (World Economic Forum) https://www. weforum.org/publications/global-gender-gap-report-2023/, accessed 29 November 2023

'Hillary Clinton Backs Saudi Women Defying Driving Ban' (GulfNews. Com, 12 October 2013) http://gulfnews.com/news/gulf/saudi-arabia/hill ary-clinton-backs-saudi-women-defying-driving-ban-1.1242231, accessed 17 November 2023

'How Long Does a Typical Social Media Campaign Last?' (Ignite Social Media – The Original Social Media Agency, 7 February 2008) https:// www.ignitesocialmedia.com/lifestyle/how-long-does-a-typical-social-media-campaign-last/, accessed 10 December 2018

'India Faces Rape Debate' (*BBC News*, 24 November 2002) http://news.bbc. co.uk/1/hi/world/south_asia/2508929.stm, accessed 29 November 2023

'India Urged to Reform Rape Trials' (*BBC News*, 23 January 2013) http://www.bbc.co.uk/news/world-asia-india-21156283, accessed 29 November 2023

'Iranian Female Soccer Fan Dies after Setting Herself on Fire' (*NBC News*, 10 September 2019) https://www.nbcnews.com/news/world/iranian-female-soccer-fan-dies-after-setting-herself-fire-n1051896, accessed 6 November 2023

'Iranian Woman Facing Prison for Sneaking into Soccer Match Burns Herself to Death' (*CBS*, 10 September 2019) https://www.cbsnews.com/news/ the-blue-girl-iran-woman-caught-sneaking-soccer-stadium-dies-setting-herself-fire-rather-than-prison/, accessed 12 December 2019

REFERENCES

'Iran: Progress on Ban for Women at Stadiums' (Human Rights Watch, 28 June 2018) https://www.hrw.org/news/2018/06/28/iran-progress-ban-women-stadiums, accessed 16 November 2023

'Iran's New Penal Code Retains the Punishment of Stoning' (18 May 2013) http://justice4iran.org/publication/call-for-action/iran-new-penal-code-stoning/, accessed 17 November 2023

'Is Life Getting Worse for Women in Erdogan's Turkey?' (*BBC News*, 4 March 2015) http://www.bbc.co.uk/news/world-europe-31709887, accessed 29 November 2023

'Is This the Year Saudi Women Drive?' (Saudi Arabia Riyadh 2009) Wikileaks Public Library of US Diplomacy 09RIYADH357_a, https://wikileaks.org/plusd/cables/09RIYADH357_a.html, accessed 23 July 2024

'It's High Time That Saudi Woman Started Driving Their Cars' http://www.alwaleed.com.sa/news-and-media/news/driving/, accessed 17 November 2023

'J&K Government Bans 22 Social Networking Sites Citing Their Misuse' (*Times of India*, 26 April 2017) https://timesofindia.indiatimes.com/india/jk-government-bans-22-social-networking-sites-citing-their-misuse/articleshow/58382769.cms, accessed 16 November 2023

'Kenya "Anti Stripping Squad" Formed' (*AGR NEWS*, 26 November 2014) https://agrfm.wordpress.com/2014/11/26/kenya-anti-stripping-squad-formed/, accessed 16 November 2023

'Kenya Arrests after Women "Stripped"' (*BBC News*, 18 November 2014) http://www.bbc.co.uk/news/world-africa-30093816, accessed 29 November 2023

'Kenya Rape Verdict World's "Worst Ever"' (*The East African*, 9 June 2017) http://www.theeastafrican.co.ke/news/Kenyan-judge-juma-chitembwe-shamed-for-worst-ruling/2558-3962770-kdwy1dz/index.html, accessed 16 November 2023

'KHRC – Joint Press Statement by Kenyan Women & Civil Society Organizations on the Sexual Offences Against Women' https://web.archive.org/web/20181020142019/http://www.khrc.or.ke/2015-03-04-10-37-01/press-releases/375-joint-press-statement-by-kenyan-women-civil-society-organizations-on-the-sexual-offences-against-women.html, accessed 16 November 2023

'Kingdom of Saudi Arabia – Statement on Female Driving Protest' (Genius) https://genius.com/Kingdom-of-saudi-arabia-statement-on-female-driving-protest-annotated, accessed 17 November 2023

'Legislating against Sexual Violence: The Kenyan Experience' (Choike.org) https://web.archive.org/web/20101207010147/http://www.choike.org/nuevo_eng/informes/4717.html, accessed 16 November 2023

'Life Sentence Requested for Three Suspects in Özgecan Murder' (*Hürriyet Daily News*, 9 September 2015) http://www.hurriyetdailynews.com/life-sentence-requested-for-three-suspects-in-ozgecan-murder------.aspx?pag eID=238&nID=88257&NewsCatID=509, accessed 17 November 2023

'The Life Span of a Tweet: Why Fast Isn't Fast Enough in a Crisis' (*Stanton Communication*, 16 March 2017) https://stantoncomm.com/life-span-tweet, accessed 10 December 2018

'Multi-Channel Marketing: How Long Should Campaigns Last?' (Technology TherapyTM Group, 12 January 2015) https://technology therapy.com/long-multi-channel-advertising-campaigns-last/, accessed 10 December 2018

'Musk Threatens to Sue Researchers Documenting the Rise in Hateful Tweets' (*PBS NewsHour*, 31 July 2023) https://www.pbs.org/newshour/economy/musk-threatens-to-sue-researchers-documenting-the-rise-in-hateful-tweets, accessed 15 November 2023

'My Dress, My Choice Protest Sparks a Lot of Questions' (*Sewa News*, 23 November 2014) https://www.sewa.news/2014/11/kandeh-mariama-seray-my-dress-my-choice.html, accessed 29 November 2023

'National Crime Records Bureau', http://ncrb.gov.in/, accessed 2 January 2019

'Nirbhaya Case: Four Indian Men Executed for 2012 Delhi Bus Rape and Murder' (*BBC News*, 20 March 2020) https://www.bbc.com/news/world-asia-india-51969961, accessed 29 November 2023

'Number of Femicide Victims in Argentina 2022' (*Statista*) https://www.stati sta.com/statistics/1102274/number-femicide-victims-argentina/, accessed 17 November 2023

'One Day Women Will Drive, Saudi King Says' (*ABC News*, 14 October 2005) http://www.abc.net.au/news/2005-10-14/one-day-women-will-drive-saudi-king-says/2124474, accessed 29 November 2023

'Open Government Around the World' (World Justice Project) https://worldjusticeproject.org/open-government-around-world, accessed 30 November 2023

'Opinion: Give Saudi Women the Right to Drive', https://edition.cnn.com/2013/10/24/opinion/begum-saudi-women-driving/index.html, accessed 17 November 2023

'Özgecan Aslan's Murderers Sentenced to Aggravated Life Imprisonment' (*Bianet – Bagimsiz Iletisim Agi*, 3 December 2015) https://www.bianet.org/english/women/169845-ozgecan-aslan-s-murderers-sentenced-to-aggrava ted-life-imprisonment, accessed 17 November 2023

'Parliament Uproar over Delhi Rape' (*BBC News*, 18 December 2012) http://www.bbc.co.uk/news/world-asia-india-20765869, accessed 29 November 2023

REFERENCES

'Platform Law Proposal Full Text to Stop the Murder of Women' (We Will Stop Femicide, 27 June 2015) https://kadincinayetlerinidurduracagiz.net/haklarimiz/2251/kadin-cinayetlerini-durduracagiz-platformu-yasa-tekl ifi-tam-metni, accessed 17 November 2023

'The Political Terror Scale' (The Political Terror Scale) https://www.polit icalterrorscale.org/, accessed 29 November 2023

'Rajya Sabha Passes Juvenile Justice Bill, Nirbhaya's Mother "Satisfied"' (*Times of India*, 22 December 2015) https://timesofindia.indiatimes.com/india/Rajya-Sabha-passes-Juvenile-Justice-Bill-Nirbhayas-mother-satisf ied/articleshow/50285328.cms, accessed 16 November 2023

'Rapist Indian Guru Jailed for 20 Years' (*BBC News*, 28 August 2017) http://www.bbc.co.uk/news/world-asia-india-41070764, accessed 29 November 2023

'Roadblocks Still in Place for Saudi Women after Five Years of Driving' (*France 24*, 7 July 2023) https://www.france24.com/en/live-news/20230 707-after-five-years-of-driving-roadblocks-remain-for-saudi-women-1, accessed 17 November 2023

'Rouhani Minister Expresses Outrage That Women Were Banned from Attending Iran-US Volleyball Match' (Center for Human Rights in Iran, 23 June 2015) http://www.iranhumanrights.org/2015/06/rouhani-minis ter-women-volleyball/, accessed 16 November 2023

'Sadece 2016'da 236 Kadın #25Kasım' (Change.org) https://www.change.org/p/%C3%B6zgecanyasas%C4%B1-%C3%A7%C4%B1ks%C4%B1n-yasalar-kad%C4%B1nlar%C4%B1-korusun-ba-yildirim/u/18584990, accessed 17 November 2023

'Saudi Activists Call for the Release of Women Detained for Driving' (*The New York Times*, 9 December 2014) https://www.nytimes.com/2014/12/09/world/middleeast/saudi-activists-call-for-the-release-of-women-detai ned-for-driving.html, accessed 29 November 2023

'Saudi Arabia Extends Detention of Women Driving Activists: Amnesty' (*The Express Tribune*, 9 December 2014) https://tribune.com.pk/story/804221/saudi-arabia-extends-detention-of-women-driving-activists-amne sty/, accessed 17 November 2023

'Saudi Arabia Issues Warning against Women's Driving Campaign' (*Foreign Policy*, 25 October 2013) https://foreignpolicy.com/2013/10/25/saudi-arabia-issues-warning-against-womens-driving-campaign/, accessed 14 February 2018

'Saudi Arabia Must Not Thwart Campaign for Women Drivers' (Amnesty, 24 October 2013) https://www.amnesty.org/en/latest/news/2013/10/saudi-arabia-must-not-thwart-campaign-women-drivers/, accessed 17 November 2023

'Saudi Arabian Women Launch Campaign For Right To Drive: But Will It Make A Difference?' (*HuffPost UK*, 17 June 2011) http://www.huffing tonpost.com/2011/06/17/saudi-arabia-women-drive_n_878884.html, accessed 29 November 2023

'Saudi Arabia to Allow Women to Drive' (*Al Jazeera*, 27 September 2017) http://www.aljazeera.com/news/2017/09/saudi-arabia-women-drive-170926190857109.html, accessed 29 November 2023

'Saudi Authorities Detain Six Women for Driving' (*ArabianBusiness.com*, 10 June 2011) http://www.arabianbusiness.com/saudi-authorities-detain-six-women-for-driving-404597.html, accessed 17 November 2023

'Saudi Clerics Protest Outside King's Palace, Blame US for Women Driving' (*Mehr News Agency*, 23 October 2013) https://en.mehrnews.com/news/56993/Saudi-clerics-protest-outside-king-s-palace-blame-US-for-women, accessed 29 November 2023

'Saudi Clerics Protest Women Driving at the Royal Court' https://riyad hbureau.wordpress.com/tag/royal-court/, accessed 17 November 2023

'Saudi Princess Lobbies For Women's Right To Drive' (NPR.org, 14 July 2011) https://www.npr.org/2011/07/14/137840538/saudi-princess-lobb ies-for-womens-right-to-drive, accessed 17 November 2023

'Saudi Woman "Arrested" for Driving' (*Al Jazeera*, 5 December 2014) http://www.aljazeera.com/news/middleeast/2014/12/saudi-woman-arres ted-driving-2014121165739368209.html, accessed 29 November 2023

'Saudi Woman Driving Blog "Arrest"' (*BBC News*, 3 December 2014) http://www.bbc.co.uk/news/blogs-trending-30316837, accessed 29 November 2023

'Saudi Woman Penalised for Driving Car before Ban Is Lifted' (*The Guardian*, 9 October 2017) https://www.theguardian.com/world/2017/oct/09/saudi-arabia-woman-penalised-driving-car-before-ban-lifted, accessed 29 November 2023

'Saudi Woman "Spared Lashing" in Driving Case' (*Al Jazeera*, 28 September 2011) http://www.aljazeera.com/news/middleeast/2011/09/2011928 20341050915.html, accessed 29 November 2023

'Saudi Woman's Lashing "Revoked"' (*BBC News*, 29 September 2011) http://www.bbc.co.uk/news/world-middle-east-15102190, accessed 29 November 2023

'Saudi Woman to Get 10 Lashes for Driving a Car' (*CBS News*, 27 September 2011) https://www.cbsnews.com/news/saudi-woman-to-get-10-lashes-for-driving-a-car/, accessed 29 November 2023

'Saudi Women Can Drive at Last but Some Say Price Is Silence', https://web.archive.org/web/20180709125334/https://uk.reuters.com/article/uk-saudi-women-driving-politics/saudi-women-can-drive-at-last-but-some-say-price-is-silence-idUKKCN1C71TJ, accessed 17 November 2023

REFERENCES

'Saudi Women Defy Ban to Take Driver's Seat' (*Al Jazeera*, 17 June 2011) http://www.aljazeera.com/video/middleeast/2011/06/201161713200141 723.html, accessed 29 November 2023

'Saudi Women Driving Ban Not Part of Sharia-Morality Police Chief' (*Reuters*, 19 September 2013) https://www.reuters.com/article/us-saudi-women-driving/saudi-women-driving-ban-not-part-of-sharia-moral ity-police-chief-idUSBRE98I0LJ20130919,

'Saudi Women Rejoice at End of Driving Ban' (*BBC News*, 27 September 2017) http://www.bbc.co.uk/news/world-middle-east-41411799, accessed 29 November 2023

'Senior Cleric Opposes Women's Presence in Sports Stadiums' (The Iran Project, 13 June 2015) http://theiranproject.com/blog/2015/06/13/sen ior-cleric-opposes-womens-presence-in-sports-stadiums/, accessed 16 November 2023

'Sign the Petition' (Change.org) https://www.change.org/p/özgecanyasası-çıksın-yasalar-kadınları-korusun-ba-yildirim, accessed 17 November 2023

'Stop the Violent Attacks on Women: #MyDressMyChoice' (*Equality Now*) https://web.archive.org/web/20181018124310/https://www.equalitynow. org/stop_the_violent_attacks_on_women_mydressmychoice, accessed 16 November 2023

'Student "Gang-Raped on Delhi Bus"' (*BBC News*, 17 December 2012) http://www.bbc.co.uk/news/world-asia-india-20753075, accessed 29 November 2023

'A Tehran Court Sentences a Young Mother to Stoning, Execution' (NCRI Women Committee, 8 November 2021) https://women.ncr-iran.org/ 2021/11/08/a-tehran-court-sentences-a-young-mother-to-stoning-execut ion/, https://women.ncr-iran.org/2021/11/08/a-tehran-court-senten ces-a-young-mother-to-stoning-execution/, accessed 16 November 2023

'Thousands March in Kabul Demanding Justice for Woman Killed by Mob' (*The Guardian*, 24 March 2015) https://www.theguardian.com/world/ 2015/mar/24/farkhunda-thousands-march-in-kabul-demanding-justice-for-woman-killed-by-mob, accessed 29 November 2023

'Thousands Protest Murder of Özgecan Aslan' (*Hürriyet Daily News*, 18 February 2015) http://www.hurriyetdailynews.com/thousands-protest-murder-of-ozgecan-aslan-.aspx?pageID=238&nID=78520&NewsCatID= 341, accessed 17 November 2023

'TransResearch Consortium' (TransResearch Consortium, 15 September 2022) https://transresearchconsortium.com, accessed 30 November 2023

'Turkey President Erdogan: Women Are Not Equal to Men' (*BBC News*, 24 November 2014) http://www.bbc.co.uk/news/world-europe-30183 711, accessed 29 November 2023

'Turkey's Femicide Problem' (17 May 2015) https://web.archive.org/web/20230120024848/https://harvardpolitics.com/turkeys-femicide-problem/, accessed 17 November 2023

'Turkey's Introduction of Chemical Castration for Sex Offenders Prompts Mixed Reaction' (*Hürriyet Daily News*, 27 July 2016) http://www.hurriyetdailynews.com/turkeys-introduction-of-chemical-castration-for-sex-offenders-prompts-mixed-reaction.aspx?pageID=238&nID=102147&NewsCatID=509, accessed 17 November 2023

'Turkish Court Jails Three to Life for College Girl's Brutal Murder' (*Hürriyet Daily News*, 4 December 2015) http://www.hurriyetdailynews.com/turkish-court-jails-three-to-life-for-college-girls-brutal-murder.aspx?pageID=238&nID=92051&NewsCatID=509, accessed 17 November 2023

'Turkish Family Ministry Plans Stronger Action Plan to Combat Violence against Women' (*Hürriyet Daily News*, 18 February 2015) http://www.hurriyetdailynews.com/turkish-family-ministry-plans-stronger-action-plan-to-combat-violence-against-women-.aspx?pageID=238&nID=78548&NewsCatID=341, accessed 17 November 2023

'Turkish Leaders Celebrate International Women's Day' (*Hürriyet Daily News*, 9 March 2015) http://www.hurriyetdailynews.com/turkish-leaders-celebrate-international-womens-day------.aspx?pageID=238&nID=79370&NewsCatID=338, accessed 17 November 2023

'Turkish PM Pledges to Act on Women Killings' (*Hürriyet Daily News*, 16 February 2015) http://www.hurriyetdailynews.com/turkish-pm-pledges-to-act-on-women-killings.aspx?pageID=238&nID=78388&NewsCatID=338, accessed 17 November 2023

'Turkish President Erdoğan Says Gender Equality "against Nature"' (*Hürriyet Daily News*, 25 November 2014) http://www.hurriyetdailynews.com/turkish-president-erdogan-says-gender-equality-against-nature.aspx?pageID=238&nID=74726&NewsCatID=338, accessed 17 November 2023

'Turkish President Erdoğan Slams Women Protesting Özgecan's Murder by Dancing' (*Hürriyet Daily News*, 17 February 2015) http://www.hurriyetdailynews.com/turkish-president-erdogan-slams-women-protesting-ozgecans-murder-by-dancing-.aspx?pageID=238&nID=78423&NewsCatID=338, accessed 17 November 2023

'Turkish Women Relate Sexual Harassment Stories via Social Media' (*Hürriyet Daily News*, 16 February 2015) http://www.hurriyetdailynews.com/turkish-women-relate-sexual-harassment-stories-via-social-media-.aspx?pageID=238&nID=78413&NewsCatID=341, accessed 17 November 2023

'Turkish Women Share Stories of Abuse' (*BBC News*, 17 February 2015) http://www.bbc.co.uk/news/blogs-trending-31504416, accessed 29 November 2023

REFERENCES

'UN Special Rapporteur Challenges Argentina to Step up Protection of Women in "Machismo Culture"' (21 November 2016) https://www.ohchr.org/fr/newsevents/pages/displaynews.aspx?newsid=20903&langid=e, accessed 2 January 2019

'Understanding India's Rape Crisis' (*The Harvard Gazette*, 20 September 2013) https://news.harvard.edu/gazette/story/2013/09/understanding-indias-rape-crisis/, accessed 16 November 2023

'The Village Where Cousins Were Raped and Hanged' (*BBC News*, 30 May 2014) http://www.bbc.co.uk/news/world-asia-27622236, accessed 29 November 2023

'Violence against Women Is Turkey's "Bleeding Wound" – Erdogan' (*Reuters*, 16 February 2015) http://www.reuters.com/article/us-turkey-women-violence-idUSKBN0LK1OH20150216,

'West's Approach to Women Issues "Profoundly Deviant": Leader' (The Iran Project, 20 April 2014) http://theiranproject.com/blog/2014/04/20/wests-approach-to-women-issues-profoundly-deviant-leader/, accessed 16 November 2023

'When Is My Tweet's Prime of Life? (A Brief Statistical Interlude)' (*Moz*, 12 November 2012) https://moz.com/blog/when-is-my-tweets-prime-of-life, accessed 10 December 2018

'WJP Open Government Index 2015' (*World Justice Project*) https://worldjusticeproject.org/our-work/wjp-rule-law-index/wjp-open-government-index-2015, accessed 20 October 2018

'Women Free to Wear Miniskirts – Lokodo' (*Daily Monitor*, 16 January 2014) http://www.monitor.co.ug/News/National/Women-free-to-wear-miniskirts---Lokodo/688334-2148738-v2a1ai/index.html, accessed 16 November 2023

'World Bank Open Data' (World Bank Open Data) https://data.worldbank.org, accessed 30 November 2023

'The World's Most Dangerous Countries for Women 2011' (Trustlaw, 15 June 2011) https://web.archive.org/web/20180711002531/http://news.trust.org/spotlight/the-worlds-most-dangerous-countries-for-women-2011, accessed 16 November 2023

'والیبال مسابقات سالن در بانوان حضور بررسی برای روحانی حسن دستور' (*Mehr News Agency*, 17 June 2014) http://www.mehrnews.com/news/2313394/دستور-حسن-روحانی-برای-بررسی-حضور-بانوان-در-سالن-مسابقات-والیبال, accessed 29 November 2023

Index

References to figures appear in *italic* type; those in **bold** type refer to tables. References to footnotes show both the page number and the note number (34n1).

A

Abdullah, King 141
adultery 3, 36–37, 40, 41, 49, 51
Afghanistan 3, **26**, 61–81, 87, 158
  Afghan Women's Network 75, 82
  end violence against women (EVAW) 67–68, 81, 88, 116
  Special Inspector General for Afghanistan Reconstruction (SIGAR) 75, 76
  and United Nations Assistance Mission in Afghanistan (UNAMA) 67, 69, 81
  see also #farkhunda campaign
aggravated sentences 84
Ahmadi, A. 44–45
Ahmadinejad 41
Ahmed, S. 6–7, 158
Alhargan, R. A. 13
Alston, P. 148–149
Alwaleed bin Talal, Prince 143
Ameerah Al-Taweel, Princess 143
Amnesty International **29**, 34, 36, 46, **47**, 67, 122–123, 142, 145, 148, 197
anti-female stereotype 77
anti-pornography bill, Uganda 74
Application Programming Interface (API) 187
arbitrary arrests 34, 46, 185
Argentina 3, 10–11, 13, 18, **26**, 66, 160
  Argentine Penal Code, Article 80 124
  gay rights movement 10–11
  gender violence law, Law 26.485 107–109
  Ministry of Women, Gender, and Diversity 109
  national action plans, against violence 77–78, 113
  National Women's Council 109, 113
  see also femicides; #niunamenos campaign
arrests 34, 34n1, 37–38, 46, 48, 85, 145, 156, 161, 185

B

Bachelard, J. Y. 16
backlash campaigns 7, 68, 76, 117, 127, 139, 141, 159, 170
  active users profile, in Twitter 56–57
  content analysis, Twitter 58–59
  context explaining 39–40
  domestic drive, lack of 157–158
  engagement metrics 55–56
  institutionalization, lack of 42–46
  law enforcement 46–48
  legal outcomes in 40–53
  legislation 40–41
  poor persistence (Tweets/day) 54–55
  UN dialogue 48–53
  see also #letwomengotostadium campaign; #stopstoning campaign
Beijing Platform for Action 79–80
Beijing Platform for Women 43
Black Wednesday protest 102
Blue Sky 188
boomerang model 8–9
Borzel, T. 14, 76
#bringbackourgirls campaign 22
Brysk, A. 11, 13–14

C

campaign groupings, based on outcomes 157–161
Castells, M. 17, 19
Chase, A. T. 11–12
Cheng, I. 11
civil society organizations (CSOs) 8, 12, 14, **29**, 66, 77–78, 103, 147
Cizre, U. 11
Clinton, H. 136, 155–156
CNN effect 18n52, 19n62, 20, 197
Colombia 11, 13, 162n7
Committee on Economic, Social and Cultural Rights 50, 90–91, 124

INDEX

Committee on the Elimination of Discrimination Against Women 87–91
Committee on the Elimination of Racial Discrimination 50
Committee on the Rights of Child 52–53
composite scores 28, 184
consistent messaging 59, 94, 97, 123, 131, 133, 151, 154, **163**, 169–170, 180, 183
constructed messaging 20
counter-narratives 20, 65, 80, 95, 96, 98–99, 152, *153*, 155, 194
COVID-19 pandemic 74–75, 80, 110
Czech Republic 15–16

D

death penalty 3, 43, 49, 51, 52, 107, 115–117
#delhigangrape campaign 3, 20, **26**, 156, 159–160, 165, 167, **186**, 193, **196**
  active users 128–129
  consistently used words 131, *132*
  content analysis 129–133
  engagement metrics 127–128
  institutionalization, lack of 110–112
  law enforcement 114–118
  legislative change 104–107
  overview 100–101
  persistence (Tweets/day) 126–127
  positivity and peaks, in sentiments 129–133, *131*
  UN reports on 120–123
detention 34, 36, 46, 48, 52, 53, 60, 135, 145, 146–147, 156, 185
diaspora effect 165
digital feminist activism 4, 5, 18, **32**, 33, 156, 158, 161, **163**, 168, 189
  counter-narratives in 65
  and fourth wave feminism 6–8, 101
  positivism in 118, 137
  and spiral model of human rights change 54, 156
discrimination 36, 38–39, 43, 50, 75n68, 91n164, 102, 144, 145, 147
  caste-based 112
  class-based 101
  gender-based 36n11, 37, 37n11, 64n11
domestic actors 10–12, 13, **32**, 162–164, **163**
domestic capacity 10, 14–15, **33**, 76, **163**, 175–178
domestic civil society 8, 12, 14
domestic drive, lack of 12, 53, 59, 94, 157–158, 161, 167, 189
domestic voices 18–19, 35, 56, 99, 165–168, 195

E

elections and regime change 11, **29**, 100, 103–104, 107, 109, 113, 120, 126, 133, 137, 159–160, **186**, 198
elimination of violence against women (EVAW) in Afghanistan 67–68, 81, 88, 116

in India 76, 110
elite, heteronormative, patriarchal platforms 168–169
engagement metrics 179–181, **180**, *182*, *183*
  backlash campaigns 55–56
  possible success campaign 151
  status quo campaigns 93–94
  tactical concession campaigns 127–128
Erdogan, R. T. 71, 83
European Union 57, 66, 77, 129
extra-marital relations 51

F

Facebook 1, 22–23, 45, 135–136, 146, 186–187
#farkhunda campaign 3, **26**, 159, 167, 173, 193, **196**
  active users, in Tweet 94–96
  consistently used words *98*
  content analysis, in Twitter 96–99
  engagement metrics 93–94
  law enforcement in 81–83
  overview 61–62
  persistence (Tweets/day) 92–93
  positive changes in institutionalization 75–76
  positive legislative changes 67
  UN reports from and to Afghanistan 87–88
  variable framing, with messaging 97
fast-track courts, India 106, 107, 114–115, 117–118
Fédération Internationale de Volleyball (FIVB) 38
femicides 3, **26**, 63–64, 70, 71, 75, 77, 81, 86, 89, 96, 114
  in Argentina 101, 118–119
  conviction rates on 119
  laws on 107–110, 124–125
  We Will Stop Femicide, Turkey 84
feminism, fourth wave 4, 5, 6–8, 33, 101
feminist cyber-activism 139
feminist voices 20
Fiscal Specialised Unit on Violence against Women (UFEM) 102n12
foreign involvement, in hashtag campaigns 13, 168, 189
framing 4, 17, 19, 25, 130, 170
  and government backlash 59
  and messaging 20, 58, 97, 99, 155, 169, 170, **186**, 196
Fraser, N. 6–7, 158
future of hashtag campaigns 185–188

G

gender equality 8, **29**, 66, 77, 95
Ghani, A. 75–76
Gilboa, E. 20
Gladwell, M. 22–23, 56
Goldsmith, J. 15, 16
Goodman, R. 12

government backlash 10, 12–13, **32**, 53–54, 56, 59, **163**, 168–172, **186**
Gulf War 137
gun violence towards women 109

H

hadd crime 40, 41
harassment laws 68, 70, 141
Hemmings, C. 6–7, 8, 22, **32**, 40, 59, 158, **163**, 168
Heo, M. 11
heteronormative patriarchy, of social media 2, 7, 17–19, 168, 169
heteroscedasticity 184
high-profile cases 117
human rights
  abuses 140
  change, theory 4, 8–9, 11–12, 33, 35, 61, 156, 160, 172
  #humanrights 58
  international mechanisms 103, 122, 123, 126, 149, 170
  international norms, violation of 42, 115
  international treaties **29**, **31**, 39, 49
  norms 11, 14, **31**, 52
  see also spiral model of human rights change theory
Human Rights Committee 43, 52, 120, 121, 124, 125
Human Rights Council 148
Human Rights Watch 69–70, 82, 107, 146, 147, 154

I

ideal Twitter campaign behaviours 185, **186**
impunity culture 62, 82, 85, 86, 92, 104
incentives, role in spiral model 10, 15–16, 23, **33**, 53, 68, **163**, 180, 181
India 3, **26**, 148, 158, 177
  conviction rates in 105, 117, 118, **119**, 119–120, 124, 126
  crime statistics 117
  criminal justice system 106–107
  Criminal Law (Amendment) Act 122
  fast-track courts 106, 107, 114–115, 117–118
  Juvenile Justice Bill, 2015 106
  juveniles, in Indian criminal justice system 106–107
  violence against women 100–101, 107, 108, 112
  see also #delhigangrape campaign
institutionalisation, lack of 112–113
international actors 9, 11, 12, 13, 16, **32**, 161, **163**, 166
international Twitter-driven hashtag campaigns 10, 15, 16, 33, 177, 185, 188
international women's rights norms 43–44, 48, 59, 158

Iran 3, **26**, 66, 68, 76, 148, 170
  backlash campaigns in *see* backlash campaigns
  Constitution, Article 167 41
  Constitution, Article 221.5 42
  Iran Human Rights 34, 37, 43, 46, 47, **47**
  Islamic Penal Code 40, 41
  Islamic Revolution (1979) 40
  Judicial and Legal Commission of the Islamic Consultative Council 42
  laws 36–37
  National Council of Resistance of Iran (NCRI) 34, 46, **47**
  New Islamic Penal Code (2007) 41
  social media in 21
  2025 mission 49
  see also #letwomengotostadium campaign; #stopstoning campaign
Ireland 18, **26**
Israel 11

J

Jackson, M. 21
Jackson, P. T. 15
Jetschke, A. 12, 13
Jinks, D. 12
Joseph, S. 20

K

Kaba, M. 7
Keck, M. E. 8
Kenya 16, **26**, 64–67, 72–75, 79, 84–86, 90, 94, 103, 110
  ban the miniskirt bill 73
  decency laws 65, 73, 95
  Domestic Violence Bill 90
  Jezebel's story 64
  Sexual Offences Act 72, 79, 85, 90
  see also #mydressmychoice campaign; public stripping
Khamenei, A. 44, 46
Krasner, S. D. 15, 16
Krebs, R. R. 15

L

legal outcomes 3–5, 185
  backlash campaigns 40–53
  negative outcomes 40–53
  positive success 138–149
  status quo campaigns 67–91
  tactical concession campaigns 104–126
#letwomengotostadium campaign 3, **26**, 34, 97, 128, 158, **196**
  active Tweet users in 57
  consistently used words in *58*
  engagement metrics 55–56
  legal outcomes in 40–53
  overview 37–39
  persistence and timeline of Tweets 54–55

INDEX

Liese, A. 13
lifespan, of hashtag campaigns 21, 25, 92, 127, 131, 155, 170
Linde, R. 15–16
lip service 75–76, 77, 78, 110

M

machismo/machista culture 3, 112, 118, 125–126, *132*
#malala 26, 27
Malala, Y. 26
marital rape 50
mass arrests 34n1, 85
material incentives 16, 178–181
media effects theory 4, 5, 6, 16, 21, 33, 61, 157, 197–198
see also social media theory
messaging, on social media 19, 20, 28, **32**, 169, **170**
  consistent 59, 94, 97, 123, 131, 133, 151, 154, **163**, 169–170, 180, 183
  constructed messaging 20
  and framing 20, 58, 59, 97, 99, 130, 155, 169, 170, **186**, 196
  off-topic messaging 96
  and outcomes 169–170, **170**, *171*
  and UN dialogue, relationship between 171
Mexico 10
Molaverdi 44, 45
Morozov, E. 56
Muñoz, A. A. 10
Musk, E. 187, 188
#mydressmychoice campaign 3, **26**, 159, 167, 173, **196**
  active users, in Tweet 94–96
  consistently used words *98*
  content analysis, in Twitter 96–99
  engagement metrics 93–94
  implementation and institutionalization, lack of 79–80
  law enforcement in 84–86
  legislative changes 72–75
  overview 64–65
  persistence (Tweets/day) 92–93
  Security Laws Act of 2014 72n53
  UN dialogue in 90–91

N

Naghibi, N. 21
Nairobi 64, 73, 79–80, 85, 159
  anti-stripping squad 85
  Forward-Looking Strategy 79–80
Namibia 65
naming and shaming concept 10, 16, 23, 160, 168, 178–179
#niunamenos campaign 3, 25, **26**, 57, 156, 159, 160, 164–165, **186**, 192, **196**, 198
  active users 126–129
  consistently used words 131–132, *132*

content analysis 129–133
engagement metrics 127–128
institutionalization, lack of 112–114
law enforcement 118–120, 167
legislative changes 107–110
overview 101–102
persistence (Tweets/day) 126–127
positivity and peaks, in sentiments 129–133, *130*, 193
UN reports on 123–126
non-governmental organizations 1, 35, 136, 197
#notacriminal 26–27
nuanced incentives **33**, **163**, 178–179

O

off-topic messaging 96
Open Government Index **30**, 177
Optional Protocols **29**, 103
Opuz case 89
organic framing and messaging 59
overall composite campaign score 181, 183–185, **184**, *184*
Özgecan's Law 64, 71

P

Pakistan 26
Perloff, R. M. 17
persistence of Tweets 172–175, *176*, 177
  backlash campaigns 54–55
  potential success campaign 149–151
  status quo campaigns 92–93
  tactical concession campaigns 126–127
polygamy 37
potential success campaign 160–161
  content analysis 154–156
  context of 137
  engagement metrics 151
  foreign active users 151–152, *153*
  framing and messaging 154–155
  institutionalization 141–145
  law enforcement 145–147, 167
  legislative change 138–141
  low level persistence 149–151
  positivity over time *154*
  pressure from US 161
  and tactical concessions campaign 144
  UN dialogue 147–149
  see also #women2drive campaign
pseudo-mob mentality 15
public stripping 64–65, 69, 80, 95, 97, 159
  see also #mydressmychoice campaign

R

religion, hard-line conservatives 37, 42, 68, 141, 146, 158
  see also #women2drive campaign
#repealthe8th 18, 26–27
reproductive rights 144

risky campaign behaviours 5, 188
Risse, T. 8–9, 14, 76

S

Saud, Prince 139
Saudi Arabia 3, 13, **26**, 158, 160, 165, 167, 177–178, *178*
  clerics protest against women driving 142–143
  guardianship laws 138, 144, 156, 160–161, 185
  Islamic law. 147
  Personal Status Law 144–145
  Shura Council 142
  Vision 2030 149
  see also #women2drive campaign
Saudi-American, active users 152
Save Darfur coalition 23–24
Schwarz, R. 11
selfie mania 62
#sendeanlat campaign 3, 26, 129, 159, 165, 173, 193, **196**
  active users, in Tweet 94–96
  consistently used words *98*
  content analysis, in Twitter 96–99
  engagement metrics 93–94
  implementation and institutionalization, lack of 77–79
  legislative outcomes 69–71
  mitigating factors 83–84
  overview 63–64
  persistence (Tweets/day) 92–93
  sentiments over time 96–97, *97*
  UN human rights mechanisms, dialogue with 88–90
sexual harassment 72, 76, 79, 117, 118
sexual politics 13–14
Shari'a law 40, 41, 143–144, 147
Shor, E. 9–10, 14–15
Sikkink, K. 8, 12–13
slactivism 22, 56, 133, 160, 179
sleeper effect 21
Snyder, J. 16
social media
  active users 2, 15
  activism 4, 5, 16, 42, 103, 157
  advocacy campaigns 2, 158
social media theory 6, 92, 105, 130
  in activism and women's rights campaign 16–24
  campaign participants, no risk to 22–24
  domestic context or voice, lacking of 22
  elite-driven, heteronormative patriarchal nature 17–18
  fickleness of 20–21
  organic and chaotic 19–20
  sleeper effect 21
societal norm 138
spark incidents **26**, 61, 74, 92, 122, 159

spiral model of human rights change theory 8–9, 168
  domestic actors 10–12, 13, **32**, 162–168, **163**
  domestic capacity 10, 14–15, **33**, 76, **163**, 175–178
  government backlash 10, 12–13, **32**, 53–54, 56, 59, **163**, 168–172, **186**
  incentives role 10, 15–16, 23, **33**, 53, 68, **163**, 178–181
  progression issues 13–14, 172, 173–175
  theoretical critique of 9–16, 126, 141, 177–179, 181, 185
statistical analysis, for campaigns 161–181
  domestic actors focus, lack of 162–168
  domestic capacity issues 175–178
  government backlash 168–172
  long-term progression, lack of 172–175
  material incentives, ignoring 178–181
  overview of tests **163**
status quo campaigns 104, 127, 157, 159, 173, 174
  active users, in Tweet 94–96
  content analysis, in Twitter 96–99
  context in 66
  engagement metrics 93–94
  institutionalization 75–81
  international norms presence in 99
  law enforcement 81–86
  legal outcomes 67–91
  legislative change 67–75
  negative sentiments in 96–97
  persistence (Tweets/day) 92–93
  UN dialogue 87–91
  see also #farkhunda campaign; #mydressmychoice campaign; #sendeanlat campaign
stoning sentences 36–37, 40–41, 43, 46, 48, 49, 51, 53
#stopstoning campaign 3, **26**, 34, 91, 129, 149, 158, 165, 167, 172, **186**, **196**, 198
  active Twitter users in 57
  consistently used words in *58*
  engagement metrics 55–56
  legal outcomes in 40–53
  moratorium, on stoning 41, 43, 49
  overview 35–37
  persistence and timeline of Tweets 54–55
  reports of stoning in Iran 46, **47**
  stoning sentences 36–37, 40–41, 43, 46, 48, 49, 51, 53

T

tactical concession campaigns 9, 13, 93, 138, 144, 157, 159–160, 168, *178*, **186**
  active users 128–129
  content analysis 129–133
  context in 103–104
  elections, role in 100, 103–104, 107, 109, 113, 120, 126, 159–160, **186**, 198

INDEX

engagement metrics 127–128
law enforcement 114–120
legislative change 104–110
meaningful institutionalization, lack
of 110–114
persistence (Tweets/day) 126–127
and potential success campaign 144
UN human rights reports 120–126
see also #delhigangrape campaign;
#niunamenos campaign
Taiwan 11
Taliban 61–62, 66, 67, 69, 76, 87
Tehran 37–38, 45, 47, 54, *55*
Tehran Islamic seminaries council 45
Thunderclap 54, *55*, 58
transnational advocacy networks (TANs) 8,
10–11, 12, 16, 20, 167
Travers, A. 158
Turkey 3, **26**, 63, 66, 67, 69, 71, 75, 77, 83,
88–90, 118, 158
awareness, on violence against women 63
Criminal Code 89
Criminal Law 71
Execution Act 71
Ministry of Family and Social Policies 78
Özgecan's Law 64, 71
Turkish law 64, 70
see also #sendeanlat campaign
Twibbon campaign 154, 155

U

Uganda 65, 73, 74
United Arab Emirates 146
United Nations
Convention on Civil and Political Rights
(CCPR) 147
Convention on Economic, Social, and
Cultural Rights (CESCR) 52n81, 147
Convention on Elimination of all forms
of Discrimination Against Women
(CEDAW) **29**, 36–37, 39, 43–44, 49, 76,
79–80, 87–90, 103, 110, 124–125, 147
human rights system 48, 50, 88–91,
120–126, 138
Resolution, rights of women and girls 87
Special Rapporteur on Violence Against
Women 49, 50, 51, 87, 121–123, 125–126
treaty bodies 39, 120
United States 12–13, **29**, 94, 143, 145
and Afghanistan 66, 75–76
foreign policy 136
Saudi-American living in 152
and #women2drive campaign 136, 161

V

variable framing and messaging 99, 130, 169,
170, 196
variables, selection and definitions of 27–28,
29–32

Verma, J. S. 106
Verma Report 114, 122
victim-blaming culture 111, 113
victim–saviour dichotomy 8, 12
Vinjamuri, L. 16
violence
colonial 8, 12, 13, 22, **32**, 40, 53, 59, 158,
163, 168, 189
and Convention on Elimination of all
forms of Discrimination Against Women
(CEDAW) **29**, 36–37, 39, 43–44, 49, 76,
79–80, 87–90, 110, 124–125
counter-narratives on 95
domestic 124
elimination of violence against women
(EVAW), government policies 67–68, 76,
81, 88, 110, 116
Fiscal Specialised Unit on Violence against
Women (UFEM) 102n12
gender-based violence 71, 75, 79, 80,
84–85, 86, 114, 125
laws on 72–74, 79, 107–109
national action plans combating
77–78, 113
sexual **26**, 79, 84, 101, 104, 106, 107,
110–111, 112, 117, 119, 122
special prosecution unit for 109
Special Rapporteur on 49, 50, 51, 87,
121–123, 125–126
#VAW 58
violent emotion 118
against women **26**, **30**, 43, 49, 50, 62,
64–65, 67, 68, 69, 80, 81, 83, 196
see also #delhigangrape campaign;
#farkhunda campaign; #mydressmychoice
campaign; #niunamenos campaign;
public stripping; #sendeanlat campaign;
#stopstoning campaign

W

Waleed, Prince 141
We Will Stop Femicide 79, 84
Western perspectives and influences 40,
42–43, 136, 158, 164, 168
Women Living Under Muslim Law
(WLUML) 54
#women2drive campaign 3, **26**, 57,
59, 160, 165, 166, 172, 185, **186**,
193, **196**
consistently used words 155
content analysis 154–156
context 137
dialogue with UN 147–149
engagement metrics 151
foreign active users 151–152, *153*
framing and messaging 154–155
institutionalization 141–145
law enforcement 145–147, 167
legislative change 138–141

low level persistence 149–151
overview 134–137
positive change in human rights 148–149

women's rights
campaign 2, 15, 66
civil society organizations 66
norms 40, 75, 123, 141, 169, 170

women's voices 7, 10, 22

World Justice Project **30**, 39, 177–178, *178*, 185

Y

Yemen 11–12
YouTube 142–143, 145

Z

Zina crime 40, 41